3/25

Commercial Recreation

Commercial Recreation

Taylor Ellis, Ph.D., M.B.A.
Associate Professor
Department of Recreation and Leisure
University of Utah
Salt Lake City, Utah

Richard L. Norton, M.B.A.
Vice President
Economics Research Associates
Fort Lauderdale, Florida

Times Mirror/Mosby College Publishing
St. Louis • Toronto • Santa Clara   1988

Editor: Ann Trump
Editorial assistant: Susan Clancy
Project manager: Carlotta Seely
Editing/production: Editing, Design & Production, Inc.
Design: Elizabeth Fett

Printed in the United States of America

Library of Congress Cataloging-in-Publication Data

Ellis, Taylor.
    Commercial recreation / Taylor Ellis, Richard L. Norton.
       p. cm.
    Bibliography: p.
    Includes index.
    ISBN 0-8016-1494-5
    1. Leisure industry—Management. 2. Recreation—Management.
I. Norton, Richard L.   II. Title.
GV188.E45 1988
790'.06'9—dc19   87-29489
                                                                       CIP

C/VH/VH 9 8 7 6 5 4 3 2 1   01-C-079

Preface

The study of commercial recreation involves more than learning how to provide activities and entertainment for people. It entails learning the necessary people skills, technical abilities, and general management sense to be successful in today's competitive world. Of the three skills mentioned, general business management is the most important, but it is often not emphasized in the commercial recreation curriculum. An individual with strong business management skills can hire personnel with the appropriate people and technical skills, and together they can operate a successful commercial recreation enterprise. The key to the success of a commercial recreation enterprise is professional business management.

Purpose of the text

The ability to operate and manage any commercial recreation enterprise is a skill that can be learned. This text is intended to introduce you to business techniques and show how they can be applied to recreation. The skills discussed are those that are considered important in the everyday operation of a business. Through such major topics as legal structures, sources of capital, pricing, financial statements, and marketing, the text emphasizes management, design, and operational aspects of a full-profit commercial recreation enterprise.

Who is this text written for?

Commercial Recreation is designed for upper-division undergraduate and graduate students in recreation, leisure studies, tourism, physical education, and business. The subject matter presented is appropriate for public recreation department managers, commercial recreation managers, and recreation business owners. All courses in recreation management can benefit from the material discussed. This book will considerably enhance any recreation program because of its thorough coverage of technical material relevant to profitable commercial recreation operation.

How is this book different?

This text reflects an extensive background in the business and recreation world. Author experience in recreation management and feasibility analyses of recreational clubs, fitness centers, and theme parks has provided a store of real-life situations and experiences used in designing this text. The topics discussed are

v

current and relevant to the world of commercial recreation. The emphasis of this text is on business aspects, not programming and other categories of commercial recreation.

Why use this text?

1. **Balanced perspective.** This book contains a balanced perspective of the field of commercial recreation. It begins by presenting a general discussion of the history of commercial recreation and an overview of the current status of the field (Chapter 1). Then the text systematically discusses the techniques needed to run a successful business. All aspects of the commercial recreation field are covered.
2. **Depth and diversity of subject matter.** The in-depth discussions of planning (Chapter 5), feasibility studies (Chapter 6), and marketing (Chapter 9) show students what is involved in properly evaluating a new business venture, establishing the key criteria that will affect present and future operation, and effectively promoting the new enterprise. The chapter that focuses on advertising (Chapter 10) discusses the advantages and disadvantages of each advertising medium and the process of selecting the best one.
3. **Systematic development.** The table of contents presents material in the order that commercial recreation managers work through the demands of their positions. The text begins with general commercial recreation information and progresses to the more technical aspects of business analysis and pricing.
4. **Case studies.** In order to put material into more practical terms, case studies are provided in selected chapters. The case studies provide the necessary information to understand the subject matter and aid the student in practicing the skills presented. Each case has successfully been used in actual university classes to ensure its usefulness and validity.
5. **Clear presentation.** The information is provided in such a way that it is easily understood. Complex business skills are presented in clear, concise language that aids in the reader's understanding and retention of the material.

Pedagogical aids

Commercial Recreation includes the following learning aids specially designed to assist the reader in understanding, retaining, and developing the subject matter:

1. **Chapter objectives,** which precede the chapter text, help direct the student in identifying the important components of each chapter.
2. **Summaries** at the end of each chapter reiterate the important points and assist the student in understanding and retaining the most salient points.
3. **Figures and tables** illustrate key ideas and topics.
4. **Practical examples** illustrate important business techniques used in the establishment and maintenance of a commercial recreation enterprise.
5. **References** provide up-to-date resources and allow students to seek further information about the content discussed in each chapter.

6. **Suggested readings** give students additional resources and offer them the opportunity to broaden their knowledge and understanding of business and recreation.

Instructor's Manual

The *Instructor's Manual* provides recommendations on how to use the text most effectively. This includes explanations of financial analysis, chapter questions, information to aid in classroom discussions, and project ideas for out-of-class assignments. Essay test questions based on chapter content are also provided.

Taylor Ellis
Richard L. Norton

Acknowledgments

Any book is the result of the efforts of many people. In the case of this book many people have been instrumental in its completion. I wish to take this opportunity to publicly acknowledge them.

I would like to begin by thanking my co-author, Richard Norton. He has provided extremely valuable background and insight for the financial feasibility chapters through his experience as Vice President of the Fort Lauderdale office of Economics Research Associates.

Nancy Ellis, who offered the editing assistance that was so greatly needed, deserves special thanks for her patience, compassion, and help.

Nancy Roberson and Susan Clancy from Mosby deserve tremendous credit for supporting this project. Without their support and constant suggestions, this book may never have been completed.

Last but not least are those individuals who provided valuable suggestions and recommendations for strengthening this text. My appreciation is extended to the following reviewers:

Michael A. Blazey
Washington State University

Carl Yoshioka
Iowa State University

Ronald J. Havard
Ithaca College,
Ithaca, New York

Tony Fedler
University of Maryland

William Johnson
University of Wisconsin–LaCrosse

Regina Glover
Southern Illinois University–Carbondale

Debra Wright
California State University–Long Beach

Taylor Ellis

Contents

5　*Planning a Commercial Recreation Enterprise,* 102

6　*The Commercial Recreation Feasibility Process,* 142

7 *Evaluating the Commercial Recreation Enterprise,* 177

10 *Commercial Recreation Advertising*, 303

Commercial Recreation

CHAPTER 1

What is commercial recreation?

CHAPTER OBJECTIVES

1. To understand what constitutes commercial recreation

2. To understand the varied history of commercial recreation

*3. To be aware of commercial recreation's effects on the economy
of the United States*

Since its beginnings, America has gone through an interesting change in leisure philosophy. The America founded on the Puritan work ethic, a country of opportunity in which a person's worth was determined by the sweat of his brow, is now defined by its recreational activities. This change is interesting because the Puritans believed idleness was evil. However, during the time left over from work the people who pioneered America created recreational activities out of harvesting and barn raising, for example. During the early 1900s the provision of recreation was considered to be the responsibility of government. Government-sponsored activities were considered to be the only legitimate forms of recreation, and all other uses of unobligated time were considered unwholesome.

Today recreation has become one of the largest industries in the United States (Fig. 1-1). Its income exceeds that of the food production industry and is over one and a half times as large as the total U.S. defense budget. Public spending on recreation and leisure exceeds the total monetary outlay for new home construction and surpasses the total corporate profits of the United States. Since 1965 commercial recreation has shown a constant increase in spending in total and inflated dollars. This book is about commercial recreation and management techniques for it.

What is this industry that has a major impact on the way we live and behave?

1

FIG. 1-1 When most people think of commercial recreation, major theme parks such as Sea World come to mind. (Photograph courtesy Sea World.)

Definition of commercial recreation

For our purposes *commercial recreation* is any for-profit or nonprofit enterprise whose business is providing recreation or leisure services not funded by tax monies or charitable contributions.

In some cases municipalities and charitable organizations use their funds to initiate recreational activities. Once the activities are operational, they are expected to return the initial investment and produce a net profit. *Net profit* is the difference between sales and costs.

Profit making is a key component of any commercial enterprise. It must not be assumed that the concepts presented in this text are applicable only to non−tax-supported agencies. In recent years the division between public and private recreation has become less distinct. *Public recreation* is any department of government—local, federal, or state—with primary responsibility for the provision of recreation facilities and programs to meet public needs. Many such programs are open to all members of the community regardless of ability to pay.

However, the trend in public recreation is to charge fees for services (Fig. 1-2). This does not mean that public agencies have gone commercial. It merely reflects the need of public agencies to draw on additional sources of revenue. Because of this trend it is no longer possible to make a distinction between public and commercial recreation agencies based solely on management techniques, cost of services, or source of payment for services. The broad continuum between purely public and purely commercial recreation contains a majority of providers some-

FIG. 1-2 The Lafayette, Indiana, Parks and Recreation Board operates an amusement park to provide revenue for its parks and recreation department. (Photograph courtesy Lafayette Board of Parks and Recreation.)

where in between. Even the most civic-minded public agencies should use some commercial techniques.

Given the similarities and differences between public and commercial recreation, it is easiest to distinguish the two through differences in definitions and philosophies (see Table 1-1).

It is important to note that public recreation as defined in this text includes the work of voluntary agencies; moreover, for our purposes, commercial recreation includes private recreation. Public recreation includes voluntary agencies because they have the same objectives as public agencies: to provide inexpensive recreation intended for a specific group but actually open to everyone. Private recreation is really commercial, the only difference being that at a private establishment the person participating must pay a membership fee instead of an entrance fee. Both types of charges should be considered commercial.

History of commercial recreation
Antiquity to the sixteenth century

Commercial recreation has existed since approximately 4000 BC, when the Phoenicians invented money. Money allowed people to trade services or commodities for currency that had a relatively fixed value. This ability to exchange goods and services led to the development of travel and trade routes, which in turn initiated commercial recreation. Also, money allowed for the payment of goods and services at a standard rate. This led to profit-making enterprises that catered to the traveler. Probably as a result of this development, the travel industry became the first form of commercial recreation. Tourism emerged around 3000 BC, when the Greeks began traveling to Egypt to see the pyramids. This was strictly pleasure travel and had nothing to do with the establishment of trade or foreign relations.

By 500 BC in the state of Rome at least one third of the days of the year were considered unlucky for work and therefore were treated as holidays. This about matches our current standard of weekends and paid holidays.

Between 500 and 400 BC, the Olympic Games became commercialized, and the popularity of spectator sports increased. The Olympics had reached the age of specialization. There were charges for admission to watch the games and also for athletic training.

In Rome during the same period the thermae were popular. These public baths were centers for leisure activity for the Roman citizens. Entertainment and exercise took place at the thermae. In the Greek culture, gymnasiums were also beginning to result in a new kind of commercial recreation, the physical fitness center.

Until AD 1000 the concept of commercial recreation developed very slowly. One of the most important contributions was the complex Roman road system that allowed rapid and convenient travel. During this period the coinage was standardized, which allowed for currency exchanges and systematic pricing.

As the western world entered the Dark Ages around AD 500, civilization de-

TABLE 1-1. Comparison of public and commercial recreation

	Public recreation	*Commercial recreation*
Definition	Government agency with primary responsibility for provision of recreation facilities and programs to the public at low or nominal cost.	Any for-profit or nonprofit enterprise providing leisure services and recreational activities that is not funded on an ongoing basis by taxes or charity.
Philosophy	Enrichment of the community through opportunities to use wholesome leisure services and recreational activities.	Profitably satisfying public demands for leisure services and recreational activities.
Objectives	To promote leisure opportunities that meet the diverse needs of a local population and to promote desirable leisure values that meet specific community social goals.	To provide activities or programs that please and attract the public and that make a profit.
Finances	Primarily tax revenue; also gifts, grants, trusts, fees, and charges.	Primarily owners or promoters using private capital for construction and development. This money is repaid from fees.
Ownership	Usually by local government based on state or local legislation. May also be by a nonprofit or service organization.	Usually by an individual, partnership, limited partnership, or corporation. Must be registered with the municipality as a business.
Program	To provide recreational activities for all members of the population.	Usually limited to specific activities popular enough to promise an adequate return on investment.
Examples of agencies	Local recreation and park departments, YMCAs, church youth organizations, boys' clubs, scouts.	Country clubs, bowling alleys, athletic groups, yacht clubs, golf clubs, travel tours, skating rinks, theme parks, amusement complexes.
Membership	Usually for all, with some emphasis on children and aging and disabled persons.	Primarily adults and young people; membership is limited by local, state, and federal laws and the ability to pay.

clined, and with it, recreation. Then, from AD 1000 to the sixteenth century, there was a resurgence in the popularity of commercial recreation. Fairs and traveling minstrel shows increased. The fairs grew out of people's need for recreation and displays of productivity. Fairs became so popular that the landowners began to charge a tax on fairs, since they undermined control over the populace.

The middle class, consisting of merchants and skilled tradesmen, began to develop and to challenge the firmly established feudal system. It was also during this period that the Moslems introduced receipts, checks, bills of lading, and letters of credit. These concepts allowed for the continued growth of the middle class and trade throughout the region.

During the twelfth century wagons and carts were reintroduced into European civilization. They were popular during the time of the Greeks and Romans but died out during the Dark Ages. Their development allowed for increased ease of travel and trade among the major cities of the western world.

At the same time that travel was becoming easier, the printing press was being developed and by the fifteenth century travel guides were being printed. These travel guides provided detailed information about new areas and enhanced the traveling ability of individuals.

The next evolution in ease of travel took place later in the fifteenth century, when coaches were invented in Hungary. For the first time there was a travel mode that allowed for the comfort of the traveler.

1600 to 1700

During the 1600s several key events took place, including the development of insurance and the stock market. These were critical to the development of commerce. The stock market allowed individuals to raise capital for investments. At the time stock issuance was used mainly for shipping and business. However, it was later to evolve to its current use in commercial recreation. Insurance took the same basic approach. It began as a way of protecting investments in goods shipped by sea. It later made it easier for commercial recreation enterprises to operate.

During this period it also became popular for the rich and well-born to take the grand tour. This was a yearlong tour during which the sons of the nobility visited the capitals of Europe to experience the art and culture in each country. This provided a cross-fertilization of ideas and inventions.

During the late 1600s Vauxhall became the first international pleasure garden in the world. It developed from an area set aside for beauty and relaxation and became the beginning of the amusement park as we know it today.

The first coffee house in America, established in Boston, Massachusetts, initiated the concept of an establishment created solely for eating and gathering.

1700 to 1800

By the early 1700s the spa concept had evolved in Europe and the United States. Individuals were encouraged to attend spas for "medicinal purposes."

These spas, or resorts, were usually located either around hot springs or on sea-coasts. It was there that the nobility and the upper middle classes went to take "the cure," a drying out of the alcohol abusers of the time. The spas were later to evolve into resort communities as we know them today. Entire social seasons, including dances and sporting events, were planned around spa activities.

A prime example of the popularity of spas was the 1780 visit of Her Royal Highness Princess Charlotte of Wales to South End in England. Her coming established South End as the place to go. This particular event was reported heavily by the British press and turned into the major social event of that year. The interesting fact was that Princess Charlotte of Wales was only five years old at the time. It was also during this period that the first golfing society was established as the Honorable Company of Edinburgh Golfers. This sport had at one time been banned because it decreased archery practice in England.

As early as the mid 1760s English sloops were carrying 60 to 70 people daily to the various resorts and spas along the English coastline. By the late 1780s at least 40,000 British subjects were traveling in Europe each year.

In 1794 the Burns Coffee House was rebuilt into the first American hotel. This was the first building redesigned into a lodging establishment. This event marked the beginning of the hotel industry in the United States.

1800 to 1850

In 1819 the first steamship crossed the Atlantic Ocean in a record 26 days. One year later, in 1820, steamships began to run on a regular schedule between the American continent and Europe. In 1825 in England the first railway for passenger transportation opened. This was a major event, since it allowed people to travel at a speed of 10 miles per hour. Some proclaimed it as terrible for people to travel at an unheard-of speed behind a fire-bellowing monster contrived by the Devil. New developments are often greeted with some skepticism.

By 1828 the Freemont Hotel was under construction in New York City. The Freemont Hotel was unique in that it was the first building designed as a hotel; the Burns Coffee House was rebuilt into a hotel.

By 1835 New York City averaged approximately 290 guests per day as the economic center and the main debarkation point for travelers from Europe. New York enjoyed a tremendous tourist business. One year later Astor House opened in New York City. This was the most luxurious hotel in the world. Completed at a cost of $400,000, it had its own gas plant, a steam lift (later to become known as an elevator) and 309 guest rooms with 17 indoor bathrooms. Also during this period, Jone's Wood was opened. This was America's first amusement park. In fact, it was the originator of the term *beer garden* due to the beverage that was most commonly served there.

In 1841 a major commercial recreation event took place in England. An entrepreneur, Thomas Cook, decided to book a train to take local residents to a temperance meeting 11 miles away. As a result Thomas Cook helped 540 people travel a total distance of 22 miles and became the world's first travel agent.

1850 to 1900

The second half of the nineteenth century was probably one of the most prolific in the development of commercial recreation. The most important event of the period was the establishment of Atlantic City, New Jersey, with its five hotels. Atlantic City has since gone through periods of increased and decreased popularity. Another milestone occurred in 1851, when Thomas Cook, in operation only 10 years, booked 165,000 people to see the first World Exposition in London, showing tremendous growth in his business in a short time.

In the late 1850s the first permanent amusement park in the United States was built at Coney Island, New York. This initiated an ongoing tradition of amusement parks, which were later to evolve into the theme park as we know it today. By the early 1860s Pullman cars carried people in comfort and style on long train trips across the United States. By the 1870s transatlantic steamship trips had decreased from the 26 days of 1819 to seven days, allowing for increased travel between the United States and Europe.

During the early 1870s Prater Park in Vienna hosted a world's fair that included the first machine ride, which changed amusement parks forever. The machine ride came to the United States 4 years later, when the first permanent amusement ride was built at Coney Island. This was a 300-foot observation tower with elevators carrying people to the top to view the surrounding countryside.

By 1880 railroad fares had decreased to the point that railroads were beginning to encourage travel as a major form of recreation. The fare from the Missouri Valley to the Hotel del Coronado in San Diego, California, was one dollar. It is interesting that the railroad owned the Hotel de Coronado, allowing it to encourage travel to one of its own properties and increase revenues.

In 1884 the switchback railway ride, the forerunner of today's roller coaster, was in place at Coney Island. This ride was so popular that it grossed over $700 per day. Two years later the first major roller coaster was installed at Atlantic City. By the 1890s camping was established as a pastime in the United States. In 1893 George Ferris invented the Ferris wheel, first displayed at the Columbian Exposition at Chicago. This Ferris wheel was 250 feet in diameter and had 36 cars, each holding 60 people. This allowed a total of 2160 people to ride the Ferris wheel at any time. They paid 50 cents each.

By 1894 Coney Island had over two dozen rides, each privately owned. One year later at Coney Island, Sea Lion Park initiated the one-owner park with one admission price. Several owners of individual rides combined to form one subgroup and provide a service at a single price. This period also ushered in several other advances such as baseball and other games, the phonograph industry and the beginning of professional sports.

1900 to 1910

During this period in America, golf courses at resorts or spas were used to attract visitors to the southern United States. Golf became one of the more popular sports among the wealthy. The first motion picture theater, the Nickelodeon, was developed. The first dark ride, wherein the patron sits in a car and goes through a series of experiences or dark panoramas, was introduced. Interestingly enough, this first dark ride was called "A Trip to the Moon."

In 1904 there were 100 amusement parks in the United States and Henry Ford had developed the Model T. In 1910 the first regularly scheduled air service in the world took place in Europe—by zeppelin, or lighter-than-air ship.

1910 to 1930

Five years after the appearance of the nickelodeon in 1905, movie attendance had increased to 10 million people per week. They came to watch the silent movies of the era. For the first time, in 1914, passenger lines began advertising holiday vacations, as transportation of immigrants had slowed to a point where a new form of revenue had to be generated.

By 1919 the total number of amusement parks in the United States was over 1500. This was the result of the development of inner-city transportation and trolley cars. The trolley lines were busy during the week carrying people to and from work. However, on weekends there was very little business for the trolley lines. As a result, many trolley companies purchased land outside of the cities and developed amusement parks in an attempt to attract additional revenue from the park and the trolleys.

This period also saw the first international air service, between London and Paris. This was a regularly scheduled flight. The phonograph industry came of age at the same time the radio was introduced, in 1919. The first international airport in the United States was established during this period, handling flights from Palm West Florida to Cuba. The first regularly scheduled air service was initiated between Boston and New York. In 1927 the motion picture took a giant step forward when talkies were introduced.

1930 to 1940

During the 1930s, in spite of the Depression, a number of major advances took place. These include the introduction of stewardesses on airlines. These stewardesses had to be qualified nurses. In case of an accident or air sickness, a nurse would be readily available to help the passengers.

Car camping became popular during this period, with over 9000 campsites being established in the United States. In 1932 the age of the airlines arrived with the DC–2, which carried 12 passengers at an unheard-of speed of 115 miles per hour. Skiing was also introduced in the United States, with the first tow established at Woodstock, Vermont, using a modified car turning a rope tow. Two years later at

Sun Valley, Idaho, the Union Pacific Railroad introduced the chair lift to the United States.

By the late 1930s the first transatlantic air service had been developed. Also, the railroads began to decline as major passenger carriers due to the development of airlines and the tremendous number of automobiles sold in the United States.

1940 to the present

The period from 1940 to the present has seen many and varied changes. It would be virtually impossible to list all of them. However, an attempt will be made to deal with the highlights of this period.

The war effort of the 1940s developed four-wheel and off-road vehicles. Off-road vehicles have become a major form of commercial recreation.

The amusement business saw a continued increase, particularly with the development of Disneyland. This first theme park opened in 1955 on 180 acres of orchard land at a cost of $26 million. This was the first time an entire amusement facility was built around a particular theme.

By the 1960s and 1970s cruise ships had begun to make a comeback. However, until the development of the TV series *The Love Boat,* the potential of cruise lines as a form of commercial recreation was not fully recognized.

Television, developed during the early 1950s, tended to decrease the use of radios. In early 1967 Six Flags Over Texas opened the first non-Disney theme park in the United States. The Kampground of America (KOA), a chain of campgrounds available for campers, motor homes, and trailers, was also developed about this time. In 1969 the Thomas Cook Agency was the largest travel agency in the world, with over 625 offices, 10,000 employees and $360 million in business. Hawaii was being discovered due to improved airline travel.

In 1971 Disney World opened on 27,400 acres in Florida at a cost of $100 million. In 1973 Holiday Inns became the largest hotel chain in the world with over 222,700 rooms.

The 1980s have seen the development of computers, VCRs and improved forms of home entertainment. These advances are spurring an increase in popularity of at-home recreational activities.

Important concepts from history

Until the early 1900s recreational pursuits were available only to the wealthiest people in society. Travel was for rich merchants on their way to purchase goods; second homes belonged only to the wealthy or the nobility; golf and tennis were pastimes of the wealthy due to the tremendous cost of equipment and facilities. Today travel, second homes, golf, and tennis have become available to nearly all people regardless of status. Increased participation has raised revenues and encouraged a tremendous increase in the number of recreation businesses.

The trend in commercial recreation is that once profits become available from any activity, additional facilities are built. This increase of facilities stimulates demand among the middle class, and as demand increases, people in the lower socioeconomic strata begin to demand access. Once this happens, public facilities spring up and provide services for the general population.

An excellent example of this is the development of golf courses in the United States. The first ones were primarily the bastions of the very rich. In order to play golf, one had to be able to afford membership in a private club. Once golf became popular among the wealthy, people in the middle classes began to demand access to golfing facilities. This resulted in the development of privately owned golf courses that were open to the public. These new golf courses provided access to golfing for a large number of people. As demand continued to increase, municipal recreation departments began to provide golf courses, operated similarly to private golf courses with the exception that there was no membership fee and that the greens fees were lower. These changes helped make golfing available to all socioeconomic levels of society. This is typical of the evolution of commercial recreation into public recreation.

This leads to three main conclusions. First, "mass follows class"; whatever the upper-class population enjoys, the middle and lower classes find desirable and make popular in one form or another. Among the best examples are resorts and spas, now available to almost everyone, and golf and tennis. These trends indicate the desire of individuals to emulate the wealthy.

Second, technology always brings major changes, as illustrated by the changes in travel patterns as newer forms of travel became available. The progression from horse and buggy to railroads, to steamships, to airlines is an example. The evolution from radio to nickelodeon to movies to television is another. As technological advances occur, they have major effects on commercial recreation.

Third, time is important to travelers. Every major decrease in travel time has engendered major changes in recreational patterns. As steamships became faster, more people traveled to Europe. With the advent of the transoceanic airlines, it became feasible to develop the Hawaiian Islands and other remote sites (Fig. 1-3).

These three concepts should be remembered and studied closely by recreation majors, since they will form the basis for many changes in our industry over the next few years.

The free-enterprise system

The economic system of the United States, often described as "free enterprise," provides for the satisfaction and needs of consumers through largely unregulated production and distribution of any goods or services, including commercial recreation. Free enterprise allows individuals and business organizations to choose what to do with their money, labor, and property. This is guaranteed by the Fifth and Fourteenth Amendments to the Constitution of the United States, which guarantee an individual the right to own property. This basic right is responsible for the

FIRST FAMILY OF COMMERCIAL JETS

737-200
110 Seats
1,900- to 2,500-mile Range
In Service—1968

737-300
128 Seats
1,900- to 2,800-mile Range
In Service—1984

727-200
156 Seats
1,900- to 2,700-mile Range
In Service—1967
Production ended—1984

757-200
186 Seats
2,600- to 4,000-mile Range
In Service—1983

767-200
216 Seats
3,300- to 4,000-mile Range
In Service—1982
Also, an Extended Range version,
216 seats, 5,300-mile range

767-300
261 Seats
4,000-mile Range
On Order
Also offered,
an Extended Range version,
261 seats, 5,000-mile range

747SP
331 Seats
6,000-mile Range
In Service—1976

747-200
452 Seats
6,100-mile Range
In Service—1970

747-300
496 Seats
5,600-mile Range
In Service—1983

Notes: • All seating capacities shown are for mixed class
• All range figures are in nautical miles

FIG. 1-3 Aircraft technology has developed to the point where larger and faster airplanes have made tourist destinations more popular and accessible. (Courtesy Boeing.)

development of the free-enterprise system. Included with the right to own property is the right to use, control, buy, and sell property or the products produced by the use of property.

In the United States economic activity is based mainly on the decisions of individuals rather than of any central body such as exists in the economic systems of communism and socialism.

Having indicated the tremendous freedom of choice that people in our society enjoy, it is important to point out that there are constraints within any system, including some on the ability to acquire goods and services and on the establishment of some businesses. For example, you may wish to develop a major resort to rival Sun Valley, Aspen, or Vail. You have every right to do that in a free-enterprise system. However, it may be extremely hard for you to acquire the necessary resources, such as land and financial backing, to realize your objective.

As you have the right to develop and use your own property, you have the right to whatever profits such development and use generate. This is the key to any free-enterprise system. Under such a system, prestige and comforts are available from profits, and the individual earning them may use them either in the development of a new enterprise or to buy the "good life."

The free-enterprise system establishes competition between people and between companies (Fig. 1-4). Anyone may enter a market where someone else has seen profit, establishing competition. Included with competition is the risk of failure. In closed economic systems, the possibility of failure is eliminated due to governmental controls.

FIG. 1-4 Free enterprise has stimulated the development of a tourist attraction based on two manufactured objects, the Queen Mary and the Spruce Goose. (Photograph courtesy of Wrather Port Properties, Ltd.)

The role of the government in free enterprise is to protect its citizens by controlling unethical practices and by encouraging competition. This is what allows you, or any citizen, to establish any resort or development you can obtain funding for with minimal restrictions except those that pertain to the health and safety of surrounding communities. This will be discussed in a later section.

The role of the entrepreneur

Free enterprise allows room for entrepreneurs to obtain the profits associated with starting a business. What is an entrepreneur? A doer, not a dreamer. An entrepreneur is willing to risk ego, capital, and time to initiate a business, in our case a commercial recreation business.

What characteristics does an entrepreneur have? According to major venture capitalists (those who fund entrepreneurs) an entrepreneur must have intellectual honesty, be willing to face the facts, whether or not he or she likes them. This individual can recognize trouble and knows what caused his or her problems.

An entrepreneur must have tremendous self-confidence, be able to tolerate uncertainty and still have few doubts of success. This characteristic relates directly to the next item, ego. This is not conceit or arrogance, but inner strength and optimism. A successful entrepreneur almost never considers failure as a real possibility. The true entrepreneur quite often does not fit well within an organization, mainly because he or she drives the boss crazy while receiving a lot of respect from subordinates.

The entrepreneur is dynamic, full of energy, but often considered by peers to be a prima donna. This person will not take "no" for an answer and does not work well in corporate politics—the doer, not the dreamer.

Finally, the entrepreneur is not afraid to associate himself with the best people to be found. This person is not intimidated by bright, energetic people. Therefore, people who lend money to entrepreneurs quite often are buying management teams, not ideas. These teams, who are often the factor that will make the enterprise profitable in the long run, are extremely important.

A new form of entrepreneur was identified in *Intrapreneur,* by Gifford Pinchot, III. An *intrapreneur* is encouraged within the corporate structure. The company encourages an intrapreneur to create new products and allows that individual to succeed or fail and reap the rewards accordingly. Under such a program it may be possible for you to develop new forms of recreational activities within existing companies and still reap the benefits from them.

Economic aspects of commercial recreation

The economics of commercial recreation should be treated with respect. Commercial recreation has grown from industry revenues totaling approximately $58.3 billion in 1965 to $262 billion in 1982 (Doan, 1982). These numbers, while impressive, are hard to fathom until you take into consideration the following facts. In 1972 $105 billion was spent on commercial recreation; this amount exceeded total corporate profits in the United States (*U.S. News and World Report,* 1972). In 1978 the $180 billion spent on commercial recreation accounted for $1 of every $8 spent in the United States (*U.S. News and World Report,* 1981). The 1981 figure of $244 billion spent on commercial recreation accounted for 9% of the net national product and 9 million jobs. In 1982 the $262 billion spent on commercial recreation was almost one and a half times as large as the total federal government outlay for national defense. If commercial recreation as a whole were to be considered one business, it would be second in size only to the food industry, which includes the growing, processing, and selling of all food within the United States.

In order to put these numbers into perspective, consider the change in spending from 1965 to 1981. Over this period total commercial recreation spending has quadrupled. This compares with increases in total government spending on recreation over the same period, 1965-1981, of just over fourfold, so the growth in the two industries has been approximately the same. However, in 1965 commercial recreation spending was $58.3 billion dollars, whereas total government spending on all recreation was $1.1 billion. In 1983 commercial recreation had grown to $262 billion, while total government spending had increased to $8.2 billion. Local city spending on recreation had grown only to a 1981 total of $3.4 billion. The fact is that in 1980 total government spending on recreation was only 3.7% of that spent by consumers on commercial recreation. Government spending on recreation is minuscule in comparison to public spending for commercial recreational activities (*Statistical Abstracts of the United States,* 1982).

Total government revenues from recreation in 1980 amounted to $1.2 billion, or slightly more than 0.5% of total public spending on commercial recreation. Is it any wonder that governments are beginning to charge fees for recreation? They are following the example set by the commercial recreation industry.

The service industries of the United States, growing rapidly and predicted to grow even faster, provide further examples of the importance of commercial recreation. In 1977 commercial recreation businesses accounted for 23% of the receipts of all service businesses. In addition, *Forbes* magazine has listed the leisure industry as one of the top four industries from 1975 through 1979 (*Forbes,* 1979). Specific commercial recreation industries have also shown substantial increases. For example, in 1981 theme parks drew nearly double the attendance of professional football, baseball, and basketball combined. They accounted for an average annual attendance of 170 million people. In 1972 24% of the population of the United States reported visiting a theme park at least once. This had increased by 1977 to 73% of the population. Of the 508 amusement facilities operating in the United States, the 40 major parks grossed over $750 million in 1977.

Another aspect of commercial recreation, the travel and tourism industry, has grown so large that in 1983 visitor and convention bureaus spent $161 million to bring conventions and visitors to their cities. In 1984 state agencies of travel and tourism spent $130 million to lure tourists. In fact, in 1981 travel and tourism accounted for more jobs in the United States than any other private industry except health care. This placed the industry as the top source of jobs in 13 states and in the top three job sources in 39 other states. Between 1981 and 1982 travel and tourism created an additional 39,000 new jobs in the United States, increasing the states that ranked travel and tourism first to 18 and placing the industry in the top three in 38 states. In fact, total traveler spending in 1982 increased to $194 billion and was responsible for 4.5 million jobs.

Travel agencies have increased at the rate of 10 percent per year from 1970 to 1981. Gross bookings are up 18 percent, or $31 billion a year. In Las Vegas, tourism has become so profitable that the Las Vegas travel and tourism bureau contributed over half a million dollars to the Clark County Parks and Recreation Department during the 1982-1983 fiscal year to help with the development of recreational facilities for residents (*Las Vegas Marketing,* Sept. 1983).

A recent survey by Knapp Communications asked, "How do you use your discretionary income?" The responses indicated that 74% used their discretionary income for vacation trips of one week or more. Vacation by car was reported by 46% and recreation or entertainment was topped by 18%. Out of the top six responses to this question, the three just listed ranked first, second, and sixth respectively (Las Vegas Convention and Visitors Authority, Sept., 1983). Some other industries have shown substantial increases in recent years: The boating industry accounted for $3 billion in equipment purchases in 1981 and a total expenditure including gas and supplies of $8 billion. Motorcyclists purchased $2 billion of equipment and spent a total of $4.5 billion on cycling in 1981. Spending on skiing has increased by six and a half times, on golf, three times.

Computers have also invaded the arcade segment of commercial recreation. Millions of dollars are being spent annually to purchase home computers and video toys. Additional millions are spent on games and software, and the total revenue generated accounted for approximately 9% of the gross national product of the United States in 1981. Commercial recreation is not only a provider of ways to use unobligated time, it is also an important source of jobs.

Summary

The history of commercial recreation has provided us with three concepts:
1. Any activity that is popularized by either the upper class or the media will become popular with the middle class.
2. As transportation time decreases and travel becomes easier, more people will travel to any location.
3. Due to advances in technology, new and different forms of commercial recreation will be invented and become popular.

The economic system of the United States is based on free enterprise. This allows individuals to determine how to allocate their resources. This translates as the ability to start any business if you have the required resources. It carries with it the right to fail in any enterprise.

An entrepreneur is any individual willing to take the risk of starting a business. This is the way many commercial recreation businesses are started.

Commercial recreation is an integral part of life in the United States, a major portion of the economy providing thousands of jobs and doing billions of dollars of business every year. The components of commercial recreation reach into virtually every aspect of our lives and are affected by virtually every decision we make.

BIBLIOGRAPHY

Amory, C.: The last resorts, New York, 1948, Harper and Brothers.

Bicentennial edition, historical statistics of the United States, colonial times to 1970, Washington, D.C., 1975, U.S. Government Printing Office.

Carleson, R.E., McKlean, J.R., Deppe, T.R., and Peterson, J.A.: Recreation and leisure: the changing scene, Belmont, Calif., 1979, Wadsworth Publishing Co.

Chubb, M., and Chubb, H.: One third of our time, New York, 1981, John Wiley & Sons, Inc.

Crandall, D.A.: Recreation fun and jobs for America, American Recreation Coalition, April 1983.

Doan, M.: $262 Billion dogfight for your leisure spending, U.S. News and World Report, July 26, 1982.

$83 billion for leisure, U.S. News and World Report, Sept. 15, 1969.

Eleventh annual Ski Magazine survey, Ski Magazine, 1983.

Leisure, Forbes, Jan. 8, 1979.

Leisure boom: biggest ever and still growing, U.S. News and World Report, April 17, 1972.

Leisure where no recession is in sight, U.S. News and World Report, Jan. 15, 1972.

Marketing bulletin, second quarter 1983 summary, Las Vegas Convention and Visitors Authority, vol. 10, no. 46, Sept. 15, 1983.

Marketing bulletin, third quarter 1983 summary, Las Vegas Convention and Visitors Authority, vol. 11, no. 47, Dec. 15, 1983.

Michigan travel information system study, Michigan Department of Transportation, 1983.

Miller, N., and Robinson, D.M.: The leisure age, Belmont, Calif., 1963, Wadsworth Publishing Co.

Recreation: A $244 Billion Market, U. S. News and World Report, Aug. 10, 1981.

Sanders, R.M.: Seaside England, London, 1951, B.T. Batsford, Ltd.

Statistical abstract of the United States, 1967, Washington, D.C., 1968, U.S. Government Printing Office.

Statistical Abstract of the United States, 1982-83. Washington, D.C., 1984, U.S. Government Printing Office.

Weiskopf, D.C.: Recreation and leisure—improving the quality of life, Boston, 1982, Allyn & Bacon.

SUGGESTED READINGS

Bitter, Gary G., Computers in today's world. New York, 1984, John Wiley & Sons.

General text discusses how computers operate and the various uses they are suitable for. Specific chapters on word processing and data base management. Assumes no knowledge on the part of the reader; easy to understand for the computer novice.

Bullaro, John J. and Christopher R. Edginton. Commercial leisure services: managing for profit. Palo Alto, Calif., 1985, Mayfield Publishing Co.

Basic knowledge and skills associated with commercial leisure services. A blend of conceptual, theoretical and practical material. Attempts to explain the leisure experience and its relation to the services of profit-oriented organizations. Offers guidelines for career development.

CHAPTER 2

Components of commercial recreation

CHAPTER OBJECTIVES

1. To gain an understanding of the components of commercial recreation

2. To identify some of the key associations supporting commercial recreation

3. To discuss employment possibilities in commercial recreation

Commercial recreation can be broken into four components: tourism (services for nonresidents), local commercial recreation, retail sales, and manufacturing. These four groupings are useful when discussing the types of users and can be applied to marketing and developing a commercial recreation enterprise.

There is a tremendous amount of overlap in the commercial recreation field. A person traveling to see a theme park such as Disneyland is an example of the tourism. However, to nearby residents Disneyland is a local attraction. This illustrates some of the problems involved in trying to sort commercial recreation into mutually exclusive categories. Please keep in mind the overlap between categories as we discuss them.

Tourism

Tourism comprises destinations, activities, and travel facilitation. Each of these components is equally important, and they are not perceived separately by the tourist. Try to think of the destination as the "magnet" or attraction that lures the tourist. Travel facilitators provide services that make it easier for the traveler to reach his desination.

Destination

When contemplating tourist destinations, we tend to think of the major travel areas of the world, which include gambling resorts and casinos. When you view a list of major resorts in the United States, the Pocono Mountains, Las Vegas, Anaheim, and southern Florida stand out. Destination areas are usually defined by their resorts, such as Disneyland and Disney World. Resort areas run by private concessionaires serve some national and state parks. Campgrounds in national parks and forest service lands may also include privately operated areas.

Conferences, conventions, sports events, and other special events can be treated as destinations. This includes major sporting events such as the Indianapolis 500, the Superbowl, the NCAA national championship playoffs, and the Rose Bowl.

Resorts. Resort hotels generally specialize in extended periods of stay. Hotels and motels specialize in overnight stays. Resort hotels are characterized by the number of services and amenities available on or near the site (Fig. 2-1). Among

FIG. 2-1 A destination resort must cater to all the needs of its guests. (Photograph courtesy Marriott's Tan-Tar-A Resort.)

these services and amenities are golf, tennis, skiing, horseback riding, water ski-ing, and sailing. You will also find ancillary services such as barber shops, beauty shops, travel agencies, and retail stores. This mix provides activities for the guests during their unobligated time.

Employment opportunities in the hotel and restaurant business are extensive. The U.S. Department of Labor, in *Career Opportunities in Hotel and Restaurant Industries,* published in 1982, indicated 19 job classifications in the hotel industry. Of these, half require a high school diploma or less. These are typically lower-paid positions requiring little or no skill. Salaries of the management staff are considerably higher, ranging from $35,000 to $50,000 for general manager in smaller hotels to over $50,000 in larger ones. Resident managers earn between $20,000 and $30,000, food and beverage directors $35,000 to $40,000, executive housekeepers around $35,000 and executive chefs in the $35,000 to $45,000 range.

Another job possibility is the social directorship. The social director plans and organizes hotel recreational activities and creates a friendly atmosphere. The convention manager is responsible for coordinating the activities of the staff and the convention planning personnel in order to make the arrangements for group meetings and conventions, including set-ups for office space, meeting rooms, banquet rooms, and so on. The promotional manager plans and administers sales policies and any programs used specifically to foster and promote hotel usage. The resort hotel manager is responsible for setting standards for personnel administration and performance. He or she is also responsible for overall service to the patrons, room rates, advertising, publicity credit, food selection, etc. In short, the manager is responsible for all activities that take place in the resort hotel.

The final position is the resort hotel services sales representative. This person solicits business for the resort hotel from various governmental agencies and businesses. His or her main job is to find additional sources of income and persuade groups to come to the hotel.

A recent innovation in resort hotels is the mixed-use complex: the resort hotel or property is part of a larger real estate development. Included are such revenue-producing units as time-share condominiums and second-home sites. Some resort hotels have converted rooms into time-share condominiums, allowing for sales to as many as 50 people per room. This allows an individual to use the room for a specified number of days per year (usually 7) during a specific period such as the second week of the year.

When the owner of the period is not using his or her condominium or second home, the owner allows the resort to rent the unit. The revenue generated is shared by the owner and the resort hotel. This provides the resort hotel with capital for development and revenue from the maintenance contracts and property rental.

Another source of resort revenues is the convention business. Businesses quite often look for a place to hold conventions away from the city. They find that by providing conventions in a resort atmosphere they make it possible for conventioneers to relax and develop a sense of camaraderie. An added benefit is the sense of isolation from the day-to-day stresses of conventioneers' business routines, which provides more effective meetings. This has proven very successful and is an ongoing strategy for many resort hotels.

Theme parks. This concept has evolved from the pleasure gardens of Europe to Coney Island to Six Flags, Great Adventure, and Disneyland. Each of these facilities has evolved from some unique theme that is prevalent to the area, such as Six Flags Over Texas (Fig. 2-2).

Recreation, Sports and Leisure, in the 1986 *Managed Recreation Research Report* indicated that in 1986 the average theme park attendance was over 25,000 per day. Theme parks have been in operation for over 30 years and have an average operating budget of almost $7 million.

Based on the 1986 *Managed Recreation Research Report,* just over 77% of the theme parks responding indicated that they would be developing new facilities. This expansion is necessary to maintain repeat business. As with resort hotels, a large proportion of jobs available are seasonal and pay minimum wage. However, an employee who rises above seasonal employment can expect salaries similar to those indicated for resort developments, depending on the positions available.

One of the main considerations of theme parks is liability insurance. Recreation is suffering a tremendous change in liability insurance, which is causing substantial problems for recreational activities in general and theme parks in particular.

A new form of theme park is the water slide or water park, based on the theme of water activities—slides, wave pools, and so on. This particular theme is enjoying rapid expansion because of its relatively low cost and the interest of the public. However, with the increase in accidents in water theme parks, the insurance issue has become critical. Accident rates have led to calls for regulations by various government agencies. It remains to be seen what effect these will have on the water-based theme park industry in the United States.

Campgrounds. Since its inception in the 1960s Kampgrounds of America, or KOA, has become the largest privately owned campground system in the United States. About 83% of the campgrounds in the United States are single, privately owned establishments (referred to as "Ma and Pa" operations, because they are usually owned and operated by a couple). Privately owned chains account for 11.5 percent of commercial campgrounds *(Managed Recreation Research Report).*

Other major commercial campground chains include Thousand Trails, Sugarloaf Mountain Corp., Boyne U.S., and Mobile Home Communities. Commercial campgrounds are returning profits of 18.5% of revenues. Facility rental accounts for 64.6% of revenue. Expenditures break down fairly evenly into advertising, promotion, and marketing at 29.8%, equipment repair and maintenance at 29.3%, and ground equipment maintenance at 29% *(Managed Recreation Research Report,* 1986).

Job opportunities are somewhat limited unless you wish to open a franchise for one of the major chains or develop your own campground. The commercial camp-

FIG. 2-2 Theme parks are based on any activity that can generate public interest in the park—in this case underwater exploration. (Photograph courtesy Planet Ocean.)

ground industry is flourishing, particularly owner-controlled and -operated camp-grounds. In some cases these have taken on the appearance of chains, as groups of owners have formed to purchase and manage campgrounds within a general loca-tion. These campgrounds can be affiliated with Camp Coast to Coast, a national organization of campground clubs, which allow members to share other areas' fa-cilities at a very low rate. This sharing is similar to the time-sharing in the resort industry.

Due to the tremendous increase in popularity of motor homes, trailers and campers as well as the resurgence of tent camping, campgrounds represent an area of the commercial recreation industry that is fairly stable and has potential for the future.

Travel facilitators

Tourism includes transportation modes such as steamships, railroads, airplanes, buses, and private automobile. These all have an important place in traveling. Another ancillary group that works with travel and transportation modes is travel agencies. They act as retail outlets for transportation companies and provide valuable help in planning vacations, including destination selection and travel arrangements. Tour wholesalers create vacation packages for resale to the public. Tour operators lead or direct the tourists on their trips. Meeting planners coordinate activities at a major meeting or convention site and are responsible for lodging, banquets, facility rooms, exhibit halls, pre- and postmeeting tours, and spouse programs.

The lodging industry provides places for people to stay while traveling and at the destination. Closely related is the food service industry. A new service, travel information, is being developed at many tourist sites by state and local governments that wish tourists to be aware of recreation information. Recently private entrepreneurs have been providing travel information through computers. These new computer services are able to supply specific information concerning such things as restaurants and entertainment. This information can be obtained at the traveler's home, hotels, information centers, and other public locations.

Transportation modes. Flying is the most popular form of commercial transportation available in the United States today due to the speed and ease of travel. The airline industry has been extensively affected by deregulation since 1978. Until then the Civil Aeronautics Board had full control over which airlines could fly to which cities. After deregulation limits on flights from one city to another, and to a certain extent fares, were tremendously reduced. Deregulation has resulted in a tremendous change in the makeup of the airline industry. A number of large carriers in the United States are merging to form supercarriers. This trend appears to ensure the continued strength of the airline industry through market control.

It now appears that there will be only about 5 major airlines flying in the United States, down from 12. However, the total number of airlines in the United States has increased almost twofold since deregulation because of the ease of entry into the marketplace.

The second most widely used form of transportation in the United States is the inner-city bus. A large portion of inner-city bus traffic, particularly as it relates to day-to-day business, is commuter traffic in the metropolitan areas of the East and West coasts. This accounts for a large percentage of bus revenue. The remaining revenue comes from people crossing the country, or traveling the large expanses of the western states. In most cases the bus is too slow for the business or recreational traveler. However, some vacation travelers find the bus an effective way to travel, especially those who prefer guided tours.

The rail system in the United States was reorganized under the Rail Passenger Act of 1970, which created the national railroad system. This was the beginning of Amtrak. The purposes of Amtrak are to provide modern, efficient intercity rail service, to develop the rail system into a profitable business.

Amtrak has succeeded in meeting only one of these goals, providing efficient intercity rail service for commuters on the East Coast. The fares charged by the railroads are comparable to those of the airlines; however, the travel time between destinations is often substantially longer for railways than for air carriers, which makes it difficult for rail carriers to compete.

In the United States the automobile is the dominant form of transportation, accounting for approximately 80% of all travel. This trend has been fostered by the rapid growth of automobile ownership, the personal attitudes of American people, and the development of the interstate highway system.

Closely connected with the automotive industry and use of automobiles for travel is the car rental industry, which was created to provide the business traveler with transport at a destination. Recently, in an attempt to increase off-season revenue, rental companies have encouraged fly-drive vacations. According to Hertz Corporation, the car rental industry grossed over $4 billion in 1985 (*Money,* 1985). Four major companies—Hertz, Avis, National, and Budget—account for 95% of the total rental car market (*Money,* Sept. 1985).

The final segment of the transportation industry is the cruise industry. This industry has enjoyed a tremendous increase in popularity since the inception of the television series *The Love Boat.* In fact, according to the Cruise Line International Association, there was a 100,000-passenger increase in use of cruise lines from 1980 to 1984 (Fig. 2-3).

Cruise times range from as little as 2 days to as long as over 106. The majority of cruises operating out of the United States are to the Mediterranean, Mexico, Alaska, and the Hawaiian Islands. Most newer cruise ships are equipped with casinos, gyms, beauty salons, shops, libraries, running tracks, bars, nightclubs, saunas, and other recreational facilities. Since there are only 18 major cruise lines operating out of the United States, job opportunities are somewhat limited, particularly since the majority of cruise lines like to foster a European flavor and require that a large proportion of their employees have foreign accents. Also, most employees must be able to perform in some manner, by singing, dancing, or some similar skill. This helps provide entertainment aboard ship. These restrictions tend to reduce the availability of jobs in the cruise industry for U.S. students. However, some positions are available, and it is a good way to see the world.

Positions available in travel facilitating range from baggage handling to travel agent, steward or stewardess, airline pilot, engineer, and general business manager. The salaries match the job titles, ranging from very low to extremely high.

Travel agents. Travel agencies, the creators of vacations, can be either whole-

FIG. 2-3 Cruise lines have experienced a tremendous increase in popularity in recent years. This is an example of Carnival Cruise Line's state-of-the-art liner. (Photograph courtesy of Carnival Cruise Lines.)

sale or retail. Wholesale travel operators put together complete tour packages, including air fare, ground transportation, hotels, and motels, and in some cases they escort groups on tour. The retail travel agency, the one you are most familiar with, is the company that sells the tickets.

The retail travel agent is the person to see for information on where to travel and what to do there. He or she provides information and tickets at a convenient location. Generally, travel agencies make their revenue from a commission on the sale of airline tickets and hotel rooms. Commissions range from 10%-15% of the price of the booking. In general, the job does not pay well, averaging $10,000 to $12,000 per year. However, the main incentive is the travel benefits available at reduced or no cost. Most travel agents take cut-rate "fam tours," or familiarization tours, which allow the agent to become familiar with a destination with the hope that this will increase bookings to the resort. Fam tours are sponsored by airlines and/or resorts.

The travel agency industry is in the process of dividing into four areas of specialization: commercial agencies, which supply services to anyone interested in traveling; agencies that work with specific organizations or conventions to supply travel; employee recreation travel agencies, which work with the incentive travel market to encourage employees to produce more; and agencies that specialize in business travel and cater to large companies.

The travel agent's job is highly stressful during peak periods. A travel agent must possess good social skills.

Starting a travel agency requires about $100,000 to establish connections with conventions, for staff training, for the computerized equipment needed to book and write tickets on site, and for advertising and salaries.

Local commercial recreation

At the local level commercial recreation can be divided into outdoor recreation, indoor recreation, and clubs. Each has a unique and important role. At first glance the distinctions may appear to be somewhat artificial. However, closer inspection reveals substantial differences in the types of activities and the characteristics of the people participating in each.

Outdoor commercial recreation

In recent years providing outdoor recreation for local residents has taken some interesting directions, including the development of amusement parks near city centers. Amusement parks have been popular since the early 1900s, and they now provide a wholesome and safe recreational experience, one that may provide thrills missing in many people's personal lives.

Amusement parks. Amusement parks are an offshoot of the recreation facilities developed by transportation companies in the early 1900s. Some of them provide exceptional facilities for recreation within a community. They are substantially smaller in size than major theme parks, drawing only from a local area, and not nationally as in the case of Disneyland. Attendance at these parks has remained fairly constant because of repeat visits from the local residents.

A variation of the amusement park is the water park. Water parks are specialized theme parks that cater mainly to local residents and are constructed around water slides and water-related activities. For the most part these parks consist of open or enclosed fiberglass slides that give the thrill of going down a high-speed twisting slide and generally ending up in some kind of landing pool. Variations include swinging ropes, nets, climbing areas, play areas in the pools, and wave pools, which simulate ocean currents.

The major difference between the local attraction and the tourist attraction is the size and extent of operation. However, it is entirely possible for community amusement and water parks to become tourist attractions. In these cases the businesses encourage tourist usage but depend on local residents for the core of their revenue.

A major problem for amusement and water parks is the relatively short season in most of the United States. A typical season runs slightly more than a third of the year. In most cases that 120 days is the entire season.

As with other forms of commercial recreation, amusement parks are having problems with liability insurance, which may seriously reduce their ability to continue to make profits given the low entrance fees. This will probably need to be changed soon.

Employment opportunities in amusement parks range from ride attendance and ticket taking to management and cash control. Although the majority of the positions are seasonal, positions in finance, management, liability reduction, and sales are year-round and fairly high paying.

Sporting events. Sports are provided through professional teams, collegiate sports, and sports clubs. These teams can be sponsored by private agencies or, in the case of professional sports, by a combination of subsidies from private companies, tax advantages, and admission fees.

Professional athletics has become a big business in the United States. It is not uncommon for major sports team members to have salaries in excess of $1 million per year nor for team traveling budgets to exceed $500,000. These costs must be offset by increasing gate receipts. A typical professional sports operation must generate approximately 75% of operating income from ticket sales. Other income derives from advertising, local promotions, sponsorships by local merchants and television and radio contracts.

Major problems facing professional athletics are increasing insurance rates, rapidly rising player salaries, and the increased costs of travel, particularly for teams with extensive road trips.

Nonprofessional sports facilities include the golf courses, ice skating rinks, playgrounds, and sports parks. All of these activities are on the increase nationally. On March 28, 1985, the *Wall Street Journal* indicated that more colleges are encouraging students to take up golfing as a career survival tool. This type of publicity will serve to increase the national interest in sporting activities in general and in golf specifically.

Another factor affecting nonprofessional sports is the increased emphasis on fitness in the United States. As this awareness increases, individuals continue to search for ways of staying fit, largely through sporting activities.

The possibilities for jobs in professional sports are somewhat limited because of small staff and high skill requirements. Most such workers are highly skilled either as coaches or players, with the exception of some general positions in the front office, including team managers (usually former players) and the marketing and public relations staff. The last is an area that commercial recreation students can explore and participate in. This is probably the best opportunity for commercial recreation students who are not highly enough skilled to play professionally. Golfing and other individual sports also require a high level of skill in players and managers. As a result, individuals need to develop their skills in these areas prior to applying for skill-related positions.

Fairs and carnivals. Some enterprising individuals are generating tremendous revenues through fairs and dance festivals for communities (Fig. 2-4). Examples range from ethnic festivals to garlic festivals and others that emphasize local events or products. Fairs and festivals are generally the responsibility of only the director or entrepreneur who originates the event. This is an extremely limited area, but one that can be very lucrative for those who possess the skills of marketing,

FIG. 2-4 Resorts often sponsor carnivals for local citizens. Wintertest is an event that appeals to the young and old alike. (Photographs courtesy Aspen Skiing Company.)

directing, and public relations, which is essential to general community support for your idea.

Festivals, fairs, and carnivals presented by local groups have increased dramatically in recent years. They range from medieval and Renaissance fairs to ethnic culture fairs, and they provide entertainment, sales booths, and food. These outdoor activities have become very lucrative.

These areas of commercial recreation pay fairly well. Therefore it is in the best interest of the commercial recreation student to prepare by developing organizing, marketing, promotional, and sales skills.

Indoor commercial recreation

Indoor commercial recreation includes movies, plays, musicals, concerts, and ballet. Sports franchises also provide a tremendous amount of indoor recreation for local residents.

Theaters. Movie theaters do the lion's share of the business, with live stage productions, plays, and concerts taking a minor portion of that income. The theater industry is characterized by a low return on its sales. The typical movie theater clears only $0.18 out of every $4.50 ticket sold. The remainder of the ticket price goes to the movie production company. The theater must therefore make the majority of its revenue on its concession sales, which yield about 85% of sales as profit.

The current trend for movies has generated tremendous profits for the movie industry and at the local level. However, the increased popularity of video recorders is probably taking business from theaters. Already some theaters are seeing decreases in revenues. Traditionally, the major movie-going population has been couples. With the advent of VCRs couples can now stay home, invite friends over and watch movies at a cheaper price. The major exceptions to this are single persons who are dating and teenagers. As a result, theater popularity is expressed mainly by teenagers through the dating years. This population, however, is decreasing, and tremendous effects may be seen at the movie theaters.

Legitimate theater has always been the realm of the upper and upper-middle classes. Increased availability of true theatrical productions on video cassettes may reduce the numbers of the theater- and concert-going public. However, the majority of people attending plays and concerts do so for the experience, and therefore this enterprise will probably continue to be profitable in the future.

Video arcade games, a more recent form of indoor commercial recreation, challenge people's coordination and in some cases their ability to think.

Clubs

There are three forms of clubs in the field of local commercial recreation: social clubs, health clubs, and sport and racquet clubs.

Social clubs. These serve the same function as bars and restaurants; in fact, some social clubs are similar to bars. However, they usually maintain a higher caliber of decoration and atmosphere, a certain ambience.

Restaurants and nightclubs are a major form of indoor recreation that is available both to the local individual and to the tourist. It is hard to determine what percentage of restaurant use is recreational and what percentage is required for subsistence. However, most studies indicate that people eating in restaurants are there for some form of social or business interaction, not simply for food. This would classify most restaurants as commercial recreation enterprises.

Pubs and bars are almost totally recreational in nature. Nightclubs are suffering from changing attitudes toward alcohol consumption. Nationwide bar sales are down 10%-20% because of the increased effectiveness of drunk-driving campaigns and some state laws holding the bar or nightclub owner responsible for accidents by drunk drivers.

In larger operations such as restaurants and food services, alcohol accounts for only about 12.5 percent of sales. This, however, can be a large revenue generator, because the markup on mixed drinks is substantial. In terms of national trends, it is expected that the food service industry will obtain 50 cents of every dollar spent on food by the year 2000. As in other areas of commercial recreation, the majority of the higher-paying jobs are held by managers of divisions or of the entire facility. This is not to say that servers cannot make good money, particularly through tips. However, the majority of high salaries and stable positions are for managers.

Health clubs. Health clubs have become very popular in recent years due to an increased emphasis on physical fitness and personal appearance. These clubs usually provide a place for people to lift weights and participate in aerobic exercise (Fig. 2-5). Some have amenities such as whirlpools, steam rooms and saunas. Although the primary purpose of these clubs is physical fitness, they are also highly social in nature, and thus have a dual function.

Sport and racquet clubs. Sport and racquet clubs build on the concept of a health club by adding additional facilities for members' use, such as tennis courts, racquetball courts, and swimming pools. A major component of these clubs, the opportunity for social interaction between members, must not be overlooked.

A recent study published by Research Forecasts for the Miller Brewing Company indicated that nearly half of the U.S. population engages in at least one athletic activity every day and 71% participate in a sport or physical activity once a week. In line with these figures, the interest in health clubs and multipurpose centers is increasing rapidly. Single persons make up the largest percentage of club memberships, a fact that underscores the emphasis on social activities in the club. In fact, health clubs have been called the alternative to singles bars.

Over half of athletic or multipurpose club revenue comes from membership fees. This makes it important to maintain repeat memberships and repeat attendance. Some of the lesser-quality clubs, however, rely strictly on new membership sales. The attempts to obtain new members can get very drastic; the larger clubs spend an average of 40% of their operating budget on promotion and advertising. This is staggering when you take into consideration that in 1985 average membership per club was 4294.

The health and fitness club industry has been characterized by several abuses.

FIG. 2-5 Fitness clubs have experienced a tremendous increase in popularity. In order to be competitive they must provide that little extra touch in either decor or service. (Photograph courtesy Jekyll Island Authority.)

Among these is the oversale of memberships in an attempt to generate revenue. Another is to declare bankruptcy, only to reopen a short time later in the same location with the same equipment under a new name. These abuses will most likely lose force, as consumers are getting more savvy in their attempts to find quality fitness clubs. In the future emphasis will probably need to be placed on social activities for club members.

A slightly different form of the fitness or activity club is the country club. The majority of the members are upper-middle-class individuals who can afford to belong to a social club as well as an athletic club. These clubs vary in the number of services offered from primarily social activities to golf courses and all other forms of athletic or sports activities. Country clubs have a higher ability to generate revenue because they can obtain funds through initiation fees, monthly dues, food and beverage sales, ratail sales, service charges, and patronage and assessments from the members. Membership in country clubs generally ranges from about 450 families in the smaller clubs up to a maximum of about 1400 members in the larger clubs in urban areas.

Professional positions in clubs are limited mainly to department or general managers. Most other positions pay minimum wage.

Retail sales

The retail sales aspect of commercial recreation provides a tremendous number of jobs and economic benefits to the community. As has been noted, retail sales provide support for other kinds of related services such as clubs, tourism, trips, and resorts.

Retail items include sporting equipment, clothing, and larger items such as motor homes and recreation vehicles needed to support commercial recreation in the community.

Retail sales of recreational equipment have increased drastically in the 20 years from 1960 to 1980. Sales of nondurable toys and expendable sporting supplies are up slightly over five and a half times the 1960 rate. Sales of durable sporting goods, toys, boats, and so on, are up slightly over seven and a half times the 1960 amount. Retail sale concerns with rapid growth and high potential for the commercial recreation major are sporting goods stores, clothing and equipment shops, and specialty stores such as ski shops.

This component of commercial recreation is usually not discussed with commercial recreation entrepreneurs. Most who pursue careers in retailing are from a business background or start with small specialty shops. Retailing is much written about, particularly relating to merchandising, stocking, inventory control, layouts, designs, and displays. This indicates the size and importance of this segment of the industry. The entrepreneur need only refer to this material for valuable information.

There are basically two kinds of retail outlet: the store and the catalog. Store sales take place in a variety of settings—from specialty shops to discount stores. The first form of recreational retail outlet includes specialty shops that support a specific activity—ski shops, bicycle stores, wind surfing stores, tennis pro shops, golf pro shops, and so on. These outlets stock high-quality items and charge a premium price. In order to justify high prices they must provide additional services to the customer, convenient location, or expertise.

The second form of retail outlet is a general sporting goods store, which provides equipment for a wide variety of games and pastimes. A general sporting goods store may carry firearms, water skis, snow skis, sports clothing, tennis equipment, and much more. Major examples of these outlets are Oshams and Herman's World of Sporting Goods. The prices in general sporting goods stores are usually lower than those in specialty outlets because they have more competition and their location is such that they must draw customers to their location.

A third form of retail outlet is a department store that carries sporting goods. Prime examples are J.C. Penney and Sears Roebuck. Both of these department stores also have catalog outlets.

A fourth category of retail outlet is the discount store. This category includes factory and warehouse outlets which provide the goods at a low cost, particularly in the case of a warehouse outlet. No services are provided. You simply go into a warehouse and select the item you want without the help of sales personnel. Once the selection has been made, you take it to a check-out stand and pay for it. The advantage here is price. Most discount stores are in large outlet centers and require some travel by the customer.

Nonstore outlets have expanded tremendously in the past several years. They include such catalog outlets as L.L. Bean, Recreation Equipment, Inc., and Eddie Bauer, Inc. Such outfits provide high-quality items to select customers through catalogue sales and, in some cases, retail stores. Most sales are generated by the catalog. This type of selling requires building and maintaining a mailing list, producing catalogs, and maintaining inventory and prices for the life of the catalog.

A newer form of catalog sales has arisen from the computer industry. This is the computerized shopping service, which allows the user to call a purchasing service by phone, using a personal computer. The buyer enters the information pertaining to a specific item. The computer system locates the lowest price available on that item. If the buyer wishes to purchase the item, he or she enters a credit card number and shipping address. In approximately one week the item will be delivered.

Another form of catalog sales now takes place on cable television. This is the TV sales promotion. During certain periods of the viewing day, various items are displayed on the television screen. Some are displayed in an auction format and the final selling price is substantially lower than the final bid; sometimes the product is shown to the viewing audience and the price is quoted while the various virtues of the product are extolled. An individual who wishes to purchase, picks up the phone, dials the toll-free number on the screen and orders the items by credit card number. The item is delivered within 2 weeks.

Job opportunities for commercial recreation majors in retail range from general sales to business ownership. Other positions include merchandise buyer, marketing manager, inventory handling, sales, sales management, and advertising. Salaries vary drastically. Pay systems can range from straight salary to salary plus commission to strictly commission. The higher-paying jobs generally go to those with better qualifications, background, and experience. The commercial recreation student must carefully assess the options when taking a business position.

Manufacturing

Equipment manufacturing, an ever-increasing industry of commercial recreation, includes the production of items from baseballs, baseball bats, and tennis racquets to motorcycles and recreational vehicles. Although manufacturing is a relatively large and unrecognized component of commercial recreation, without it most activities would cease to exist.

A commercial recreation major has numerous skills that can be beneficial to future employers in manufacturing. The research and development phase requires design and development of new markets and products, which must be tested before sale to the general public. The testing phase can extend to the actual use of the product throughout a season. In many cases manufacturing companies, particularly in the ski industry, pay highly skilled skiers to use and evaluate their equipment, either during races or while instructing. The people using the equipment provide feedback to the manufacturer concerning possible changes in the development of the product.

Another possible area of employment for a commercial recreation major in manufacturing is in developing a distribution network to move products from the factory to the retail outlet. The distributor manages the shipping and development, such as bringing sport clothing from foreign countries to the United States for sale in retail outlets. Distribution jobs also include that of manufacturer's representative, who is charged with approaching the retail sales outlet and selling various product lines, thereby supplying the retailer with the goods needed for sale to the public.

Since a commercial recreation major knows why people participate in recreation, he or she is an excellent choice for a marketing position in a manufacturing company. Such a person is better able to identify the true reasons for purchasing some good that the company is manufacturing than most general marketing professionals. Knowledge of the industry and why people play can be valuable in getting to the psychological reasons concerning why people purchase certain manufactured goods.

Jobs available in commercial recreation manufacturing are varied. It is the responsibility of the commercial recreation majors to convince future employers of the important contribution they can make to the company. Commercial recreation majors are sometimes in position not only to sell themselves, but to determine their own salaries in the manufacturing industry.

Nearly all of the recreation activities that people participate in today require some form of equipment. Hence manufacturing is an extremely large segment of the commercial recreation industry, possibly one the commercial recreation student has not fully explored. Job potential in manufacturing for the commercial recreation major appears to be mainly at the managerial level. Generally the most available positions are the lower-paying line jobs (such as on an assembly line). Commercial recreation majors through their understanding of recreation and why people participate in it, combined with skills in particular sports, may find it possible to move into the manufacturing sector at the managerial level.

Job opportunities

Job opportunities are readily available to those who have the ability to sell themselves. This is a skill that must be developed by the job seeker. Individuals with recreation backgrounds and degrees have been successful in obtaining positions in a large variety of areas, not all of which are closely related to recreation. The key point in obtaining a position always appears to be the ability of the individual to convince an employer that he or she has a substantial background in business, which must be translated to advantages for the individual employer. This almost entirely depends on the ability of the job seeker. We strongly encourage students in commercial recreation actively to pursue methods by which they can hone their skills in job seeking, resume writing, and interviewing techniques. This will ensure their ability to obtain a position in the future.

The job seeker in commercial recreation will most likely not be able to obtain a high-level management position directly out of school. Most commercial recreation enterprises make you "pay your dues." However, once the employee is in the industry, it is relatively easy to move between positions. This is particularly true in resorts and ski areas.

It is to your advantage to spend whatever time you can working in the industry in which you wish to pursue a career. This strategy can be extremely useful for developing contacts and proving your experience and background to future employers.

Commercial recreation associations

The following is a list of most of the major associations dealing with commercial recreation. It is by no means exhaustive. In addition, due to the possibility of movement and subsequent change of address, there can be no guarantee that the addresses provided are current. The majority of the organizations can be found in books located at the reference desk of any major library. The two best sources of information are *Gayle's Encyclopedia of Associations* and *The National Trade and Professional Associations of the United States.* Either of these books is an excellent source of current addresses, phone numbers, and services provided by each association.

Since these two books are published yearly, this list should be used as a starting point and specific information obtained from either of the two publications listed.

Air Traffic Conference of America
1709 New York Ave. NW
Washington, DC 20006
(202) 626-4218

Air Transportation Association
of America
1709 New York Ave. NW
Washington, DC 20006
(202) 626-4000

American Amusement Machine
Association
205 The Strand, Suite 3
Alexandria, VA 22314
(703) 548-8044

American Association of Health,
Physical Education, Recreation
and Dance
1900 Association Dr.
Reston, VA 22091
(703) 476-3472

American Automobile Association
8111 Gatehouse Rd.
Falls Church, VA 22042
(703) 222-6000

American Boat and Yacht Council (BYC)
P.O. Box 806
Amityville, NY 11701
(516) 598-0550

American Boat Builders and Repairers
Association
715 Boylston St.
Boston, MA 02116
(617) 266-6800

American Bus Association
1025 Connecticut Ave. NW
Washington, DC
(202) 293-5890

American Camping Association
5000 State Rd., 67 N.
Martinsville, IN 46151
(317) 342-8456

American Health Foundation
302 E. 43rd St.
New York, NY 10017
(212) 953-1900

American Hotel and Motel Association
888 7th Ave.
New York, NY 10106
(212) 265-4506

American Professional Racquetball
  Organization
8303 E. Thomas Rd.
Scottsdale, AZ 85251
(602) 945-0143

American Recreation Coalition
Suite 700
1915 Eye St. NW
Washington, DC 20006
(202) 466-6870

American Recreation Equipment
  Association
307 W. Venice Ave.
Venice, FL 33595
(813) 484-8574

American Ski Federation
207 Constitution Ave. NE
Washington, DC 20002
(202) 543-1959

American Society of Travel Agents
4400 MacArthur Blvd. NW
Washington, DC 20007
(202) 965-7520

Amusement and Music Operators
  Association
111 E. Wacker Dr., Suite 600
Chicago, IL 60601
(312) 644-6610

Association for Fitness in Business
965 Hope St.
Stamford, CT 06907
(203) 359-2188

Association of Independent Camps
60 Madison Ave.
New York, NY 10010
(212) 679-3230

Association of Marine Engine
  Manufacturers
401 N. Michigan Ave.
Chicago, IL 60611
(312) 836-4747

Association of Physical Fitness Centers
600 Jefferson St., Suite 202
Rockville, MD 20852
(301) 424-7744

The Athletic Institute
200 Castlewood Dr.
North Palm Beach, FL 33408
(305) 842-3600

Bicycle Manufacturers Association
  of America
Suite 316
1055 Thomas Jefferson St. NW
Washington, DC 20007
(202) 333-4052

Bicycle Wholesale Distributors
  Association
North Plaza Building
99 W. Hawthorne Ave.
Valley Stream, NY 11580
(516) 825-3000

Boat Owners Association of the United
  States
800 S. Pickett St.
Alexandria, VA 22304
(703) 823-9550

Boating Industry Associations
401 N. Michigan Ave.
Chicago, IL 60601
(312) 836-4747

Club Managers Association of America
P.O. Box 34482
7615 Winterberry Pl.
Bethesda, MD 20817
(301) 229-3600

Council on Hotel, Restaurant and
  Institutional Education
Human Development Building, Rm. 5208
University Park, PA 16802
(814) 863-0580

Cruise Line International Association
17 Battery Pl.
New York, NY 10004
(212) 425-7400

Hotel Sales and Marketing Association
Suite 810
1400 K St. NW
Washington, DC 20005
(202) 789-0089

Intercollegiate Yacht Racing Association
  of North America
8893 Melinda Ct.
Milan, MI 48160
(313) 434-0746

International Air Transportation
  Association
2000 Peal St.
Montreal, Quebec, Canada H3A 2R4

International Association of Amusement
  Parks and Attractions
4230 King St.
Alexandria, VA 22302
(703) 671-5800

International Food Service Executives
  Association
Suite 600
111 E. Wacker Dr.
Chicago, IL 60601
(312) 644-6610

International Passenger Ship
  Association
17 Battery Pl.
New York, NY 10004

International Racquet Sports
  Association
132 Brookline Ave.
Boston, MA 02215
(617) 236-1500

National Air Transportation Association
4226 King St.
Alexandria, VA 22302
(703) 845-9000

National Association of Skin Diving
  Schools (NASDS)
641 Willow St.
Long Beach, CA 90806
(213) 595-5361

National Association of Sporting Goods
  Wholesalers
P.O. Box 11344
Chicago, IL 60611
(312) 565-0233

National Association of Underwater
  Instructors (NAUI)
P.O. Box 14650
Montclair, CA 91763
(714) 621-5801

National Association of Golf Club
  Manufacturers
200 Castlewood Dr.
North Palm Beach, FL 33408
(305) 844-2500

National Bicycle Dealers Association
P.O. Box 3450
Mission Viejo, CA 92690
(714) 951-3451

National Campground Owners
  Association
804 D St. NE
Washington, DC 20002
(202) 543-6260

National Club Association
Suite 609
1625 Eye St. NW
Washington, DC 20006
(202) 466-8424

National Golf Foundation
200 Castlewood Dr.
North Palm Beach, FL 33408
(305) 844-2500

National Inn Keeping Association
122 E. High St.
Jefferson City, MO 65101

National Marine Representatives
  Association
16-2 St.Thomas Colony
Glen Ellyn, IL 60020
(312) 587-1253

National Recreation and Parks
 Association
3101 Park Center Dr.
12th Floor
Alexandria, VA 22302
(703) 820-4940

National Restaurant Association
311 First St. NW
Washington, DC 20001
(202) 638-6100

National Ski Areas Association
P.O. Box 2883
20 Maple St.
Springfield, MA 01101
(413) 781-4732

National Sporting Goods Association
Lake Center Plaza Bldg.
1699 Wall St.
Mt. Prospect, IL 60056
(312) 439-4000

Professional Association of Diving
 Instructors (PADI)
1243 E. Warner Ave.
Santa Ana, CA 92705
(714) 540-7234

Recreation Vehicle Dealers Association
 of North America
3251 Old Lee Hwy.
Suite 500
Fairfax, VA 22030
(703) 591-7130

Recreation Vehicle Industry Association
P.O. Box 2999
1896 Preston White Dr.
Reston, VA 22090
(703) 620-6003

Recreation Vehicle Rental Association
3251 Old Lee Hwy.
Suite 500
Fairfax, VA 22030
(703) 591-7130

Souvenir and Novelty Trade Association
401 N. Broad St., Suite 226
Philadelphia, PA 19108

United States Yacht Racing Union
P.O. Box 209
Newport, RI 02840
(401) 849-5200

Yachting Club of America
P.O. Box 487
Islamorada, FL 33036
(305) 664-4102

Summary

The field of commercial recreation is extremely broad and varied. The career you choose is strictly up to you and your ability to sell yourself. In this industry, salaries can range from minimal to very high. Students who are contemplating moving into commercial recreation should contact some of the associations and businesses in their area for additional information pertaining to possible careers.

BIBLIOGRAPHY

Barbati, C.: Meetings at mountain resorts, Meetings and Convention, Feb. 1985, p. 87.
Benson, F.: A space-age swimming hole, Parks and Recreation, Oct. 1977.
Bicycling Magazine's 1985 study of U.S. retailing bicycle stores, Marketing and Merchandising, July 1985.
Bueltena, G.L., and Wood, V.: The American retirement community: bane or blessing?, Journal of Gerontology **24:**209–217, 1969.

U.S. Department of Labor Career Opportunities in Hotel and Restaurant Industries. Washington, D.C., 1982, U.S. Printing Office.
Cornish, G.S. and Whitten, R.E. The golf course, New York, N.Y., 1982, Rutledge Press.
Fasta, G.: The Five Hundred Pannel, Restaurant Hospitality, vol. 66, no. 6, June 1982.
Gift and decorative accessories. vol. 87. Dover, N.J., 1986, Geyer-McAllister Publications, Inc.

Girtch, C.M.: The economics of racquetball, Parks and Recreation, Oct. 1982, pp. 47-50.

Hawes, J., and d'Amico, M.: Developing a planned retirement community, Journal of Property Management **47:**14, 1982.

Loro, L.: Radio Only, Radio Programming, March 1986.

Manning, R.E., and Powers, L.A.: Peak and off peak use: redistributing the outdoor recreation/tourism load, Journal of Travel Research Fall, 1984, pp. 25-31.

Manuson, Ed.: If Its Flat, Develop It, Time, Jan. 13, 1986, p. 20.

Squri, J.: The movie business book, Englewood Cliffs, N.J., 1983, Prentice-Hall, Inc.

Students take up golfing, Wall Street Journal, March 28, 1985.

Swartz, S.: Here today, gone tomorrow, Wall Street Journal, April 21, 1986, Sec. 4, p. 21D.

Trunzo, C.: The royal rail to romance, Money, Sept. 1985, p. 53.

Visual merchandising and store design, vol. 117. Cincinnati, Oh., 1986, Signs of the Times Publishing Co.

Wade, G.: Projecting the need for new sports facilities, Parks and Recreation, July 1982, pp. 40-43.

Welling, B.: Why basketball is having a championship season, Business Week, March 4, 1985, pp. 75-76.

SUGGESTED READINGS

Bolles, Richard N. What color is your parachute?, Berkeley, Calif., 1986, Ten Speed Press.

This book is updated annually and provides excellent background information on interest identification, job search, selling yourself, and resume construction. Invaluable to the commercial recreation student.

Lattin, Gerald W. The lodging and food service industry, East Lansing, Mich., 1985, The Educational Institute of the American Hotel and Motel Association.

An excellent resource for the hotel and food service industries. Provides background information on careers, growth, and future of these industries. Also covers various jobs available.

McIntosh, Robert W. and Charles R. Goeldner. Tourism: principles, practices, philosophies, 4th edition, Columbus, Oh., 1984, Grid Publishing, Inc.

Oriented to the more technical aspects of travel and tourism, but some sections pertain to history and general organization of the industry.

Leisure Industry Digest.

This biweekly publication continually updates information on all forms of commercial recreation, from new trends to recent data and surveys.

Managed Recreation Research Report. Recreation, Sports and Leisure, Minneapolis, Minn., Lakewood Publications.

This yearly report provides updates on new purchases, size of the industry, income of managers, salaries, satisfaction, and general facility profiles, along with trends in commercial recreation. This publication is in its third year providing historical as well as current data. The special issue is usually published in July and August.

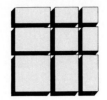

Legal structures for commercial recreation

CHAPTER OBJECTIVES

1. To discuss the advantages and disadvantages of each form of business organization

2. To help select the most appropriate business organization

3. To introduce the concepts of contractual law

4. To introduce the concepts of risk and risk reduction

People in commercial recreation are intimately involved with the concept of games. In any game there are rules that must be followed in order to compete successfully. As with a game, in business there are rules that must be followed, often designated by business organizations. The selection of the form of business organization establishes the rules by which an individual must play the game of business.

Let's take the game concept one step further, to video games, where various levels of play can be selected by a player. Each skill level requires different techniques to avoid pitfalls and to win the game. This is also true in business. Various sets of rules can be selected by the player, and as with video games, the rules can be easy, medium, or very hard.

As an entrepreneur learns about the game of business and progresses through various stages of participation, he or she may eventually achieve a managerial position, or higher level of difficulty in the game. A manager must be aware of all of the rules and their relationship to the strategies of the business. The manager must be aware of the different rules required for each business organization. How the rules are determined depends on the objectives of the player. Once the player/ manager has determined the most important components of the game, he or she is able to select the most acceptable business organization.

Business organization selection is dependent on two factors: business control and tax consequences. It is important to realize that an organizational form can leave the player with very little control over the business yet still require total responsibility for running the organization. Taxes are based on the type of business and its returns. Income fluctuation can play a very important role in the selection of the tax year. If taxes are due during the slack season, there may not be sufficient funds to pay them. It is important to understand how much of the company resources can go to pay taxes. These costs can be significant and possibly damaging.

This chapter discusses different business organization forms as they relate to a business manager. Specific sections will deal with control and taxes. Others discuss the advantages and disadvantages of each business form. Business organizations range from simple to complex in the following order: sole proprietorships, partnerships, and corporations. In addition to these general forms there are numerous hybrid forms that combine the advantages and disadvantages of each. Later sections will deal with contracts and risk management.

Sole proprietorship in commercial recreation

The sole proprietorship is the oldest and simplest form of business organization. It is also the most common form in use today. Sole proprietorships may also be called individual proprietorships or individual enterprises. In a sole proprietorship, one person is the owner, with legal title and exclusive rights to the business. As well as these rights, the owner has certain responsibilities and liabilities.

Probably the most common example of a sole proprietorship in commercial recreation is the retail outlet (for example, sporting goods store) created out of the owner's interest in a specialized activity. To illustrate, we will discuss the hypothetical sole proprietorship called Wind Sailing, Inc., a wind-surfing shop started by a recent commercial recreation graduate. All of the information pertaining to Wind Sailing, Inc., in the following pages is applicable to sole proprietorships.

The commercial recreation graduate begins the business based on her experiences as a participant in the sport while going to school. Perceiving a lack of competition in the area, she decides to start her own wind surfing shop. As the sole proprietor, or owner, she needs to be aware of all business concepts that relate to her business, such as equipment purchasing, advertising, sales, and management.

The owner must obtain funding for the business, establish the organization, do the buying and selection of the merchandise, run the business, keep the books, take any losses, and settle any liabilities. Any relatively small commercial recreation enterprise that does not need extensive capital can be organized as a sole proprietorship like Wind Sailing, Inc.

Advantages of a sole proprietorship

Ease of formation. A sole proprietorship is the easiest and least expensive business organization to establish. All that is needed to establish a sole proprietorship is the desire and the capital. Depending on local and state laws, some sole owners are required to obtain special licenses and permits. The minimum basic permit is a business license obtained from the city and a tax permit obtained from the state. Other requirements may be more complicated, depending on the type of product being sold, as in the case of restaurants, for which food handling permits and health licenses are necessary. However, in our case this is not necessary. Wind Sailing, Inc., is very inexpensive to establish, since there are few if any legal fees when only one person is responsible for the company and its actions.

Owner keeps all profits. Since there is only one person responsible for Wind Sailing, Inc., that person is allowed to reap the profits, which are passed directly on to the owner in the form of income. Wind Sailing, Inc., does not pay any taxes as such; however, the revenue generated from the business is taxable as regular income to the owner. In this case, the tax regulations are similar to those pertaining to individuals and are relatively easy to compute.

Uncomplicated control and decision making. Since there is only one person responsible in Wind Sailing, Inc., that person has the right to make necessary and appropriate decisions. There is no need to consult anyone about decisions concerning product lines, expansion, or borrowing capital. Some laws pertain specifically to business units and the Uniform Consumer Product Code. The sole proprietor should be familiar with these laws.

Flexibility. Since Wind Sailing, Inc., has a very simple legal structure and there is only one owner, the company is able to respond rapidly to changing situations. Management decisions are made by the owner. Since the legal structure is extremely flexible, the owner of Wind Sailing, Inc., is able to dissolve the sole proprietorship and enter into a new form of organization if it appears more advantageous to her. This usually takes place when a business has become sufficiently complicated to warrant the introduction of large amounts of new capital. Other situations that prompt a change in organization include needing new expertise and becoming so profitable that personal tax rates become prohibitive. In each of these situations a different form of business organization may be wiser.

Less government control. Wind Sailing, Inc., is responsible only to state and local governments. Laws pertaining to proprietorships attempt to ensure fair business practices. In other forms of business organizations, such as corporations, numerous reporting laws must be followed in order to maintain the business. These laws are required by the federal government to help maintain an estimate of the economy.

Confidential operations. There is no need to prepare complex balance sheets for circulation to stockholders in sole proprietorships because there are no stockholders. This allows the owner to maintain confidentiality about the way the business is operated. This is particularly desirable when patents and special processes must be protected. Confidentiality is much more difficult to maintain in other forms of business organizations since the owners (stockholders) of the company have the right to know what is taking place. Lack of confidentiality can be carried to an extreme in a publicly held organization.

High personal incentive. The owner of Wind Sailing, Inc., has a high personal stake in its success. This incentive is not only financial but also psychological. If the business succeeds, the individual also succeeds. This personal involvement has the tendency to create a strong need for success on the part of the business owner. As a result, he or she may work long hours to ensure success.

Disadvantages of a sole proprietorship

Unlimited liability. Since Wind Sailing, Inc., and the owner are not considered separate legal entities, the total assets of the owner can be used to pay off the liabilities of the business. These liabilities can take two forms: (1) personal injury claims from people who are on the business property, and (2) losses due to economic downturns or mismanagement. To prevent catastrophic losses due to liability for injury occurring on the property, the purchase of sufficient insurance to cover the cost of anticipated lawsuits or damages is mandatory. However, you cannot insure against poor management. Because of this, it is wise to consider the ramifications of a sole proprietorship. If Wind Surfing, Inc., generates large losses, the creditors are legally able to lay claim against the owner. This allows creditors to obtain and sell the personal assets of the owner including her car, home, and all other personal assets. It is quite possible for the owner of Wind Sailing, Inc., to be liable for losses that exceed her personal wealth. In this case she may labor for years to pay off her business debts. For this reason one should be careful about selecting a sole proprietorship as a form of business.

Availability of capital. There are only two ways that Wind Sailing, Inc., can raise funds for creation or expansion: by borrowing against the owner's personal assets and from income generated by the business. This limiting factor should be taken into consideration when trying to establish a business. Most people find it very hard to generate the capital needed to begin a business out of their personal assets. In addition, banks hesitate to lend to people who have no business record. Normally a bank will use personal assets as collateral on a loan for the business. Once Wind Sailing, Inc., is functioning properly, there is a possibility that increased funds for expansion can come from profits. However, profits are subject to income tax. Once the owner has paid herself a salary (the usual practice) and paid taxes, there may not be enough left from profits to pay for expansion and development.

Limited life. Since Wind Sailing, Inc., is the responsibility of one person, illness,

death, or bankruptcy of the owner of the business would terminate the sole proprietorship. This is the reason sole proprietorships are not usually passed on from
generation to generation. This consideration also severely limits the size of the organization. It is rare that any business can become very large in one generation.
Moreover, if the owner is incapacitated through illness or injury, the company may
not survive.

Limited viewpoint and managerial expertise. Since the sole proprietorship is
most often a one-person operation, that person must be responsible for all aspects
of the business, including finance, advertising, marketing, buying, credit references, etc. Rarely does one person possess all of these skills. As a result, it is unlikely that all areas of the business will receive premium input and expertise. Most
people with well-developed business skills will not work for a sole proprietorship,
since there is little or no opportunity for advancement. This is a major drawback of
the sole proprietorship and one that requires recognition. There are numerous
cases of sole proprietorships that failed just when they were becoming successful
because the owner did not realize the need for additional expertise in time.

Lack of unobligated time. Since the owner of Wind Sailing, Inc., is responsible
for all operations, quite often she does not feel able to be away from the business.
This is especially true in commercial recreation because most of the people in the
field are there because they enjoy participating in the activity their businesses
support. Quite often, due to lack of time, the sole proprietor needs to give up the
very activity he or she has enjoyed enough to warrant the establishment of the
business. This problem can be dealt with in a number of ways, but usually it is not.
Among the ways that unobligated time for participation can be increased is by hiring people to help in the operation and management of the business, by reducing
expectations on the owner's part in order to free up time, by operating the business on a part-time basis, and through teaching the activity to others. The reasons
for this perceived lack of time are lack of funds and the feeling of the owner that no
one else can do the job as well as he or she can.

Partnership

The Uniform Partnership Act, which has been adopted by most states, defines
partnership as "an association of two or more persons to carry on as co-owners of a
business or businesses for profit." This form of business organization solves many
problems evident in the sole proprietorship. These include the inability to raise
capital and the lack of general expertise in one person.

There are many partnership forms for use in commercial recreation management. The most common is general partnership, in which the partners share
equally in the operation, management, and liability of the business. In an active
partnership, all the co-owners work in and share responsibility for the business.
One or more of the partners, however, may not be publicly identified as such; they
are known as *secret partners.*

In some partnerships, one or more of the co-owners of a business are not involved in day-to-day operations and are not publicly identified as partners; they are called *dormant partners*. *Silent partners* are not involved in the operation of the business and may or may not be publicly identified as partners.

Secret, dormant, or silent, all the above are true partners; that is, they are co-owners and share in the profits and liabilities of the enterprises. *Nominal partners* (or partners by estoppel), on the other hand, do not really share in ownership. Nominal partners allow their names to be associated with businesses for advertising or public relations purposes. It is important to note that a nominal partner, while not a co-owner, is as liable for damages as a true partner or full participant in the partnership agreement. Anyone contemplating nominal partnership should think carefully of the consequences.

A limited or special partner because of a contractual agreement has only limited liability in the company, while a general partner has unlimited liability. Liability is limited to the amount of money the special (or limited) partner has contributed. This limited-liability clause is valid as long as the limited or special partner does not participate in the management of the company. If the limited partner becomes an active participant in the management process, he or she loses limitations on liability and is treated by the law the same as any general partner.

In any of these forms of partnership, there is always *at least one* partner who has unlimited liability for the actions of the company. In all cases the assets are co-owned by the partners in general, and the partners share in the profits from the company. Partnerships differ from sole proprietorships because two or more people own the company. This necessitates that a contractual agreement be established prior to the development of a partnership.

We cannot emphasize enough that people establishing a partnership need to seek legal counsel before attempting to develop any form of partnership. Many subjects addressed in partnership agreements should be discussed by prospective partners. When the partners have reached an agreement on each item, a contract should be drawn up. It should include each of the following articles: names, purposes, domiciles, duration of agreement, character of partners (general or limited, active or silent), contributions by partners, business expenses (how handled), authority (individual partners' authority to conduct business), separate debts, books, record keeping and methods of accounting, division of profits and losses, draws or salary, rights of continuing partners, death of a partner, employee management, release of debts, sale of partnership interest, arbitration, additions, alteration or modification of partnership agreements, settlement of disputes, required and prohibited acts, absence, and disability. These contractual articles should be used only as guides; circumstances may dictate additional articles.

A partnership is initiated when one or more partners have special attributes to bring to the business. These attributes can include capital assets, specific business knowledge, and business connections. It may be beneficial to form a partnership when two companies with people of complementary backgrounds and expertise can get together to save costs and to increase operational efficiency.

There are also tax advantages. A partnership is a contractual agreement, and the character of the income can be contractually changed. It is possible for different proportions of business income to go to the partners, allowing for maximum tax benefits based on the total income of both partners.

For example, one of the partners may be very wealthy, while the other has a moderate income. In this case the partnership agreement could allow for the partner with the higher income to lower his or her overall tax burden by sustaining some of the losses from the company to offset income from other sources. The partner with the lower income could assume more of the profits from the company. In this case the company would pay less tax than a sole proprietorship.

To illustrate, let's consider a partnership of two people. One partner, the commercial recreation major, supplies the expertise; the other partner supplies the capital. This is not an uncommon situation. The business is to rent motor boats to the general public at Lake Tahoe. The name of the company is to be Tahoe Boats. The provider of capital is to be a limited partner; therefore, her liability, if the business should fail, is strictly limited to the amount of money that she has invested in the company—provided she does not participate in the day-to-day business. The managing partner's liability is unlimited, since he is the one who is doing business in the company name.

Advantages of partnership

Ease of formation. While a partnership is more complicated than a sole proprietorship, it is less so than a corporation. The main requirement for formation of Tahoe Boats is a contract between the partners. The business initiation and development is similar to a sole proprietorship. A partnership may have no contract between partners, but we strongly advise against this.

Ease of raising capital. Since a partnership comprises two or more people, it is easier for partners to raise capital for initial costs than it is for sole proprietors because both partners' assets can be used for collateral.

Strength of organization. Since more than one person is involved in a partnership, it is likely that the partners will bring different backgrounds and expertise. Consequently, it should be easy to draw on the strengths of both partners to create a much stronger organization than would exist in a sole proprietorship and so allow for rapid development and specialization of tasks. Specialization is usually accomplished by splitting the managerial duties among the partners based on individual experience and expertise—except in the case of limited partnerships such as Tahoe Boats, where the partner does not want to become involved in the operation of the business.

Tax advantages. Since Tahoe Boats is able to disperse profits and losses among the partners based upon the contractual agreement, it maximizes revenue to the partners. For example, the sole proprietor is taxed on the full income amount at the appropriate tax rate. However, if a partnership agreement disperses the profits on a fifty-fifty basis, each partner is liable for his or her personal portion of the taxes. This may result in a lower tax rate, which saves personal revenue for reinvestment into the company.

Flexibility. A partnership is less flexible than a sole proprietorship but much more so than a corporation. Since only the partners need to agree on changes, they can be executed very rapidly. The partnership allows one partner to leave the business to take vacations, eliminating some of the feelings of being tied down prevalent in the sole proprietorship.

Personal incentive. Like the sole proprietorship, the partners in a business are personally involved in its success.

Disadvantages of partnership

Unlimited liability. Partnerships have liabilities similar to those of sole proprietorships. The same insurance plans must be considered. If the company's assets are not sufficient to cover losses, the partners' personal assets become available for the payment of the debt. If this takes place, the partners are assessed based on their share of the business. If one partner's assets are not sufficient to cover his or her portion of the debt, the other partner is held liable. This is the case in most forms of partnerships, the exception being the limited or special partner. The limited or special partner is liable only for the amount of capital invested in the company. Creditors are not able to collect any additional funds from his or her personal assets. Remember, in partnerships, at least one partner always has unlimited liability for the company.

Difficulty in raising funds. As noted earlier, Tahoe Boats has a greater potential of obtaining loans than does a sole proprietorship. However, a partnership suffers numerous disadvantages in comparison with a corporation. A partnership is not able to go to the capital funds market and generate additional revenue through the sale of stocks and bonds. The only methods available to a partnership are to add more partners, to borrow funds, and to use company profits.

Limited life. The life of a partnership depends upon the contractual agreement. On the death or disability of one of the partners, the partnership automatically dissolves. Since more people are involved, the life of a partnership is somewhat less than that of a sole proprietorship because of the increased chance of one partner becoming disabled. As the number of partners increases, the expected life of the company decreases.

Once the partnership has been dissolved because of death or the disability of one of the partners, the remaining partners may purchase the former partner's portion of the company and the company may continue to operate as a new partnership or as a sole proprietorship. In many cases the remaining partners do not have sufficient funds to purchase the assets of the deceased partner, so the company is terminated.

Disagreements among partners. Since two or more people are involved in the partnership, it is possible for disagreements to evolve. Once this happens, the partnership is on shaky ground. The majority of partnerships that fail do so because of disagreements between the partners brought on by personality and conceptual differences.

Disposing of partnership interests. There is no secondary market for the sale of partnership interests. Upon termination of the partnership, it becomes necessary for the remaining partners to find a replacement, to purchase the partner's interest, or to dissolve the company.

Bound by acts of one partner. Since a partnership is a company directed by two or more people, the acts of any one partner is sufficient to bind the remaining partner(s) in a contractual agreement. This can have severe consequences if one of the partners is not wise. This possibility is a very severe drawback to any partnership agreement.

Corporation

Corporation was defined in 1819 by Chief Justice Marshall in the decision in *Dartmouth College v. Woodard.* He wrote, "A corporation is an artificial being, invisible, intangible and existing only in the contemplation of the law." This decision has had tremendous impact on the organization of corporations and has created many responsibilities for corporate advisors. It defined a corporation as a being with rights and responsibilities separate from those of the owners of the corporation. This means that a corporation is responsible for its own debts and is also taxed on its own revenue. In addition, the ruling indicated that the corporation exists under the law. This means that it is subject to numerous local, state, and federal laws that do not pertain to any other business form.

Because of these responsibilities, a corporation is the most complex form of business to establish. However, it also provides a business person with numerous protections and advantages that are not available in the other forms of business organizations. It is advisable that you seek legal counsel before you attempt to establish a corporation. However, for purposes of this text, the general requirements of corporations will be discussed.

The corporation must be licensed to do business within the state of its origin. Licensing can be handled by incorporating in the state in which the business is to be conducted or by filing as a foreign corporation doing business within a state. There are advantages and disadvantages to each of these actions, depending on which states are involved. Incorporation involves complex issues that need to be dealt with by legal counsel and are well beyond the scope of this text. However, the fact that the corporation must be registered to do business within a state is important. The filing requirements usually include the name and address of the corporation, the articles of incorporation, the bylaws, the directors and officers of the company, the kind and duration (which can be listed as perpetual) of the business, the maximum number of shares of stock it can sell, and the par value of that stock.

Usually corporate officers consist of a president, a vice president, a secretary and a treasurer, who together are responsible for day-to-day operations. Their duties, titles, and responsibilities are outlined in the articles of incorporation, and generally the officers report directly to a board of directors, who are in turn elected by the stockholders. The board of directors is required by law to meet at least once a year, and the minutes of the meetings must be maintained. If not, the corporate veil may be pierced by the Internal Revenue Service, and the corporation may be judged to be a partnership or a sole proprietorship.

The articles of incorporation, or bylaws, should include a list of organizers of the corporation; how, where, and when stockholder meetings are to be called; the name of the corporation; its objectives and purposes; how directors and officers are to be elected; duties and compensation of directors and officers; when and how dividends are to be declared; methods of transferring shares of stock; location of the corporation; the names of the officers; procedures for amendments to the articles; and the signatures of incorporators, witnesses, and a notary public. Again, let us stress that these requirements vary from state to state and it is in your best interests to obtain the services of a lawyer to handle these specifics.

Advantages of a corporation

Limited liability. Since the corporation is a legal entity and is responsible for its own debts, the liability of the stockholders is limited to their investment in the company, that is, the amount of money they have paid for stocks. If the corporation faces financial difficulties or liabilities, the debtors cannot collect from the assets of the stockholders. This is a major factor in the development of any corporation and is one of the reasons people are willing to purchase stock. However, this limited liability should not be thought to mean limited liability in terms of insurance. The same forms of insurance are needed for a corporation as for any other form of business organization.

Unlimited life. Since a corporation is a legal entity, it has an unlimited life, so the death or retirement of any of its principal members, directors, or officers does not terminate it. This allows corporations to enter into long-term contracts, since their stability is relatively ensured and is not dependent on the lives and health of officers of the company.

Transfer of ownership. It is easy to transfer ownership through the purchase and sale of stock. This allows people to trade their shares in the company for cash. Consequently, it is easy to sell shares in a company and yet maintain the viability of the company.

Ease of raising capital. Because of the advantages of perpetual life, the simplified transfer of ownership, and the limited liability to the owners, it is relatively easy to raise long-term capital for a corporation. In fact, through the sale of stock in a corporation, the owners are able to raise *equity capital*. Equity capital is money paid for a part ownership in a company; this does not have to be repaid to the investor. Equity capital has a definite advantage when establishing a business, since it provides large amounts of capital with no personal liability. Also, stock may be sold to numerous people, allowing for many small purchases to make up the total capital needed for the formation of the company. As a result, the increased number of people willing to participate in the corporation eases the acquisition of funds.

Efficiency of management. Since a corporation is a large organization, it has the cash to attract and keep people. Because of this it is able to divide responsibilities and optimize the performance of each individual. The result is a more effective organization and operation of the business.

Disadvantages of a corporation

Expensive to organize. Due to extensive legal work and the number of legal entities involved in corporate management, such as local, state, and federal governments, corporations are very expensive to create. It is also extremely expensive and difficult to destroy corporations due to the legal ramifications. Because the corporation has its own life, it must be destroyed, not dissolved. This requires the legal processes of state and federal governments. In addition, all stockholders must be notified.

Governmental control. Because of the legal status of a corporation, the government is involved in all aspects of corporate life. Most of the pertinent laws were established to protect the public from unscrupulous business practices. The result of these legal requirements is a cumbersome and complex organization that does not allow rapid change and that requires extensive legal involvement. Regardless of the reasons for corporate laws and their complexity, compliance is time-consuming and expensive.

Business restrictions. When a corporation files its articles of incorporation, the business of the corporation is specifically stated. As a result, the corporation is limited to certain types of enterprises. It can change the charter through amendments, but this is time-consuming and costly. This requirement does not allow for rapid expansion into new areas of business. Suppose a commercial recreation business's articles of incorporation indicate that it is specifically developed to sell skis on the wholesale market to retail manufacturers. This company cannot expand into ski manufacturing without changing its articles of incorporation, which may take up to a year and accrue extensive legal fees.

Control of company. Since the corporation is owned by stockholders, they are the final decision makers in any changes by the corporation. It can be time-consuming to get the stockholders to agree to changes in direction or management policy. When a corporation has a major decision to make, it must be made by means of a vote of the stockholders. This is usually accomplished by mailing a ballot, referred to as a proxy. Therefore, when the actual voting takes place, the stockholders need not be present but can cast their votes by proxy.

There can be abuses by stockholders in proxy fights. Dissatisfied stockholders may gain a majority of the votes and completely change the officers and organization of the company. Control of a company may rest with the major stockholders and not with the people who developed the company.

Taxation. As a separate entity, the corporation is subject to corporate tax laws. Any profits received by the corporation are taxed at the corporate level. In addition to corporate taxes, any dividends to stockholders are taxed as ordinary income, which results in double taxation. This results in generally high taxation of corporate profits. When issuing stock in a company, it is imperative for the board of directors to be extremely aware of the tax laws. We highly encourage individuals developing a commercial recreation corporation to identify and explore the ramifications of stock issuance with a qualified investment banker or securities lawyer.

Subchapter S corporations

It is possible to organize a business venture as a corporation but to pay tax on the revenue as a partnership. This provides all the limitations on liability of a corporation but eliminates the tax disadvantages of a corporation. Such corporations must be developed under Subchapter S of the Internal Revenue Code. The basic considerations are as follows:

1. There can be no more than 25 shareholders, and each must consent to the election of this type of business organization.
2. Only persons, estates, and certain trusts can hold stock in the corporation; specifically, there can be no corporate or partnership shareholders.
3. There can only be one class of stock.
4. All shareholders must be U.S. citizens or resident aliens.
5. Not more than 80% of the firm's gross receipts may come from sources outside of the United States.
6. Not more than 20% of the firm's gross receipts can come from interest, dividends, rents, royalties, annuities, and gains from the sale or exchange of securities.

Advantages of a Subchapter S corporation

The major advantage of a Subchapter S corporation is that it provides limited liability to the owners of the company. At the same time it helps in the establishment of long-term capital due to the unlimited life of the corporation and its ability to sell stock.

Disadvantages of a Subchapter S corporation

Specific regulations cover cash disbursement, reporting, and legal requirements. It is in the best interest of a person seeking to establish a business to look into the possibility of a Subchapter S corporation before deciding on any type of organization.

How to select the business organization you need

Before you select a business organization, a series of questions need to be answered. The answers will help you decide which organizational form is best suited to you. Be sure to seek competent legal aid when starting your business. The questions that follow are intended only as examples of areas you should consider.

1. How big is the risk? That is, what is the amount of the investors' liability for debts and taxes?
2. How important is the continuity of the firm? What if something happened to the principal or principals?
3. What legal structure would insure the greatest adaptability in administration of the firm?
4. What are the influences of applicable laws on the business?
5. What are the possibilities of attracting additional income if it is needed, and what are the capabilities of raising capital now?
6. What are the needs or the possibility of attracting additional expertise to run the business?
7. What are the costs and procedures involved in starting the proposed business?
8. What is the ultimate goal and purpose of the enterprise and what legal structure can best serve its purpose?
9. How much control of the business does the developer wish to have in the long run?

It is possible by answering these nine questions to go back to the advantages and disadvantages of the different legal organizations that we have discussed and select the most appropriate one. These questions will help you focus your attention on the important aspects of a business. To help remind you of the advantages and disadvantages of each business form, refer to Table 3-1.

Contracts and commercial recreation

A contract is one of the most important business documents. Contracts are involved in almost every aspect of a commercial recreation enterprise (Fig. 3-1). There are contracts to purchase goods, to perform specific duties, between employees and employers, for the delivery of goods, for behavior, and for concession arrangements—to list a few. The nature of and requirements for a valid contract are of vital importance.

Before any discussion of contracts certain things must be clear. First, we are not lawyers but educators. As Betty van der Smissen said, "There is a difference between a lawyer who is interested in recreation and a recreation educator who is interested in law" (van der Smissen, 1983). We concur completely. Law is a human institution and the machinery for its administration is human machinery. There are imperfections, uncertainties, variations, and inconsistencies in the law, especially as it relates to contracts. It is imperative that this writing not be

TABLE 3-1. Forms of business organization

	Proprietorship	Partnership	Corporation	Subchapter S corporation
Risk	Unlimited	Share of total liability	Investment	Investment and loans
Continuity	Lifetime	Lifetime of one partner	Unlimited	Unlimited
Adaptability	High	Moderate	Low	Moderate
Legal requirements	Low	Moderate	High	Moderate
Capital	Owner only	Loans from partners or from new partners buying in	Sell stock or bonds	Sell stock
Staffing	Poor	Poor	Good	Fair
Cost to establish	Low	Moderate	High	Moderate
Ultimate goal	Depends on desires of owner			
Control	High	Moderate	Depends on amount of stock owned	Moderate

construed as legal advice. The material presented is the summation of research into contracts and contractual law. Any situation involving ambiguities must be judged in a court of law based on the specific facts involved in a contractual agreement. The intent of this section is to make you aware of questions to ask a lawyer in reference to contracts.

What is a contract?

You need to know what a contract is, the different types, and the requirements for a valid contract. What constitutes a contract? In a number of definitions three factors in various combinations are present:

1. A contract is a series of operative acts of the parties and an expression of their assent to these acts.
2. A contract is a physical document executed by the parties and is lasting evidence of other necessary acts expressing their intentions.
3. A contract defines the legal relationships resulting from the operative acts of the parties, always including the relation of the right in one party to the duty in the other (Corbin, 1952).

Simply stated, a contract is a promise enforceable by law, either directly or indirectly. For example, A promises to operate B's ride at an amusement park, and B promises to pay A. This definition is important, since it specifically identifies the

FIG. 3-1 Contracts should be established for every aspect of a commercial recreation enterprise, including the rental of bicycles during the off-season. (Photograph courtesy of Copper Mountain, Inc.)

duties of the parties in a contract. A party is an individual, or a business. Under the law, a business entity has the contracting power of an individual, provided that the contracting member of the corporation or business has the authority to act for the organization.

The three most common forms of contracts are unilateral, implied and bilateral. Let us discuss an example of each.

Suppose A is representing a resort and offers B this proposition: "I will give you $20 a day to be a lifeguard at the swimming pool." Is a contract in force? The answer is yes. Under the law, A, as the representative of the resort, has entered into a unilateral contract. This is one in ". . . which, although a legal obligation is created, one party receives as consideration for his promise the performance or forbearance of some act" (Wyatt, 1971, p. 37). Unilateral contracts are important for several reasons, one of which is the fact that the other party does not have to agree to the terms. A unilateral contract stays valid until you revoke it or until it is executed by the other party. The next day B could arrive to lifeguard the swimming pool, and A would have entered into a valid contract and owe the lifeguard $20 per day. A unilateral contract does not have to be agreed on by both parties; the contractual relationship is not established until the actual performance of an act. Once this happens, the legal obligation on A's part to pay for the services rendered is in force.

Let's look at another type of contract. Say you have been approached by an individual selling shirts with the name of your business silk-screened across the front. He offers to sell them to you, and you take the goods. You have not agreed to purchase the goods. Have you entered into a contract? Yes, an implied contract. The key to an implied contract is that the terms are implied through the acts of both parties. Accepting shipped goods implies agreement to buy. This is especially true if you have done business with this supplier in the past.

The third type, the bilateral contract, is probably the most common. In a bilateral contract "each party receives as consideration for his promise a promise from the other party" (Wyatt, 1971, p. 37). This is most commonly executed by two people negotiating the terms of the contract, as when A agrees to lease to B a beachfront property if B agrees to operate a concession stand to rent sailboats on it.

A bilateral contract must be composed of the following items:

1. An agreement, both an offer and an acceptance
2. Some *consideration,* or exchange of goods, services, or money
3. Parties who have the capacity to contract
4. Legal objective or objectives

The following sections will discuss each of these items.

What is agreement?

To enter into a contract, both parties must reach an agreement.This agreement must have three separate parts: the formation of an offer, the determination and duration of the offer, and the acceptance of the offer (Wyatt, 1971, p. 40). An offer is a proposal made by one party to another to enter into a contract. Be careful what you offer, because if your offer is accepted, a contract has been established. This offer may be oral, written, or implied. However, it is essential that it be made with the intent to enter into a contract, that it be communicated to the *offeree,* or person to be contracted with, that it be definite and certain, and that it not be an invitation to negotiate.

The intention of entering into a contract must be established in a formal setting. The law has determined that a person who enters into a contract at a social engagement is not thinking of legal obligations. Therefore statements or assertions made in jest, under strain, stress, or excitement are not offers.

The second part of the offer is communication. This means more than that the offeree learns of the offer. It must be expressed by words, writing, or conduct. This communication must be made directly to the other party of the contract or by an authorized representative. An offer is not communicated when one person tells another that he intends to make an offer to a third person, and the hearer, without authority, conveys that information to the putative offeree.

You should always remember that an offer must be clear, definite, and certain in such essential terms as the time of performance, the price to be paid, the work to be done, and the identification of the subject matter. These are critically important, especially if the contract should be questioned and litigation is necessary.

When dealing with contracts, it should be noted that an offer must be distinct from an invitation to negotiate. Quite often in business transactions one party would like the other to make an offer first. This allows the first party to find out what the other party thinks would be a fair offer. However, acceptance of an offer would result in a contract. If you enter into an agreement to negotiate, the other party is required to present the offer first and you have the option to present a counteroffer or to accept the offer.

One term should be clarified when used with the offer of a contract. It is quite common for an individual to make a *firm offer*. A firm offer is an irrevocable offer, in which an expiration time is clearly stipulated. This offer cannot be revoked until that time period has passed. Be careful when you use the term "firm" in connection with an offer, especially if you do not specify an expiration date.

Once an offer has been made, it may be terminated by one of the following:

1. Revocation of the offer. The offerer must communicate revocation to the offeree *prior to* acceptance of the offer.
2. Acceptance of the offer.
3. Expiration of the offer. This occurs when the stipulated expiration date of a firm offer passes before the offer is accepted.
4. Termination by implied terms. In the absence of an expressed limitation, an offer expires after a reasonable time has elapsed. Determination of a reasonable time by the courts depends on what the offer relates to. If you were dealing with a highly perishable commodity, an offer would terminate much sooner than if the commodity were nonperishable. In deciding what is a reasonable time, the courts take into consideration the nature of the proposed contract and the usages of business in addition to other circumstances.
5. Rejection of the offer, with or without a counteroffer. A rejected offer cannot be revived by any act on the part of the offeree. However, having rejected the offer, he or she is free to make a counteroffer by indicating the desire to enter into a contract with terms different from those made by the offeror. A counteroffer reverses the relationship of the parties: the offeree becomes the offeror.

Acceptance of the offer must be communicated to the offeror. This can be done in a number of ways. Probably the most common is oral acceptance. A contract entered into orally is valid. A written contract is merely a manifestation of the contract.

Silence or inaction on the part of the offeree does not amount to an acceptance of an offer, except in a few instances when the law imposes a duty to speak. It is wise for the offeree to accept or reject the offer in writing.

There are two common instances in which silence implies assent to a contract. The first is when the offeree has had previous dealings with the offeror. In this case the offeree's conduct on previous occasions may give the offeror reason to believe that silence amounts to acceptance of the contract. The second is the retention of property, in which case silence as acceptance is applicable if the offeree takes benefits, goods, or services offered with the expectation of pay. As you will remember, these are both instances discussed above relating to an implied contract.

The third type of contract is unilateral. Remember, the unilateral contract is defined as a promise for an act. Courts sometimes allow the offeree to recover on a quasi contract if there has been a benefit to the offeror. The courts also hold that the start of performance constitutes a legal bilateral contract when there is doubt whether the contract is bilateral or unilateral. There is also an increased willingness on the part of some courts to enforce a promise: (1) if the offeree has suffered extensive damage, (2) if the offeror actually made the promise that was the cause of the offeree's reliance, and/or (3) if the detrimental reliance by the offeree was foreseen by the offeror. Once an offeree has started the work specified by the person offering the unilateral contract, the contract becomes bilateral.

Sometimes an offer has ambiguous acceptance terms. When this happens, the law generally provides that an offer may be accepted in any manner and by any reasonable medium. Therefore you must be very careful when accepting any shipment. The Uniform Commercial Code makes it mandatory that the buyer notify the seller when acceptance of a shipment is not acceptance of a contract, but that acceptance is made only as an accommodation to the buyer. The acceptance of goods without such notification is an acceptance of a contract. Ordinarily, if you accept a shipment from a supplier, you have entered into a contract.

Considerations

A contract, whether oral or written, is not binding in the absence of consideration. *Consideration* may consist of any of the following: an act, forbearance, *or a return promise.* Consideration must be sufficient in the sense that it has legal value in the eyes of the law. In a bilateral contract a promise for a promise constitutes the consideration, and each party is both a promisor and a promisee. In a unilateral contract, a promise for an act, the offeror is a promisor and the offeree is a promisee.

The general rule is that "the mutual promises must be stated in terms such that both parties are bound and that an action could be maintained by each against the other for a breach of the contract" (Wyatt, 1971, p. 64). An agreement that enables one party to reserve the right to cancel the agreement at his pleasure imposes no liability on that party if he takes advantage of the reservation clause and terminates the contract. There is no promise for a promise and therefore no contract.

The forbearance of a legal right is considered to be sufficient consideration to warrant a contract, providing that the forbearance does not involve an act that the forbearer is legally entitled to perform and that is not contrary to public policy. However, the peformance of a preexistent duty is not sufficient consideration. The promise to perform something a person is already under legal obligation to perform does not constitute consideration. Since the courts make no attempt to determine value, the term *adequate consideration* pertaining to the value of property is considered to be legal and binding on both parties.

Once a contract has been entered into and consideration and acceptance of the offer have taken place, there are two ways to change a contract. One is to modify the contract, as when both parties enter into a new contract pertaining to the same subject or introduce new terms into the old contract. This makes the former contract invalid and constitutes a new agreement. A second method is the mutual rescission of a contract. A contract that has not been fully performed by both parties may be rescinded by the parties. This rescission is possible provided the rights of a third party have not intervened. If there is a third party involved, they all must agree to the rescission.

Capacity to contract

A contract may be invalid in certain situations because of the condition of one of the parties entering into the contract. These conditions include infancy, insanity, intoxication, and being under sentence for a crime. These conditions are important to commercial recreation enterprises because contracts may need to be executed with individuals in questionable condition.

Infancy is defined as any age under the age of majority. This varies from state to state, usually ranging from 18 to 21. A contract entered into by a person under the age of majority may be held invalid at any time until that person reaches majority or in some cases after his or her majority. Be careful when entering into a contract with underage individuals.

Insanity is any mental defect rendering a person incapable of understanding the nature and consequences of his or her actions. An insane individual may affirm or disaffirm a contract after it has been shown that the person has regained sanity. It is doubtful that anyone would enter into a contract with an insane individual unless that person appeared to be sane. The burden of proof of insanity falls on the person who wants to terminate the contract. Intoxicated persons are treated by the law as insane. They may either affirm of disaffirm the contract once sober.

Convicts cannot enter into any contract while they are serving their prison terms. This is important when prisoners are used in work-release programs. It is wise to have the courts appoint a trustee to act for a convicted individual and to contract with the business.

Contract illegalities

No contract entered into for illegal purposes is valid. However, there are some forms of contract illegalities you may not be aware of. The most common of these is the Sunday law. Many state legislatures have enacted Sunday laws, or "blue laws," that hold that contracts entered into on Sundays are invalid or illegal. The courts have determined that if the terms of a contract are agreed upon on Sunday, but the contract is not entered into until a weekday, the contract is valid. Check the law in your state.

Another illegal contract is one based on a wager, in which the promises are dependent on the outcome of an uncertain event or a fact. This could have ramifications for raffles, door prizes, and similar arrangements. Check your state laws regarding wagers and raffles. If you are running an event in which you give away prizes based on games of chance or uncertain events, you should consider your contractual obligations.

Another type of illegal contract is one that acts as a restraint of trade. This is any contract entered into to eliminate competition or to slow down the development of competition. For example, if a number of resorts in a specific location got together to establish rates, they would be making an illegal contract.

Contracts that are required to be in writing

The statutes on frauds require certain types of contracts to be in writing to be valid. A contract that cannot be completely executed within one year must be in writing. The year begins on the day after the contract is made and ends at the close of the anniversary of the day of contracting. Remember, the year begins on the day after the contract is entered into, not the date that performance is started.

A second kind of contract that must be in writing is one for the sale of real estate or any interest therein. The words "any interest in land" include the fee simple acquisitions, easements, leases, mortgages, and contracts to sell real estate.

Finally, any contract involving the sale of goods for $500 or more must be in writing; if not, it is not enforceable. The form of the contract can be informal and incomplete and still satisfy the Uniform Commercial Code, providing there is sufficient written material for the courts to interpret the intent of the parties. Since the Uniform Commercial Code has been adopted by all 50 states, all commercial recreation students should become familiar with it.

There is one exception to the $500 rule. Sales of specially manufactured goods are enforceable by oral contracts if the goods are made specifically for the buyer. This contract is enforceable under these conditions:

1. The goods are made especially for the buyer.
2. The goods are not suitable for sale in the ordinary business of the seller.
3. The seller, before receiving notice of any repudiation of the contract, has made a substantial commitment toward manufacture.

A written contract is the best protection for any business arrangement. Any writing that accurately names the contractors or describes the parties and the contractual considerations will suffice. It is not necessary for both parties to sign a contract. In general, the printed names of the parties involved either at the top or in the body of the memorandum is sufficient, providing the memorandum is signed by an individual with the authority to enter into a contract.

Risk management

In business three types of risk are of concern to the owner/operator (Fig. 3-2). Business risk, or the risk of failure of the enterprise, is the first. A risk due to un-

FIG. 3-2 In every commercial recreation enterprise there is some risk. It is the duty of each recreation manager to minimize any risk to consumers. (Photograph courtesy Busch Gardens, Tampa, Florida.)

foreseen natural events such as floods, fires, and storms is the second. These risks can be covered by adequate insurance. The third type of risk is liability to a customer who has been injured by the product or service. This form of risk is covered in this section.

It is impossible in this text to cover all of the intricacies of liability as thoroughly as is needed by a business owner. Two excellent textbooks on the subject are *The Law of Parks, Recreation Resources and Leisure Services,* by Frakt and Rankin, and

Liability and Law in Recreation, Parks and Sports, by Kaiser. These books are suggested for individuals contemplating any kind of recreational enterprise.

One of the major issues in the field of parks and recreation today is liability and liability insurance. Numerous causes (outlined in the January 1987 issue of *Parks and Recreation* magazine) have made liability insurance for recreational enterprises extremely expensive or impossible to obtain. The main problem is tort law. Kaiser described a tort as "a civil wrong, other than a breach of contract, for which the court will provide a remedy in the form of an action for damages" (Kaiser, 1986, p. 40). Three elements must be present in all tort cases: breach of legal duty, causation, and injury.

Breach of duty stems from the fact that the law applies the "reasonable and prudent man doctrine" to commercial recreation enterprises. This doctrine states that if you behave other than as a reasonable and prudent operator would, you have breached your legal duty to operate the business in a safe manner.

The courts have identified three different standards of care for individuals using a commercial recreational facility. In declining order of care provided, these are the invitee, the licensee, and the trespasser. Kaiser (1986, p. 92) says,

> (1) An invitee is either a public invitee or a business visitor. (2) An invitee is a person who is invited to enter or remain on land as a member of the public for a purpose for which the land is held open to the public. (3) A business visitor is a person who is invited to enter or remain on land for a purpose directly or indirectly connected to business dealing with the possessor of the land.

The invitee is the person whom you are enticing to come onto your property so you can make money. This classification requires the highest standard of care, including but not limited to maintaining all facilities in a safe operating manner. Constant inspection of the premise for any possible hazard is required and if such hazard is noted, repair should be expedited. You must also anticipate any foreseeable use of your facilities and attempt to make them as safe as possible. Any hazards existing on the facility must be totally removed or the invitee must be warned of the possible danger.

A licensee receives the next strictest standard of care. Frakt and Rankin (1982, p. 135) define *licensee* as an individual whose entry onto the premise is permitted and who is not there to engage in business. Note the difference in the definitions of invitee and licensee. The owner's responsibility to the licensee is much less than to an invitee. In fact, it is presumed by law that an individual entering the premise as a licensee takes the facility or the operation as he finds it, including dangers and hazards.

The lowest standard of care is due a trespasser, someone who has entered the property without permission or who is there illegally. The owner's duty to a trespasser is not to injure him or her through any personal act.

There is a different classification when children enter the premise. This is the *attractive nuisance*. The law has stated that the natural curiosity of children makes certain types of attractions by their nature of interest to children. The owner of the property has a higher standard of duty to prevent children from entering an area where they may be injured.

Kaiser (1986, p. 104) identifies *attractive nuisance* as

(1) The place where the condition exists is one upon which the possessor knows or has reason to know that children are likely to trespass leaders. (2) The condition is one which the possessor knows or has reason to know and which he realizes or should realize will involve an unreasonable risk of death or serious bodily harm to such children. (3) The children because of their youth do not discover the condition or realize the risk involved intermeddling with it or in coming within the area made dangerous by it. (4) The utility to possessor of maintaining the condition and the burden of eliminating the danger are slight as compared to the risk of the children involved, and the possessor fails to exercise reasonable care to protect the children.

As a result of these conditions the landowner has a much higher standard of care in order to prevent children from becoming injured.

In tort law, the most common form of lawsuit is for *negligence;* a legal duty existed due to the nature of the activity and that legal duty was not performed. The result of the nonperformance was an injury that can be compensated for monetarily. The law has identified the following elements of negligence:

(1) A duty or obligation recognized by law requiring the actor to conform to a certain standard of conduct for the protection of others against unreasonable risk. (2) A failure to conform to the standard required. (3) A reasonably close causation connection between the conduct and resulting injury. (4) Actual loss and damages resulting to the interest of another (Kaiser, 1986, p. 52).

The legal duty stems from the type of visitor who is using the premise. It is in the best interest of the commercial recreation operator to treat all individuals on the property as invitees. If you are treating everyone with the highest possible standard of care, you should reduce your risk.

The second issue, the failure to perform, has been briefly addressed earlier. In all cases the courts will apply the "reasonable and prudent man" doctrine. That is, the courts will try to determine what would have been the standard of care due the individual by other businesses operating similar facilities. Once this has been established, it will be compared to the way you performed in your business.

The third requirement for negligence is concerned with the cause of the injury to the individual. If a link can be made between your failure to perform a duty and an injury, the case for negligence is complete. You do not have to be solely responsible for the injury; your action or failure to act need only be a substantial factor in the cause of the injury.

The final element in negligence is that an injury must result in damage to the injured party. An injury can include the invasion of a legal right. However, if that invasion does not result in damage, then there is no basis for recovery by the injured party. The courts have been lenient in determining monetary damages for everything from pain and suffering to loss of companionship. This makes it hard to identify what is true damage resulting from negligence.

In any action resulting from negligence there are eight defenses:

1. *Contributory negligence* is conduct on the part of the injured party that helped to cause the accident.
2. *Comparative negligence* is the amount of contribution to the accident assessed each party, with damages assessed accordingly.
3. *Assumption of risk* means that the injured party assumes part of the responsibility or participates in the activity knowing that harm may happen based on the activity and actions of others.
4. *Governmental immunity* holds that the government cannot be sued for its wrong action. However, this defense is not being as strongly upheld as in the past.
5. *Statutes of limitations* are the legal requirements for filing a lawsuit within a specific period of time.
6. *Notice of claim* is required in many states. This requires an injured party to notify the operator of the business of any injury within a specified time. This allows the operator to mitigate or solve the problem prior to legal action.
7. *Failure of proof* occurs when the injured party is unable to demonstrate negligent action.
8. In *waiver* or *release* the party participating in the recreational activity waives their rights to bring a suit in the case of an injury. This is a very touchy issue and has been interpreted differently by various courts. It is *not* suggested that by simply signing a waiver, a person gives up rights to any legal action.

This section briefly covers the elements of risk that face a commercial recreation entrepreneur. It does not attempt to cover the subject thoroughly or to replace legal counsel. Consulting legal counsel is the best method of mitigating the risk of negligence suits. Insurance can also cover negligence suits. It is in your best interest to work with the insurance company, since it can provide expert counsel to help in the design, development, and operation of your facility to minimize the risks of negligence suits.

Summary .

Business organizations take one of three forms, from the sole proprietorship, which is the easiest to form and the shortest in life, through partnerships to corporations, which are more complicated in nature. It is important to study before starting a business the numerous legal and tax consequences attached to the business structure you select. These need to be fully understood and analyzed based on their relevance to the proposed business organization form.

It is important for a new business developer to seek competent legal help before attempting to initiate any kind of business and to make sure that all legal requirements of forming the business as well as applicable federal, state, and local regulations are met before the business opens.

There are three types of contracts: unilateral, implied, and bilateral. To be valid a contract must consist of an agreement supported by consideration and entered into by parties with the authority to contract for legal purposes. A contract must be in writing if it takes over one year to complete, concerns real estate or an interest therein, or is for over $500.

Liability is the main area of risk faced by a recreation business. The standard of care provided a visitor depends on his status—invitee, licensee, or trespasser. A special category for children is called the attractive nuisance doctrine. In order to prove negligence, it must be shown that an obligation existed and that a failure to conform to a standard resulted in an injury sufficient to cause damage. There are eight defenses to negligence ranging from contributory negligence to waivers or releases. For any legal issue always seek competent legal advice.

BIBLIOGRAPHY

Briskin, R.A.: Use of Subchapter S corporations to shift income among family members, Taxes, Aug., 1981.

The business lawyer, A quarterly publication, Chicago, Ill., 1982, American Bar Association, Section on Corporation, Banking and Business Law.

Clarkson, K.W., and LeRoy, R.: West's business law: text and cases. St. Paul, Minn., 1986, West Publishing Co.

Collins, J.W.: Business law: text and cases. New York, 1986, John Wiley & Sons, Inc.

Corbin, A.L.: Corbin on contracts. St. Paul, Minn., 1952, West Publishing Co.

Diamond, J., and Pintel, J.: Introduction to contemporary business, Englewood Cliffs, N.J., 1975, Prentice-Hall, Inc.

Finston, I.L., and Mehr, R.I.: Pension funds and insurance reserves: a resource for financial officers, Homewood, Ill., 1986, Dow Jones-Irwin.

Frakt, A.N., and Rankin, J.S.: The law of parks, recreation resources and leisure services, Salt Lake City, Ut., 1982, Brighton Publishing.

Fulcher, W.: Advantages and disadvantages of incorporating a small business, National Public Accountant, April, 1981.

Hagen, W.W., and Johnson, G.H.: Digest of business law. St. Paul, Minn., 1979, West Publishing Co.

Jubenville, A.: Outdoor recreation management, Philadelphia, 1978, W.B. Saunders Publishing Co.

Kaiser, R.A.: Liability and law in recreation, parks and sports. Englewood Cliffs, N.J., 1986, Prentice-Hall.

Sommerfeld, R.M.: Federal taxes and management decisions, Homewood, Ill., 1981, Richard D. Irwin, Inc.

Tomczak, S.P.: Making the proper decision: sole proprietorship, partnership, corporation, Steven P. Tomczak and Associates, 1979.

van der Smissen, B. Personal conversation, Nov. 15, 1983.

Wyatt, J.W., and Wyatt, M.B.: Business law principles and cases, New York, 1971, McGraw-Hill Co.

SUGGESTED READINGS

Turner, L., editor, Doing business in Utah, Salt Lake City, 1983, Coopers and Lybrand. 1983.

This handy little book provides background information on the basics of doing business in the United States. For some areas of the country Coppers & Lybrand have produced a supplement titled *Doing Business in a Particular State*. This source of information is excellent for people doing work in the business field.

Stillman, R.J.: Small business management—how to start and stay in business, Boston, 1983, Little, Brown and Co.

This text presents a good basic background on all aspects of business, with particular focus on a chapter on legal requirements in business.

U.S. master tax guide, Publisher's Clearing House, 1984.
Reprinted yearly, this guide discusses the implications of tax law changes. It is valuable in helping you determine the tax consequences of business organizations.

CASE STUDY

When you develop a company, there are many decisions to make. In the case of The Bike Lock Company *it appears that most of the critical decisions have already been made. But have they? After reading the information in this chapter, evaluate this case. While reading it please keep in mind the material pertaining to business organizations, contractual law, and liability.*

The Bike Lock Company*

At their third official meeting, Joe Last, Mike Mulligan, and Carl Reily addressed the topic of money and ownership as the first order of business.

Organization

It was agreed that a corporate form of ownership should be used for several reasons. Ownership transfer via stock was fairly simple compared to making changes in a partnership. Most potential outside investors would be used to dealing with corporations, and a position on the required corporate Board of Directors could be used to sweeten a deal with an investor if necessary. Finally, there was a reasonable amount of flexibility in spreading the ownership among different types of early investors by using promotion stock and options for key people in the new company. During the discussion, a question was raised about "1244" shares. Mike agreed to look into the tax considerations surrounding such shares.**

Money

Mike Mulligan took the lead in summarizing the initial cash needs of the company. His figures on cash requirements are shown at the top of the next page.

*Reprinted with permission of the Stanford University Graduate School of Business, 1975 by the Board of Trustees of the Leland Stanford Junior University. This case was written by Steven Carl Brandt, Lecturer in Management, as a basis for class discussion. Names and details have been modified.
**"1244" share owners are allotted favorable tax treatment by the IRS under certain conditions. A corporation can issue only a limited amount of "1244" stock during its early days of existence.

Equipment	$ 3,000
Inventory	2,500
Working Capital	5,000
Marketing	5,000
Total	$15,500

Mike indicated that he and Joe felt this was a "bare bones" budget aimed at getting the business launched. Neither of the two had much cash to invest at the start and they wanted to minimize the early dilution of their stock ownership, i.e., they wanted to own all they possibly could of the corporation.

Mike went on to outline the cash flow picture he saw for the business.

Fixed expenses/month

Rent	$ 500
Utilities	100
Salaries	2,000
Insurance	150
Phone	100
Miscellaneous	150
	$3,000

Variable costs per lock

Cable	$1.45
Lock	1.60
Noise Generator	.95
Labor @ $4.00/hr	1.00
Packaging	.10
	$5.10

Exhibit 1 contains Mike's projected cash flow for the first six months. He felt that it was quite conservative in that it didn't show any increase in volume after the fourth month.

After examining the cash flow figures, Mr. Reily noted that the July low point figure was probably too optimistic because it didn't include cash out for adequately restocking the cable and electric lock inventories that had to be purchased well in advance of the big volumes Joe talked about. (Joe was extremely confident that the volume of locks sold would actually be at least 2,500 per month by September.) Mike commented that the company had not made any use of bank debt in the cash projections. Bank debt, he felt, was the emergency reserve for the company until the viability of the noisy, electric lock concept was proven with volume and profitability.

Ownership

Discussion now turned delicately to the question of where and how the $15,500 from investors was to be obtained. Mr. Mulligan outlined a proposal to Mr. Reily.

Mike had a total of $2,500 he could invest in the company. Joe felt he could borrow $1,500 in cash to contribute directly. The part time employee whom Joe hired from time to time also wanted to invest $1,500 in the company. So, in total, this employee group could put up $5,500.

Mike went on to say that he and Joe would like Carl Reily to loan the company $7,500 at 9%, interest only for three years. Carl could then buy $2,500 worth of stock to fill out the remaining need for $15,500.

In summary, the cash investment proposal put together by Mike and Joe looked like this:

	Cash invested	%
Joe Last	$ 1,500	18
Mike Mulligan	2,500	32
Employee	1,500	18
Carl Reily	2,500	32
	$ 8,000	100%
Loan	7,500	
Cash In	$ 15,500	

Then, Mike continued, additional ownership would be provided for as follows:

- Joe Last would receive shares for the $3,300 Net Worth of the existing company.
- Both Joe and Mike would receive promotional stock for a total of 20% of the initial issue.
- All three (Joe, Mike, and Carl) would receive stock options totalling another 20% of the initial issue.

Mike indicated that he had received the information on the twenty percent figures from an attorney friend. Twenty was typically the maximum the State Corporate Commissioner would allow.

Summarized, using a share per dollar, the proposed ownership pattern would look like this:

Shares for:	Cash	Assets	Promotion	Options	Total Shares	% Ownership After Conversion
Joe Last	1,500	3,300	1,500	1,625	7,925	51
Mike Mulligan	2,500		760	500	3,760	24
Carl Reily	2,500			135	2,635	16
Employee	1,500				1,500	9
	8,000	3,300	2,260	2,260	15,820	100 %

Any cash to the company for the founders' option stock would, of course, come at a later time.

Mr. Reily reviewed the figures carefully. Finally, he said quietly that he had absolutely no interest in loaning the company $7,500, and further, that he doubted that anyone else would either. Carl went on to say that he felt the percentage ownerships resulting from Mike's and Joe's proposal did not adequately reflect the risks being assumed. Mike, seeing himself as something of a mediator, asked Carl for what his idea of a fair split would be.

Taking a piece of paper and the information on what cash Joe and Mike could invest, Carl sketched out the following picture, using the same one share per dollar assumption for discussion purposes.

Shares for:	Cash	Assets	Promotion	Options	Total Shares	% Ownership After Conversion
Joe Last	1,500	3,300	600	1,000	6,400	27
Mike Mulligan	2,500		600	2,000	5,100	21
Investors	11,500		600	500	12,600	52
	15,500	3,300	1,800	3,500	24,100	100 %

Carl felt the option stock should be at a higher price than the original issue; he also felt that Mike, as the principal operating management person, should be given the largest portion of the stock options. (Although titles had not yet been discussed, Carl felt that Mike should be the chief operating officer or general manager.) Carl went on to point out that between them, the two brothers-in-law held 48% of the stock after conversion and that they would be given preferential treatment on any new stock issued.

"What about my employee who wants to put in $1,500?" asked Joe. "My recommendation is that we don't bring in any junior or amateur investors as stockholders at this time," Carl replied.

It was clear that there was a significant gap between the position of the management, Joe and Mike, and the position or point of view of the investor, Carl Reily, as to the matter of ownership. Following a few moments of silence, Carl suggested that they all sleep on the matter and discuss it further the next day. This was agreeable to everyone. Carl proposed also that Joe and Mike review his strategic ideas for the company. He passed out copies of the plans contained in Appendix A.

APPENDIX A

The Bike Lock Company

1. **Business definition:** Provide superior, light-weight security to cycling activists who own cycles retailing at over $100. The activists can be anywhere in North America. The theme for the company should be: "Make your bike last forever" or "Make yours a one-owner bike."

2. **Basic business strategy:** Build high quality, original equipment locks for sale to cyclists directly or through specialty bike shops at a retail cost of no more than 10% of the cost of a new bicycle.

3. **Marketing strategy:** Be first into the North American market to establish the company name and the noise lock concept by using space advertising that reaches cycling activists and progressive cycling retailers.

4. **Advertising strategy:** Use heavy visual approach that stresses toughness of cable, the security aspects of the noise emission, economy (cheaper than a new bike), and the quality of construction. Use specialty publications and point of purchase displays.

5. **Distribution/pickup:** Emphasize direct mail order approach on wide geographic

basis first. Build dealer (stores, shops, etc.) network second on a region by region basis starting in fourth quarter of 1973 in time to test Christmas appeal of lock.

6. **Production strategy:** Seek high level of automation; minimize direct labor costs. Limit product line to a single size, color, weight, etc. By end of year, determine economic plant size in relation to production efficiency.

7. **Materials:** Have complete inventory of finished locks, supplies, and materials at all times so that locks ordered can be shipped or mailed within 24 hours of receipt of order. Explore possibility of eventually manufacturing own electric locks.

8. **Personnel:** Minimize dependence on non-management personnel. Locate any new facilities in low labor cost areas. Promote from within. Use 24-hour operation (3 shifts) as necessary.

9. **Financial strategy:** Round No. 1 will be used to establish production capability for minimum of 2500 locks per month, to complete regional market test with advertising campaign, and to build finished goods inventory. Money will be obtained through a private placement limited to professional investors and the founders.

Round No. 2 will be used for broader advertising (entire USA), volume production, cost controls, and inventory expansion. Private placement.

Round No. 3, based on the success of company, will be used to add a second plant (East Coast), expand sources of supply, develop distribution and dealer system. Investments by professional venture capitalists would be sought at this stage.

EXHIBIT 1

Cash flow

	May	June	July	August	September	October
Cash In - Investors	$15,500					
Locks Sold - Units	112	500	700	1,000	1,000	1,000
@ $8.00/each	$ 900	$4,000	$5,600	$8,000	$8,000	$8,000
Cash On Hand	700					
TOTAL IN	$17,100	$4,000	$5,600	$8,000	$8,000	$8,000
Expenses:						
Salaries	$ 1,600	$2,000	$2,000	$2,000	$2,000	$2,000
Rent	1,000	500	500	500	500	500
Utilities	100	100	100	100	100	100
Insurance	150	150	150	150	150	150
Phone	150	100	100	100	100	50
Miscellaneous	250	200	150	100	100	50
Labor	—	315	875	1,250	1,250	1,250
Materials	1,000	1,500	—	—	3,000	—
Packaging	500	—	500	—	500	—
Delivery/Freight	60	300	420	600	600	600
	$ 4,810	$5,165	$4,795	$4,800	$8,300	$4,800

	May	June	July	August	September	October
Purchases						
Equipment	1,000	1,000	1,000	—	—	—
Supplies (Indirect)	200	100	50	50	50	—
Bonding Material	100	—	50	50	100	—
	$ 1,300	$1,100	$1,100	$ 100	$ 150	—
Marketing	$ 500	$2,000	$2,000	$ 500		$ 500
Total Out	$ 6,610	$8,265	$7,895	$ 5,400	$ 8,450	$ 5,300
Net Cash	$10,490	−4,265	−2,295	+2,600	−450	+2,700
Cumulative Cash on Hand, End of Period	$10,490	$6,225	$3,930	$ 6,530	$ 6,080	$ 8,780

Questions

1. What advice would you give Mike Mulligan to help him protect his idea and hard work?
2. If you were Carl Reily, would you accept Mike's proposal? If not, why not? If you were to accept the proposal, what stipulations would you place on the agreement?
3. Is the proposed organizational plan the best one for this business? If so, why? If not, which form of organization would you recommend and why?
4. Are there any possible liability questions to be evaluated? What are they?
5. In your opinion does this business venture have the possibility of succeeding? Why?

CHAPTER 4

Funding sources for commercial recreation

CHAPTER OBJECTIVES

1. To discuss the differences between fixed and working capital

2. To understand the differences between debt and equity capital

3. To identify the various methods of funding a commercial recreation enterprise

4. To know where to obtain funding for a commercial recreation business

5. To be familiar with the various types of funding that can be used in the establishment of a commercial recreation enterprise

6. To be aware of what a lender requires of a commercial recreation borrower

When contemplating starting a commercial recreation business, consider the amount of funding required and whether this money can be obtained. Many sources of capital are available to the small business person. The key to obtaining these funds is a thorough and innovative search for possible sources coupled with a viable, well organized business plan.

In this chapter we will discuss sources and uses of capital, equity and debt in commercial recreation, sources of advice on borrowing, and keys to obtaining the necessary financing.

Sources and uses of capital

Capital, or money available for investment, can be classified two ways: by the use to which it is put and by the source from which it is obtained.

Uses for capital

Capital is put to use in two ways:

1. *Fixed capital* includes assets to be used for a considerable length of time, such as land, buildings, machinery, equipment, furniture, and fixtures. It may be easier to think of fixed capital as the resources needed to produce your goods or service.
2. *Working capital* includes cash assets or assets that can easily be converted into cash, such as inventory and accounts receivable. These are consumed through the normal operation of your business.

Sources of capital

There are also two basic types of source capital:

1. *Equity capital* is money invested in the business and carries no legal obligation to pay back principal or interest. Equity is most often obtained through the sale of stock in a company. The owners of the stocks become part owners in the business and are not entitled to a return on their capital. However, they share in the profits of the company.
2. *Debt capital,* or *borrowed capital,* must be returned with interest or other compensation for the use of the funds.

The balance between equity capital and debt capital

Whether to use equity or debt capital is an important consideration. The tradeoff lies between relinquishing ownership, and thus control, of your business through the use of equity and the burden of having to repay debt. Because equity capital need not be repaid, it is "safe" for the entrepreneur, who may not achieve profitability as quickly as predicted. Use of equity also avoids the need to pay interest in addition to the sum borrowed. The major drawback of obtaining outside investments is the loss of complete control and flexibility.

Debt capital, on the other hand, enlarges the funds under ownership control. Interest is tax-deductible as a business expense. Debt is even more attractive in time of inflation because repayment is made in depreciated dollars. The reverse is true during deflation. The use of debt brings on the risk of being unable to repay creditors when money is due. This is especially dangerous for a new business person, as it may damage your credit rating, force you to yield control of the business temporarily to creditors, or cause liquidation through bankruptcy. The optimal level of equity of the owners in a business varies depending on experience, risk, return on investment, and other elements of the particular situation. A minimum target is often 20% equity and 80% debt. Accepted guidelines for each line of business may be obtained from bankers, accountants, or trade associations.

Let us consider a sporting goods store to illustrate the many funding options open to the commercial recreation entrepreneur. Frank, our prospective store owner, is beginning to search for the necessary funding to initiate the business and acquire inventory. This store, called All Seasons Sporting Goods, will carry a variety of sporting equipment, small boats, clothing, shoes, and accessories.

Frank doesn't want to be too highly leveraged (a business is *highly leveraged* when the ratio of debt to equity is high). At the same time, he does not want to share control of his business. In consultation with some trusted financial counselors, Frank arranges to hold 50.1% of the equity stock of his business. He offers equity shares to others, but he retains control. He also targets 30% of his total prospective investment as equity contribution and 70% as debt.

The innovative search for funds

The sources from which All Seasons Sporting Goods can obtain funds may include Frank, his family and friends, equity investors, banks, savings and loan institutions, the government, and venture capitalists. It is vital to keep in mind that investors are not standing ready to dispense cash. Frank's search for investors will most likely involve great effort and stamina as he "sells" All Seasons Sporting Goods. No matter what the business venture, if your proposition is a good one, investors will recognize that there is an opportunity for them to benefit. The search for such willing investors demands professionalism and creativity, both in locating funding sources and in convincing them that the business opportunity is a good idea. For "selling" the good business opportunity represented by your business, the feasibility study and business plan are critically important tools.

Equity in commercial recreation

In order for Frank to be identified as the owner of All Seasons Sporting Goods, it is necessary for him to establish an ownership (or equity) position. This is done by using private money to establish the business. In All Seasons' case, this money could be used for the purchase of land, development of the building, or the outright purchase of the display cases, lighting fixtures, or inventory. There are various methods that Frank can use to obtain equity funds. Be aware that we will be moving from the most common to the least common as we go through these examples.

Personal ownership. It is often necessary for entrepreneurs to invest their own savings when starting a business. Using private money to start All Seasons Sporting Goods is extremely important to potential investors. Investors like to see personal savings invested in the business. To gain the necessary private funding, Frank may borrow against his house through a second mortgage, borrow against his life insurance policy, or sell any stocks and bonds he owns. By investing personal assets in his business, Frank may avoid some of the pressure of turning the quick profit needed to repay creditors, and he can keep control of the business.

Friends, relatives. Friends and relatives may be a good source for funding, as these people are informed of Frank's integrity and ability to work and achieve success. Friends and relatives may have more confidence in Frank's ability than would bankers or other investors. This advantage, however, is often outweighed by the dangers of borrowing from such sources. Good relationships may be harmed if these investors expect their payoff sooner than is feasible. Frank may receive unsolicited and uninformed business advice, and well-meaning relations may desire to "get a hand in the pot." It is wise to make every attempt to repay these debts within the first six months of operation.

Local investors. Sometimes it is possible to obtain financial backing from well-to-do individuals such as lawyers and physicians. However, it is often difficult to find local capitalists because they typically do not advertise their desire to invest. Another consideration is that such investors will not invest in a highly risky venture unless they are convinced that the potential return is better than could be achieved elsewhere and that the prospective management team has a good "track record."

Local investors do not receive interest payments because they are purchasing a part ownership in the company, so the return they expect is a share of the profits. In this respect it is much harder for Frank, as the owner of the company, to project long-term continued return, since reinvestment of profits from the company is probably needed to insure growth and continued profitability.

Selling stock to individual investors. During times of high interest rates, entrepreneurs may choose to raise capital by selling stock to individual investors. *Private placement* is the sale of stock to selected individuals, such as employees, acquaintances, local residents, customers, and suppliers. Private placement is difficult for a new company because the majority of investors don't learn of the availability of the stock, but it is a way of avoiding the many public stock sale requirements of the securities law.

Selling stock to the general public. Selling stock to the general public is typically done only by the larger, established business firms because the general public is less likely to invest in small enterprises. There are more regulations on the sale of stock to the public than on private placement. The Securities and Exchange Commission does, however, permit *Regulation A* offerings for small sales; such transactions require minimal financial data and information. To avoid getting involved in the details and the risk of selling such stock, Frank can sell common stock to underwriters, who guarantee the sale of securities. This is usually expensive, however, as fees of 10% to 30% are required to cover the uncertainty and risk associated with public offerings of the stock of small unknown firms such as All Seasons Sporting Goods.

Section 1244 stock. Equity or stock investment can be structured to obtain maximum tax benefits should All Seasons Sporting Goods fail to reach the operating stage. According to Section 1244 of the Internal Revenue Code, if the stock in small companies is sold at a loss or becomes worthless, losses are deducted from ordinary income. The deduction limit for Section 1244 stock is $50,000 per year per individual. This tax advantage is attractive to investors, since it reduces the risk they assume in contributing funds.

For its stock to qualify under Section 1244, All Seasons Sporting Goods must be a domestic small business corporation that obtains less than half of its income from passive sources such as rents, dividends, and interest. The stock must be nonconvertible common stock purchased by means other than securities. The purchaser must be an individual or a partnership. The value of all stock issued under Section 1244 cannot exceed $1 million.

Debt capital in commercial recreation

Now that Frank has obtained some equity capital to begin developing and establishing All Seasons Sporting Goods, it is necessary to obtain the rest of the funding through traditional borrowing. Debt or borrowing sources include trade credit, equipment loans or leases, banks and savings and loan institutions, venture capitalists, small business development companies, and the government. Let's look at how each of these types of loan can be used to establish All Seasons Sporting Goods.

Trade credit. Credit from vendors of materials, merchandise, and other supplies is a major source of financing. It enables business owners to obtain large portions of their working capital needs, especially in retail. By this method Frank may be able to obtain merchandise—sweatsuits, tennis racquets, racquetball equipment, and even some larger items such as skis and firearms. A loan between business owners and suppliers exists if the supplier does not demand payment until delivery. It is common for vendors to allow 30, 60, or 90 days for payment. Often suppliers offer a discount for early payment, typically 2% for payment within 10 days. If the discount is forgone, it may be considered as interest expense on the "loan," or delayed payment. The decision to gain the discount must be weighed against other uses of the money for the period before payment. Suppliers tend to be less exacting than other lenders, such as banks, in enforcing credit terms and are more likely to extend credit freely to new firms because of their interest in developing customers.

Equipment loans and leases. All Seasons Sporting Goods needs equipment, which may be purchased on an installment basis. After Frank makes a down payment of 25% to 35%, the remainder of the contract can be extended for 3 to 5 years with regular installment payments. The supplier will usually extend this credit based on a conditional sales contract, or mortgage, on the equipment. During the loan period the equipment cannot serve as collateral for a bank loan.

Equipment leasing is another method of stretching capital by paying for business necessities out of operating funds rather than using equity capital. Leasing presents several advantages. For the entrepreneur in need of funds, the overriding advantage may be that if you do lease, you don't have to buy. In some cases a considerable part of the rental can be applied against eventual purchase. Another cost advantage is maintenance of the equipment by the owner; also, lease payments are classified as a business expense, which can be deducted from income tax. If lease payments are spread out over time, they can provide a hedge against inflation. By leasing equipment that is at high risk of obsolescence, the entrepreneur avoids risk of owning obsolete equipment. Leasing has only a short-term advantage, however, because long-term lease payments will eventually exceed the value of the equipment. There are other disadvantages to leasing. Some leases require the use of the same manufacturer's supplies and accessories, which may be more expensive than those of another company. By leasing equipment, you forgo the opportunity to acquire an asset that may be traded in or used as collateral for some other purpose. Such considerations must be weighed and balanced in relation to the specific type of business and the nature of the equipment.

Banks. Commercial banks are the most common source of financing for businesses. A commercial bank is characterized by the wide variety of services it offers, although its major functions are to receive and protect deposits, to pay checks, and to lend money. Small businesses may also rely on investment and estate advisory services, customer credit references, night depositories, and discounting of accounts and notes receivable.

Because the commercial bank was established to earn a profit, the new entrepreneur will find that loans are not readily handed out. Business people who have a good financial relationship with a bank are those with the ability to put up collateral or provide a cosigner for a loan. Keep in mind, however, that these institutions have a responsibility to use their depositors' money wisely. However, commercial lenders are in the market for business opportunities and do have funds available for such purposes.

Loans are available in varying forms according to the use to which they will be put and the amount and type of compensation to be exchanged for the funds. *Secured loans* are backed by collateral of greater value than the amount of the loan. *Unsecured loans* are backed only by a good credit rating and the character of the borrower. They tend to cover shorter periods and smaller amounts of money than secured loans. Banks do not often make unsecured loans to entrepreneurs. Short-term loans—for less than 1 year—are the most common form of loan from a commercial bank. A substantial number of "semi-term" loans are made by banks on a 60- to 90-day basis and are subject to virtually continuous renewal under favorable circumstances. Intermediate-term loans mature in 2 to 5 years. Long-term loans usually mature in 10 to 30 years.

Because obtaining a loan is often a time-consuming process, entrepreneurs should arrange in advance for a *line of credit.* This is the amount of credit a bank is willing to extend to a borrower at a given time according to specific conditions. Banks extend credit only when they are well informed. For this reason it is wise to have a line of credit arranged prior to the beginning of operations in the maximum amount likely to be needed for carrying out business plans.

Self-liquidating loans, used very commonly by commercial lenders, are made to borrowers with good financial status with the bank. The money is used as working capital or to acquire assets capable of being converted quickly into cash. Self-liquidating loans are usually used to purchase inventory prior to a large buying season such as Christmas.

Loans for buying assets of long-term value such as buildings, machinery, and furniture are called *capital loans*. The purchase of these fixed assets is usually secured by a mortgage.

Inventory loans are used when the bank requires collateral to secure a loan for working capital. Inventory on hand is the collateral. *Floor planning* specifies that the articles pledged as inventory must be kept in a specified area and items sold from this area must be replaced with other inventory items of equal or greater value. In the case of All Seasons Sporting Goods, floor planning could be used to finance the sale of boats. Boats are ideally suited for floor planning because each boat has a serial number. As All Seasons Sporting Goods sells each boat, the title can be transferred from the bank to the purchaser and the funds available from the purchase used to stock a new boat.

Under a *bonded warehouse receipt*, the pledged inventory goods are held in sealed storage and cannot be moved until the loan is repaid. As with floor planning, bonded warehouse receipts are generally used with items of greater value. This may be the case with firearms sales; the firearms are purchased using the bank's money and are stored in a sealed, bonded warehouse. This lets Frank continually replenish his stock in the store from the bonded warehouse. Inventory loans are useful when presented with favorable buying conditions or in planning ahead for seasonal business.

Accounts receivable loans entail an advance by the bank of 75% to 80% of the money owed to a company by customers who have made purchases on time or credit. They are usually for merchandise with a high initial cost, including boat motors and expensive exercise equipment. In some cases customers are notified that their debt has been assigned to the bank and they should make direct payment to that institution. In other cases companies prefer to avoid letting customers know that funds are being borrowed from the bank, so payments continue to be made to the company and turned over to the bank.

Other collateral arrangements may be formed in exchange for funds borrowed from a bank. A borrower may sometimes pledge business property or personal assets in order to secure a loan. This type of collateral is the least desirable to either party, because resale cost is usually lower than value, and owners prefer not to part with such possessions. A more acceptable method is to borrow against the cash surrender value of a life insurance policy. Should the borrower die, the bank will receive a portion of the policy equal to the amount borrowed. If the loan cannot be paid off, the bank may claim the value owed from the cash value of the policy.

Term lending, or *installment lending*, is used when there is a need for intermediate- to long-term credit, generally over several years. Regular installment payments are made against the amount outstanding, unlike short-term loans, which are usually repaid in a lump sum. This type of loan is usually secured to finance a major expansion of capital facilities. For All Seasons Sporting Goods intermediate loans may be taken out to ensure funding for remodeling of the facility or expansion of square footage to allow room to take on a new line of equipment. More than one bank may be involved if the sum is very large. The borrower usually agrees not to incur other debts until the loan is paid off.

Savings and loan banks. Traditionally the savings and loan bank (chartered by state or federal government) has not provided as wide a range of services as the commercial bank and has primarily concentrated on home loans. However, this distinction is blurring as savings and loans increasingly provide banking services characteristic of commercial banks. Recently savings bank services have been extended to include small trust funds, life insurance, safe-deposit boxes, commercial property, checking accounts, and credit cards as well as personal, inventory, and equipment loans. Under banking rules passed by Congress in 1982, savings and loans are now permitted to invest up to 10% of their assets in business loans, 10% in equipment financing, 30% in inventory financing, and 40% in commercial real estate lending.[1] Savings and loans should be considered when evaluating sources for financing.

Venture capital companies. *Venture capital enterprises* are usually partnerships or corporations that operate as investment groups. Venture capital is usually used for relatively new businesses that are somewhat risky but have a good potential for high growth and return on investment. Computer and high-technology businesses have been prime benefactors of venture capital. As opposed to banks, venture capitalists are mainly concerned with the features of the product or service and its market potential. The other major factor for a venture capitalist is the management of the company. Since such investors are not likely to be involved in day-to-day operation, management is an integral part of the reason they invest in a commercial recreation enterprise. As a result, it is extremely important to have the best management possible. A drawback to keep in mind is that venture capitalists usually insist on owning more than half of the business, although they are not usually interested in running the business on a daily basis or in controlling management. Pressure may result from the use of this method of financing, as venture capital companies typically demand a return of three to five times their investment in only 5 to 7 years. Because venture capitalists require higher risk return investment opportunities than are generally available in commercial recreation, venture capitalists are not usually good prospects as investors in commercial recreation enterprises.

Small business development companies. SBDCs are similar to the small business investment companies under the jurisdiction of the Small Business Administration except that they are capitalized entirely by private sources. Such sources include banks, large manufacturers, utility companies, and transportation firms. SBDCs provide loans on a long-term basis and also purchase stock in commercial

[1]*Inc.*, July 1983, p. 99.

enterprises. You can contact your local chamber of commerce for specific information about small business development companies.

Government-sponsored programs

In assessing his need for capital, Frank needs to cover all possible sources. Frank has learned that the government is an excellent source of funding. Government-sponsored funding programs have been many and varied. Selected government-sponsored programs are discussed in the following paragraphs.

Small business administration. Established by an act of Congress in 1953, the Small Business Administration helps small businesses by providing funds and free assistance and counseling. From its 100 field offices throughout the country, the SBA helps small firms obtain government contracts, sets up small business institutes, provides financial counseling, conducts courses, and distributes management literature. Addresses and telephone numbers of SBA offices are shown in Fig. 4-1.

A small firm is defined according to the type of help sought, the type of business, and the industry in which the firm operates. "Small" in the United States often means medium or large in other countries. Thus, the criteria are conveniently flexible provided your enterprise is not disqualified for reasons such as having more than 50% of net receipts come from the sale of alcoholic beverages, deriving its gross income from gambling, or having inadequately secured loans. To apply for help from the SBA, applicants must show proof that at least two banks have turned down loan requests. Assets and part ownership in the company cannot be sold to obtain money, and loans from credit sources and other government agencies are forbidden.

If you are denied a loan by a bank, you may request that the bank make the loan under the SBA Loan Guarantee Plan. The SBA will guarantee up to 90% of the loan, and it is to the bank's advantage to participate in this type of lending. The largest proportion of SBA loans are guaranteed loans. The SBA Preferred Lenders Program should reduce the time it takes to obtain an SBA-guaranteed loan from 6 to 4 weeks. Participating lenders can set their own rates rather than charge the usual SBA maximum of 2.75 points over prime. *Participation loans* are made jointly by a bank and the SBA. The bank is expected to provide at least 25% of the loan. *Direct loans* are funds provided solely by SBA with no help from a bank. The interest charged by SBA on its direct loans is set by Congress and changes periodically, but it is approximately two thirds of the bank's maximum rate. Historically, 25% of SBA's business loans have been allocated to new businesses. Of all its business loans, only about 3.5% have been written off by default.

As well as the commonly used business loans, the SBA makes loans to help small businesses repair damages and economic injuries caused by natural disasters. Economic injury loans may also assist small firms forced to relocate because of federally aided urban renewal and highway construction programs. SBA provides financial assistance to local corporations formed and supported by at least two

FIG. 4-1. Field Offices of the Small Business Administration

Region		City	State	Zip Code	Address	Commercial Telephone Numbers for Public Use Only
I	RO	Boston	MA	02110	60 Batterymarch Street, 10th Floor	(617) 223-3204
	DO	Boston	MA	02114	150 Causeway St., 10th Floor	(617) 223-3224
	BO	Springfield	MA	01103	1550 Main Street	(413) 785-0268
	DO	Augusta	ME	04330	40 Western Avenue, Room 512	(207) 622-8378
	DO	Concord	NH	03301	55 Pleasant Street, Room 211	(603) 224-4041
	DO	Hartford	CT	06106	One Hartford Square West	(203) 722-3600
	DO	Montpelier	VT	05602	87 State Street, Room 204	(802) 229-0538
	DO	Providence	RI	02903	380 Westminster Mall	(401) 351-7500
II	RO	New York	NY	10278	26 Federal Plaza, Room 29-118	(212) 264-7772
	DO	New York	NY	10278	26 Federal Plaza, Room 3100	(212) 264-4355
	BO	Melville	NY	11747	35 Pinelawn Road, Room 102E	(516) 454-0750
	DO	Hato Rey	PR	00919	Carlos Chardon Avenue, Room 691	(809) 753-4002
	POD	St. Croix	VI	00820	4A La Grande Princesse	(809) 773-3480
	POD	St. Thomas	VI	00801	Veterans Drive, Room 283	(809) 774-8530
	DO	Newark	NJ	07102	60 Park Place, 4th Floor	(201) 645-2434
	POD	Camden	NJ	08104	1800 East Davis Street, Room 110	(609) 757-5183
	DO	Syracuse	NY	13260	100 South Clinton Street, Room 1071	(315) 423-5383
	BO	Buffalo	NY	14202	111 West Huron Street, Room 1311	(716) 846-4301
	BO	Elmira	NY	14901	333 East Water Street	(607) 734-8130
	POD	Albany	NY	12207	445 Broadway-Room 236B	(518) 472-6300
	POD	Rochester	NY	14614	100 State Street, Room 601	(716) 263-6700
III	RO	Philadelphia	PA	19004	231 St. Asaphs Rd., Suite 640	(215) 596-5889
	DO	Philadelphia	PA	19004	231 St. Asaphs Rd., Suite 400	(215) 596-5889
	BO	Harrisburg	PA	17101	100 Chestnut Street, Suite 309	(717) 782-3840
	BO	Wilkes-Barre	PA	18701	20 North Pennsylvania Avenue	(717) 826-6497
	BO	Wilmington	DE	19801	844 King Street, Room 5207	(302) 573-6294
	DO	Clarksburg	WV	26301	109 North 3rd St., Room 302	(304) 623-5631
	BO	Charleston	WV	25301	628 Charleston National Plaza	(304) 347-5220
	DO	Pittsburgh	PA	15222	960 Penn Avenue, 5th Floor	(412) 644-2780
	DO	Richmond	VA	23240	400 North 8th Street, Room 3015	(804) 771-2617

	City	State	ZIP	No.	Address	Phone
DO	Towson	MD	21204	8600	LaSalle Road, Room 630	(301) 962-4392
DO	Washington	DC	20036	1111	18th Street, N.W. 6th Floor	(202) 634-4950
IV						
RO	Atlanta	GA	30367	1375	Peachtree St., N.E., 5th Floor	(404) 881-4999
DO	Atlanta	GA	30309	1720	Peachtree Road, N.W., 6th Floor	(404) 881-4749
POD	Statesboro	GA	30458	52	North Main Street, Room 225	(912) 489-8719
DO	Birmingham	AL	35203	2121	8th Avenue North, Suite 200	(205) 254-1344
DO	Charlotte	NC	28202	230	S. Tryon Street, Room 700	(704) 371-6563
POD	Greenville	NC	27834	215	South Evans Street, Room 102E	(919) 752-3798
DO	Columbia	SC	29202	1835	Assembly, 3rd Floor	(803) 765-5376
DO	Jackson	MS	39269	100	West Capitol Street, Suite 322	(601) 960-4378
BO	Biloxi	MS	39530	111	Fred Haise Blvd., 2nd Floor	(601) 435-3676
DO	Jacksonville	FL	32202	400	West Bay Street, Room 261	(904) 791-3782
DO	Louisville	KY	40201	600	Federal Place, Room 188	(502) 582-5971
DO	Miami	FL	33134	2222	Ponce De Leon Boulevard, 5th Floor	(305) 350-5521
POD	Tampa	FL	33602	700	Twiggs Street, Room 607	(813) 228-2594
POD	West Palm Beach	FL	33407	3550	45th Street, Suite 6	(305) 689-2223
DO	Nashville	TN	37219	404	James Robertson Parkway, Suite 1012	(615) 251-5881
V						
RO	Chicago	IL	60604	230	South Dearborn Street, Room 510	(312) 353-0359
DO	Chicago	IL	60604	219	South Dearborn Street, Room 437	(312) 353-4528
DO	Cleveland	OH	44199	1240	East 9th Street, Room 317	(216) 552-4180
DO	Columbus	OH	43215	85	Marconi Boulevard	(614) 469-6860
BO	Cincinnati	OH	45202	550	Main Street, Room 5028	(513) 684-2814
DO	Detroit	MI	48226	477	Michigan Avenue, Room 515	(313) 226-6075
BO	Marquette	MI	49885	220	West Washington Street, Room 310	(906) 225-1108
DO	Indianapolis	IN	46204	575	North Pennsylvania Street, Room 578	(317) 269-7272
BO	South Bend	IN	46601	501	East Monroe Street, Room 160	(219) 232-8361
BO	Madison	WI	53703	212	East Washington Ave., Room 213	(608) 264-5261
DO	Eau Claire	WI	54701	500	South Barstow Street, Room 17	(715) 834-9012
POD	Milwaukee	WI	53203	310	West Wisconsin Ave., Room 400	(414) 291-3941
BO	Minneapolis	MN	55403	100	North 6th Street, Suite 610	(612) 349-3550
BO	Springfield	IL	62701	Four	North, Old State Capital Plaza	(217) 492-4416

Continued.

FIG. 4-1—cont'd.

Region	City	State	Zip Code		Address	Commercial Telephone Numbers for Public Use Only
VI RO	Dallas	TX	75235	8625	King George Drive, Bldg. C	(214) 767-7643
DO	Dallas	TX	75242	1100	Commerce Street, Room 3C36	(214) 767-0605
POD	Marshall	TX	75670	100	South Washington Street, Room G-12	(214) 935-5257
DO	El Paso	TX	79902	10737	Gateway West, Suite 320	(915) 541-7678
BO	Ft. Worth	TX	76102	221	West Lancaster Ave., Room 1007	(817) 334-5463
DO	Albuquerque	NM	87100	5000	Marble Avenue, N.E., Room 320	(505) 766-3430
BO	Harlingen	TX	78550	222	East Van Buren Street, Room 500	(512) 423-8934
BO	Corpus Christi	TX	78408	400	Mann Street, Suite 403	(512) 888-3331
DO	Houston	TX	77054	2525	Murworth, Room 112	(713) 660-4401
DO	Little Rock	AR	72201	320	West Capitol Avenue, Room 601	(501) 378-5871
DO	Lubbock	TX	79401	1611	Tenth Street, Suite 200	(806) 762-7466
DO	New Orleans	LA	70112	1661	Canal Street, Suite 2000	(504) 589-6685
POD	Shreveport	LA	71101	500	Fannin Street, Room 6B14	(318) 226-5196
DO	Oklahoma City	OK	73102	200	N.W. 5th Street, Suite 670	(405) 231-4301
DO	San Antonio	TX	78206	727	East Durango Street, Room A-513	(512) 229-6250
POD	Austin	TX	78701	300	East 8th Street, Room 780	(512) 482-5288
VII RO	Kansas City	MO	64106	911	Walnut Street, 13th Floor	(816) 374-5288
DO	Kansas City	MO	64106	1103	Grande Avenue, Room 512	(816) 374-3419
BO	Springfield	MO	65803	309	North Jefferson, Room 150	(417) 864-7670
DO	Cedar Rapids	IA	52402	373	Collins Road N.E.	(319) 399-2571
DO	Des Moines	IA	50309	210	Walnut St., Room 749	(515) 284-4422
DO	Omaha	NB	68102	300	South 19th Street	(402) 221-4691
DO	St. Louis	MO	63101	815	Olive Street, Room 242	(314) 425-6600
POD	Cape Girardeau	MO	63701	339	Briadway, Room 140	(314) 335-6039
DO	Wichita	KS	67202	110	East Waterman Street	(316) 269-6571
VIII RO	Denver	CO	80202	1405	Curtis, Street, 22nd Floor	(303) 844-5441
DO	Denver	CO	80202	721	19th Street, Room 407	(303) 844-2607
DO	Casper	WY	82602	100	East B Street, Room 4001	(307) 261-5761
DO	Fargo	ND	58108	657	2nd Avenue, North, Room 218	(701) 237-5771

Type	City	State	ZIP	Street Address	Phone
DO	Helena	MT	59626	301 South Park, Room 528	(406) 449-5381
POD	Billings	MT	59101	2601 First Avenue North, Room 216	(406) 657-6047
DO	Salt Lake City	UT	84138	125 South State Street, Room 2237	(314) 524-5800
DO	Sioux Falls	SD	57102	101 South Main Avenue, Suite 101	(605) 336-2980
IX					
RO	San Francisco	CA	94102	450 Golden Gate Avenue, Room 15307	(415) 556-7487
DO	San Francisco	CA	94105	211 Main Street, 4th Floor	(415) 454-0642
DO	Fresno	CA	93721	2202 Monterey Street, Room 108	(209) 487-5189
BO	Sacramento	CA	95814	660 J Street, Room 215	(916) 440-4461
DO	Las Vegas	NV	89125	301 East Stewart Street	(702) 385-6611
POD	Reno	NV	89505	50 S. Virginia Street, Room 238	(702) 784-5268
DO	Honolulu	HI	96850	300 Ala Moana, Room 2213	(808) 546-8950
BO	Agana	Guam	96910	Pacific Daily News Bldg., Room 508	(671) 472-7277
DO	Los Angeles	CA	90071	350 S. Figueroa Street, 6th Floor	(213) 688-2956
BO	Santa Ana	CA	92701	2700 North Main Street, Room 400	(714) 836-2494
DO	Phoenix	AZ	85012	3030 North Central Avenue, Suite 1201	(602) 241-2200
POD	Tucson	AZ	85701	300 West Congress Street, Room 3V	(602) 629-6715
DO	San Diego	CA	85701	880 Front Street, Room 4-S-29	(619) 293-5540
POD	San Jose	CA	95113	111 West St. John Street, Room 424	(408) 275-7584
X					
RO	Seattle	WA	98121	2615 4th Avenue, Room 440	(206) 442-5676
DO	Seattle	WA	98174	915 Second Avenue, Room 1792	(206) 442-5534
DO	Anchorage	AK	99501	701 C Street, Room 1068	(907) 271-4022
BO	Fairbanks	AK	99701	101 12th Avenue	(907) 452-0211
DO	Boise	ID	83701	1005 Main St., 2nd Floor	(208) 334-1696
DO	Portland	OR	97204	1220 S.W. Third Avenue, Room 676	(503) 221-5221
DO	Spokane	WA	99210	W920 Riverside Avenue, Room 651	(509) 456-5310

Disaster Area Offices (DAO)

Type	City	State	ZIP	Street Address	Phone
DAO 1	Fair Lawn	NJ	07410	15-01 Broadway	(201) 794-8195
DAO 2	Atlanta	GA	30303	75 Spring Street, S.W., Suite 822	(404) 221-5822
DAO 3	Grande Prairie	TX	75051	2306 Oak Lane, Suite 110	(214) 767-7571
DAO 4	Sacramento	CA	95825	77 Cadillac Dr., Suite 158	(916) 440-3651

REGIONAL OFFICE (RO)   DISTRICT OFFICE (DO)   BRANCH OFFICE (BO)   POST-OF-DUTY (POD) small business firms for making joint purchases or establishing common research and development facilities. Indirect assistance through state and local development companies is available for the acquisition of land, for construction, conversion, and expansion of buildings, and for the purchase of machinery and equipment.

Small business investment companies. In 1958 Congress authorized a program under the Small Business Investment Act to allow small business investment companies (SBICs), licensed by the SBA, to provide equity capital to companies unable to raise funds elsewhere. The SBICs are privately owned, profit-oriented companies chartered under state law. SBICs make long-term loans, purchase capital stock and debt securities, and purchase debentures which are convertible into stock of the business. The maximum SBIC investment in any single firm cannot exceed 20% of its combined capital and surplus. Several SBICs may jointly finance a company. To encourage the growth of SBICs, the government does not tax the dividends received by these organizations from their investments in small businesses. Losses suffered by an SBIC and its stockholders may be charged against ordinary income instead of capital gains.

Minority enterprise small business investment company (MESBIC). Similar to SBICs, MESBICs are privately capitalized venture capital firms, licensed and regulated by the Small Business Administration, specially formed to aid minority businesses.

Area redevelopment administration. The Area Redevelopment Administration was formed to make loans and grants to businesses to stimulate new permanent employment. The goal of this program is to alleviate unemployment and underemployment. Labor-intensive businesses may be able to secure funds from this source.

Economic development administration. The Economic Development Administration, created in 1965 to promote industrial and commercial development, is an arm of the U.S. Department of Commerce and represents another potential source of funding for small businesses in areas of substantial unemployment or low median family incomes. These businesses can receive loans of up to 25 years at an interest rate substantially less than current market rates. Over the last few years the amount of money appropriated for EDA activities has steadily diminished. The EDA has decreased its lending activity and appears to be focusing its efforts on the capitalization of local revolving loan funds.

State business and industrial development corporations. Many states fund their own development corporations. Rather than equity investments, the SBICs provide loans of 20 to 45 years for facility expansion and equipment purchase. Some states concentrate on high-risk loans for businesses that cannot otherwise obtain bank loans. Others lend only at minimal risk. Specific interest rates and priorities can be obtained from state business development offices, chambers of commerce, and SBA offices.

Local development companies. Local development companies (LDCs) are resident-organized and -capitalized, but they solicit SBA loans and bank loans or build facilities for small local businesses. LDCs are eligible for one SBA loan or guarantee up to $1 million annually as well as unlimited bank loans for each small business they assist. An LDC usually supplies 10% of the project cost, and the remainder is financed by SBA and bank loans or by an SBA-guaranteed bank loan. An LDC can finance a company's facilities but may not provide working capital such as for inventory or freestanding fixtures and equipment. Nonprofit LDCs charge minimum interest on their 10% of the funds, while profit-oriented LDCs charge rates comparable to those of banks. Applicants are evaluated by the SBA and the participating bank before acceptance by the LDC.

Conclusions—government funding sources. In Frank's case, SBA loan programs represent the most viable of the government-sponsored loan programs for his particular business enterprise. However, he would need to request SBA financing only if he were denied conventional financing at a commercial bank.

Other sources of funds

To make sure no stone is left unturned, Frank has also reviewed additional sources of funding outside of government and commercial lending institutions. These are discussed in the following paragraphs.

Insurance companies. Insurance companies are playing more visible roles in financing American business developments. Small businesses can sometimes obtain term loans through the small business loan department of insurance companies. Considerable effort and evaluation takes place as the companies scrutinize financial statements and projections of the potential borrower.

Factoring companies. Factoring companies purchase the accounts receivable of businesses on either a notification or nonnotification basis. When a company such as All Seasons Sporting Goods enters a notification agreement with a factoring company, it turns over the collection and notification of debt to the factoring company. The factoring company is responsible for all billings and collection of the debt. In a nonnotification factoring agreement, All Seasons Sporting Goods retains the responsibility of collecting the debt from the customer, including billing procedures. The latter is usually less expensive, as Frank and his company retain the responsibility for collection. Usually the business pays the factoring company a percentage of the face value of the accounts purchased plus an annual percentage. Rates are usually higher than for bank loans. As a commercial financier, a factor may handle equipment loans, finance mergers and acquisitions, purchase real estate, and participate with banks in loans to clients.

Franchises. Some ventures adapt well to franchising. If you plan on franchising, your business should be a going concern in order to demonstrate economic viability. A franchiser may be willing to pay you for permission to sell your item or idea at another location or to expand into new territory. On the other side of the coin, purchasing a franchise is another way to start a new business. Such costs as finding a location, hiring and training employees, and designing the facility are lower for franchises than for independent businesses. The tradeoff between the loss of independence and the greater assurance of success must be carefully considered.

Credit card companies. Depending on the credit card company and the line of credit on the card, several thousand dollars may be available to the cardholder. This credit can be used for the purchase of supplies or materials, or a cash advance may be obtained. This type of credit is easy to obtain, but the interest rate is usually extremely high.

Real estate developers and owners. People with property interests can sometimes be encouraged to aid beginning enterprises by aiding in the construction of buildings and securing initial financing for equipment and fixtures. Real estate owners, especially developers and shopping center promoters, occasionally help finance small entrepreneurs who buy or lease through their companies.

Other businesses. An entrepreneur may sometimes be able to determine other businesses that would profit by the proposed venture. For example, a tennis racquet manufacturer may be seeking a dealer outlet in your area. This could benefit All Seasons Sporting Goods, as the community may lack a specialized shop or facility. By locating these interested parties, the potential commercial recreation business owner may be able to secure investment from these other businesses.

Commercial finance companies. Commercial finance companies provide secured loans for small business firms. The loans may be backed by such items as inventories, accounts receivable, and equipment. Interest rates usually are higher than those of commercial banks. Commercial finance companies are usually a last resort for short-term financing.

Miscellaneous other sources. Other financial institutions and groups sometimes provide financing for small business firms. Some possibilities include credit unions, mutual savings banks, personal finance companies, universities, and investment bankers. These potential investors may be sold on your venture if they hold a related interest or may somehow benefit from its implementation.

Conclusions—additional sources. Of the additional funding sources reviewed, Frank will be more inclined to consider those best suited for his type of retail business. Frank sees definite opportunities with factoring companies and perhaps making a leasing deal with the shopping center developer.

Sources for advice on borrowing

Many entrepreneurs are wise to seek the advice of experts for financial information. Frank is wise enough to seek help in reviewing All Seasons' financing methods, in developing general proposals for financing strategy, in preparation of a written presentation, and in locating contacts in the money market. Where to turn for such assistance depends on the size of the loan needed as well as the complexity of the situation.

Free advice

Many sources offer free advice for companies needing up to $500,000. These sources may be more valuable than the often used and comparatively expensive accountant or attorney, who may not have the daily experience needed for sound advice on such matters. Examples of these free sources of information:

1. National Association of Management and Technical Assistance Centers—emphasis on government financing
2. Service Corporations of Retired Executives (SCORE)—retired persons with experience in financing small businesses
3. Small Business Administration Management Assistance Program—financial advice
4. Small Business Institute—graduate business schools—free advice from faculty members and graduate students
5. Farmers Home Administration (FmHA)—small businesses in population areas of less than 50,000
6. Economic Development Administration—branch of U.S. government
7. Active Corporations of Executives (ACE)—executives offering advice in free time

Paid advice

Paid consultants can help you negotiate terms and review lenders' documents. Lenders welcome this professional involvement, as it helps to eliminate unsuitable borrowing prospects. The paid consultant acts as the intermediary to keep disagreements on both sides from multiplying. The paid advisor could be an attorney, accountant, investment banker, professional consultant, or private investor. Reputable advisors have built up contacts with the right people and will be practiced in knowing how to package your company.

Another source of help is a *finder*. A finder is an individual financial consultant who is paid a percentage of the loan in exchange for locating a loan. Finder's fees can vary from 1% to 15%. They can be found through advertisements or by recommendations from other business people, attorneys, accountants, and bankers.

Obtaining the necessary financing

Obtaining financing involves assessing the compatibility of capital sources and uses and the preparation of a sensible financial and business plan.

Compatibility of sources and uses

As well as maintenance of a desirable balance between debt and equity financing, a number of other factors come into play when selecting sources and types of financial assistance. The length of time for which you will need the money is an important consideration. Short-term loans such as for building inventory should be repayable with the income from the investment. In other words, short-term loans should pay for themselves. In the case of All Seasons Sporting Goods, an example of a short-term loan that pays for itself is one for purchase of the latest in sportswear during the season. The sale of the sportswear should bring in enough to repay the loan and make a profit. An extra margin of profit or other benefits should be gained, of course, to justify the loan. With regard to longer-term loans, the advantage gained by taking out the loan should be greater than its cost.

Also of vital concern is the risk to which your business is exposed as a result of borrowing. If there is a high probability that you will be unable to meet the terms of the agreement or that damages will arise from it, the risk is too great to bear, especially for a business that is just starting and is tight with its funding.

Flexibility may be affected in various ways, depending on the source of funding. Limitations may be placed on ways the capital may be used or on seeking additional capital. Some long-term loans must be paid off before any other borrowing can take place. These requirements are generally written into the terms of the loan. For example, All Seasons Sporting Goods may require a piece of equipment to refinish ski bottoms and to mount bindings. Since this is a costly item, the loan agreement may require that this loan be paid off before All Seasons Sporting Goods can enter into any additional loan agreements. This helps ensure repayment of the loan.

Some funding sources may affect the control of the business. Venture capitalists, for instance, usually demand more than 50% ownership of the business. It must be predetermined whether such loss of ownership may also affect daily operations and management procedures that are in the business's best interest.

A final primary consideration in selecting funding sources is availability. Some funds are more abundant than others, depending on various qualifications. Availability may also be affected by economic factors or business practices of the lending institution.

These factors work together rather than independently in helping the business manager to select a funding source. Tradeoffs among the factors must be weighed and ranked by importance and the future of the business.

Preparing a financial plan

A financial plan is critically important to obtaining funds. Regardless of whether you are requesting financial assistance from a friend or a banker, professionalism is vital for gaining faith and financing from your potential investors. To minimize perceived risk, Frank must present his business proposal in a manner that is carefully organized and credible. A good financial plan is naturally produced in the process of creating a good business plan. Reversing the order is commonly yet fruitlessly attempted. Planning your operation around a predetermined amount of financing is as foolish as building a house according to the amount of paint you have. If the structure and support of All Seasons Sporting Goods is to be strong and long lasting, it will be necessary to begin with a solid foundation rather than skimp on the necessities in order to minimize borrowing.

The business plan encompasses the financial plan. The level of detail presented to funding sources will vary accordingly, but for your own determination of what you will need, a detailed survey of your operation-to-be must be conducted.

Inadequate financing is one of the most frequent yet easily avoidable causes of business failure. Underfinancing can lead to problems so severe that the business may be doomed before it begins. This is so because financing is the heart of the business enterprise and business plan; it affects every part of the operation. Such a grave error can most easily be avoided by methodical planning. In Frank's case with All Seasons Sporting Goods, good preparation for seeking financing gives him an advantage over others with potential investors and begins his operation with a firm foundation.

The financial planning process consists of six basic steps, addressed below.

Identify all needs for funds

The first step in forming a business plan is to identify all needs for funding. This can be done by studying similar businesses' operating guidelines or by asking bankers or accountants. The operation must be thought through systematically to evaluate the amount needed for different purposes and activities.

In the case of All Seasons Sporting Goods, this includes different lines of stock for each type of activity. For example, firearms could include Rugar, Winchester, Black Hawk, Smith & Wesson, and Colt. Since each of these is specific and unique in its requirements for funding, each needs to be identified. In addition Frank must cover such expenses as advertising, personnel costs, utilities, and insurance. Each of these drastically affects the amount of funding required and must be thought through well in advance of putting together a final proposal for the investors.

Determine the needed capital. The prospective business owner must next estimate the total amount of capital needed. A range can be established by setting a minimum and maximum cost for each item listed. Items to include are capital assets, working capital, and reserve for contingencies (unplanned events and emergencies).

Determine the types and mix of financing. Choices between debt and equity, short- and long-term borrowing, and secured and unsecured loans must be weighed. Undercapitalization may be a result of securing the wrong kind of financing. Too little starting capital results in negative net worth, which will result in the need for new investment. A proper balance of debt and equity, determined with the assistance of a banker or accountant, enables faster growth than an extremely conservative no-debt policy.

Identify future financing needs. Last-minute financing, or "Friday night financing," is hard to get and usually wasteful, because the expense is high and the use was not carefully preplanned. Thus, a timetable of financial needs should be determined and shown to bankers and other financiers before you actually need the loans. This will allow input and advice from these sources and will emphasize your managerial strength.

Develop the financial plan. Next comes the time to develop a financial plan. The business person must know where to obtain loans and what to do in order to assure that the financing will be forthcoming. Financing proposals can vary in complexity from thorough financial plans to a sketchy cash flow and balance sheet. New and risky operations require more planning and documentation than established ones, as do seasonal requests for financial assistance. The plan should be updated periodically regardless of whether more financing is needed. Financiers should be kept informed of your situation and activities both in strong times and in weak so as to avoid dealings only in times of need. Two alternative financial strategies may be useful: a capital-conservative plan and a more highly leveraged plan. Bankers and other lenders will respond most favorably to good financial planning.

Implement and review the plan. The final step is to implement and review the financial plan. Funds secured for specified purposes must be used for such. If the financial plan is good, there is no excuse for not abiding by it. The plan should be periodically reviewed with financiers to ensure that it remains strong.

What your prospective investors will want to know. Bankers and other prospective investors scrutinize the business person and financial plan in which they are contemplating investment. They must be assured a fair chance of earnings on the deal. This will be calculated by a tradeoff between risk and return. The wise business person plans ahead for the investor's information needs.

In the case of All Seasons Sporting Goods, financiers will want to know about Frank's character—background, criminal record, credit rating, and management skills. The use to which the money will be put is another key consideration. Investors will demand to know when and how Frank plans to pay the money back. They want to be assured that there is some cushion in the loan amount for unplanned events. Finally, prospective financiers need to determine the outlook for Frank's business and the general economy in which it will operate. By preparing for these questions, Frank will save time and gain credibility.

Summary

The financing for commercial recreation enterprises is a very complex and individualized undertaking. Many considerations must be dealt with prior to the presentation of a proposal to a lending institution. Among them are whether the capital will be used for the acquisition of fixed assets such as buildings or land, or for purchase of inventory or goods that will generate profits for the business. As a result of this, capital can be divided into two general categories: equity capital, which is ownership capital, and debt capital, which must be repaid with interest. There are many avenues along which the commercial recreation entrepreneur can pursue funding sources. Among these are individual investors such as friends, relatives, and stock sales; business supplies through trade credit, equipment loans, and leases; financial institutions, including banks and venture capitalists; and government-sponsored loans through the Small Business Administration and other state and federal agencies.

When creating the financial plan, the commercial recreation entrepreneur must obtain the best possible advice. This can be had from many free small business agencies or from a paid business consultant. Regardless of the form of help obtained, the lending proposal should take into consideration a number of specific considerations. These include time, money needed, risk, and flexibility.

How the funds will be used is extremely important when trying to match the type of loan with the use to which it will be put. Other considerations are debt versus equity, short versus long term, and the schedule of borrowing and repaying. If it is a seasonal business, this is extremely important. Included are the plan for repayment, the character of the borrower, and the economic climate.

It is very important for the commercial recreation entrepreneur to identify the areas in which he or she needs help and to establish a plan to meet those objectives.

BIBLIOGRAPHY

Baumbeck, C.M., and Lawyer, K.: How to organize and operate a small business, ed. 6, Englewood Cliffs, N.J., 1979, Prentice-Hall, Inc.

Cohen, W.A.: The entrepreneur and small business problem solver, New York, 1983, John Wiley & Sons, Inc.

Fishman, A.E.: Obtain expert advice on borrowing from free sources, Merchandising **9**: 80-84, Feb., 1983.

Fishman, A.E.: Second mortgages can help finance business needs, Merchandising **9**:80-85, Aug., 1984.

Good news for entrepreneurs, Money **12**:182, 1983.

Greisman, B., editor: How to run a small business, New York, 1950, McGraw-Hill Book Co., 1950.

Murphy, T.P.: Franchising, Forbes **130**:244, Sept. 13, 1982.

Osgood, W.R.: How to plan and finance your business, Boston, 1980, CBI Publishing Co.

Rausch, E.N.: Financial management for small business, New York, 1979, AMACOM.

Ray, G.H., and Hutchinson, P.J.: The financial control of small enterprise development, New York, 1983, Nichols Publishing Co.

Walbert, L.R. The up and comers, Forbes **133**:142, March 26, 1984.

SUGGESTED READINGS

Dermer J., and Wertheimer, S., editors: The complete guide to corporate fund raising, New York, 1982, Public Service Materials CTR.

Essays on how to improve the chances for success in winning corporate grants. Pg. 7: "Corporate Giving in America: An Overview." Corporations gave more than $3 billion to philanthropy in 1981. President Reagan and his advisors call on business leaders to fill the gap where critical public needs are no longer funded by the government.

Changes in 1981 tax laws included 5%-10% of the amount deductible from corporate taxable income for charitable contributions. Direct support no longer restricted to good works.

Corporate contributions for 1980 represent 1.1 percent of net income: 34% to health and welfare, 37.8% to education, 10.9% to culture and art; 11.7% to civic activities; 5.6% miscellaneous.

Fram, E.H., editor: Small business credit and finance, New York, 1966, Oceana Publications, Inc.

An old, still good outline of sources in direct, understandable language.

Gross, H.: Financing for small and medium sized businesses, Englewood Cliffs, N.J., 1969, Prentice-Hall, Inc.

Osgood, W.R.: How to plan and finance your business, Boston, Mass., 1980, CBI Publishing Co.

Determine the amount and kind of financing most appropriate to your business.

Rausch, E. N.: Financial management for small business, New York, 1979, AMACOM.

Chapter 3, "Seeking Funds to Finance Your Profit Plan." Discusses bank financing, venture capital, insurance company financing.

Ray, G.H., and Hutchinson, P.J.: The financial control of small enterprise development, New York, 1983, Nichols Publishing Co.

Choosing from short-term, long-term and equity funds

Hayes, R.S., and Howell, J.C.: How to finance your small business with government money: SBA loans, New York, 1980, John Wiley & Sons, Inc.

Shows what resources you need and where to find them; steps to take; how to prepare financial analysis, what information the banks and the SBA want.

Parris, A.W.: The small business administration, New York, 1968, Frederick A. Praeger.

Financial assistance programs; SBIC venture capital.

Rubin, R., and Goldberg, P.: The small business guide to borrowing money, New York, 1980, McGraw-Hill Book Co.

For newcomers and experienced entrepreneurs; avoid pitfalls of borrowing; obtain fastest and best financing. Chapter 4, Private Lenders: Who They Are and How to Approach Them; Ch. 5, Borrowing from the Government.

Shapiro, E.D., Needham, R.A., and Arrowsmith, J.V., editors: Small business financing library, Ann Arbor, Mich., 1966, Institute of Continuing Legal Education.

Advice about financing a small business when it is inappropriate to go public.

Vepa, R.K.: Joint ventures—a new technique for industrial growth, India, 1980, Ramesh Jain.

Potential entrepreneurs assisted by a government promotional agency. Industrial unit jointly run by private sector, entrepreneur, and government agency is in the joint sector, not public or private sector.

Surf Queen illustrates how you, as the seeker of funds for your business, must place yourself in the position of the lender. There are two necessary considerations when making a loan: how the loan will be repaid and how to help a customer's business grow. As a loan officer, you must possess the ability to make profitable loans. While reading this case, place yourself in Mr. Lawson's position. Evaluate Mr. Hamlin's request from this perspective.

Surf Queen*

On September 12, 1956, Mr. Howard Lawson, Assistant Vice-President of the Eastern National Bank, was considering a loan application from Neill Hamlin, proprietor of Surf Queen, a New York manufacturer of women's swim suits and beachwear. Mr. Hamlin had requested a factoring credit line of $100,000, and an unsecured credit line of $75,000, both expiring August 31, 1957. This financing was needed for an anticipated 50% increase in sales of the spring swim suit line. In addition to these larger credit lines, Mr. Hamlin also asked the bank to reduce the discount rate on the factoring line from 2% to 1.5% because of the general improvement in the company's financial condition during the past three years.

The Eastern National Bank, established in 1910, was a large unit bank which in 1955 had total resources slightly over $2 billion. It was progressively managed and had been expanding rapidly in recent years. Eastern National offered a complete range of banking services, with emphasis on loans to industry. Since competition was particularly keen among New York financial institutions, the bank aggressively sought new customers and lending opportunities. As one of its services to business, Eastern National had established an Accounts Receivable and Factoring Department. Industries in the New York area which raised working capital through factoring included leather, textiles, plastics, furniture, chemicals, electronics, and industrial machine manufacturers.

Mr. Howard Lawson, 46, Assistant Vice-President, was manager of the Factoring Department at Eastern National. He had been employed at the bank for 7 years, during which he had worked primarily in the credit department. Mr. Lawson was promoted to Assistant Vice-President in 1954 shortly before assuming supervision of the Factoring Department.

Mr. Neill Hamlin, 51, was born in Yonkers, New York in 1905. After graduating from the New York Academy of Art, he entered the field of women's fashion design and for several years worked with a number of New York salons and style shops.

In 1946, Mr. Hamlin organized Surf Queen, using personal savings of $15,000 to finance the venture. The company manufactured women's swim suits and terrycloth

*Reprinted with permission of the Stanford University Graduate School of Business, 1957 by the Board of Trustees of the Leland Stanford Junior University.

93

beachwear for sale through manufacturer's representatives in the New York City area. The beachwear and swim suits designed by Hamlin were high style merchandise which sold under the trade mark "Surf Queen." Retail prices of the swim suits ranged from $15 to $35. Company offices were on one floor of a small three-story building in the downtown New York textile district. The company averaged 50 employees in 1956 — 8 in the sales department, 36 in production, and 6 in the general office.

The swim suit business was heavily seasonal; production of the spring line began in September, but about 75% of the year's sales occurred between January and April. In 1948, direct selling of the Surf Queen line began with a sales force of five men who covered the middle Atlantic states. Customers included department stores, clothing stores, and women's specialty shops, which usually ordered on terms of 1 to 4 months. The company offered 4-month credit terms early in the year, with the dating decreasing as May and June approached. Datings usually matured June 10. May and June invoices, normally for small "fill-in" orders, carried regular monthly terms.

In 1950, Mr. Hamlin signed contracts with Giant Stores, Inc., and American Federated Stores, two nationwide retail chains, to design and produce a line of lower priced women's swim suits for sale under the chains' brand names. Surf Queen usually submitted sample lines each year during September. Both Giant and Federated had steadily increased their purchases; in the 1956 season the two chains accounted for nearly $200,000 of Mr. Hamlin's total sales volume of $500,000.

Surf Queen had almost continually needed additional working capital because of its small initial investment and the pronounced seasonal nature of the business. Large sales increases in the 1956 season had caused an especially severe pressure on working capital. In addition to the seasonal sales pattern, extended terms of sale, a competitive characteristic of this industry, magnified the shortage of working capital. Nearly 75% of the company's sales carried terms of from 60 to 120 days; hence, it became necessary for Surf Queen to factor its accounts to maintain a satisfactory current position.

The company's annual financial requirements were divided into two parts. The first important need for funds arose from October to February to cover the costs of materials and production of spring lines. In the 1956 season, the bank had extended an unsecured line of $50,000 to Mr. Hamlin to finance inventory and production requirements. He asked for an unsecured line of $75,000 to cover these requirements during the 1957 season.

The second major need for funds began with the spring selling season which usually lasted from January through April. Surf Queen obtained funds during this period through factoring of accounts receivable. Mr. Hamlin had factored his accounts with Eastern National for the past five years. Recently his factoring lines had increased substantially: in 1954 from $40,000 to $60,000; in 1955, to $75,000; and the current request was for a line of $100,000. Exhibits I and II present financial and operating details of the business from 1953 to 1956.

Surf Queen used the following procedure in factoring its accounts with Eastern National:

1. *Preliminary Credit Check.* As he received orders the clerk would telephone the bank to check the credit rating of the customer. If the bank was unwilling to purchase particular accounts, the clerk would refer these orders to Mr. Hamlin for his credit approval. Occasionally, Surf Queen shipped merchandise on a guarantee or

"house risk" basis. Thus, if the account did not remit, Mr. Hamlin would repay the bank. This contingent liability was generally minor and chargebacks had been small. In addition, the company normally financed approximately 10% of its own receivables. Bad debt expense incurred on these accounts had been relatively slight.

2. *Invoicing.* A clerk prepared original invoices and as many copies as required by the customer. This clerk also typed one extra copy of the invoice for the bank's files. He also stamped all invoices with a notice stating that these had been sold and were payable to the Eastern National Bank. The bank would not accept invoices covering consigned merchandise, C.O.D. or export shipments.

3. *Evidence of Shipment.* The bank requested evidence of shipment or delivery of the merchandise. The delivery receipt or the shipping documents issued by the carrier were preferred. If the customer requested the original evidence of shipment, the order clerk would prepare a duplicate delivery receipt for the bank.

4. *Preparing the Transfer List.* The clerk next sorted invoices into alphabetical order typing the name and address of the customer on a Transfer List which conveyed to the bank the legal title to the invoices. (See Exhibit III) The Transfer List was mailed to the bank daily.

5. *Credit Memos.* If the day's billings included Credit Memos, the clerk added these to the Transfer List following the last invoice. He then subtracted the total of the Credit Memos from the total of the day's invoices. The resulting figure was used by the bank to compute the NET amount credited to Surf Queen's deposit account. The bank mailed an advice showing these computations and a record of the amount deposited for the company on the same day that the Transfer List was received by the bank.

6. *Payments.* Surf Queen's customers mailed all checks in payment of factored invoices directly to the bank. Any checks inadvertently mailed to the company were forwarded to the bank.

7. *Factoring Reserve.* The bank required Surf Queen to maintain a factoring reserve of 20%. This reserve was used to provide funds to cover any returns or disputed invoices, to establish a reserve to charge back guaranteed invoices, and to help the bank earn a higher rate of return on its funds. The factoring reserve could be compared in some respects to a compensating balance.[1]

---

[1] Eastern National calculated the factoring reserve as follows: Assume a schedule of purchased invoices totaling $1,000, selling terms 2%-10, net 30, bank discount 1.5%, factoring reserve 20%. The 1.5% rate is based on 30-day terms (no dating in this instance).

Invoices (dated 5/10)	$1,000.00
2% Cash Discount	20.00
Net Invoices	980.00

Discount (1.5)	14.70	
20% Factoring reserve	196.00	
		210.70
Net credit to the Surf Queen account		$ 769.30

The 20% factoring reserve is released after expiration of the discount period, in this case on 5/20.

After reviewing the loan application and the most recent audited financial statements, Mr. Lawson was undecided regarding his recommendation on the increased lines of credit. Accordingly he telephoned Mr. Hamlin asking for more detailed information about the sales outlook for the 1957 spring selling season. Mr. Hamlin discussed the forthcoming season in general terms and promised he would send the bank a letter describing his sales prospects and needs for additional funds. Hamlin also repeated his request for a reduction in the factoring discount rate from 2% to 1.5%. He referred to the satisfactory profits shown by Surf Queen in the past two years and to the general improvement in his financial condition. Mr. Hamlin stated he could obtain a lower rate from a commercial factor in the city. After the telephone conversation, Mr. Lawson dictated the following memorandum summarizing the loan application and bringing the credit file up to date:

Factoring Department
New York
September 12, 1956

Mr. Neill Hamlin, d.b.a.

Surf Queen

Outstanding debt
Not now in our debt. Previously had a factoring line of $75,000, expired July 31, 1956, 2% discount, 20% reserve, ½ of 1% per month for each month of additional dating. Account also had an unsecured line of $50,000, rates prevailing at time of advance, expired July 31, 1956. Notes drawn on a 90-day maturity basis, rates generally 6¼%.

Current application
Increase of the factoring line to— 100,000, 20% reserve, discount to be reduced from 2% to 1½%, additional charges of ½ of 1% for each month of extended dating. Line to expire July 31, 1957.
Increase in unsecured line to—$75,000 rates prevailing at time of advances, but not less than 6%, notes drawn on a 90-day maturity basis, line expiring July 31, 1957. Continuing guarantee of wife.

History and business data
This is a sole proprietorship manufacturing a line of ladies swim suits. Factoring arrangements have been in effect for several years with satisfactory relations. Collateral performance has been good with nominal losses and average invoices in excess of $100.

Financial
From an unqualified report prepared by Sessions and Co., CPA., dated July 31, 1956:

Current Assets	$147,115
Current Liabilities	56,008
Net Worth	170,375

Comparatives (000 omitted)

	12/31/54	12/31/55	7/31/56
Current Assets	120	185	147
Current Liabilities	70	131	56
Working Capital	50	54	91
Net Worth	118	136	170

Comments

Sales for the current year increased substantially over last season and have resulted in a good profit with over half retained in the business. Payables are current and unsecured borrowings have previously been liquidated before maturity. Collateral performance has been satisfactory, returns minor and reserves adequate. Additional financial and operating information has been requested from Mr. Hamlin per telephone conversation of 9/12/56. Hamlin is asking for a rate reduction from 2% to 1½% claiming a lower rate is available to him elsewhere.

Two days later, Mr. Lawson received a letter from Hamlin describing the outlook for Surf Queen. The letter said in part:

In regard to the increase in my secured and unsecured lines of credit, the following is a summation of the facts discussed on the telephone today: Concerning chain store sales, Giant Stores picked five styles last year and we did $67,012. This year they tell me they will pick ten styles in a better price range for a larger volume and we expect to do at least $120,000. In samples alone, we have already shipped $3,600, which is three times greater than last year.

American Federated Stores is reviewing 11 styles all in a very popular price range and in samples we will ship $4,400. Last year they had 6 active numbers and we did $101,327. From the 11 styles submitted this year, we expect a volume of at least $180,000.

On the Surf Queen label, we did $348,600 last year and very few orders were booked during September and October. This year we already have booked $34,800.

We will probably add approximately 150 new customers this year, which should account for about $50,000 of the increases in the Surf Queen line. The remaining $50,000 will result from larger sales to established accounts.

In summary, we did $500,000 for the 1956 season, and for 1957 we expect to do the following:

	1956-57 Season	1955-56 Season
Surf Queen Line	450,000	348,600
Giant Stores	120,000	67,012
American Federated Stores	180,000	101,327
	750,000	516,939

Consequently, I am going to need the larger credit lines requested. The earlier receipt of orders this year is the best indication we have of a greater year for us, and along with the increase in chain stores sales, we must increase our working capital. Also, last year we had to work a night shift and almost every Saturday to handle the increased volume. We want to start a little earlier this year to avoid so much overtime and night work. . . .

◻

EXHIBIT A

Comparative income statements, audited, seven months ended July 31, 1955-1956

	7/31/55	Percent of net sales	7/31/56	Percent of net sales
Sales	413,126		522,041	
Less returns	27,244		22,633	
Net sales	385,882	100	499,408	100
Cost of Sales				
Material	130,768	33.9	171,992	34.5
Labor	89,016	23.1	119,976	24.0
Factory burden	35,599	9.2	51,552	10.3
Total cost of sales	255,383	66.2	343,520	68.6
Gross profit	130,499	33.8	155,888	31.2
Selling, General, and Administrative Expenses				
Selling expenses	40,884	10.6	46,801	9.4
General and admin. expenses	12,935	3.4	15,052	3.0
Operating profit	76,680	19.8	94,035	18.8
Other Charges, Net				
Interest expense	664	.2	2,345	.5
Factoring expense	5,886	1.5	9,390	1.9
Sundry other expenses	204	.1	7,149	1.3
Gain on sale of fixed assets	(302)	(.1)	(100)	
Discounts earned	(371)	(.1)	(508)	(2.1)
Sundry other income	—	—	(38)	
Federal income taxes	23,341	6.0	26,265	5.3
Net profit	47,258	12.2	49,532	9.9
Withdrawals	20,000		21,206	

EXHIBIT B

Comparative balance sheets, audited July 31, 1953-1956

	7/31/53	7/31/54	7/31/55	7/31/56
Assets				
Cash	445	3,628	22,285	11,446
Accounts receivable, net	20,386	28,195	27,901	11,936
Factoring reserve	12,368	17,492	12,182	11,612
Inventory	67,139	80,954	77,515	112,121
Total Current assets	100,338	130,269	139,883	147,115
Fixed assets	23,910	29,876	36,641	64,468
Less: reserve for depreciation	(11,652)	(15,162)	(17,960)	(18,502)
Fixed assets, net	12,258	14,714	18,681	45,966
Accts. receivable, other	3,185	—	1,139	3,256
Other assets	768	—	12,691	21,381
Prepaid and deferred	7,906	6,776	6,554	8,665
Total assets	124,455	151,759	178,948	226,383
Liabilities				
Notes payable—bank	5,468	—	—	—
Accounts payable	26,717	27,250	30,344	40,865
Fed. & state payroll taxes payable	4,523	3,594	2,845	8,095
Accruals	3,901	6,124	3,710	7,048
Total current liabilities	40,609	36,968	36,899	56,008
Capital	62,558	79,404	114,791	142,049
Current profit and loss	21,288	35,387	27,258	28,326
Total liabilities and net worth	124,455	151,759	178,948	226,383

⌐

EXHIBIT C

Original transfer list

This is to certify that the persons named below are indebted to the undersigned in the sums set opposite their respective names, for goods, sold, shipped and delivered.

LEAVE BLANK	NO.	NAME, TRADE STYLE AND ADDRESS IN FULL	DATE OF INVOICE	INVOICE NUMBER	TERMS OF SALE	GROSS AMOUNT OF INVOICE	APPROVAL NUMBER
	1						
	2						
	3						
	4						
	5						
	6						
	7						
	8						
	9						
	10						
	11						
	12						
	13						
	14						
	15						
	16						
	17						
	18						
	19						
	20						
	21						

Definitions

Accounts receivable. Money owed to the business by customers.

Factoring. A method of financing accounts receivable where a business sells its accounts receivable to a financial institution. This is usually done at less than face value of the accounts receivable.

Datings. A process by which merchandise can be shipped to a customer before the bill is written. Often used in the clothing industry to allow the customer to sell some of the product before payment is due.

Working capital. A business investment in short-term assets (i.e. cash, short-term securities, accounts receivable, and inventories).

Payables. Money that the business owes its creditors; usually for such items as raw materials, inventory, and short-term loans.

Unsecured. Usually applied to a loan. This means that there is no lien placed on specific property that can be sold to pay back the loan.

Questions

1. As Mr. Lawson, would you approve the loan to Surf Queen? If not, why not? Would you change your mind if you could apply certain stipulations? If so, what would they be? If you decide to grant the loan, why? What factors lead you to this decision?
2. What suggestions can you make to Mr. Hamlin to strengthen his request for the loan?
3. If you were Mr. Hamlin, what other avenues are open to you to obtain the needed funding?
4. It it possible for Surf Queen to continue its growth without the additional capital? If so, how?

CHAPTER 5

Planning a commercial recreation enterprise

CHAPTER OBJECTIVES

1. To understand the role of government in a commercial recreation enterprise

2. To understand the concepts of infrastructure and superstructure and how they relate to commercial recreation

3. To be familiar with the concepts of static and dynamic planning

4. To be able to select the best method for planning the commercial recreation enterprise

Planning is the most important and least understood component of commercial recreation. During planning a number of key criteria are established and decisions are made that will affect the operation of any recreation enterprise. A slight miscalculation concerning the products or kinds of services to be offered can produce the fatal result of not meeting consumers' needs. Once this happens, management must attempt to undo the mistakes and hazards associated with a poorly planned opening season. Because of the critical importance of planning, considerable time and thought must be given to it.

In order for you to understand the planning process completely, we must discuss the raw materials of commercial recreation. These are land resource, financial resource, personnel resource and planning. An effective combination of these four components brings together a functional and profitable commercial recreation enterprise.

In some cases an abundance of one of these four components can be used to compensate for the lack of one of the others. Abundant financial resources can compensate for deficiencies in the physical resource by creating an attractive environment for the commercial recreation enterprise established. Abundant financial resources can also be used to bring in outside labor or to pay for extensive training for the personnel involved in the operation of the enterprise. Exceptional physical resources and/or personnel can often compensate for small financial resources. In all cases, the planning phase is used to establish the operating perspectives for the enterprise. For this reason, planning is the most important component in development.

As an example, let's establish a resort development (Fig. 5-1). Resorts are popular places to work as well as visit. To a casual observer they have a definitely romantic aspect, especially when the majestic mountains, ocean sunsets or broad green expanses provide panoramic backdrops for the resort. However, the real resort operation is concerned with the day-to-day business of unifying resources—physical, human, and natural—with the varied needs and demands of an inconsistent public. The resort makes a good example because it is the most complex form of commercial recreation enterprise. Our resort development is a year-round facility, specifically a winter and summer resort like the one in Sun Valley, Idaho.

In order to develop this facility, we must consider all planning aspects as they relate to the physical facility.

FIG. 5-1 Resorts such as Snowbird offer the ultimate in scenic beauty and excitement. These types of destination resorts must be very carefully planned to blend into the surrounding natural resource. (Photograph courtesy Snowbird Corp.)

Legal aspects

The legal requirements of any commercial recreation enterprise are the same as for any business. They exist at all three government levels—federal, state, and local. Examples of the legal requirements of the different government levels include the following:

The federal government requires that you register with the Internal Revenue Service to acquire an employer identification number. You must withhold federal income tax and report it to the IRS on a monthly basis. There are also corporate laws and requirements that must be met when establishing a corporation.

State requirements include health regulations and collection of sales tax, recreation taxes that may be applicable to the business, and unemployment insurance tax to cover fired employees, as well as withholding of state income tax.

Local regulations that cover businesses include business licensing requirements, local sales tax collection, and another set of health and safety regulations.

Federal government

Sometimes, because of its perceived distance from the facility, it is difficult to see how the federal government affects a commercial recreation enterprise. However, the federal government has tremendous impact on all commercial recreation enterprises.

For example, if our resort is developed on federal land or uses federal funds, it must meet the requirements of the Environmental Protection Act. This can delay a project for up to five years. During this delay inflation can substantially increase the costs of proposed development.

Other federal agencies, such as the Department of Transportation, can substantially affect the ability to attract consumers. The Department of Transportation grants licenses to bus companies and railroads and would be involved in the establishment of any airports close to our facility. Once the Department of Transportation has granted the necessary licenses, we are in a much better position to attract customers.

The list of federal laws that can relate to recreation is so extensive that it cannot be included here; however, these are some of the laws you need to be aware of:

The Securities Act regulates the ways in which stocks and bonds can be offered
    to the public for sale.

The Occupational Health and Safety Hazard Act (OSHA) specifies standards
    that must be observed in the workplace, including cleanliness, design, and
    employee working conditions.

The Fair Labor Act controls union activities.

The Truth in Advertising Act states that an individual who advertises that he
    uses your product must actually use it and that you must be able to prove
    any claims you make concerning your product.

The National Environmental Protection Act (NEPA) concerns natural resources as they relate to commercial recreation enterprises and how those enterprises obtain permits for use of government property or federal funds for recreational purposes. This is particularly important when dealing with environmental impact statements and environmental impact analysis.

These examples are illustrative of the role the federal government plays in the planning process and the legalities associated with it.

As well as laws, federal policies can also have substantial effects on a commercial recreation enterprise. The policies of the federal government or of foreign national governments can substantially increase tourism. Government policies can result in tremendous tax and financial breaks to the entrepreneur or they can disrupt the business climate.

Some prime examples of the effect of government policies relate directly to travel and tourism, particularly in foreign countries. As a government's currency fluctuates, travel and tourism to that country also fluctuate. Thus, it is best for a commercial recreation and/or travel and tourism business to locate in an area where the government is sympathetic to the needs of the entrepreneur and does everything in its power to establish a stable government, both economically and politically.

State government

Like the federal government, state government has substantial influence on travel, tourism, and commercial recreation. Almost all state governments in the United States have some kind of tourism promotion agency to attract tourists and tourist dollars. A tourism promotion agency would have a tremendous impact, not only on the tourism industry but on all related commercial recreation enterprises, including hotels, motels, food services, and special attractions. Because these enterprises benefit from the increased numbers of tourists coming to the state, the state tourism agency can have substantial benefits for them.

Some states, such as Colorado, impose entertainment and amusement taxes that pertain strictly to commercial recreation enterprises. The revenue from these taxes is used either to attract additional visitors to the state or to reduce the tax burden of local residents.

In addition to attracting tourists and levying taxes, state governments regulate health and safety. These laws can apply specifically to a commercial recreation facility and to its ongoing management. For instance, all states have regulations concerning the operation and management of water-based facilities such as swimming pools and water slides. Regulations include specifications on the slope of the pool (which must not become too deep too quickly), the steps and ladders in the pool, recirculation systems, chemical feeders, chlorination systems and quality of the water.

There are many state health laws and regulations that a commercial recreation entrepreneur must be aware of when establishing a facility. If food is served, for instance, a number of sanitation regulations pertaining specifically to food and food service operations must be obeyed. Further regulations generally control the size and number of toilet facilities on any premise, particularly those that provide food services.

State employment and tax laws can also affect commercial recreation. The specifics of laws affecting commercial recreation vary from state to state.

In most cases the recreation entrepreneur can be sure that state regulations include a requirement that the company name and business be filed with the secretary of the state. There are regulations about the establishment of the business and procedures for filing state income tax returns. Regulations similar to the federal government's OSHA standards can be dealt with through the state occupational and safety office. The entrepreneur must also meet the state requirement that the employer carry workman's compensation insurance. These rules vary from state to state and need to be thoroughly researched.

Local government

Local government can be extremely supportive or restrictive to the development of a commercial recreation enterprise. Some local governments do not want visitors attracted to the area. There can be conflicts between residents who do not wish to see development and residents who do. Local restrictions can limit improvements needed for the development of the enterprise on such public utilities as streets and sewer and water systems. Zoning regulations can also restrict development.

Communities that are supportive of a commercial recreation enterprise can be very cooperative. Some may even issue renovation or industrial revenue bonds to provide funding for the enterprise at a much lower rate than would be available from regular financial institutions.

This is a very brief summation of some of the ways in which government can affect a commercial recreation enterprise. The ways in which governmental actions can encourage the development of a recreation business can include (in a foreign country) the government's willingness to grant major tax benefits and concessions to a commercial recreation business. Such concessions have at times included the total elimination of sales tax and/or income tax for the corporation. It must be noted that such concessions are usually made by foreign countries. The United States, however, does have various agencies concerned with the development of economically depressed areas. In these cases federal funds can be made available to encourage new development. Such funds can include planning funds, wage and salary subsidies, and grants for utility development.

Conversely, negative impact by governmental agencies can be exemplified by the trouble that is arising in the ski industry. Most ski resorts are on federal land and must file an environmental impact statement. This process can be time-consuming and costly. From the beginning to the final approval of an environmental impact statement may take as much as 3 to 5 years, not counting possible delays due to lawsuits.

Importance of infrastructure in commercial recreation

The term *infrastructure* includes all facilities on or under the ground, including the land, environment, roads, highways, and airports. The infrastructure is related to the land that the recreational facility will be developed on, and it is important to deal with this component of the enterprise in a number of ways. Let's go back to our example—the development of a major destination resort. This facility will offer skiing and summer activities. Therefore, land use and site selection are important to this operation (Fig. 5-2).

Site selection must be undertaken with an understanding of the terrain suitable for the type of venture. The site must be accessible by airline, freeways, and other forms of transportation. Without linkages to other populations the venture is doomed to failure. An operation of this type requires very careful site selection especially for the physical and transportation aspects.

Once a suitable site has been selected, it is necessary to develop the land. This requires matching the facilities to the land, both physically and aesthetically, to provide the desired ambience. This includes hiding the maintenance structures from public view and locating lodgings to optimize the view. At the same time development must consider the layout of the ski runs, golf course, tennis courts, and swimming pool. These must not affect the beauty of the landscape. After all, this is what the vacationing people will be looking for.

Now we need to consider zoning laws. Most counties and cities have specific requirements concerning what can be built on which piece of land. These requirements pertain to everything from type of building, specifically residences and commercial buildings, to the size of signs and height of buildings. These are specified by the planning committee or the governing body. Any deviation must be approved by the governing body and go through a public hearing process.

In our example, it is to the developer's advantage to encourage strict zoning regulations to control development on the land he or she is using. This can be done by creating a zoning commission or by working closely with the local governing body to establish suitable zoning regulations.

Land

The land for a year-round resort can be its most important feature. Commercial recreation developers must understand that people will travel long distances to a scenic location providing there is something for them to do when they get there, and the environment is part of the experience. The recreation entrepreneur must be extremely careful about the way in which the land is developed. Since the environment and the beauty of the land are probably what attracts visitors to the area in the first place, it is of vital importance that nothing be done to mar that scenic attraction. All too often in commercial recreation and resort development, the scenic beauty is destroyed in an attempt to increase profits. This is often due to improperly planned and located hotels, condominiums, and resort developments. It is

FIG. 5-2 Notice how the infrastructure blends into the natural terrain of Amelia Island Plantation. An infrastructure should never intrude on the landscape, only complement it. (Photograph courtesy Amelia Island Plantation.)

of utmost importance that the land base be maintained in its proper, natural, scenic state.

In some cases the land resource is less important. Prime examples of this are Disneyland and Disney World. In this type of enterprise construction costs are substantially higher than for resorts using the natural environment. However, the developer is more able to control the experience and create an illusion instead of reality. In developments of this nature, financial resources take precedence over land resource.

Underground facilities

Elements of the infrastructure such as sewer lines, water lines, electrical power, gas lines, and roads, are extremely important to commercial recreation. Other elements of the infrastructure might include airports and landing facilities for boats. Today people do not talk about travel in terms of miles but in terms of time. An attraction is often of better value if the consumer can get there more rapidly than by driving, so the facilities necessary for landing planes and making visitors comfortable immediately on arrival are of extreme importance.

Visitors to a facility require modern conveniences such as flush toilets and electrical power. It is important that utility plants to support these facilities be provided unobtrusively; of course they must also work well and be easy to repair.

Planning for underground facilities and infrastructure must take place prior to construction of the above-ground facilities, or the developer will be constantly trying to redo his design and development of the area.

Seasonal considerations

Seasonal conditions must be considered during the planning stage. Transportation into and out of the area during bad weather must be designed to cover all emergencies including avalanches and times when the road is not usable. It may be better to plan for inability to use conventional transportation methods like roads and develop exceptional transportation methods such as subways that allow easy year-round accessibility.

Amenities related to comfort such as air conditioning, heating, and entertainment systems (radio and television) must function flawlessly. These points may seem minor, but there are instances of facilities that have not been able to function properly because of insufficient power to run the amenities required by visitors. This is particularly true when developing a resort.

Superstructure

It is important to discuss the *superstructure,* or above-ground facilities and equipment needed for the operation of the enterprise. In a resort setting, this means buildings, hotels, restaurants, shops, ski lifts, and all equipment necessary to keep the resort operating smoothly. Equipment, such as snow cats, lawn mowers and snow plows, is also considered part of the superstructure. These need to be planned and budgeted for, since maintenance is very important. It is wise to arrange maintenance equipment and procedures so that they are unobtrusive yet highly effective.

Types of planning in commercial recreation

Commercial recreation planning can be broken down into static and dynamic planning. Static planning, the most commonly used in the United States, takes a commercial recreation enterprise through its various phases to completion. Once the facility has been designed, the plans drawn, and the architectural renderings and blueprints completed, the planning phase is over. Once planning stops, the facility is constructed and goes into operation.

In dynamic planning, the process never stops. Once a facility has been designed and construction begins, the planning goes on to determine what the consumer wants. As needs are identified or new information becomes available, plans evolve to allow for constant checks and improvement in the design of the facility. An excellent in-depth discussion of these planning concepts is available in *Tourism and Recreation Development,* by Fred Lawson and Manuel Baud-Bovy.

Static planning

The physical planning approach

This approach was developed in the 1960s to deal with some of the needs related to the development of resort facilities. It begins with the creation of a map of the area that notes the specific characteristics considered important to the development: major roads, suitable land and terrain, existence of other attractions, locations of suitable utilities, and so on (Fig. 5-3). Once these key criteria have been identified, each is placed on a separate map, often a transparency allowing the maps to be overlaid on each other. This process identifies the key areas that need further research.

When this phase is completed, a detailed land use plan is developed. This includes drawings of the proposed facility, including blueprints of the building. These blueprints are used in the final phase, an evaluation of the costs and revenues to be generated. If the plan is determined to be profitable, construction begins and planning ceases.

The unit use standard approach to planning

Some key issues are not addressed by the physical planning approach. Particularly, this includes the market aspect, and so the unit use standard approach was developed (Fig. 5-4). In this approach market consideration for such a facility is included. The use standard approach takes the market into consideration in five steps.

First the planner studies present recreation activities in an area. Once these activities are identified, a unit of measure, or standard, is established for each activ-

Attributes in the Great Lakes area

Geology

Archean
Huronian
Keweenawan
Cambrian
Ordovician
Silurian

Soils

Mountainous, rocky loam
Sandy clay
Dry, wet sands, bog muck
Sandstone, gravel

Land relief

Major hills
Crystalline uplands
Ridge and swamp belt

Forests

Forest-covered land

Water

Shoreline
Inland lakes

Climate

Average annual snowfall
in inches

Development

Cities
   15,000-20,000
   5000-15,000
   under 5000

History

Distribution of historic
sites

FIG. 5-3 The physical planning approach.

ity. Then an inventory of the current available resources, including site locations and raw acreage, is taken. Current demand is evaluated to determine whether existing facilities are overused, and based on the evaluation, an estimate of future demand is established. When future demand, available resources, and present demand have been evaluated, a program for satisfying additional needs is estab-

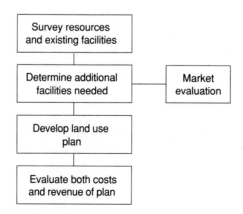

FIG. 5-4 The unit use standard approach to planning.

lished. This program should identify needed facilities and make plans to construct them. Construction should be timed to coordinate with the rise in the number of visitors to the area.

The economic policies approach to planning

A major drawback to the standard use approach is that it does not consider alternatives. As a result, the economic policies approach was developed (Fig. 5-5). In the example of our ski resort, it may be feasible to find a suitable location and a market for such a development. However, the size and economics of the project and its profitability have not yet been considered. These issues are explored with the economic policies approach, which is based on an extremely thorough analysis of the market segment and forecast needs. It is followed up by a survey of resources and existing facilities, which results in a comparison between the two. This comparison should direct the entrepreneur through a series of alternative actions ranging from building needed facilities to completing totally new concepts.

Each possibility for development is evaluated according to market forces, programs, economic feasibility, physical site available, and social and economic impact. The subsequent selection process compares multiple options to determine an optimal economic return. Once the most profitable option is selected, detailed planning of the project, including developing blueprints, is begun.

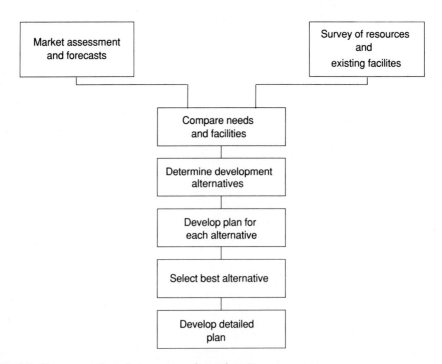

FIG. 5-5 The economic policies approach to planning.

The systems approach to planning models

Helped by the increased accessibility of computers for use in research and planning, many researchers have begun to view the recreation enterprise as a complex socioeconomic model. Computer simulations predict where people will travel and what factors are relevant to the decision to visit a specific recreation site.

Computer models and gravity flow models identify distance as the key to participation. Computer models such as Symapping deal with advanced statistical techniques, such as analysis of variance, to describe customer behavior. Unfortunately, each model has flaws that detract from its effectiveness as a predictor of attraction to a commercial recreation enterprise (Fig. 5-6).

Dynamic planning models

The PASOLP approach to planning

Products analysis sequence for outdoor leisure planning, or the PASOLP method, was developed in the late 1970s. It is based on maximum attractiveness and maximum feasibility (Fig. 5-7). PASOLP considers the attractiveness of the enterprise to be important to profitability. In addition, maximum feasibility evaluation weighs political ramifications and defines the concept of *critical mass,* which determines whether an area or facility has sufficient attractions to create demand. PASOLP consists of four steps.

1. A survey analysis identifies existing markets, potential resources, and policies and priorities of government to create a base for analysis of potential alternatives.
2. Once policies and priorities have been determined, options for commercial recreation products for the site are listed.
3. Possibilities are subjected to feasibility and economic analysis. This results in a priority listing of commercial recreation enterprises to be developed.
4. The development of the physical plan and the construction of the facility are based on the needs of developer, tourist, and government.

First the facility is constructed; then the effects of the development are measured. These are protection and improvement of the environment and community social and economic results. In the PASOLP approach there is no attempt to monitor the effectiveness of the original plans.

The dynamic commercial recreation plan

Many resorts have changed ownership or gone out of business because of inability to use their resources to meet public needs. Usually this is because the resort manager does not rapidly identify problems that discourage visitors from coming to the resort. This lack of identification can be complicated by an inability to pinpoint the origin of management problems. The dynamic planning and management model (Fig. 5-8) identifies operational or resource problems and supports a means of correcting them once they have been identified. The advantage of a dynamic model is its ability to identify changes and correct them in an ongoing process.

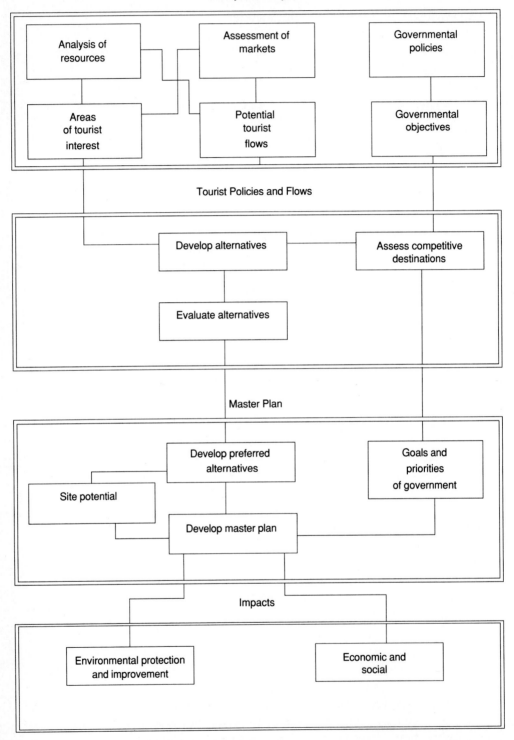

Survey and Analysis

Analysis of resources

Assessment of markets

Governmental policies

Areas of tourist interest

Potential tourist flows

Governmental objectives

Tourist Policies and Flows

Develop alternatives

Assess competitive destinations

Evaluate alternatives

Master Plan

Develop preferred alternatives

Goals and priorities of government

Site potential

Develop master plan

Impacts

Environmental protection and improvement

Economic and social

FIG. 5-6 The systems approach to planning.

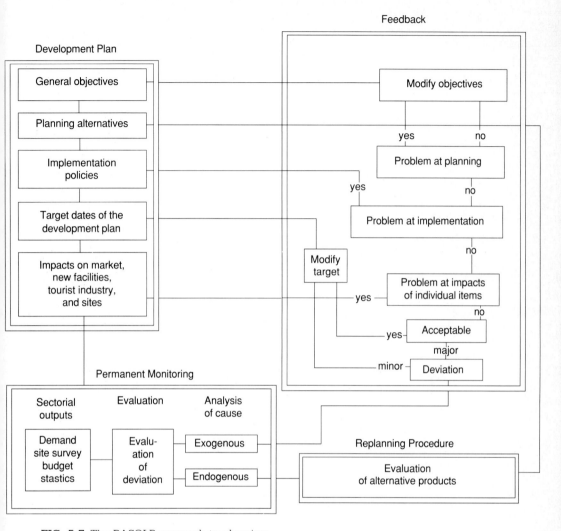

FIG. 5-7 The PASOLP approach to planning.

Development of the model

In order for a planning model to be dynamic, it must include an evaluation and feedback phase that suggests changes within the project itself. The model can be divided into four major components.

1. The planning and development phase, basically a modification of existing planning models.

2. The monitoring and evaluative phase, in which profitability criteria are monitored on an ongoing basis and an evaluation of them is performed through a modification of managerial accounting.

3. The modification phase, in which answers to a series of questions determine where in the planning model the manager should correct the problem.

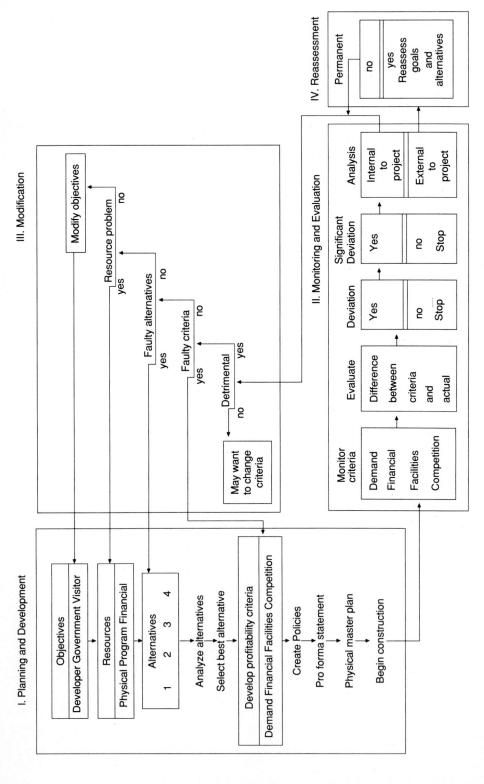

FIG. 5-8 The dynamic planning approach.

4. The reassessment phase, which takes place when the analysis indicates that the deviation from the developed criteria is external to the project and is probably based on a permanent shift in the economy or habits of the consumer. A shift of this type should lead to a reassessment of the entire project.

The planning and development stage

Once a project has been conceived, the developer must determine objectives. For any given resort, there are three interested groups, each with its own set of objectives that must be reconciled and accommodated in project objectives. These groups are the developer, concerned government agencies, and the visitor population. For example, one objective of the developer is to create a profitable enterprise. Local, state, and federal government objectives may range from unemployment reduction to increasing prestige, and visitors have certain preconceived objectives for visiting a resort.

In the ski resort used in this example, the stated objective by the developer is to turn a profit. The governmental objective is to increase local employment through the winter months. The visitor's objective is to obtain the best possible skiing on challenging terrain and with excellent snow quality. One challenge to the developer is to meet the objectives of the visitor while maintaining the environmental quality of the site. Environmental quality consists of such things as scenic beauty and an uncrowded, natural environment. This is extremely important because many studies have indicated that a major consideration in any recreational facility, particularly a year-round resort, is the scenic quality and uniqueness of the area.

These three sets of objectives are accommodated in the project objectives, which are to develop a profitable, high quality resort, to employ local people in the winter season, and to provide challenging terrain and superior snow quality to the skier.

Once the project objectives are defined, the developer can analyze the available project resources, consisting of (1) physical resources, or natural amenities and infrastructure; (2) program resources, or activities; and (3) financial resources of the developer. These three resources are combined to aid in the development of multiple planning choices.

In our example available sites are varied. The physical resources are somewhat limited on land that can be purchased outright by the developer. However, physical resources available through government leases are excellent. The lack of resources available for outright purchase by the developer will severely limit the variety of programs that can be initiated. For example, one of the options conceived prior to site acquisition was to develop an 18-hole golf course. The very small amount of land available will not allow this; therefore, summer activities must be deemphasized.

The developer is a multimillionaire with a very large credit line who can afford the expensive design and the costly construction of permanent facilities. The owner's financial resources will provide for an excellent management team to run the resort. Multiple planning options can be identified and evaluated by economic, financial, and physical techniques such as feasibility and site studies. It is important to be sure that all options are evaluated by the same procedure. This allows them to be compared to each other and provides a basis for selecting a single best choice.

Profitability criteria

Profitability criteria are the standards that will insure a profitable operation. They are divided into four categories:

1. Demand, which includes visitation, visitor days, and occupancy rates.
2. Competition, which concerns who the competition is, what percentage of the market the resort can draw, and what percentage of the market the developer anticipates obtaining.
3. Finance, which includes return on investment, internal rates of return, fixed costs, and variable costs.
4. Facilities, which includes the number of beds, the type of recreational and support facilities, and the usage rates.

Profitability criteria must be developed in a testable format. To be effective the criteria in the dynamic model must be quantifiable—that is, measurable. (See Table 5-1 for examples of criteria.) To illustrate, one example of each profitability criterion will be discussed. Demand will be defined as an occupancy rate of 95% throughout the skiing season. *Occupancy rate* is the percentage of rooms occupied on any given night by guests of the resort. The competition criterion is that at least 33% of the skiers at the resort are from the East Coast. The financial criterion will be return on investment (ROI). *Return on investment* is the yearly profit from the resort divided by the original investment. It should be at least 10%. A sample facility criterion is: The wait in lift line is not to exceed 15 minutes. These four examples of profitability criteria are relatively common in the resort industry and have been identified as critical to the success of a resort. In a realistic situation many additional criteria would be identified.

Once the profitability criteria are identified, the next step is to create policies for operation based upon those criteria. Once these policies are stated, it is possible to proceed to the preparation of a five-year pro-forma statement (projected financial statement). This should provide the basis for a financial analysis and suggest whether or not the project is feasible.

Monitoring and evaluation

A resort operation must be monitored on a regular basis, usually monthly and sometimes weekly or daily. In our example we will evaluate each of the criteria for the following periods: Demand should be determined daily. Finances should be evaluated yearly. Lift line waiting time should be evaluated as the average time waited in line per week. The competition factor should be determined on a monthly basis. Management should monitor the profitability criteria of demand,

TABLE 5-1. Examples of profitability criteria.

Facilities	
Number of beds at base	2557
Average days of operation	154
Number of rooms ÷ total revenue	58
Terrain (%)	
Beginner	22
Intermediate	48
Expert	30
Demand	
Average skier visits	378,000
Average peak day crowds	6952
Vertical transportation feet (VTF) per hour (demand per skier visit)	1613
Occupancy rate (%)	72.7
Financial	
Average daily room rate per guest	$30
Average revenue per skier visit (lift ticket)	$15
Revenue per skier visit (other than lift ticket)	$10
Monthly revenue as % of gross fixed assets	7
Ratio of debt to cash flow	2.2:1
Competition	
Local market share (%)	48
East coast market share (%)	22
Share of out-of-state skiers in local market (%)	50

competition, finance and facilities to insure that the criteria are being met. This is why the profitability criteria must be in measurable form.

Next we need to determine whether there is any significant deviation from the criteria. If there is, management needs to analyze the reasons for that difference. If there is no deviation from the criteria, management has adequately planned and defined profitability criteria.

Whether a deviation from profitability criteria is significant depends upon the judgment of the management. Most resorts consider a deviation of 10% or more to be significant. If the deviation is significant, detailed analysis will determine whether or not it is internal or external to the project. Internal deviations arise from factors under the manager's control. External deviations, such as the 1970s gas shortage, are not under direct management control. This was a situation that sharply reduced resort revenue, but the resorts had no control over gasoline allocations to their region.

If analysis indicates that the deviation is internal, the manager should proceed

to phase three, modification. Suppose in the ski resort illustration all four areas, demand, finance, facilities, and competition, varied significantly from the criteria.
Analysis indicated that all four deviations were internal. The occupancy rate for
lodging was 62% during peak season instead of the 95% projected. With regard to
competition, 22% of the skiers were from the East Coast instead of the 33% required. For facilities, the wait in the lift lines was 30 minutes, not 15. The return on
investment was negative instead of the 10% required. This means that all four of
our criteria are subject to modification.

Modification

Once an internal deviation from profitability criteria has been identified, management can determine whether the difference is detrimental to the project. A difference can be either beneficial or detrimental. If it is not detrimental, management
may want to keep the criteria and policies or modify them the better to reflect actual conditions. If the difference is detrimental, the criteria may not reflect actual
conditions, and the criteria may need to be modified. If the events are accurately
measured, management needs to look at whether or not it has chosen an appropriate option. If the selected option is viable, perhaps additional resources are needed. If neither the criteria nor the chosen option is at fault, management should return to the beginning and modify the objectives of the entire resort.

In this example, the developer placed the criteria on the modification portion of
the model and found the facilities insufficient, not because of a shortage of rooms,
but because the support facilities did not keep pace with the number of rooms
available. A number of studies indicate that the occupancy rate of hotels is dependent on availability of support facilities in the area. There were only enough liquor
outlets to serve 46% of the population. More liquor stores were opened, which led
to an increase in the occupancy rate. In addition, the restaurants and eating facilities were insufficient to serve more than 66% of the guests, so the criteria were
changed to monitor those support facilities more closely. This does not mean that
the occupancy rate criterion was eliminated, but additional criteria relating to support facilities were developed.

The negative return on investment was determined to be the result of new condominiums in the area. The owners were not providing sufficient revenue to provide for the desired return to the resort. Consequently, the alternatives were reeval-
uated, and instead of a third time-share condominium project, a new hotel was
built and run by the resort management. This increased the return on investment.

The lift line wait was determined to be a physical resource problem. The type of
lift serving the resort allowed large portions of the mountain to be accessible only
through one lift that lacked the capacity to handle the skier population. Analysis
indicated that an additional lift should be provided. This would make the prime
skiing area more accessible. This physical resource change required a financial
correction. Therefore it was necessary to return to the resources portion of the
planning and development section.

A major problem with competition was that approximately 9% of the total skier population were from the East Coast and were very cost-conscious. It became evident that Eastern skiers found it cheaper to go to resorts on the East Coast. However, it is possible through advertising to modify visitor objectives and to promote the idea that skiers receive a high-quality skiing vacation at a relatively low cost. It is to be hoped that additional analysis and new marketing plans will provide a visitor increase.

This takes our example through the analysis phase, which has indicated that the significant differences were internal to the project. However, what happens if the evaluation indicates that the problem is external to the resort?

Reassessment

If the problem is external, the developer must determine whether or not the situation causing the problem is permanent or temporary. If temporary, the problem should be treated as if it were internal to the project and a change anticipated. If the cause of the problem is permanent, the developer needs to return to the beginning of the model and reassess the options and objectives.

Here is an example of an external problem. Suppose the return on investment for the whole resort, not just the lodging portion, is found to be insufficient, but analysis planning showed that the ski season was plagued by lack of snow. The reason for the poor return on investment was temporary, external to the project, and beyond management control. As a result, no permanent change is indicated.

Summary

This section presents various methods used to plan commercial recreation enterprises. The key components in any such planning development:
1. The policies of government at the federal, state, and local levels, important in determining whether or not a commercial recreation enterprise is feasible.
2. The infrastructure and superstructure.
3. Financial and personal resources, which need to be planned thoroughly. This is true particularly for the infrastructure, which must be in place prior to the development of any superstructure.

This chapter covers analysis of the different planning concepts available, from the physical approach to the more complex PASOLP approach, in which effects are determined. There is no method by which to evaluate the effectiveness of the planning model in any of these approaches. Only the dynamic planning model evaluates effectiveness because it allows the developer to create a feedback loop that implements changes in the planning process. Each of the methods identified is an outgrowth of the previous methods, including the dynamic planning approach. By no means should the dynamic planning approach be considered definitive. As improvements become available, this approach will evolve.

It is important to understand the overall importance of planning in developing a commercial recreation enterprise. It can have the most lasting effect on the commercial recreation enterprise.

BIBLIOGRAPHY

Albrecht, J.G.: Planning as social process: toward a normative definition of planning, Ann Arbor, Mich., 1980, Princeton University.

Basche, J.R.: International dimensions of planning, Conference Board, 845 Third Ave., New York, New York, 10022, 1981.

Branch, M.C.: Comprehensive planning: general theory and principles, Pacific Palisades, Calif., 1983, Palisades Publishers.

Clarkston, A.: Toward effective strategic analysis: new applications of information technology, Boulder, Colo., 1981, Westview Press.

Journal of the American Planning Association, American Planning Association, Washington, D.C.

Mason, R.O., and Mitroff, I.I.: Challenging strategic planning assumptions: theory, cases and techniques, New York, 1981, John Wiley & Sons, Inc.

Preston, P.W.: Theories of development, Boston, Mass., 1982, Routledge & Kegan Paul.

Simmons, W.W.: Exploratory planning: briefs of practices, Oxford, Oh., 1977, Planning Executives Institute.

Tourangeau, K.W.: Strategy management: how to plan, execute, and control strategic plans for your business, New York, 1981, McGraw-Hill.

Vasu, M.L.: Politics and planning: a national study of American planners, Chapel Hill, N.C., 1979, University of North Carolina Press.

Wilson, D.E.: The national planning idea in U.S. public policy: five alternative approaches, Boulder, Colo., 1980, Westview Press.

SUGGESTED READINGS

Gunn, C.A.: Tourism planning, New York, 1979, Crane Russak & Co.

Examines the planning process for a large regional area. Emphasis is mainly on travel and tourism. The concepts can be applied directly to local commercial recreation.

Gunn, C.A.: Vacationscape designing tourist regions, Austin, Tex., 1972, Bureau of Business Research, University of Texas.

Extensive documentation of earlier planning processes such as the physical resources model. Introduces the concept of the planning model and modes. This concept is extremely important in the development and design of commercial recreation enterprises. Lays the framework and presents different concepts for the planning process.

Kaiser, C., Jr., and Helber, L.E.: Tourism planning and development, Boston, Mass., 1978, CBI Publishing Co.

Insight into government operation, conceptual planning, master plan development, on-site development. Excellent background information, extremely useful to any commercial recreation planner. Particularly important are the lists of factors to be considered in the planning process.

Lawson, F., and Baud-Bovy, B.: Tourism and recreation development: a handbook of physical planning, London, England, 1977, Architectural Press, Ltd.

If you must choose one text dealing with planning in commercial recreation, this would be the book. Loaded with pertinent information, designs, and plans for recreation enterprises throughout the world. Extensive, detailed information from refreshing and seldom-seen texts produced in the U.S. Important considerations and hints for the planning process. Numerous values relate strictly to the planning process and its characteristics.

MacIntosh, R.W., and Goldner, C.R.: Tourism: principles, practices and philosophies, Columbus, Oh., 1984, Grid Publishing.

Several chapters deal with tourism. Its main strength is in the chapters on marketing and in the integration of all concepts of commercial recreation into a complete package. Many articles by people other than the authors are valuable to commercial recreation entrepreneurs.

In any land development project, many groups must come to an agreement. Ward Valley is an excellent example. The planning process usually requires several years and numerous permits. Sometimes, as in the case of Lake Tahoe, there are substantial personal and emotional issues to be resolved. One such issue is addressed in this case. As you read this case place yourself in Mr. Conroy's place. Also pay special attention to the various phases that are planned for the development. Are there any important aspects of the case that have been left out?

Ward Valley Resort Community*

Evaluation of a condominium proposal

In the Spring of 1972, Mr. Parker Conroy, an experienced and successful investor in real estate, was considering an investment in a resort development at Ward Valley, near Lake Tahoe in California. Two weeks earlier, George Reston, the developer, had invited him out to dinner to explain the project. In the past, Reston had provided Conroy with some very successful ventures, so Conroy had been happy to go. He had received extracts from the investment prospectus and a long-winded "pitch" over dinner.

Alpine Peaks Development Corporation
Confidential

Alpine Peaks Development Corporation seeks initial capitalization for the construction and sale of condominium and commercial properties in the Ward Valley region of the California Lake Tahoe area. To accomplish this task, the corporation wishes to sell 100,000 shares at $10 per share. In order to avoid registration and other fees, it is planned that no more than 25 investors will be allowed to participate. This would mean that an investor must purchase a minimum of 4000 shares for $40,000. Profit projections indicate that such an investment would be worth in excess of $346,000 at the end of five years.

Ward Valley is situated 8 miles west of Lake Tahoe and about 12 miles southwest of Tahoe City. Within the confines of the valley lies one of the finest natural undeveloped ski bowls in all of the Sierra. The corporation plans to develop the ski area in conjunction with the condominium community, eventually yielding a total "ski village" con-

*Reprinted with permission of the Stanford University Graduate School of Business, 1972 by the Board of Trustees of the Leland Stanford Junior University.

cept. This idea has already been used by Boise Cascade's Incline Village development and the Fiberboard project, and the success has been phenomenal.

Lake Tahoe offers both winter and summer recreation, as well as gambling and entertainment on the Nevada side. The ski areas, campsites, boating and swimming areas, and nightlife have attracted visitors and tourists in excess of four million visitor-days per year. At the same time, the location has become an ideal spot for second homes of upper-income families from all over California. Various studies have shown that the demand for condominium type second homes has grown with the increase in discretionary income of American families. This demand is not expected to abate during the 1970s, and indeed will probably rise dramatically. Exhibits A, B, C, and D show the market projections for incomes and the second home demand in the Lake Tahoe Basin over the next ten years. Clearly, the condominium development in Ward Valley contemplated by the corporation will serve to meet this growing demand.

Presently, Alpine Peaks Development has obtained the zoning, options, and plans which are required to begin the development project. A small area of the valley (297 acres) was successfully subdivided and sold during 1969 for single family residences. The remainder of the area has been zoned for higher density and included on the Lake Tahoe Regional Master Plan. Furthermore, paved road, water, sewer, and power are already available to the residential area, requiring only minimal further investments to service each of the condominium areas.

The land in the valley is owned presently by a few individuals and the S.P. Land Company, a subsidiary of Southern Pacific. All parties involved have agreed to sell the property to the corporation on a specified timetable. These owners have set the price of the property at 9% of the sale values of the condominiums built on the land. In total, the sale price would amount to over $4.8 million in the five year development plan.

This entire land area has been analyzed by Barry C. Thompson, FAIA, AIP, to determine the optimal density and utilization for developmental purposes. Based on this analysis, the corporation has designed a long-range plan for the gradual development of the area. This step-by-step program was instituted so that the initial investment would be as low as possible, and the market would not be flooded with any more than 300 new condominiums for sale in any one year.

Phase I. The initial step will be to develop Parcel #1 (27.7 acres) with 100 condominium units. The 800 foot extension of the road, water, sewer, and power services for this area will cost approximately $100,000. This amount, plus the total of the direct construction costs, will be financed through a 12% construction loan for the building period of about ten months. A good portion of sales revenue can be realized even before the completion of construction, because customers will view the model and purchase a condominium in order to have it for the upcoming ski season.

Phase II. This phase will mark the beginning of the build-out of parcel #2 (33.8 acres). This land will support a much greater density, and the entire project will produce 800 condominium units. This project will entail the extension of the service facilities only 1000 more feet than already available from Phase I. This project will also include the addition of two Riblet chair lifts to the one already existing, the construction of ski lodge and shop, and the completion of a 500-car parking lot. It is planned that the skiing facilities and 200 condominium units will be ready for sale in 1973, with an additional 300 units completed and sold in 1974 and 1975. The ski facility will be operated by Alpine Meadows Ski Corporation on a lease arrangement from the corporation. (It must be noted here that all condominiums will have $2000 added to the sale price to cover the cost of these ski facilities. Other ski community condominium developments have assessed up to $4000 per unit for captive ski facilities.)

Phase III. This step in the developmental plan would include the use of parcels 3, 7 and 8 (totalling 77.6 acres) for more lower density condominium construction. The total will be 300 units, which will be available in 1977. At the same time, two more chair lifts and additional ski facilities will be constructed. This will bring the total capacity of the bowl to 4500 skiers per day, which is all that the area could handle.

Phase IV. The plans for the last phase are as yet incomplete. Parcels 4, 5, and 6 would allow adequate space for 300 additional units, and a large amount of commercial development (envisioned as a ski village). This phase would complete the entire valley development and bring the total units to 1500. At 3 persons per unit, the area would provide enough skiers to support the ski bowl so that the area could be closed to day-skiers. This would, in turn, reduce the parking and transportation requirements for the valley as a whole. Moreover, the remainder of the valley would remain public Forest Service land so that the scenic beauty of the area would be relatively untouched.

Exhibit E displays the income statements projected through Phase III of the development project. It shows that the profits will indeed be handsome, with an average annual return of 50% to the investors. The sales price represents $42 per square foot (1000 square foot units) for the condominium. This price and the expenses have been illustrated as growing at 3% per year. All estimates are based on costs experienced by competent local construction companies, so that there is no reason to suppose that they will not be met. It is assumed that construction loans will be available for 90% of these costs at 12% interest per year. The actual direct construction will be contracted so that any overruns will be borne by the contractors and not the corporation.

The foregoing is only an extract from the massive amount of market, construction, and architectural analysis which has been conducted over the past two years. The details, including research studies, drawings, and construction estimates, are available to interested investors. For a more complete report of how to invest in the Ward Valley Development Project, contact:

George M. Reston
Alpine Peaks Development Corporation
3107 Sand Hill Road
Menlo Park, California
Confidential

Parker Conroy had seen some very lucrative proposals over the years, but this Ward Valley development project at Lake Tahoe took the prize. He could not help but think that the profits looked just too good. Conroy knew that developments in the Tahoe area had been providing substantial returns to investors, but not in the neighborhood of 50% per year. He decided to conduct some research of his own into developments in the Lake Tahoe region.

Background

Conroy travelled to Lake Tahoe in order to get the background on the area and Ward Valley in particular. In looking over the Ward Valley region and surrounding area, he noted that both Alpine Meadows, immediately to the north, and Squaw Valley, eight miles to the north, had extensive day use and residential developments related to skiing. Furthermore, these areas, as well as Ward Valley, were serviced by California Highway 89, a wide-shoulder two-lane highway connecting Truckee to Tahoe City on the west shore of the lake. The roads around the perimeter of the lake itself were two-lane, uncontrolled access highways with numerous blind turns and narrow shoulders.

It was evident to Conroy that accelerated commercial development had been geared totally to the tourist trade. This meant that all municipal facilities (roads, sewers, etc.) experienced highly irregular demands, peaking on weekends through the summer and winter seasons. The pressures of recreational and commercial development had severely taxed the existing transportation, sewage, and water supply capabilities of the area. The problem was compounded by the fact that a high proportion of the property owners were nonresident. Their presence at peak periods necessitated the design and construction of municipal facilities with capacities greatly in excess of "normal" daily use by the resident population. The heavy traffic and the number of visitors at peak periods also created problems with air pollution and littering.

⌐

EXHIBIT A

Trends in household income by market area 1960-1980 (thousands)

Level of household income	Number of households[1]					Increase in high-income households[2]			
	1960	1965	1970	1975	1980	1960-1965	1966-1970	1971-1975	1976-1980
Primary market									
Less Than $10,000	981	1,059	1,036	1,068	1,097	—	—	—	—
$10,000-$14,999	205	274	335	409	499	69	61	74	90
$15,000-$24,999	61	116	167	226	299	55	51	59	73
$25,000 and more	27	41	56	77	99	14	15	21	22
Primary market total	1,274	1,490	1,594	1,780	1,994	138	127	154	185
Secondary market									
Less than $10,000	582	667	629	660	688	—	—	—	—
$10,000-$14,999	72	84	98	113	130	12	14	15	17
$15,000-$24,999	20	30	42	55	70	10	12	13	15
$25,000 and more	9	12	15	18	23	3	3	3	5
Secondary market total	683	793	784	846	911	25	29	31	37

Level of household income	Number of households[1]					Increase in high-income households[2]			
	1960	1965	1970	1975	1980	1960-1965	1966-1970	1971-1975	1976-1980
Tertiary market									
Less than $10,000	2,004	2,181	2,141	2,215	2,275	—	—	—	—
$10,000-$14,999	419	565	692	849	1,034	146	127	157	185
$15,000-$24,999	125	240	346	469	620	115	106	123	151
$25,000 and more	55	86	116	158	207	31	30	42	49
Tertiary market total	2,603	3,072	3,295	3,691	4,136	292	263	322	385
Total market									
Less than $10,000	3,567	3,907	3,806	3,943	4,060	—	—	—	—
$10,000-$14,999	696	923	1,125	1,371	1,663	227	202	246	292
$15,000-$24,999	206	386	555	750	989	180	169	195	239
$25,000 and more	91	139	187	253	329	48	48	66	76
Grand total	4,560	5,355	5,673	6,317	7,041	455	419	507	607

Note: Projections for 1975 and 1980 are in 1970 constant dollars.
[1]Average household size equals 3.5.
[2]Considers only households with incomes in excess of $10,000.
Source: U.S. Bureau of the Census; Sales Management, *Survey of Buying Power;* California Franchise Tax Board; and Economics Research Associates.

◻

EXHIBIT B

Past and projected increase in demand for second homes in the market area by level of household income 1960-1980 (thousands)

Household income level	Increase in second-home demand[1]			
	1960-1965	1966-1970	1971-1975	1976-1980
Primary market				
$10,000-$14,999	3.5	3.1	3.7	4.0
$15,000-$24,999	5.5	5.1	5.9	7.3
$25,000 and more	2.1	2.3	3.2	3.3
Primary market total	11.1	10.5	12.8	14.6
Secondary market				
$10,000-$14,999	0.6	0.7	0.8	0.9
$15,000-$24,999	1.0	1.2	1.3	1.5
$25,000 and more	0.5	0.5	0.5	0.8
Secondary market total	2.1	2.4	2.6	3.2
Tertiary market				
$10,000-$14,999	7.3	6.4	7.8	9.3
$15,000-$24,999	11.5	10.6	12.3	15.1
$25,000 and more	4.7	4.5	6.3	7.4
Tertiary market total	23.5	21.5	26.4	31.8
Grand total	36.7	34.4	41.8	49.6

[1]Based on second-home demand equivalent to 5 percent of households earning $10,000-$14,999, 10 percent of households earning $15,000-$24,999, and 15 percent of households earning $25,000 and more. Source: Economics Research Associates.

EXHIBIT C

Projected second-home development at Lake Tahoe (thousands)

Second-home inventory	1960	1970	Increase
Market area	100.3	171.4	71.1
Lake Tahoe	5.6	11.5	5.9
Lake Tahoe as percentage of market area	5.6	6.8	8.3
Annual rate of increase			7.5%

Projected	1970-1980
Increase in second homes	91.4
Lake Tahoe penetration	8.3
Demand at Tahoe	7,550

□

EXHIBIT D

Characteristics of selected condominium developments on Lake Tahoe's north shore

Price Year	Development	Price range (thousands)	Price per square foot
1964	Crystal Shores West	$31.0–$36.0	$23.75–$25.75
1965	Creekside East	$22.5–$25.5	$17.25–$19.50
1965	Creekside West	$22.5–$25.5	$17.25–$19.50
1965	Crystal Shores Villas	$32.0–$36.0	$26.50–$30.00
1965	Incline Manor	$20.0–$22.0	$22.25–$24.50
1965	Squaw Valley West (A)	$32.5–$35.0	$27.00–$29.25
1965	Tahoe Tavern #1	$26.5–$60.0	$22.00–$33.25
1966	Northwood Estates (B)	$30.0–$33.0	$17.50–$19.25
1966	Alpine Manors	$27.5–$30.0	$27.50–$30.00
1966	Heritage Cove #1	$35.0–$40.0	$22.75–$27.75
1966	Tahoe Tavern #2	$35.0–$70.0	$25.00–$39.00
1967	Incline Crest #1	$18.5	$19.00
1967	Tavern Shores #1 (A)	$40.0–$55.0	$28.50–$31.00
1968	Mountain Shadows #1	$30.0–$43.5	$27.00–$27.25
1968	Tyrolean Village #1 (C)	$31.0–$35.0	$25.00–$28.25
1968	Incline Crest #2	$19.5	$20.00
1968	999 Lakeshore	$30.0–$60.0	$18.75–$28.50
1968	Tahoe Tavern #3	$30.0–$45.0	$25.00–$32.00
1968	Tahoe Tavern #4	$40.0–$60.0	$26.75–$33.25
1968	Alpine Place #1 (D)	$30.0–$37.0	$26.50–$33.25
1969	Woodmere (E)	$50.0+	$30.50+
1969	Creekside Circle	$27.0	$20.25
1969	Tyrolean Village #2 (C)	$32.0–$36.0	$25.75–$29.00
1969	Tyrolean Village #3 (C)	$34.0–$38.0	$27.00–$31.00
1969	Mountain Shadows #2	$32.0–$45.0	$28.00–$29.00
1969	Tyrolean Villas	$31.5–$32.5	$17.50–$18.00
1969	Tahoe Tavern #5	$45.0–$75.0	$30.00–$41.50
1969	Tavern Shores #2 (A)	$45.0–$75.0	$30.00–$41.50

		Unit Sizes (square feet)			
One-bedroom	Two-bedrooms	Three-bedrooms	Four-bedrooms	Five-bedrooms	Special Features
—	1,300	1,400	—	—	Lakefront
—	—	1,300	—	—	
—	—	1,300	—	—	
—	1,200	—	—	—	Lakefront
—	900	—	—	—	
—	1,200	—	—	—	Lounge, pool
—	1,200	1,500	1,800	—	Lounge, pool, beach, tennis courts, boat piers
—	—	1,720	—	—	
—	—	1,000	—	—	
—	1,260	1,400	1,760	—	Lakefront
—	1,200	1,500	1,800	—	Lakefront, lounge, pool, beach, tennis court, boat piers
970	—	—	—	—	
—	1,200	1,500	1,800	—	Lakefront, lounge, pool, beach, tennis court, boat piers
—	1,100	1,300	1,600	—	Pool, some view sites, near golf course
—	1,100	1,250	1,400	—	
970	—	—	—	—	
—	1,600	1,700	2,100	—	Lakefront
—	1,200	1,600	1,800	—	Lakefront, lounge, pool, beach, tennis court, boat piers
—	1,200	1,600	1,800	—	Lakefront, lounge, pool, beach, tennis court, boat piers
—	900	1,280	1,400	—	
—	—	1,640	—	—	Near golf course
—	—	1,300	—	—	
—	1,100	1,250	1,400	—	
—	1,100	1,250	1,400	—	
—	1,100	1,300	1,600	—	Pool, some view sites, near golf course
—	—	1,800	—	—	
—	1,200	1,600	1,800	—	Lakefront, lounge, pool, beach, tennis court, boat piers
—	1,200	1,600	1,800	—	Lakefront, lounge, pool, beach, tennis court, boat piers

Continued

Exhibit D, Continued

Price Year	Development	Price range (thousands)	Price per square foot
1969	Chateau Chamonix	$20.0–$60.0	$20.00–$33.25
1970	The Cedars	$42.0	$26.25
1970	Crystal Bay Cove	$79.5–$100.0	$35.50–$39.75
1970	Crystal Tower	$79.5–$127.0	$49.00–$62.00
1970	Lakeshore Terrace	$65.0–$89.5	$40.50–$40.75
1970	Mountain Shadows #3	$34.5–$46.5	$29.00–$31.25
1970	Tyrolean Village #5 (C)	$35.0–$40.5	$29.00–$34.50
1970	Incline Crest #3	$24.5	$22.25
1970	Squaw Valley North (A)	$32.0–$40.0	$26.50–$28.50
1970	Squaw Peak Aprts.	$22.5–$23.5	$33.50–$34.50
1970	Alpine Place #2	$35.0–$40.0	$28.50–$39.00
1970	Tahoe Tavern #6	$50.0–$95.0	$41.75–$52.75
1970	Rocky Ridge	$58.0–$75.0	$34.50–$40.25
1970	McKinney's Landing	$45.0–$62.5	$28.50–$29.75

(A) This project is on leased land. Prices reflect unit only.
(B) Resale prices now at $36,000–$37,000 ($21.00–$21.50 per square foot).
(C) Includes average lot price plus average cost to construct one of the units offered.
(D) Two remaining two-bedroom units priced at $27,000 ($30.00 per sq. ft.).
(E) Resale prices now at $54,000–$57,000 ($33.75–$35.75 per sq. ft.).
Source: Economic Research Associates

Unit Sizes (square feet)

One-bedroom	Two-bedrooms	Three-bedrooms	Four-bedrooms	Five-bedrooms	Special Features
1,000	1,200	1,600	1,700	—	Lakefront, lounge, pool, beach
—	—	—	1,600	—	
—	—	2,000	2,400	—	Lakefront, beach, piers
—	1,280	1,860	2,100	2,600	Lakefront, high-rise building, beach, piers
—	1,600	1,700	2,200	—	Lakefront, boat deck
—	1,100	1,300	1,600	—	Pool, some view sites, near golf course
—	1,100	1,250	1,400	—	
—	1,100	—	—	—	
—	—	1,200	1,400	—	
700	—	—	—	—	
—	—	1,280	1,400	—	
—	1,200	1,600	1,800	—	Lakefront, lounge, pool, beach, tennis court, boat piers
—	—	1,700	1,860	—	View sites, pool, lounge
—	—	1,500	1,900	2,200	Lakefront, beach, pier, putting green

EXHIBIT E

Pro forma income statements, Alpine Peaks Development Corporation

	1972	1973	1974	1975	1976
Units sold:					
Phase I	100				
Phase II		200	300	300	
Phase III					300
Total	100	200	300	300	300
			(in thousands)		
Revenues:					
Condominium sales	$ 4200	8600	13,200	13,500	13,800
Skiing, etc.	100	500	750	1,000	1,000
Total Revenue	4300	9100	13,950	14,500	14,800
Expenses:					
Land	400	800	1,200	1,200	1,200
Direct Construction	1,800	3,700	5,700	5,850	6,000
Improvements	160	330	525	540	555
Lodge		100			
Parking Lot		50			
Lifts, Facilities, etc.	30	600	600	600	600
Fees, Taxes	100	205	310	315	320
Sales Expenses	300	600	900	900	900
G & A	120	240	360	360	360
Interest	200	410	620	640	660
Total Expenses	$3,110	7,035	10,215	10,405	10,595
Net Profit	$1,190	2,065	3,735	4,095	4,205
Tax (50%)	595	1,030	1,865	2,045	2,100
Net Income	$ 595	1,035	1,870	2,050	2,105
			(in thousands)		
Shares					
Investors					
Management	100	100	100	100	100
	10	10	10	10	10
Total	110	110	110	110	110
Earnings/Share	$5.40	$9.40	$17.00	$18.66	$19.14

Recent development along the west and north shores of Lake Tahoe had been increasingly oriented toward condominium "second home" residences. Developers presently perceived high-density residential (i.e., condominium) development to be more lucrative and desirable than commercial development—a turnabout from the immediate past and a new pressure on zoning authorities. Waterfront condominium developments in the area of Tahoe City frequently included plush appointments, underground utilities, permanent management staffs and exterior grounds maintenance, tennis courts, private piers, and so forth, with unit prices ranging from $60,000 to $115,000. Virtually no lakefront property on the west and north shores remained undeveloped; private homes and newer condominium complexes dotted the waterfront. Property values declined somewhat with distance from the shore. Virtually all development on the north and west shores followed the perimeter highway or centered in developed mountain ski bowls. Residential development had historically catered to upper-middle-class or wealthy people throughout the Tahoe Basin. Service staff or blue-collar workers typically commuted from Truckee, because land and property values in the immediate Tahoe area made residence there prohibitively expensive for all but the well-to-do.

Ward Valley was relatively undeveloped. The area was divided into numbered parcels, each one square mile (640 acres) in area. Most of the parcels belonged to government agencies ("U.S.A.") or to a subsidiary of the Southern Pacific Railroad ("S.P. Land Company"). The "checkerboard" pattern of land ownership derived from federal legislation in 1862, which granted alternate square mile blocks of land to railroads (consequently called "land grant railroads") which the railroads could sell to private business interests to finance construction of railroads across the country. Alternate square mile blocks for twenty miles on either side of the tracks over the Donner Pass had thus been granted to the predecessors of Southern Pacific. The United States Forest Service had acquired several contiguous parcels in Ward Valley through an active acquisition and exchange program and was the area's largest landowner. The U.S. Forest Service controlled key slope areas, whose access was important for any developer planning improvements related to skiing.

Lack of transportation facilities into Ward Valley had also impeded its development. Recently, the first step toward residential development had been taken: General American Development Corporation had engineered, financed, and marketed a single-family subdivision of 297 lots (approximately 100 acres) in 1969-70. The developer had to build a two-lane paved road one-and-a-half miles long, drill a private well for water supply, and build a sewer trunk connecting at Sunnyside. Underground power was bonded for installation in 1972.

General American had halted operations in 1970 when its principal financial backer had withdrawn financing to bolster his own business operations. General American had, however, managed to sell 297 1/3-acre lots at prices of approximately $8,000 to $10,000 (the market value of the undeveloped lots carried on the Placer County tax rolls). Each unimproved lot incurred a county tax bill of approximately $150 per year. Placer County appled the same tax rate to residential or commercial property. Taxes were computed as a fixed dollar amount per dollar of assessed value; "assessed value" equaled one-quarter "market" or "cash" value. Only three lots had been improved, each with lavish single-family structures.

Conroy also noted developments on the legislative and regulatory fronts. An article in *Business Week* noted the formation of the Lake Tahoe Regional Planning Agency, a group of ten men from both California and Nevada with ultimate responsibility for all proposed new developments in the Lake Tahoe area. Conroy discovered that TRPA had worked with Placer County (the California county, seated in Auburn, in which Ward Valley was located) to formulate a detailed master plan for Ward Valley. A developer thus faced two tiers of approved authority for proposed property improvements in Ward Valley: the five-man Placer County Board of Supervisors and the ten-man Tahoe Regional Planning Agency. Both groups would judge the individual proposal on the basis of an area master plan that specified allowable development types and density given land capability, transportation, and municipal services.

Placer County's perspective

With these discoveries in mind, Conroy decided to stop in Auburn to find the view of Placer County toward the development proposal for Ward Valley. He found first that Board of Supervisors in Placer County based all its decisions on proposed developments on a 58-page document, the "Ward Valley General Plan (1970)," which had been financed by contributions from property owners, including the Southern Pacific Company, General American Development Corporation, and Alpine Meadows. The Plan gave a detailed analysis of the vegetable cover, land form, geological make-up, watershed, etc., from which was derived a land capabilities map specifying the area's development potential and "living unit intensities per acre." LUI data for Ward Valley designated the area for the development proposal for three living units per acre throughout. Commercial zoning was not presently included, Conroy learned, and it would be necessary to appeal to the Board of Supervisors to get it.

He talked to Mr. William Cramer, Placer County Senior Planner and the architect of the plan, who stressed that the county had enforcement authority to demand conformity with the plan. "The pressures on the developer are far greater," he said. "When a developer comes to us now, he must collapse his tentative and final proposals into one detailed proposal—with environmental impact studies and his detailed plans to meet our specifications."

Cramer pointed out that ordinances were becoming more strict, with severe ramifications for day skiing. A "bedroom intensity" ordinance had been proposed for neighboring Squaw Valley, because the county was concerned with the fact that many 2-4 bedroom condominiums and houses had become "mini-motels." This had created problems with roadside parking (which interfered with snow removal) and an added burden on all municipal and county facilities. The Plan specified that all new condominiums should have 1 1/2 parking spaces per unit, preferably underground.

Present policy indicated that the practical limit on the number of skiers in Ward Valley was 5,000, although this capacity might be raised to 8,000 if an alternative transportation system were developed. Bus lines, or a reactivated "ski train," could provide such an alternative. In either case, Cramer emphasized the necessity to look beyond Ward Valley to the entire North Shore and the traffic burdens on Highway 89. Merely parking the additional automobiles at the mouth of Ward Valley would not solve the problem. Nor would widening the road in the area; added congestion would still choke Tahoe City and its access roads.

Cramer informed Conroy that the existing private well in Ward Valley would serve the present 297-acre subdivision, but that it would not be sufficient for any additional development. Connections with Tahoe City would be the only alternative in the event of a large-scale development.

"The General Plan could provide the impetus for an improved transportation system," Cramer stated. "If the plan serves to halt more development in the area and limit day use to a certain point, maybe it will force the San Francisco Bay Area to see the light. You can have more day use only if you cause a new transportation system to be financed and implemented.

"There's still more to it. Look at the added burdens on the county that accompany day use—the need for police protection and snow removal, to name two. And an additional social problem: What can we do for the people who work at the casinos, hotels, and so on at the Lake, but can't afford to live there? These are the kinds of concerns we have as planners for Placer County."

Conroy thought that he could learn even more by talking with one of the county supervisors. The Fifth District, which was the area of Tahoe that lay within Placer County, was represented by William Briner. Since Briner was a resident and businessman at Lake Tahoe, his voice carried the most weight in decisions affecting the area. Conroy learned that Briner was giving up his position by not running in the next county election. But Briner was able to detail a number of problems faced by the Board of Supervisors.

"Lake Tahoe has always been a rich man's paradise. Now many groups want the lake opened up as public land so everyone can enjoy it. What they don't realize is that the wealthy people with their large estates have saved Lake Tahoe's natural beauty from being spoiled by overdevelopment. Kick out the rich and put in the poor and you'll kill the lake—and it'll cost like hell to correct. A good balance between the rich and the poor must be kept in order to save the lake."

Briner also alluded to the fact that most of the county's tax revenue came from the developed areas at Lake Tahoe. "Sure, the lake is the county's gold mine. The Fifth District has 45% of the county's property values and only 30% of its population. So the county benefits from any development that might go on. But don't forget that Placer County was the first to put controls on development.

"If the man from Colfax wins the next election, he won't understand the lake's problems. The only way for a man from the lake to win is for second-home owners to register to vote up here. I've talked to many of them about it, but when something comes up in their home districts, they'll switch their registration again."

Conroy asked Briner about Ward Valley in particular and Briner replied, "Some people want to prevent any development of the valley. But to do that would take a lot of money to buy all the privately-held land. But that isn't likely, so it has to develop. No matter what restrictions we put on, a developer could meet them and still make a healthy profit. I see the natural ski bowl at Ward Valley as a rare God-given resource, and there is no reason not to develop it. Transportation is the only constraint. Highway 89 cannot handle the extra traffic. A tram over the hill from Alpine Meadows is not the answer, because they will probably run out of parking space. I would like to see an extension of BART from Concord to Sacramento and on to Reno. There could be an extension down to Tahoe with a loop around the lake, but no one has any idea how long that will take."

Tahoe Regional Planning Agency

Conroy felt that he could find out more from the second step in the process of governmental approval—the regional agency. He found the executive director of TRPA, Richard Heikka, in his offices at South Lake Tahoe. Conroy soon learned the view that the agency took toward development in the Tahoe area in general and Ward Valley in particular.

"The agency came into being," Heikka explained, "primarily because the five counties bordering Lake Tahoe could not agree upon the standards or degree of development that would be in the public interest. The lake was a cash register for them because the land values provided high tax revenues without any great social service costs to them. The second homes were only occupied about 65 days a year.

"In devising the regional general plan, we first had to show that the land here has physical limits. Look at what has happened to Yellowstone and Yosemite. They have so many people there, they have to close the gates. Right now we are facing that same problem. Originally, the area would have been developed with densities that gave a total population of 700,000. But now our plan shows that the eventual population will be only 250,000. We have specified that the entire area will be about 15% private and 85% public land. But there still remains the problem of 'bedroom intensity' and the enormous number of visitors to campgrounds and hiking areas.

"Although there are some problems with water, sewage, power, and environmental impact," Heikka continued, "the number one difficulty is transportation. You'll notice that the plan does not call for any new interstate or state highways into the area. That's because we think the capacity of the present system is the largest number of cars we can handle in the area. Right now, on peak weekends, Interstate 80 over Donner Pass reaches its practical capacity of 2,500 cars per hour. That means we're saturated."

Conroy asked about the Agency's view toward Ward Valley development. Heikka replied, "Right now, we don't think the ski bowl there should be developed for another ten years. As I said, the transportation system is already strained, and we just don't need any more ski areas without some means of getting people there. In fact, the area would probably just split off the available supply of skiers from other areas. Besides, a ski area can't exist without all of the support facilities in the base area. Right now, one half of the land in the proposed area is public land, so I don't think a big commercial ski area development is very likely. Look at Alpine Meadows. They don't have any of these base facilities, and they're in financial trouble.

"Sure, the area is zoned for development. But we think that the development should be a function of the transportation system improvement. Maybe for a while a parking area outside the basin with buses running into the recreational areas will do. But eventually, we will need some kind of mass transit, like a train or monorail to bring people down the California side. But that's a long way off, and until it comes, I don't think Ward Valley should be developed on a large scale.

"Because of these problems, we would like to acquire all of Ward Valley for public use. Of course, there is a lot of other land that is already zoned general forest, which we must buy from private landowners, but Ward Valley is high on the list of possible acquisitions. We have asked the federal government for $50 million dollars to begin this acquisition program, and I think there is a good chance we'll get it.

"I know that, above all, Reston wants to build the ideal ski area. He was in Europe this winter touring their ski resorts, and he sent me a picture of a condominium development up in the French Alps. And the way the market is now, a developer could meet all the requirements we could place on him and still turn a profit. A developer could even afford to clear ski runs without disturbing the slopes by logging with helicopters."

The U. S. Forest Service's perspective

Of the total 202,030 acres of land in the Tahoe Basin, some 127,000 were in public ownership (115,658 owned by Federal Government, 9,599 owned by California and Nevada as State Parks). Lands in public ownership were held as open space, with occasional public day-use facilities (campgrounds, picnic tables, etc.) constructed. At its discretion, the U. S. Forest Service may grant timber or mineral rights to business interests, with lease proceeds flowing to the U. S. Treasury. Twenty-five percent of such receipts are returned to the appropriate county government as a partial substitute for county property taxes lost.

Mr. Joseph Flynn, Chief of the Division of Lands, U. S. Forest Service, commented to Conroy that "Most counties come out ahead with public ownership. They lose potential assessed value for tax purposes, but there is an offsetting benefit in maintenance services which they need not provide; the federal government assumes operating responsibility.

"Public attitudes toward the Forest Service have recently swung 180 degrees, now favoring our acquisition of land for public ownership," Flynn continued. "We've been active in Ward Valley, taking title to 692 acres just last fall in a negotiated sale from a private owner."

There were several ways the Forest Service could acquire land. The first method, condemnation through the exercise of eminent domain, was avoided because of legal complications. The second method was negotiated sale, dealing directly with the selling party. Under the Uniform Land Acquisition Act of 1969, however, all government agencies (federal, state, and local) must offer the full appraised price; dealing is prohibited. Appraisals must be conducted in the company of the owner; the result must be shown to him. The transaction could be consummated at a price below appraised value only if the seller recognized the fact and signed a statement to that effect. "Frequently, public-spirited citizens will do this for us," Flynn noted, "but there is a better way.

"The Nature Conservancy and other nonprofit organizations like it can often facilitate acquisition of natural lands. They were involved in the Holmwood acquisition in Ward Valley; we paid only $800,000 for the 692 acres."

The Nature Conservancy was a private, nonprofit national organization whose purpose was to acquire and hold—or pass on to public ownership at their cost—such natural areas as wildlife preserves. Begun in the East by the Dupont and other families, it operated with volunteer help, frequently from very high-calibre exbusinessmen, and with wholly private funding. It could bargain for land in a nonofficial capacity, explain tax advantages to the seller, and frequently exert considerable private influence to encourage private sale. Normally it would tie down a piece of property through a purchase option, backed by a $6 million "line of credit" from the Ford Foundation. Through cooperation with public agencies, the Conservancy was frequently able to pass prime natural lands along to the government at prices well below the appraised value of the lands.

A fourth method of land acquisition was property exchange; land in one area was obtained in exchange for land or timber and mineral rights in another. Exchanges were done on a dollar-for-dollar basis rather than acre-for-acre and could involve private individuals or corporations. Flynn told Conroy, "Since we initiated land exchange in 1935, we have acquired 8.9 times as much [acreage] as we have given up. Our current stance is that we will consider trades only if the dollar values are compatible and TRPA and county plans are served. For the time being, TRPA has asked us not to consummate land trades which would allow developers or private interests to consolidate large tracts in the Tahoe Basin. We might consider exchanges if what we give up is outside the basin.

"We'd like to acquire more land in Ward Valley," he continued, "but we're constrained by the federal budget. We've made some major purchases on the Nevada side, and presently we're out of funds." For fiscal 1972 (ending 6/30/72) the U. S. Forest Service had a $30 million budget for nationwide "recreational area" land acquisition; for fiscal 1973 (ending 6/30/73) the allocation was budgeted at $10 million. TRPA recently had petitioned Congress for $50 million over five years for the Tahoe region *alone,* but it had thus far been unsuccessful. "Ward Valley is high on our list for land acquisition," Flynn concluded, "but we don't have the money right now."

The Forest Service took pains to involve the public in public land use decisions. The major issue facing the U. S. Forest Service over Ward Valley was whether access rights for ski lifts and parking facilities would be granted to developers. A planning team was working with county and regional authorities to help develop a proposal which would be aired in public meetings through the summer of 1972. By autumn, the Forest Service hoped that a decision on the ski lift and parking access rights would be possible.

The local community's perspective

Conroy felt that he had better check with some of the local residents to find out what the local opinion was toward development of Ward Valley. He talked to Rod Stollery, editor of the *Tahoe World,* a weekly newspaper for the north and west shores, who offered his thoughts on the issue:

"Ward Valley is the only undeveloped area in the Tahoe City region, and it's our last chance to do everything right. The pressures are certainly building for planned and reasonable development; developers are becoming gun-shy in the Tahoe Basin. Approval from all the authorities can take three to four years; it's not the one-summer deal it used to be.

"Given the tax rates and property values here, I think this will always be a rich man's paradise. As for attitudes here, I'd call it the 'gangplank syndrome.' By that I mean someone gets his property at Tahoe and then wants to draw the line on any more development.

"There are some tough issues involved here. Public access to the beach is virtually nonexistent. Should we press for public acquisition or private developments to provide it? If we do, look at the demands we place on our sewage and garbage disposal systems, not to mention the transportation problems. Poor man's use versus rich man's use poses an inevitable conflict when a finite amount of land is involved.

"Sewage treatment is a tough problem that most people don't think of, and new development adds stress to an already strained system. Here in Tahoe City we now face the need for expanded pumping and treatment facilities. To spread the fixed costs of new sewer hook-ups, utilities base their tax assessments on the highest value use of a given lot. People who buy four contiguous lots to provide some space around their houses discover that the sewer assessment might be $3,500 per lot, or $14,0C0 assessed at the front end of their purchase. That's a strain on anyone."

The League to Save Lake Tahoe

Once back in the San Francisco Bay Area, Conroy thought that he ought to see what kind of opposition might be represented by the League to Save Lake Tahoe. He stopped by to visit Steven Brandt, the League's executive director. He soon learned that, although Brandt did not own any land at Tahoe, almost all of the League's members did. He found that about 70% were second-home owners and 30% were year-round residents of the Lake Tahoe area.

"It's difficult to organize a constituency at Tahoe," Brandt remarked. "The residents don't have a strong political voice 'downhill' in the county government, but there's a new flow of benefits down to the county from the high property taxes at Tahoe.

"Through government agencies people are starting to appraise development from a standpoint of 'what can the land take' rather than 'what do the people want?' That's a tough transition; people have difficulty viewing land as anything other than a private good. The reason is simple: Land has historically been taxed privately, while air and water have not.

"I think the 'gangplank theory' and the 'rich man's paradise' arguments are straw men. I'm as often accused of saving the lake for hippies as I am of saving it for private landowners. There is a point of contention as far as the shoreline is concerned. But there's plenty of room for public day use in forest lands. Most people won't venture very far from the road anyway.

"Cars are the worst intrusion in the basin. I don't feel that we have a social responsibility to make it easy for people to drive to the edge of the lake. And, generally speaking, I'm most concerned about the transportation problems which the development of Ward Valley would create. We need a new system down from Truckee. Forget wider roads or superhighways.

"Looking at regional government as an experiment in the Tahoe Basin, I prefer to work with the Agency. State and federal government empire-builders would love to come in here to take over planning and jurisdiction, saying that regional government is wrong. I'd rather not close the door on the TRPA; I think they'll do the right thing if shown the way."

Conroy thumbed through the development proposal again as he thought over what he had seen and heard. With so many interest groups involved, whose views would prevail? What ramifications would there be for Reston's proposal if pressure increased from one or more of the groups?

He noted that costs could rise by $250,000 per year in order to comply with any restrictions that might be placed upon Ward Valley and the project would still be extremely profitable. But Conroy could not make up his mind whether to invest.

Questions

1. As Mr. Conroy, would you purchase the land and proceed with the development? What are your reasons for this decision?
2. Identify what you think are the goals of the various governmental agencies involved. Can these goals be met in the development of Ward Valley? How?
3. What type of planning has been employed in the case? What does this style of planning leave out that you consider to be important? Why are these omissions important?
4. Is the phasing of the development logical? What criteria should be applied to each phase in an attempt to monitor the effectiveness of each phase? What levels of profitability should be reached before the next phase is begun?

CHAPTER 6

The commercial recreation feasibility process

□

CHAPTER OBJECTIVES

1. *To understand the nature of the feasibility process*

2. *To understand why a feasibility study is needed*

3. *To understand the role of the feasibility process*

4. *To understand the key components of the feasibility process*

□

Objectives of the feasibility process

The objective of the feasibility process is to examine the suitability of a business decision, a program, or a commercial development opportunity. The feasibility process may include many detailed steps or it may be very simple, depending on the nature and complexity of the project. Understanding the feasibility process is extremely important to commercial recreation managers. The process enables managers to evaluate the potential of a new business opportunity and on an ongoing basis to test the viability of new ideas, programs, and facilities.

This chapter reviews the feasibility process and provides specific examples of how to use it. You as a future commercial recreation manager may use the feasibility process or may hire others to do so. The important thing is to understand the feasibility process and to be able to ask appropriate questions not only of yourself, but of others who may assist you. A simplified outline of the feasibility process:

1. Know your audience
2. Set study objectives and outline research tasks
3. Understand your potential users
4. Identify comparable or competitive facilities or programs
5. Identify demand (use) potential
6. Draw market feasibility conclusions based on research
7. Conduct financial analysis

Each step in the feasibility process is discussed below.

Know your audience

At the beginning of the feasibility process the commercial recreation manager should ask, "For whom is the study being prepared? How is the study to be used?" The answers will dictate the form and content of the study. Potential audiences for the study may include one or more managers, a board of directors, potential investors, and a financial institution. A study prepared for in-house management may include only those tables containing sufficient information on which to base an in-house decision.

In comparison, a study prepared for potential investors or a financial institution typically needs to be well written with plenty of backup information to support specific conclusions and recommendations. The depth and professionalism of the report's presentation are particularly important when the report is being used to secure financing.

Set study objectives

Clear and concise study objectives provide study direction, save research time, and communicate the study's purpose. Let us illustrate the objective statement using an example from the aquatic park industry. Susan is the manager of Banzai Aquatic Park, which includes a wave pool, four serpentine flumes, an inner-tube rapids ride, and two speed slides. Her park charges a one-price admission of $9 per adult and $7.50 per child under 12. She wants to raise the admission fees. Her principal study objective is to determine the admission price level that will increase total admission revenues.

Prepare research outline

In order to accomplish her objective, Susan must break it down into a research outline:

Task 1. Define the market area. This is simple. Susan knows from experience that her market area is the metropolitan region.

Task 2. Review the population trends and demographics (age, income, employment status, and household size) of the area. Has the population grown? Has the average household income increased or decreased? Are households able to pay more for recreation?

Task 3. Review pricing of other recreation activities in the area. Susan checks aquatic parks in other towns as to whether or not they have raised prices in recent years and how price increases have affected attendance. She also reviews other recreational activities such as golf, tennis, and theme parks in her market area for price increases and attendance figures.

Task 4. Make conclusions as to the price elasticity of demand[1] based on the socioeconomic review and the review of comparables. Susan does not do a detailed survey of her market. Instead, she draws some conclusions based on review of her market area and the experience of comparable recreation businesses in her region. From this she sets a price and estimates the effect it will have on attendance and total revenues.

Understand potential users

In conducting a feasibility analysis, it is very important to understand the characteristics of potential users. Primary research (surveys) and secondary data sources are the principal sources for understanding potential users.

Primary research. Primary research may be a short questionnaire or a detailed survey, depending on the sophistication of the analyst. Visitor/guest surveys at recreation establishments are commonly used to help identify the market. Commercial recreation managers use surveys to identify the principal age groups of visitors, visitor origins, length of stay, and favored activities. An example of a user survey for an aquatic park is shown in Fig. 6-1.

Secondary sources of information. Almost all commercial recreation enterprises belong to some type of industry group. Most aquatic parks and theme parks belong to the World Waterpark Association and the International Association of Amusement Parks and Attractions. Golf, tennis, racquetball, skiing, and other recreation enterprises belong to their specific industry trade groups. These trade groups are often good sources for user profile information.

Other good sources of information include national research companies, such as the A.C. Nielsen Company, which provide demographic profiles on various commercial recreation activities.

To understand user markets, it is important to understand the demographics and trends of the local population for a given market area. Population trends are important because the rate of growth or decline in a population often has direct influence on the viability of commercial recreation enterprises. Similarly, demographics (age, income, sex, and employment) affect the feasibility of an enterprise. Census and regional planning agencies typically have very good population and demographic information available to the public.

In the case of Banzai Aquatic Park, Susan is most interested in understanding whether or not the socioeconomics of her market area have improved since the last time she adjusted her prices. In order to find out, Susan went to a local regional plan-

---

[1]Price elasticity of demand is the quantitative expression of the effects of a change in price on attendance and on total revenues.

BANZAI AQUATIC PARK GUEST QUESTIONNAIRE

(The questionnaire is filled out by Park Management.)

My name is _____. I am on the management staff of Banzai Aquatic Park. We thank you for your visit to the Aquatic Park today. In order that we might make your future visits more enjoyable, we are asking a few short questions of our guests today.

For Survey Administrator Only (   )

(Today's Date: _____)

(Sex: Male _____   Female _____)

Age: _____

Home Address Zip Code: _____

Is this your first visit to the park? (Please circle.)   YES   NO

If no, how many times have you been to the park?   Last Season: _____
                                                                    This Season: _____

How many hours do you plan to stay in the park today? _____

Which of our activities do you like best?

_____

_____

_____

_____

What areas do we need to improve?

_____

_____

_____

_____

THANK YOU!

FIG. 6-1 Example of a park questionnaire.

TABLE 6-1. Population growth, attendance growth, penetration rate, and median household income growth Banzai Aquatic Park and market area

	1986	1987	1988	Compounded annual growth rate (%)
Population of Waterville metropolitan statistical area (MSA)	1,870,000	1,907,400	1,945,600	2
Banzai Aquatic Park attendance	411,400	438,700	440,800	3.5
Penetration rate of Banzai Aquatic Park in Waterville MSA population (%)	22	23	22.7	—
Median household income of Waterville MSA	$29,745	$31,861	$34,127	7.1

TABLE 6-2. Demographic changes 1986-1988 Waterville MSA

	Percentage distribution		Growth segments
	1986	1988	
Waterville age distribution			
Less than 17	27.3	26.9	
18–24	11.3	11.6	+
25–34	20.4	21.0	+
35–49	21.3	20.6	
50 and above	19.7	19.9	+
Median age	30.6 years	31.3 years	
Income distribution			
Less than $10,000	15.5	10.0	
$10,000–$19,999	20.0	21.0	+
$20,000–$34,999	26.8	28.0	+
$35,000–$49,999	18.7	20.0	+
$50,000 and above	19.0	21.0	+
Median household income	$29,745	$34,127	+

ning council and obtained population and demographic information for her metropolitan region for the last three years. An example of this information is shown in Table
6-1 and Table 6-2. From the information she collected, Susan learned:

- Park attendance was growing faster than the metropolitan population.
- The market penetration rate of the total Waterville population had remained
  fairly constant between 22 and 23%.
- Median household income for the Waterville market had increased 7.1% over
  the period, from $29,745 to $34,127.
- The age distribution and the median age of her market area were rising. This
  alerted Susan that she would need to provide activities and promotions that
  would appeal to older age segments as well as to teenagers.
- Income distribution and median household incomes indicated that there
  would be increases in household incomes. Higher incomes support Susan's
  objective of raising admission prices.

Identify comparable or competitive facilities or programs

The key to a good feasibility study is a thorough review of comparable and competitive facilities and programs. In fact, the feasibility study is sometimes defined
as a comparability study. Ideally an analyst identifies at least four or five comparables for the facility or program. Returning to Banzai Aquatic Park, Susan has identified four aquatic parks in her state and in neighboring states that have similar
attractions to hers and that have recently (within the past two years) changed their
admission pricing. She called the managers of these aquatic parks and asked for
their prices and how the new fee levels had changed attendance levels. The review
of those figures is found in Table 6-3.

From the information in Table 6-3 Susan learned that:

- Price increases in two of the four parks did not reduce attendance.
- At the two parks where attendance declined after a price increase, the decline
  was minimal.
- Price increases overall had little or no effect on attendance.

Susan also examined some of the recreational enterprises in her own city. She
noted whether prices had risen and the effect of price increases on attendance lev-

TABLE 6-3. Price changes and attendance impacts at comparable aquatic parks

Comparable aquatic parks[1]	Admission pricing			Attendance		
	1986	1988	% change	1986	1988	% change
Aqualand	$9.50	$10.00	+ 5.3	225,000	235,000	+ 4.4
Waterland	9.50	10.50	+10.5	400,000	390,000	− 2.5
Atlantis	10.00	11.00	+10.0	510,000	500,000	− 2.0
Aquaworld	8.50	9.50	+12.0	240,000	275,000	+14.6

[1]All parks are similar to Susan's Banzai Aquatic Park in variety and mix of water attraction elements.

TABLE 6-4. Price change comparisons—selected other recreation activities
Waterville MSA

	1986	1988	% change
Waterville public golf courses			
Course #1 (greens fees)	$10.00	$12.00	+20
Course #2 (greens fees)	7.50	9.00	+20
Theme park—Waterville (adult admission fees)	12.00	15.00	+25
Waterville Tennis Center (hourly court fees)	2.50	2.50	No change

els. An example of this is in Table 6-4. Susan learned from conducting this exercise
that in general, user prices had increased over the period of 1986 to 1988 for other
recreational enterprises in her area.

Identify demand (use) potential

After the review of the demographics of an area and the experience of comparable facilities, an analyst can determine demand and use potential of a selected
facility or program. Below is a schematic highlighting the demand process:

Population → Participation rate → User (attendance) potential
and/or
penetration rate

Demand potential goes from general to specific. The key is being able to identify
what percentage of the population is likely to participate in a particular activity or
program. National statistics from A.C. Nielsen Company, trade publications, and
private research are generally available for identifying the propensity of a given
population to participate in a given commercial recreation activity. Participation
rate[1] figures exist for skiing, tennis, golf, aquatic parks, racquetball, and a large
number of other recreation enterprises. Participation rates can be adjusted according to the actual experience of comparables or one's own experience.

When there is more than one facility in a given market area, an analyst will also
need to determine the penetration rate[2] (market share) the subject facility can be
expected to achieve. In the latter part of this chapter, a case study illustrates in
more detail this aspect of the demand analysis process.

Susan has had a few years of operating history; thus, she knows what her attendance has been and what her market population is. Her operating experience has
facilitated her understanding of the park's penetration rate of the total population

[1]*Participation rate* or *incidence of participation* is the percentage of the population likely to participate
at least once in a year in a given activity.
[2]*Penetration rate* of the total available market for a given activity is the percentage (or market share)
likely to participate at a specific facility or location.

TABLE 6-5. Penetration rate comparisons after price changes for selected comparable aquatic parks

	1986	1987	1988
Aqualand			
Adult admission price	$9.50	$9.50	$10.00
Child admission price (under 12)	$8.00	$8.00	$8.50
Market area population	932,800	946,800	963,800
Park attendance	225,000	220,000	235,000
Penetration rate (%)	24.1	23.2	24.4
Waterworld			
Adult admission price	$9.50	$9.50	$10.00
Child admission price (under 12)	$8.00	$8.00	$9.00
Market area population	1,735,000	1,743,700	1,747,200
Park attendance	400,000	375,000	390,000
Penetration rate (%)	23.1	21.5	22.3
Atlantis			
Adult admission price	$10.00	$10.50	$11.00
Child admission price (under 12)	$8.50	$9.00	$9.50
Market area population	2,000,000	2,034,000	2,064,510
Park attendance	510,000	525,000	500,000
Penetration rate (%)	25.5	25.8	24.2
Aquaworld			
Adult admission price	$8.50	$9.00	$9.50
Child admission price (under 12)	$7.50	$7.75	$8.00
Market area population	872,100	885,500	907,300
Park attendance	240,000	260,000	275,000
Penetration rate (%)	27.5	29.4	30.3

(Table 6-1). Likewise, she has been able to determine the penetration rates of her selected comparables for periods before and after the price changes. The penetration rate comparisons shown in Table 6-5 help Susan to understand the potential result of a price change.

Drawing market feasibility conclusions based on research

Critically important to any feasibility study are conclusions that are well documented and justified based on the market evidence. Findings and conclusions should flow directly from the analysis. Susan concluded that she could raise admission prices from $9 to $10 without reducing attendance. Her analysis is shown in Table 6-6 and her conclusions are highlighted in the following list.

TABLE 6-6. Susan's worksheet on price increase estimated impact on attendance

	Actual			
	1987	*1988*	*1989*	*% change*
Average adult admission price[1]	$9.62	$10.25	$10.25	+ 6.5
Average child admission price[1]	$8.18	$8.75	$8.75	+ 7.0
Banzai Aquatic Park adult admission price	$9.00	$9.00	$10.00 (proposed)	+11.1
Banzai Aquatic Park child admission price	$7.75	$7.75	$8.50 (proposed)	+ 9.7
Attendance	438,700	440,800	440,000 (estimated)	+ 0.3
Market area population	1,907,400	1,945,600	1,974,800 (estimated)	+ 3.5
Penetration rate (%)	23.0	22.7	22.3	Not applicable
Median household income	$31,861	$34,127	$36,554 (estimated)	+14.7

[1]Average of the four comparable parks.

- Admission prices at comparable facilities are at similar levels.
- Price increases at comparable facilities have not resulted in loss of attendance or revenues. Therefore, Susan does not anticipate an attendance drop at her park.
- Household income has increased commensurately with the proposed price change.

Financial analysis

The financial analysis normally is the key indicator of whether a project is feasible. The financial analysis typically represents two components, revenue and cost analysis. In a new venture it is critically important to get good information on which to base financial projections. With an ongoing venture, it is a little easier to conduct the financial analysis, since historical operating figures are usually available.

This chapter merely sets the stage for conducting the financial analysis. Subsequent chapters present specific guidance as to how to conduct a detailed financial analysis. For the purpose of this particular chapter, it is most important to focus on the revenue side of the revenue/cost equation.

Susan wanted to ascertain whether an increase in price would result in an increase in revenues. She was addressing the elasticity of demand. She concluded from the market analysis that an increase in price would not affect her attendance levels and would indeed increase total revenues. Her comparable analysis indi-

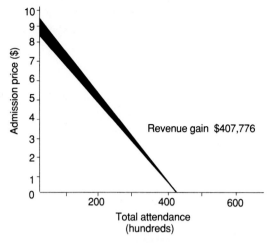

Revenue gain=price change vs. price status quo

	1989 Price increase	1989 Price status quo	Difference
Average admission price	$9.22[*]	$8.31[*]	+$0.91
Estimated attendance	440,000	440,800	-800
Total admission revenues	$4,064,176	$3,656,400	+$407,776

[*]Assumes 80% adult and 20% children; assumes a 20% discount for 25% of all attendance to take into consideration group business and special promotions.

FIG. 6-2 Revenue gain for Banzai Aquatic Park.

cated that price increases did not noticeably affect attendance as long as the increases were reasonable and commensurate with gains in disposable income. Susan compared the expected revenues from her proposed pricing schedule against expected revenues from keeping admission prices the same (Fig. 6-2). The graph indicates that Susan indeed will make more money by increasing prices than by keeping them at current levels.

Conclusions

Although every feasibility study is different, all follow a similar process. Using the process allows the manager to make informed decisions by asking the appropriate questions. The only way to become proficient at conducting good feasibility studies is to do them. The following case study applies the feasibility process to a new business opportunity.

Case study: a new business opportunity

A recreation manager may at some point decide to open a new enterprise—golf club, tennis club, health and fitness center, or any other recreation business. The manager/entrepreneur may or may not be experienced in the field, but he or she will be required to put together a rational market plan and financial justification in order to attract investment capital.

Background

John wants to open up a new racquetball and health/fitness club in a nearby town. He is a fitness enthusiast and is very much interested in becoming his own boss. John, having graduated recently from a good academic program in a local college, remembers being taught the feasibility process in his commercial recreation class. John reviews the feasibility process as follows:

- Know your audience.
- Set study objectives and prepare research outline.
- Understand potential users.
- Identify comparable or competitive facilities.
- Identify demand (use) potential.
- Make market feasibility conclusions based on research.
- Conduct financial analysis.

Know your audience

John is preparing a study to be used as an aid in securing financing. Knowing that either his bank or investors will be reviewing the study, John is prepared to provide his audience with a detailed report that will answer their major questions with respect to the market and the financial potential of his proposed enterprise.

Set study objectives/prepare research outline

The principal objective of John's study process is to determine the membership/user potential and financial viability of a proposed racquetball fitness center. In order to accomplish this objective, John prepared a research outline.

Task 1. Understand potential users.
Task 2. Identify comparable or competitive facilities.
Task 3. Identify demand/user potential.
Task 4. Make market feasibility conclusions based on research.
Task 5. Conduct revenue and cost analysis.
Task 6. Estimate level of warranted investment.

Understand potential users

From John's own experience as a health/fitness enthusiast, he understands that his principal market is persons age 12 to 50 with greater than average income levels. John's first step is to review population characteristics for the town in which he is to open his center. John goes to the census bureau, city and county planning departments, and regional planning agencies for age and income demographics. This shows John the size of his market and the relative age breakdowns and helps him to identify portions of the market that are relatively good targets. Examples of

TABLE 6-7. Population growth comparisons for subject city, nearby city, and state

	Population			Compounded annual growth rate (%)	
	1985	*1990*	*1995*	*1985-1990*	*1990-1995*
Subject city in which John is planning the development	55,000	65,800	74,200	3.7	2.4
Nearby city	45,000	51,000	56,000	2.3	1.9
State	4,500,000	5,000,000	5,600,000	2.1	2.3

Source: Bureau of Census, Regional Planning Agency.

how John would portray this information in tabular form are shown in Tables 6-7, 6-8, and 6-9. These are his findings:

- His city is growing faster than a nearby city and the state as a whole. This is very encouraging for future support for racquetball and fitness centers (Table 6-7).
- The age distribution and median age of his area are generally older than either the nearby city or the state. This indicates that the prime age groups (12–50 years) for health/fitness facilities are less dominant than in the nearby city and the state as a whole (Table 6-8).
- His city's household income distribution exhibits more strength (in the $15,000 to $45,000 range) than either the nearby city or the state as a whole. This is particularly pleasing to John because it means that his market may be better able to afford memberships (Table 6-9).

John has identified his market area as the city in which his proposed development will be located. Sometimes it is not so easy to identify the boundaries of the

TABLE 6-8. Age distribution—1990 estimates

Age group	Subject city (location of John's development)	Nearby city	State
Less than 12 years	19.8	19.2	18.6
12–17	11.2	10.5	9.6
18–24	8.9	16.0	13.2
25–34	13.2	16.5	16.0
35–49	16.7	17.0	16.5
50 and over	30.2	20.8	26.1
Median age	33.7 years	30.5 years	32.6 years

Source: Bureau of Census; Bureau of Economic Research, local university.

TABLE 6-9. Household income distribution for subject city, nearby city, and state 1988 estimates

Income group	Subject city (location of John's development)	Nearby city	State
Less than $15,000	10.7%	9.6%	10.7%
$15,000 to $29,999	20.1	18.6	19.2
$29,999 to $44,999	32.0	26.5	27.5
$45,000 and above	14.4	23.4	21.2
	100.0%	100.0%	100.0%

Source: Statistical yearbook.

market area to be analyzed. Market areas are typically best defined by comparison with the market areas of existing facilities in similar locations.

Identify comparable or competitive facilities

The next step John undertakes is to identify comparable or competitive facilities. It so happens that there are no existing racquetball/fitness centers in his city. However, a number of comparables in other cities help John understand:

1. The market characteristics of the user groups
2. The market radius of comparable facilities (distance from which the facilities draw people)
3. Revenue characteristics—membership prices, court fees, rental income, concession income, and program fees
4. Operating costs associated with the development

John has selected clubs with a high degree of comparability to his. Since his proposed club would have racquetball courts as well as weight equipment, he studies fitness clubs that have these characteristics. Examples of the types of information that John has collected on selected clubs are presented in Tables 6-10 and 6-11.

John collected this information in his discussions with other club managers:

- Guidelines for membership fees, number of memberships, public play rates, and health memberships. All this will help John set prices.
- The relationship between full racquetball memberships and health memberships. This is important because John needs to understand what percentage of his members will not play racquetball.
- The distribution between family memberships and single memberships. This is particularly important because family memberships are priced differently from single memberships.

Identify demand/user potential

John's analysis of potential market support for his facility depends heavily on national studies reviewing health/fitness support for selected U.S. population groups. A national opinion company, A.D. Sports, Inc., has conducted periodic sur-

TABLE 6-10. Comparable racquetball/fitness clubs

	Health/fitness only memberships as a percentage of racquetball memberships	Distribution of memberships (%)			
		Racquetball/full		Fitness only	
		Couple/family	Single	Couple/family	Single
Comparable #1 Galaxy RB	26	30 (2.2 members per membership)	70	10 (2 members per membership)	80
Comparable #2 World RB	23	70 (2.5 members per membership)	30	50 (2 members per membership	50
Comparable #3 Universe RB	25	45 (2.3 members per membership)	55	25 (2 members per membership)	75
Comparable #4 Cosmos RB	28	50 (2.2 members per membership)	50	20 (2 members per membership)	80

veys of the U.S. population, broken down by region, to indicate propensity to use or participate in certain sports. A review of the A.D. Sports, Inc., statistics are presented in Table 6-12. Without A.D. Sports, John would need to find propensities to use health/fitness facilities from other sources. Such statistics could be generated by analyzing comparables and understanding how many individuals within a given market area use comparable facilities. This would enable John to compare the propensity to use a health/fitness facility in a neighboring city with that of his city. This analysis provides justification for estimates of demand for the facility John plans to build.

Table 6-13 applies the health/fitness racquetball propensities to the local population. From this John is able to identify the number of potential participants from whom he is likely to attract memberships.

Table 6-13 shows the potential number of full racquetball memberships. In order to ascertain that number, John needed to review the salient conclusions from his previous tables and apply these conclusions to the four analysis steps shown in Table 6-13.

1. John showed total population for his market area on the first line of Table 6-13.
2. The majority of John's market is people ages 12–50. This segment of the total population is the total relevant market.
3. Next John estimated an incidence of participation for this group to give him the total number of expected participants in the 12- to 50-year-old range. The percentage that John used reflected in part the income levels and the age distri-

TABLE 6-11. Survey of selected racquetball clubs and fitness centers

	Number of courts	Memberships			Membership fees		
		Opening date	To date	Per court	Initiation	Dues	Hourly rate
Comparable #1: Galaxy RB	8	1983	1,200	150	single $150	$45	None
					couple $200	$65	None
					Corporate rates less 15 percent to 30 percent		
Comparable #2: World RB	12	1981	3,000	250	single $120	1/ $60	$4 prime
					couple $160	1/ $80	$3 non- prime
					family $180	1/ $90	
					junior $55	1/ $35	
Comparable #3: Universe RB	7 RB 6 tennis	1982	1,200	171	single $300	$ 42	none
					couple/ family $450	$ 63	
					corporate $750	$114	
Comparable #4: Cosmos RB	15	1980	2,500	167	single $275	$45	none
					couple/ family $400	$65	

| Public play rates | | | Health club membership | | | |
Prime time	Non-prime time	Health only	Initiation	Dues	Hourly racquetball rate	Facility description
$10 guest			single $75	$35	$5 prime time	Two glass-enclosed viewing courts, lounge with snack bar, luncheon specialties and television, full amenity locker rooms, social activities, weight room, dance/ exercise classes, pro shop, half-court gym for basketball, volleyball, or exercise classes.
			couple $125	$50		
$7	$5	$5				Also offer quarterly play cards for active players at $35/month single and $50/month couple.
$6 guest	$4					Semi-complete Nautilus exercise class run by outside operator— charges $2.50 per class. Facility offers sauna and whirlpool bath. Nursery available. Very family-oriented.
$7.50 hotel guest						Part of Atlas Hotel. Offers full amenity health club and recreation opportunities to hotel visitors and residents.
$7	$5	$5	single $100	$50	$5	Four glass walled courts, health snack bar, club lounge for cocktails, dancing, games, television, dining room, full amenity locker room, complete pro shop, children's playroom. Pool, whirlpool bath, full weight room, multipurpose exercise room, dance/exercise classes.
			couple $150	$75	$5	
$6 guest	$4 guest					

TABLE 6-12. Demographic profile of racquetball players as determined by A.D. Sports, Inc.

	Percent of participants		Incidence of participation	
	1985	*1988*	*1985*	*1988*
Sex				
Males	72.0%	70.0%	8.1%	7.0%
Females	28.0	30.0	3.0	3.0
Total/composite	100.0%	100.0%	6.7%	6.4%
Region of the United States				
Northeast	20.0%	20.8%	5.0%	5.0%
North Central	34.0	33.2	7.4	7.1
South	23.0	21.2	5.0	5.0
West	23.0	24.8	9.0	8.1
Total /composite	100.0%	100.0%	6.7%	6.4%
Age group				
17 and under	17.0%	16.0%	5.0%	5.0%
18-34	65.0	66.0	8.6	8.3
35-54	14.0	14.0	1.5	1.2
55 and over	4.0	5.0	1.0	0.8
Total/composite	100.0%	101.0%	6.7%	6.4%
Annual income				
Under $15,000	0.0%	20.0%	5.9%	6.0%
$15,000-$30,000	0.0	30.0	7.1	7.0
$30,000 and over	35.0	50.0	8.5	8.0
Total/composite	35.0%	100.0%	6.7%	6.4%

Note: A.D. Sports, Inc. is a fictitious name. The information, although fictitious, is similar to historical data developed by the A.C. Nielsen Company.

TABLE 6-13. Projected market support for racquetball/health/fitness center

	1990	1995
Total population in market area[1]	65,800	74,200
Percentage of people age 12 to 50	50	50
Total relevant market[2]	32,900	37,100
Incidence of participation[3] for racquetball	.07	.07
Number of racquetball participants	2300	2600
Capture rate (%)[4]	30	30
Total racquetball membership potential	690	780

[1]See Table 6-7.   [2]See Table 6-8.   [3]See Table 6-11.
[4]See Tables 6-9 and 6-12. John has ruled out memberships from those with incomes of less than $15,000. His capture rate represents a judgment based on income and information from discussions with managers of comparable racquetball clubs.

TABLE 6-14. Projected membership levels — John's proposed club

	1990	*1991*
Total racquetball member demand[1]	690	780
Allowance for nonracquetball[2]	173	195
(fitness-oriented) members		
Total member demand	863	975
Distribution of racquetball memberships		
Single (50%)[3]	345	390
Couple/family (50%)[4]	150	170
Total racquetball	495	560
Distribution of health/fitness membership		
Single (80%)[3]	136	156
Couple/family (20%)[5]	17	20
Total health only	153	176
Total club memberships	648	736

[1]Final line of Table 6-13.
[2]Estimated to be 25% of total demand based on comparable facilities (see Table 6-11).
[3]One member per membership.
[4]2.3 members per membership based on comparables (see Table 6-11).
[5]Two members per membership based on comparables (see Table 6-11).

bution of the area, and was consistent with the A.D. Sports, Inc., incidence of-participation for income levels over $15,000 (bottom of Table 6-12).

4. The final line item, the total number of potential racquetball memberships, is the critical item for John. John used a capture rate of 30% of total potential participants. This gave him a total membership potential of 690 in 1990, growing to 780 in 1995. John's capture rate represented a judgment based on his income and age distribution tables and on discussions with managers of comparable racquet clubs.

Table 6-14 represents John's estimations of total membership demand. These are based on the experience of the comparable facilities.

Financial analysis

The objective of the financial analysis is to forecast revenues and expenses. From interviews with club managers at comparable facilities, John discovered that revenues were produced from a variety of sources:

- Memberships
- Guest fees
- Snack bar sales
- Locker rentals
- Pro shop sales
- Lessons

TABLE 6-15. Recommended membership and day use pricing for John's proposed club

| | Memberships | | | | |
	Charter[3]	Regular	Monthly dues	Public use fees	Member guest fees
Racquetball[1]					
Single	$150	$175	$37.50	$7.00 prime	$6.00 prime
Couple/family	200	225	45.00	5.00 nonprime	4.00 nonprime
Health club[2]					
Single	90	110	25.00	4.00	3.00
Couple/family	120	150	32.50		

[1]Includes all club facilities.
[2]Includes use of exercise, spa, and support areas only.
[3]Charter rates apply to preopening sales of memberships.

Membership and guest revenues. Based on the analysis of comparables, John has a very good understanding of what individuals are willing to pay for memberships and public court time. Taking comparable information into consideration, John has set membership and guest prices that he thinks are reasonable. Prices for comparable clubs are shown in Table 6-11. John's pricing schedule is shown in Table 6-15.

The proposed price schedule shown in Table 6-15 represents a synthesis of John's own experience and his experience reviewing membership pricing at the comparable clubs. John has added an additional category, charter membership. John anticipates selling charter memberships at a discount before opening the club in order to ease his cash flow burden and to show the potential lending institution sales progress before final capital commitment.

Other review sources. In addition, John has estimated per capita expenditures for other revenue sources, such as health, snack bar, locker rentals, pro shop sales, and lessons, from data from the comparable facilities. Although other revenue sources are not shown in the data tables on comparable facilities, John's estimates are based on conversations with the managers of the comparable clubs. These revenues are summarized in Table 6-16.

Total revenues. At the bottom of Table 6-16, John has indicated total revenues from all sources, expected to range from $441,000 to $467,000.

Operating expenses. In order to estimate operating expenses for his proposed club, John had many detailed discussions with the friendly management of the selected comparable clubs. Based on these discussions, John prepared Table 6-17, showing reasonable estimates of the operating percentages of the comparable clubs.

TABLE 6-16. Total annual revenues

	Preopening	1987	1988	1989	1990
Membership revenues[1]	$63,150	$301,830	$277,925	$284,125	$295,095
Guest revenues[2]		78,700	80,400	82,200	84,300
Subtotal member/user revenues		$380,530	$358,325	$366,325	$379,395
Health/snack bar sales (net)[3]		$30,800	$31,500	$32,100	$33,000
Locker rentals[4]		17,100	17,500	17,900	18,500
Pro shop sales[5]		26,000	26,500	27,100	28,000
Lessons (net)[6]		7,400	7,600	7,750	8,000
Subtotal other operating revenues		$81,300	$83,100	$84,850	$87,500
Total revenues	$63,150	$461,830	$441,425	$451,175	$466,895

[1]Number of members multiplied by achievable membership fee based on comparable clubs.
[2]Guest revenue based on membership to guest ratios of comparable clubs.
[3]$2.50 per visit, 25% of gross revenues to club from concession.
[4]One permanent locker per 1.3 memberships; $3.00 monthly fee.
[5]$7.00 average monthly expenditure per membership; 50% net after cost of goods.
[6]Two lessons per membership per year, $15 per lesson, 60% to pro.

Net operating income before debt service and taxes. Using the operating expense percentages shown in Table 6-17 as benchmarks for his own projections, John developed reasonable ratios for the proposed operation. John applied his estimated operating ratios to the total project revenue stream and prepared a net operating income statement for a five-year period, as shown in Table 6-18. After the preopening year his net cash flow before debt service and taxes ranges from $183,000 to nearly $203,000.

Implementation steps

John is ready to hire an architect to design a club and to place an option on the site of his choice. With input from John, the architect can estimate the size and cost of the facility needed to meet John's projected demand.

Armed with land and building costs, John is ready to meet with a banker or investor group. John can ask for a specific loan amount and show the retirement of the financing as an additional line item on his balance sheet.

Optional—warranted investment analysis. Instead of going directly to the bank with only a predebt cash flow, John conducts a warranted investment analysis to get an idea of what level of investment his predebt and taxes cash flow will support. The primary intent of this analysis is to indicate the level of investment warranted by the projected income flow from club operations. The warranted investment level is a function of operational cash flow and the desired return on investment. John has chosen 1992 as a typical or stable income year.

TABLE 6-17. Operating cost data comparisons

	Comparable #1 Galaxy RB	Comparable #2 World RB	Comparable #3 Universe RB	Comparable #4 Cosmos RB
Wages and salaries				
Manager	$2,800/month	$2,600/month	$2,200/month	$2,800/month
Assistant manager	$2,400/month	$2,200/month	$2,000/month	$2,500/month
Staff	$6-$8/hour	$5-$7/hour	$5-$7/hour	$6-$8/hour
Total	30% of Total revenues	33% of Total Revenues	28% of Total revenues	32% of Total Revenues
Payroll and **benefits**	12% of Wages & salaries	10% of Wages & salaries	10% of Wages & salaries	12% of Wages & salaries
Insurance	2.5% of Total revenues	3% of Total revenues	2% of Total revenues	3% of Total revenues
Maintenance **and repairs**	2% of Total revenues	1.5% of Total revenues	2.5% of Total revenues	2% of Total revenues
Club supplies, **laundry, and** **towels**	1.6% of Total revenues	1.8% of Total revenues	1.4% of Total revenues	1.6% of Total revenues
Advertising **and promotion**	2% of Total revenues	.5% of Total revenues	1.5% of Total revenues	1.0% of Total revenues
Legal and **accounting**	1% of Total revenues	1% of Total revenues	1% of Total revenues	1% of Total revenues
Miscellaneous	1% of Total revenues	1% of Total revenues	1% of Total revenues	1% of Total revenues

Based on projected revenues for 1992, John has estimated his net operating income as follows:

Annual operating revenues	$466,895
Less operating expenses	− 264,974
Net operating income/Predebt service and taxes	$201,921

The next step in the warranted investment analysis is to determine a capitalization rate. John's effective capitalization rate is the weighted average of his desired return on equity and the rate for long-term debt based on a 20 percent equity commitment.

	Percentage of project funded	Desired return	Weighted average
John's equity commitment	20%	20%	4.0%
Long-term bank debt	80%	12%	9.6%
			13.6%

TABLE 6-18. Income and operating expense summary (1988 dollars)

	Preopening 1988	1989	1990	1991	1992
Revenues[1]	$63,150	$461,830	$441,425	$451,175	$466,895
Operating expenses:[2]					
Wages and salaries[3]	18,945	138,549	140,000	140,000	140,000
Payroll benefits and taxes[4]	2,084	15,240	15,400	15,400	15,400
Utilities and telephone[5]	5,052	36,946	35,314	36,094	37,352
Insurance[6]	0	11,546	11,036	11,279	11,672
Property taxes[7]	0	17,500	18,500	19,500	21,000
Maintenance, repairs, and replacement[8]	0	12,469	11,918	12,182	12,606
Club supplies, laundry, and towels[9]	0	7,389	7,063	7,219	7,470
Advertising and promotion[10]	5,000	5,080	4,856	4,963	5,136
Legal and accounting[11]	5,000	4,618	4,414	4,512	4,669
Miscellaneous[12]	2,000	4,618	4,414	4,512	4,669
Allowance for doubtful accounts[13]	0	5,000	5,000	5,000	5,000
Total operating expenses[14]	$38,081	$258,957	$257,915	$260,660	$264,974
Net operating income	$25,069	$202,873	$183,510	$190,515	$201,921

[1]Last line of Table 6-16.
[2]Based on experience of comparable clubs shown in Table 6-17.
[3]Estimated at 30% of total revenues. Includes manager, $2,500 per month; assistant manager/professional, $2,200 per month; plus 2.5 full-time equivalent positions at 98 hours per week at $6.00 per hour to staff, reception, sales/tours, exercise/weight training, and janitorial/maintenance functions.
[4]Estimated at 11% of wages and salaries.
[5]Estimated at 8% of total revenues.
[6]Estimated at 2.5% of total revenues except in preopening year.
[7]Estimated at 17,500 to 21,000 based on applicable millage rates.
[8]Includes $5,000 annual capital reserve allocation plus 2.7% of maintenance and repair.
[9]Estimated at 1.6% of total revenues except in preopening year.
[10]Estimated at 1.1% of total revenues except in preopening year.
[11]Estimated at 1.0% of total revenues except in preopening year.
[12]Estimated at 1.0% of total revenues except in preopening year.
[13]Allow for $5,000 reserve each year except in preopening year.
[14]Does not include interest, depreciation, or income taxes. Management fees are not included.

The 13.6% rate represents John's weighted cost of capital. This means that John and his lender must achieve a 13.6% return on money invested in order to participate in the project.

John's projected 1992 income level is capitalized at 13.6% to approximate the maximum amount of investment the stable year income will support.

$$\frac{\$201{,}921}{13.6\%} = \$1.48 \text{ million warranted investment}$$

The \$1.48 million represents the maximum level of investment that John can make in land and building improvements and still yield a 13.6% average return on investment. Armed with his warranted investment of \$1.48 million, John is prepared to meet with architects, engineers, and potential investors. From the architects and engineers John wants to determine whether \$1.48 million is sufficient to build the facility he needs to meet his market. For potential investors John will support his request for funds with a well-written feasibility study based on his own research.

Summary

The feasibility analysis is a process. From a market perspective the most important element of a feasibility study is the comparability analysis, which consists of selecting existing similar facilities and studying them. A manager can learn much by taking a look at comparable facilities and operations and then applying what he or she has learned to his or her own proposed project. The most important element of this chapter is the recognition that a feasibility study is a test of reasonableness. In doing any kind of feasibility study, present the facts in a logical and rational way that leads to the correct decision.

BIBLIOGRAPHY

Brooks, J.K., and Stevens, B.A.: How to write a successful business plan, New York, 1987, American Management Association.

Justis, R.T., and Kreigsmann, B.: The feasibility study as tool for venture analysis, Journal of Small Business Management, Jan. 1979, Vol. 17, no 1.

Kelsy, C., and Gray, H.: The feasibility process for parks and recreation, Reston, Va., 1985, American Alliance for Leisure and Recreation.

Papanek, G.F., Schydlowsky, D.M., and Stern, J.J.: Decision making for economic development: text and cases, Boston, Mass., 1971, Houghton Mifflin.

Peattie, L.R.: Thinking about development, New York, 1981, Plenum Press.

Raising venture capital: an entrepreneur's guidebook, New York, 1982, Deloitte, Haskins & Sells.

Roemer, M., and Stern, J.J.: The appraisal of development projects: a practical guide to project analysis with case studies and solutions, New York, 1975, Praeger.

Wagner, K.C.: Economic development manual, Jackson, Miss., 1978, University Press of Mississippi for the Mississippi Research and Development Center.

SUGGESTED READINGS

Business plan

Amara, R., and Upinski, A.J: Business planning for an uncertain future: scenarios and strategies, New York, 1983, Pergamon Press.

Gevertz, D.: Business plan for America: an entrepreneur's manifesto, New York, 1984, Putnam's.

Mancuso, J.: How to write a winning business plan, Englewood Cliffs, N.J., 1985, Prentice-Hall, Inc.
Roberts, D.: Business planning guide, Florida, 1984, Florida Economic Development Center, College of Business, State University of Florida.

Resource allocation

Donaldson, G.: Strategy for financial mobility, rev. ed., Cambridge, Mass., 1986, Harvard Business School Press.
Neale, M.A., and Northcroft, G.B.: Opportunity costs and the framing of resource allocation decisions, Organizational Behavioral & Human Decision Processes, 1986.

Recreation planning

Farrell, P., and Lundegren, H.M.: The process of recreation programming: theory and technique, 2nd ed., New York, 1983, John Wiley & Sons, Inc.
Fesenmaier, D.R., and Lieber, S.R.: Recreation planning and management, State College, Pa., 1983, Venture Publications.
Hjelte, G., and Shivers, J.S.: Planning recreational places, Madison, N.J., 1977, Fairleigh Dickinson University Press.

There are two possible users of a feasibility study, the owner or person who has commissioned the study and the person who may lend the money. The perspective of each is slightly different. The individual who commissioned the study wants to know if the business is feasible, how to improve the business, and if the money can be spent more profitably. The lender is interested in determining if the loan can be repaid and what the return will be. The Great X Sailing Company gives you the opportunity to look at a brief feasibility study from both perspectives. When reading the case keep both of these perspectives in mind.

The Great X Sailing Company Business Plan*

1.0 The concept

Recreational sailing is moving from a class sport to a mass sport in the same manner as golf, skiing, and tennis before it. The capital costs of sailing have dropped due to technological advances in materials—fiberglass for hulls and Dacron for sails; society in general has more discretionary time for recreational activities; and wind is a relatively inexpensive source of power. These factors have produced a virtual flood of new sail boat designs, including product introductions by some large corporate giants like AMF. The end result is a healthy wave of advertising that will augment the natural growth of the demand in the mass market for sailing craft from 6 to 40 feet in length.

Sailboats need sails. Sailmaking has long been a cottage industry, i.e., sails have been made by tiny companies serving limited markets. Typically, a lot of handwork, mystique, and personal attention have been involved. In the last few years, several sail lofts have been corporatized; they are today set on a promotional course to develop a national brand identity and to sell sails through multiple locations. The fact is that among the half-dozen leading sailmakers, there is really very little product difference— at least not any that would be discernible to the less experienced sailors buying the new fiberglass, one design production boats. So cosmetics (speed, personalities, etc.) will be used to sell sails to the new market. In order for X Sails to just stay even with the past percentage of business it has done, it must do something to compete with North, Hood, and perhaps Sutter—local competitors going heavily into national advertising and promotion.

Analysis by Jim X and others associated with his loft indicates that there is an opportunity for the Great X Sailing Company (proposed new name) to become the San Francisco Bay Area Sailing Expert. This *geographic specialization* appears feasible because (a) no one else is doing it; (b) X is well located and experienced to do it; (c) the

*Reprinted with permission of the Stanford University Graduate School of Business, 1978 by the Board of Trustees of the Leland Stanford Junior University.

cost of promotion is within reach for the Company; (d) it is unlikely that either North or Hood would try to pick up on the same theme; (e) a body of distinct Bay Area sailing lore and knowledge is developable.

In summary, the concept behind this plan is that the Great X Sailing Company is to grow vigorously in the future by utilizing its broad experience base to become the Bay Area Sailing Expert for the new, one-design boat buyer. As its theme, the Company intends to "make sailing fun" for its customers. Hence the proposed new company name: The Great X Sailing Company.

2.0 Objectives

The X Company has been around for more than 15 years. It enjoys today a good local reputation and very modest financial success. Except for the increase in competitive activity, chances are that the Company could continue as is indefinitely as long as Jim X is willing to participate directly and fully in the business. However, competition and the desire of Jim X for more freedom from day-to-day operations make change necessary. Change is also stimulated by the sense of economic opportunity in the air and some feeling of obligation to help the legions of new Bay Area sailors.

Translating into more definite terms, the Company wishes to get to a volume of sales and profits where it can support a competent loft operations management team and still show a significant return to the owner(s) at the end of each fiscal year.

Roughly, such a sales volume would appear to be around $450,000.

Sales, Net	$450,000
Cost of Goods (65%)	290,000
Gross Profit (35%)	$160,000
Loft Management	$ 30,000
Marketing Expenses	15,000
Operating Expenses	70,000
Net Operating Profit, BT	$ 45,000

So, the primary objective is to achieve the above sales and profit goals. From a $200,000 sales volume starting point, a progression to $450,000 in two years can probably be accomplished without a huge addition of investment or debt capital to finance the marketing effort if: (a) X gives full attention to the marketing effort, (b) the Company is run profitably on a tight budget, and (c) President X has regular contact with at least one businessperson interested in and familiar with the business.

In summary, the objective of this plan is to achieve a steady state $450,000 in sales volume and $45,000 in profit, before tax, by the end of two years, without a large injection of capital requiring dilution of ownership. The associated one-year objective is $300,000 in net sales and $25,000 in profit, before tax.

3.0 Analysis of the market

There are no industry statistics, but Jim X estimates that he has less than 20% of the sails market in the Bay Area. This would indicate a total market of $1,000,000 to $2,000,000 in sail sales per year at retail. (Note: X's 20% appears reasonable based on a look at the physical facilities of local competitors.)

3.1

Estimating that an average sails purchase (when sails are bought separately) for all kinds of boats is $500, the number of purchasers in the Bay Area divides out to be 3,000 per year.

3.2

Looking ahead, most new purchasers coming into the market will be buying one-design boats. In the past, X Sails has sold 60% of its business to the following one-design classes: Challenger, Cal, Catalina, 5-0-5, Ranger, Islander, Coronado, Columbia, Santana. The question is: Which class of boat will be most popular in the Bay Area during the years immediately ahead? The answer logically is: Those boats that (a) are built on the West Coast, (b) are heavily promoted, (c) have a good outlet/dealer in the Bay Area, (d) have a strong class organization and (e) get a lot of publicity via winning races. The various boats stack up as follows:

Name	Use sails	Made on West Coast	Heavy promotion	Local dealer	Class organization	Publicity	Primary sail company
1. *Cal	yes	yes	yes	Berry		yes	North
2. Ranger	yes	yes	med.	Berry	yes	yes	North
3. Erickson	no	yes	yes	Albatross		yes	North
4. Catalina	yes	yes	no	Eagle	yes	no	VH
5. Islander	yes	yes	med.	Wilson		no	
6. Santana	yes	yes	no			no	
7. Challenger	yes	yes	yes	Chal Yachts		no	
Acquarius	no	yes	no			no	
Balboa	no	yes	no			no	
Clipper	no	yes	no			no	
Newport	no	yes	no	San Leandro			
Coronado	yes	no	no				
5-0-5	yes		no				
Columbia	yes	no	yes	Sailbt, Inc.			Watts
C & C	no	no	yes	Dr. Dorch			
Seafarer							
Tartan				San Leandro			
FJ	yes						
One tens	yes						
Jesters	yes						

*Note: The numbers are the ranking by Jim X.

3.3

Historically, about 50% of X Sails sales are to individuals. The other half is through dealers. It is fair to say that the dealers, or dealers' salespersons, heavily influence the new boat buyer's choice of maker for a boat's first set of sails. It also stands to reason that the new boat owner is likely to return to his first sailmaker for new or additional sails. Dealers are motivated by various incentives to do business with a specific sail-maker. In the Bay Area, the lineup appears to be as follows:

Dealer	Current sail source		Reason
Berry	North		Real Estate
Albatross	North		Inventory
Sailboats Inc.	Watt		
Glaser	North & Dewitt and X		
Eagle	VH		
Wilson	X (in part—90% estimated)		
Challenger	X	70	
San Leandro	X	10	
Seafarer	X	10	
O'Neills (Monterey)	X	?	
Tradewinds (Sacramento)	X	5	
Fourdeck (Sacramento)	X	90	
Steve's Mar. (Stockton)	X	?	
Monterey Bay Yacht Sales	X	5	

While a larger percentage discount on sail sales may be of some value to promoting dealer loyalty, it is not of much long-run value. (Other lofts can duplicate the deal.) The best single way to get dealers to sell more X sails is for the X Sails Company to *help the dealer sell more boats.* Various possible approaches to this dealer assistance include:

- X advertising featuring the dealer (expensive)
- X advertising featuring the dealer's boats (expensive)
- X sailing school to which dealers could send new boat buyers
- X-supplied brochures or sailing hints
- X special programs that aid the dealers

The best approach, given a strategy of specialization *in sails for selected boats sailing in the Bay Area,* appears to be to develop a draft of printed material (brochures, posters, etc.) on each selected boat for which X wishes to make sails, and then to solicit and sign up the desired dealer and feature him in the brochure through over printing. The dealer gets the printed material to use in selling boats; he gives the printed material to prospective customers; X gets the sails orders for the boats sold. (Note: The same brochures can be used for direct mail pieces and for the marina "doorknob" program.)

3.4

Competitive conditions are not expected to change in the near future. North and Hood will continue as national advertisers using a racing theme and lots of technical stuff on sail design. Hood is likely to open in the Bay Area soon. Sutter appears to be following along on the national advertising and racing themes. Mitchell's advertising is sporadic. Chances are good that all other local sailmakers are too undercapitalized and undermanaged to initiate any strong campaign to offset X's dealer-oriented effort.

Significant new sailmakers are not expected on the scene. The Great X Sailing Company is to be positioned as the big, local loft—"X knows the Bay best!"

3.5

Pricing appears to be a "black art" in the industry. Strategy should be to quote just under the North, Hood, (and perhaps, Mitchell) figures with a firm knowledge of what X's internal costs are. *One* person in the Company should be responsible for all pricing (quotes, discounts, etc.). That person should be the loft General Manager.

3.6

No direct government influence is present or expected.

3.7

The X Company needs to evolve from a service business in which every sail made is seen as a unique event, to a product business in which repetitive items are made efficiently, hence, the concentration on sails for a limited number of boats that will be sold (hopefully) in volume. It is possible that within a year or so, certain sails will be able to be shipped "off the shelf" from X the same day they are ordered. To the extent that sails delivery is a bottleneck to yacht dealers today, X should work in its dealer program to eliminate it. The above does not preclude making special sails, racing sails, etc. The point is that the business pursued via the marketing effort is going to be selective.

3.8

From the information available, X Sails appears to be breaking even on about $200,000 in sales volume. Marketing expenses will increase costs, but tighter internal controls will tend to bring costs down. To reach its profit objectives, the X Sails Company needs to move in the next few years to the point where it is selling at least 25% of the sales volume in the greater Bay Area. (25% × 2 million = $500,000 in net sales.)

4.0 Marketing

Marketing and selling in the Company have been done on a hit-and-miss basis at best. Aside from the advertising and brochures being done by Dewitt, North, Hood, and Sutter, a systematic, continuing approach to the market place is not expected from any of the local sailmakers.

4.1

For purposes of this plan, assume that five brands of boats have been selected by the X Company for primary attention, and five others for secondary attention. The boats will be selected on the basis of:

a. West Coast manufacture/competitive price/boat features
b. Level of sustained advertising to end users
c. Compatibility of local dealer with Jim X
d. Range of boat sizes offered
e. Gross margin on sales of sails for the boat
f. Level of publicity accorded to boat
g. Projected volume of boats to be sold in Bay Area
h. Jim X's opinion of the boat design

A dealer program will be drafted under the general idea: "Here's how X is going to help you sell boats when you promote X sail sales." The Program will be presented to the desired dealers, and those making the requested commitment to sell X sails will be signed on. The Program will be produced, and regular (weekly) contact with the dealer maintained, by the Company's Customer Service Supervisor.

In the meantime, a pilot, direct mailing to Yacht Racing Association and yacht club members, or other lists of sailing people will be made using the "X knows the Bay Best" or "Sail for Fun" theme. The Club Jib idea will be promoted and results monitored. The Club Jib package and program will be launched by September and aimed at generating fall/winter business.

Finally, a Doorknob pilot program will be tried at six selected marinas using the dealer program materials to promote the specific service. Results will be monitored.

4.2

All promotion will be oriented to the idea that X knows the Bay best for your kind of boat with five to ten "your kinds." Details for proper sails and sailing information will have to be developed and tested (same as the 5-0-5 letter done in Seattle). Budget permitting, a brochure outlining "Known and Little Known Places to Sail on the Bay—by The Great X Sailing Company" should be produced for general usage and tied into Jim X's personal appearances, as well as those by Jim W., Bob S., Joe C., Rudy D., and Sallie R.

4.3

In summary, the major events in the marketing program are as follows:

- Dealer Program
- Club Jib Program
- Places on the Bay

4.4 Schedule

Who	July	Aug.	Sept.	Oct.	Nov.	Dec.
A.						
Select boats and dealers	x					
Develop dealer program	x	x				
Sell dealers			x			
Produce dealer program			x			
Deliver dealer program				x		
Follow through				x	x	x
B.						
Prepare Club Jib program	x	x				
Mailing list		x				
Mail to pilot			x			
Monitor results			x	x	x	
Additional mailing				?	?	
Jim X presentations			x	x	x	x
C.						
Use A and B in marina Doorknob pilot			x	x		
Monitor results				x	x	
More Doorknob				?	?	
D.						
Prepare "Bay Places" Production			x			
Jim X's presentations				x	x	x
Pilot mailing				x		
Monitor results						x

	July	Aug.	Sept.	Oct.	Nov.	Dec.
Who						
Distribution					x	
E.						
Ad format				x	x	
Plan space at boat show					x	

4.5 Budget for direct expenses other than Jim X and personnel time

		Total
Dealer program		
Development	$ 500	
Production	2,500	$ 3,000
Club Jib		
Development	100	
Production	300	
Mailing (200 pcs. @ $.20)	400	800
Places on Bay handbook		
Development	200	
Production	3,000	3,200
Doorknob campaign		
Total (1,000 pcs.)		500
Boat shows		1,300
Slide show for talks by Jim X		200
Local publications		1,000
Decals, miscellaneous supplies		500
Contingency		1,500
	TOTAL	$12,000

4.6 Results expected

The purpose of the dealer program is to produce and keep a complete set of boat dealers who recommend X sails for specific lines of boats. Next year's objective is $150,000 in net dealer sales volume.

The Club Jib mailing and Doorknob campaigns from the X Company should produce $25,000 in sales volume during the four winter months starting in October and help generate part of the $150,000 in sales to individuals projected for next year.

Some of the purposes of the Places to Sail in the Bay program are to support the dealer program, the direct contact program by the President, and boat show participations, but its primary objective is to generate $150,000 in sales volume from individuals next year. Possibly, it can become a staple item in bookstores, marine stores, and yacht clubs.

4.7

If results do not meet expectations, several options are open:

1. Shift emphasis to or away from dealers or individual purchasers

2. Go directly after boat manufacturers for an arrangement of some kind
3. Cease all media (direct mail, etc.) activity; rely on personal contacts
4. Spread efforts over a wider geographic area
5. Establish lofts in other cities
6. Pursue selected classes of boats in areas beyond the Bay

5.0 Production

Current floor space and production equipment are estimated to be capable of producing a volume in excess of $300,000 a year on a single shift. Additional volume is probably possible if: a) efficiencies are made in the production and scheduling process; b) sales volume can be spread somewhat into the non-summer months; and c) the planned specialization on a limited number of one-design boats is achieved.

5.1

Necessary equipment is on hand.

5.2

No major changes in the current facilities are anticipated.

5.3

Sailcloth and other supplies purchased need to be tightly controlled. Sailcloth, in particular, must be purchased at the best price consistent with quality requirements and inventory. The loft General Manager should be in charge of all sailcloth purchases; a meeting with major suppliers is an early item of business.

5.4

A quality control check sheet should be completed for each sail finished. Packaging and transportation costs are to be controlled by the loft manager (Production Leadperson), who will be measured on the gross margin generated.

5.5

A list of the major events to be completed in order to ensure timely, cost-conscious, sail production is as follows:

From existing data and experience

1. Determine current costs (labor and material) per square foot of sail for the high volume items.
2. Determine standard costs for the items.
3. Review pricing.
4. Review purchasing procedures and policies.

Then

5. Establish a production scheduling process.
6. Establish a cost budgeting procedure.
7. Review and adjust as necessary.

5.6 Schedule

	Who	July	Aug.	Sept.	Oct.	Nov.	Dec.
Current costs		X					
Standard costs			X				
Review pricing		X					
Review inventory			X				

	July	Aug.	Sept.	Oct.	Nov.	Dec.
Who						
Review purchasing		X				
Scheduling			X			
Budgeting			X			
Trial of new procedures				X	X	
Adjust standards						X

5.7 Budget

The total, nonpersonnel costs to install the above systems and procedures is estimated to be less than $500 for forms and, perhaps, for consulting advice.

5.8

As a result of the above, *all production work will be scheduled at least two weeks in advance at a budgeted figure for materials, labor, and supplies.* Significant variances between budgeted production and costs will be identifiable on the day they occur. Customers can be given precise status reports and shipping dates. Prices can be adjusted weekly if necessary to reflect changes in costs. Quotes can be made with a definite delivery commitment. Work force and inventory planning becomes relatively simple. *Product costs* are minimized.

5.9

There are no contingency plans for the above. If existing personnel are unable to adjust to planned production, changes in personnel will have to be considered.

6.0 Organization

Increasing the sales volume of selected products is the primary responsibility of Jim X, President. Sail design (special orders) and quality control are his other part-time tasks. Jim and one or more directors of the company will review sales and profit results weekly between September and December, at a minimum.

Reporting to Jim and responsible for the Operating Profit of the Company will be a General Manager. The General Manager is responsible for production, pricing, purchasing, accounting, customer service, and loft overhead—everything except marketing, the president, and interest on debt expenses.

Reporting to the General Manager will be a production leadperson, a bookkeeper, and a customer service supervisor

- The production leadperson will schedule and supervise the employees in order to ship completed, quality sails on time, within the budgeted labor and materials costs.
- The customer service supervisor will handle all customer inquiries, quotes, production scheduling, and Jim X's schedule for marketing activities.
- The bookkeeper will process all paperwork including payroll and management reports.

6.1 Organization Chart

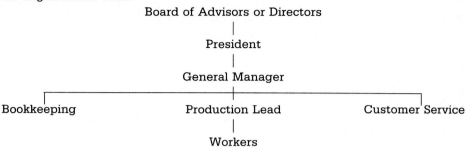

6.2

Current staff is deemed capable of filling most of the senior slots, but job descriptions and training must be developed along with systems and procedures for the various items in section 5.0. The following is the staffing: Joe C., General Manager; Rudy D., Customer Service Manager; the Production Lead will have to be Joe until the new systems are installed. A part-time bookkeeper will have to be hired.

6.3

No staffing schedule is required. However, training of existing people should be done in July and August.

6.4 Budget

Annual salaries for the first year for the four top people are estimated to be as follows:

President*	$12,000
General Manager	10,000
Customer Service	9,000
Bookkeeper	5,000
	$36,000

6.5 Results expected

The President is responsible for the Net Profit Before Taxes of the total Company. The General Manager is responsible for the operating profit percentage of the loft. The Production Lead is responsible for the gross margin percentage. The Customer Service Manager is responsible for the number of quotes, phone orders, customer complaints, meeting shipping dates, and the dealer phone contract program to be developed. Both the General Manager and the Customer Service Manager will have some field contact with dealers and potential customer groups.

Example:

Net sales and cost of goods
Production Lead ⎯⎯⎯⎯⎯⎯⎯⎯⎯⎯⎯→ Gross margin percentage

Loft overhead and staff
General Manager ⎯⎯⎯⎯⎯⎯⎯⎯⎯→ Operating profit percentage

Marketing and interest
President ⎯⎯⎯⎯⎯⎯⎯⎯⎯⎯⎯⎯→ Net profit before tax

*Jim X will spend four days/week on X Company business. He will have use of the company car and primary use of the company boat.

7.0 Funds flow and ownership

As the plan in the previous sections is implemented and produces the expected re-sults, additional money will probably be needed in the Company to facilitate further growth. This is one reason to incorporate the Company, i.e., to facilitate raising money from investors. Another reason to incorporate is to separate the Company from Jim X's personal income and activities more clearly so that employees can readily identify with the entity—The Great X Sailing Company. A third reason to shift from a proprietorship is to help attract outside advisors, possibly through stock options.

The current balance sheet for the company is approximately as follows:

Assets		Liabilities and Capital	
Cash	$ 1,000	Notes, Current	$ 7,000
A/R, Net	17,000	Advances	12,000
Inventory	28,000	A/P	10,000
Prepaid	1,000	Taxes Payable	3,000
	47,000		32,000
Furniture	5,000	Boat Note	6,500
Power Boat	6,000	Other Notes	11,000
Auto	2,000	Car	2,500
Improvements	3,000		20,000
	16,000	Capital	26,000
Goodwill	10,000		
Flowerpot	5,000		
	15,000		
TOTAL	$78,000	TOTAL	$78,000

Since a minimum of $15,000 is needed at this time to carry out the program as planned, the choices between debt and equity financing must be made. Debt is recom-mended since a minority equity ownership would probably be difficult to sell until such time as results from the new marketing effort are forthcoming. Equity now would only make sense from someone who is going to work directly in the business to "make it happen."

Therefore, $15,000 in debt money should be raised on the most favorable terms pos-sible. Ten percent interest only for two years, principal interest only for two years, prin-cipal payable in 30 monthly installments starting in two years might be a saleable pack age. Warrants to buy stock or to convert to stock could be used to make the deal more attractive if necessary. An SBA loan should also be explored.

Questions

1. Evaluate the potential of the Great X Sailing Company based on the material provid-ed. What additional material, if any, do you need to make an evaluation on the po-tential profitability of Great X Sailing Company?
2. If you were Jim X what would you do differently from the strategy presented in the case study? Why?
3. Put yourself in the place of an investor. Would you invest $15,000 in this business? Why or why not?
4. What would you expect Great X Sailing's competition to do if this proposal is carried out? How will this effect Great X's profitability?

CHAPTER 7

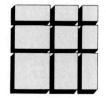

Evaluating the commercial recreation enterprise

CHAPTER OBJECTIVES

1. To understand the basic financial documents relevant to a commercial recreation enterprise

2. To be familiar with the basic forms of balance sheets and income statements

3. To know where each type of cost or revenue belongs on a company's financial documents

4. To determine where money is spent and where it comes from

5. To be able to develop pro forma financial statements

Any commercial recreation operator needs to know exactly where he stands financially. This is accomplished through the use of the bottom line, or profit.

In order to determine profit, the manager must be familiar with common financial statements. These statements have been standardized by the Federal Accounting Standards Board and are relatively consistent throughout the United States. Financial statements may be more or less complex depending on sources of income, funding, and debt. They include three separate documents: (1) The balance sheet, which summarizes the resources of a firm at a specific time. (2) The income, or profit and loss, statement, which measures how successfully management has been able to use the resources identified in the balance sheet during a specific time period. (3) The funds flow statement, or statement of changes in financial position, which indicates where the company obtained its resources and how it used them during a specific period.

Each financial statement covers a specific time period. The balance sheet tells the manager what resources are available to him on a specific date, which always appears at the top of the balance sheet. The balance sheet does not represent an ongoing situation; it is a picture of the company's status on the date shown.

The income statement covers a specific period during which the manager used the resources. Income statements can be developed quarterly, semiannually or annually. It is important to note that the period of an income statement is variable. However, the periods listed above are the most commonly used.

The funds flow statement relates to a period during which funds have been acquired and expended by the firm. The period it covers should be consistent with that of the other financial statements.

In order to understand financial statements and financial analysis, we will create a hypothetical business, World Travel, Inc.

World Travel is a large wholesale/retail travel agency specializing in corporate and incentive travel. (Incentive travel comprises trips awarded for sales performance and meeting sales quotas.) World Travel is a fully integrated company. It creates travel packages and sells them wholesale to other travel agencies or to the public. In the case of incentive travel for corporations, it also conducts group tours.

World Travel is located in downtown Metropolis, U.S.A. It has been established at its present site for approximately 30 years. Due to the dilapidated condition of its original building, a new building was constructed on the old site in 19X0, which upgraded its image substantially. In addition to its wholesale and retail trade, World Travel owns a fleet of buses and cars to transport customers between airports and destinations and on local and regional sightseeing tours.

World Travel's balance sheet and income statement will form the basis of all examples and textual material in this chapter. You should become familiar with each line item of these two documents. It is important to note that the balance sheet and income statement cover the years 19X2 and 19X3. This allows for perspective by providing two years of financial information in one statement.

Balance sheet

Our analysis of the financial documents begins with a detailed look at the basic components of any balance sheet.

First, this is a balance sheet for World Travel at the end of the calendar year 19X3 (Table 7-1). Remember, this is the position of World Travel on December 31, 19X3 (Fig. 7-1).

Usually the balance sheet is broken into three components: assets, liabilities, and shareholders' equity. The assets of a company are its economic resources, used to generate income for the company. These resources are always expressed in monetary terms, as are all other aspects of the financial statements. Therefore,

TABLE 7-1. World Travel, Inc, balance sheet Dec. 31, 19X3

	19X3	19X2
Assets		
Current assets		
Cash	$ 450,000	$ 300,000
Securities	850,000	460,000
Accounts receivable	2,000,000	1,900,000
Inventories	2,700,000	3,000,000
Total current assets	$6,000,000	$5,660,000
Fixed assets		
Land	$ 450,000	$ 450,000
Building	3,800,000	3,600,000
Machinery	950,000	850,000
Office equipment	100,000	95,000
Gross fixed assets	$5,300,000	$4,995,000
Less accumulated depreciation	1,800,000	1,500,000
Net fixed assets	3,500,000	3,495,000
Prepayments	100,000	90,000
Intangibles	100,000	100,000
Total assets	$9,700,000	$9,345,000
Liabilities		
Current liabilities		
Accounts payable	$1,000,000	$ 940,000
Notes payable	850,000	1,000,000
Accrued expenses payable	330,000	300,000
Taxes payable	320,000	290,000
Total current liabilities	$2,500,000	$2,530,000
Long-term liabilities		
First mortgage bonds 10% interest due 19X5	$2,700,000	$2,700,000
Total liabilities	$5,200,000	$5,230,000
Shareholders' equity		
Capital stock		
Class A Common:		
$100 par value; 6,000 shares authorized	600,000	600,000
and issued		
Class B common:		
$5 par value; 300,000 shares authorized	1,500,000	1,500,000
and issued		
Capital surplus	700,000	700,000
Accumulated retained earnings	1,700,000	1,315,000
Total stockholders' equity	$4,500,000	$4,115,000
Total liabilities and stockholders' equity	$9,700,000	$9,345,000

FIG. 7-1 World Travel, Inc., sells trips to such famous destinations as Niagara Falls. (Photograph courtesy Niagara Falls, Canada, Visitor and Convention Bureau.)

on the asset side of the ledger we will list all of the goods and property owned by the company as well as uncollected claims against other businesses and individuals. Some examples of these assets are buildings, equipment, prepayment for future services, cash, and other assets such as inventory and accounts receivable.

Assets in a company are always listed in order from most to least liquid. (*Liquidity* refers to ease in converting the asset into cash.) This is why cash always appears first under assets. The asset portion of the balance sheet shows items that are not readily converted into cash: buildings, equipment, and intangible items such as goodwill, patents, and trademarks, which may never be converted into cash.

Liabilities comprise all debts and obligations against the firm. These represent creditors' claims on the firm's assets. Liabilities are listed in the order in which they fall due. Short-term accounts are payable first, then long-term liabilities, then shareholders' equity. Shareholders', or owners', equity is ownership in the company and as such is not repaid.

Owners' equity is cash exchanged for a portion of the profits in the future and is a liability that is never repaid. The owner may sell his equity (stock) to another person, but in most cases the company does not buy back the stock. In fact, *retained earnings,* or profits not dispersed to the owners are added to the owners' equity, thereby increasing shareholders' investment and the value of each owner's holdings.

A general relationship always exists on the balance sheet. You will notice that the liability side equals the asset side. This is an accounting convention and must always be observed on the balance sheet. This equation is expressed thus:

$$\text{Assets} = \text{Liabilities} + \text{Owners' equity}$$

The asset portion of the balance sheet can be broken down into three components: current assets, fixed assets, and other assets. *Current assets* are used during normal business operation. They include cash, marketable securities, accounts receivable, and inventories.

Fixed assets are integral to production of the good or service. They include buildings, land, and equipment.

Other assets are anything else of value to the company. They should be listed, since they relate to the development of the business. Examples will be explained in greater detail later.

The resources of the business must always be equal to the claims of people outside of the business plus the claims of the owners of the business. The balance sheet shows where the resources of the business originated, whether from outside sources, from revenue, or from the owners of the company. Let's review the balance sheet.

Assets

Current assets

Assets are listed in the assets column of the balance sheet in order of liquidity, from the most to least liquid, beginning with current assets. These include items used during the normal course of business or ones that can be quickly turned into cash. Usually current assets are converted to cash within a year of the date of the balance sheet.

Current assets consist primarily of cash, marketable securities, accounts receivable, and inventories. All of these items produce revenue.

Cash. A *cash account* holds readily available money. There is one difference between company cash and personal cash: company cash includes the contents of the cash register and any money in a demand deposit or passbook bank account.

Marketable securities. It is not wise for a commercial recreation business to hold more cash than necessary, because cash earns little or no interest. It is usually wiser to place funds in excess of day-to-day operating capital into marketable securities and earn a much higher rate of return than available for demand deposits. These securities may be certificates of deposit, stocks or bonds. Marketable securities must be of high enough quality to convert readily to cash when needed. Marketable securities are always shown on the balance sheet at cost, though actual value may be considerably more or less depending on the market.

Accounts receivable. *Accounts receivable* are sales made on credit and not yet paid for. Credit sales vary widely from company to company. In a water park, where the majority of sales are cash (with a few people using credit cards), there are next to no accounts receivable. However, a manufacturing company that produces a high-cost item usually sold on time (such as a recreational vehicle) carries substantial accounts receivable. In the case of World Travel, accounts receivable consist of tickets and tours purchased on credit. Depending on the type of business involved, the accounts receivable collection period may range from a few days, as with credit card sales, to over a year in the case of motor homes or recreational vehicles. It is important to consider the type of business when you try to determine how large the accounts receivable should be.

Inventories. *Inventory* is goods for sale. This item on a balance sheet has a wide range of meanings for commercial recreation. It may be nothing for a ski resort or water slide park, where no goods are sold, or very high for a retail store. A pure service cannot have an inventory because a service is consumed as it is produced. However, there may be no such thing as a truly pure service. There are three different forms of inventory for a manufacturing company: raw materials, partially finished goods, and the finished product available for sale. World Travel's inventory is trips and room bookings that have been purchased from wholesalers but not resold.

The value of the inventory is based on the cost of the goods or the market value, whichever is lower. This is a conservative, hence safer, method of estimation. The actual value of the inventory may be higher or lower depending on the length of time it has been held and the ease of selling it.

Fixed assets

Fixed assets are used repeatedly in order to manufacture, display, or sell the product. These assets are not intended for sale but are used for the normal operation of the business. They include a building and land on which it is built, the computers in a travel agency, and a bus company's buses. In a baseball bat factory fixed assets include lathes and conveyor belts.

Fixed assets are referred to as "plant, property, and equipment." Fixed assets are valued at the actual cost of the item.

In the fixed assets account there are three other general headings: depreciation, prepayments, and intangibles.

Depreciation. Since fixed assets are used during production of goods for sale, they wear out over time. *Depreciation* is the allocation of an asset's cost to the period of use of the asset. Depreciation allows the company to obtain the purchase price of the new equipment by saving a portion of its income for this purpose. Land has an indefinite life and therefore is carried at book value.

Depreciation is often calculated from the purchase price and an estimate of the useful life of the asset. A newer method of calculating depreciation is to use the Internal Revenue Service's tables showing the expected life of an asset and to subtract a portion of the value from operating expenses (Table 7-2). Suppose a $10,000 truck for the delivery of sporting goods is considered by the IRS to have a useful life of five years. Depreciation by the straight-line method would be $2,000 a year. At the end of five years the truck would have no value on paper.

Certain important definitions of terms:

The *gross value* is the original cost of the property without allowance for depreciation.

Book value is the figure obtained after deducting accrued depreciation from gross value.

When property is retired or sold, its gross value is deducted from the property account and the depreciation accrued against it is deleted from the accumulated depreciation account. Accumulated depreciation on the balance sheet may or may not increase during a given period. On the balance sheet fixed assets are carried at full purchase price. (In the case of World Travel, these are land, buildings, machinery, and office equipment.) Accumulated depreciation is subtracted, leaving net fixed assets, or the current value of the fixed assets of World Travel as of December 31, 19X3.

Prepayments and deferred charges. World Travel carries fire insurance on the building. In most cases businesses pay for insurance in advance. World Travel has

TABLE 7-2. Examples of depreciation ranges in years allowed by IRS 1986 guidelines

Asset	Lower limit	Guideline	Upper limit
Office furniture	8	10	12
Computer equipment	5	6	7
Typewriters	5	6	7
Automobiles	5	6	7
Light trucks	3	4	5
Airplanes, except commercial	5	6	7
Airplanes, commercial	9.5	12	14.5
Recreation equipment used to provide amusement for a fee	8	10	12
Amusement park equipment	10	12.5	15
Buildings (Section 1250)		15	
Equipment used to build boats	9.5	12	14.5
Boat dry docks	13	16	19
Equipment used to make athletic goods	9.5	12	14.5

probably paid the fire insurance premium for the next 2 to 3 years. Since World Travel has paid for insurance but not yet received it, that payment appears in the balance sheet as a *prepayment,* a good or service that has been purchased but not received.

Deferred charges are expenses that the company has incurred but not yet received the benefit from. For example, when the Wind Surfer was first developed, there was a marketing plan instituted to persuade the public to use them. This was expensive. Most managers feel that in situations like this, it is not fair to the company to write off the total cost of the advertising expense in the year in which it is incurred. Rather, it is wiser to delay at least a portion of that marketing expense for future years, when the benefit of the advertising will be realized. This allows the company to write off marketing expenses over the next several years. This is a deferred charge.

Intangibles. Intangibles are assets that have no physical existence yet have substantial value to the company. Intangible assets include goodwill, patents, and trademarks. Let's look at some examples of intangible assets and how to place them on a balance sheet.

Suppose you developed the beeper ball, which allows blind people to play softball. The law allows you to patent the idea and claim exclusive rights to the manufacture of this product. It is virtually impossible to determine the value of that patent, yet it is of great value to the company. It makes sense that this asset be placed on the balance sheet.

Another example is cable TV marketing. In most cases a city or county will grant a franchise to a particular company allowing it the exclusive right to market cable TV in a specific area. This is an asset to the company, but it is impossible to calculate the value of that franchise.

In another example, one company acquires another and the purchase price exceeds the book value of the assets of the company being acquired. The reason for the inflated price is that the acquiring company is purchasing the goodwill of the customers toward the company being acquired. This goodwill (the purchase price minus the book value) is written on the balance sheet as an asset under intangibles.

These are all examples of intangible assets. Because it is impossible to place a value on intangible assets, some companies list intangible assets at a nominal value such as $1. Of course, this does not accurately reflect the situation, since it undervalues the assets of the company, but it is very important in accounting to be conservative in estimating company assets.

Liabilities

Liabilities comprise all the obligations the company is expected to meet. This section of the balance sheet is generally divided into two portions. One is *current liabilities,* or all debts that fall due within one year. The second includes long-term liabilities, or debts due over a period longer than one year. Current liabilities reflect day-to-day operating expenses. Long-term liabilities are usually the capitalized loans used by the company in establishing the business.

Current liabilities

Current liabilities consist of accounts payable, notes payable, accrued expenses payable, and unpaid taxes. Current liabilities are a companion to current assets. The reason for this is that current assets generate the funds used to pay off current liabilities. The relationship between these two can be revealing.

Accounts payable. Accounts payable reflect the amount of money owed by the company to those with whom it normally does business, usually companies from which you buy assets or goods for resale. For example, World Travel must purchase tickets from suppliers. If the trips and tickets are purchased on credit, they appear on the balance sheet as accounts payable. Another example is a snack bar at a water park. It must stock soft drink mix, buns, and hamburgers, to name a few items. These suppliers usually require you to pay for the goods in 30, 60, or 90 days. When you delay payment, you are borrowing money from the supplier in order to generate revenue.

Notes payable. If you borrow money on a short-term basis, the amount appears in the notes payable section of the balance sheet. It indicates that a promissory note has been signed and that you must repay the loan. This money is used to purchase goods for resale or for operations. Loans appearing in this section should never mature in more than one year.

Accrued expenses payable. It is virtually impossible for any company to have no debts to employees. *Accrued expenses payable* include salaries and wages that are due and interest on bank loans coming due. These liabilities appear on the balance sheet as accrued expenses payable. Remember, a balance sheet is the statement of your company's position at a given time. Since that point in time reflects something other than full payment of employees or bills, this line is a necessity on any balance sheet.

Taxes payable. Every company must pay taxes. Federal tax due dates depend on the company's fiscal year, and the amount payable is based on earnings. State and local tax rates and due dates vary widely. Check the laws under which you are operating.

The total current liabilities line is the sum of the listed items.

Long-term liabilities

Long-term liabilities include all forms of borrowing that are repaid over a period in excess of one year from the date of the balance sheet. They include bonds and long-term bank debts. Usually these debts are incurred by the purchase of major capital assets and are paid back over several years. Long-term liabilities are added to current liabilities to generate the last line of the liabilities section, or *total liabilities*. This should be looked at as it relates to the total assets of the company. Total liabilities should be less than total assets.

Stockholders' equity

The difference between total assets and total liabilities is balanced by *stockhold-ers' equity*, or the portion of the company owned by investors. Stockholders' equity consists of capital stock, capital surplus, and accumulated retained income.

Capital stock

Capital stock is the number of shares in the company that have been sold. Pre-ferred stock is listed first and followed by common stock. The par value of the stock must be listed on the balance sheet. In the past par value was set at the lowest selling value of a stock. In current terminology par value is established arbitrarily and appears on stock certificates only out of historical preference.

The number of shares of each type of stock authorized must also be listed, along with the number of shares of each kind issued. The difference between authorized and issued shares of stock is an indication of the company's ability to raise funds.

The dollar value of stock is determined by multiplying outstanding shares by the par value of each share. This is the *capital stock value* of each type of stock.

Capital surplus

Once a company has been in operation for any length of time, the value of its stock should increase. For example, Disney stock has risen over the last 20 years due to the tremendous profitability of Disney's theme parks. If Disney should sell stock today, the amount received would exceed the par value of the stock. This difference would appear on the balance sheet under capital surplus. Remember that capital stock on the balance sheet is shown as the par value of the stock times the shares issued. Once a company's stock sells for more than its par value, the difference between the two amounts appears under capital surplus. World Travel received over $700,000 more than the par value of its 306,000 shares of common and preferred stock.

Accumulated retained earnings

Retained earnings is the portion of profit kept in the company over the life of the company. For example, the first year that a small boat rental concession at a state park was in operation, there was a zero balance in the accumulated retained earn-ings portion of the balance sheet. At the end of the first season the company had turned a profit of $30,000. A dividend was declared to the stockholders, allowing them a portion of the profits as a return for their investment. The remainder of the profits appeared in the retained earnings account. Let's say the $30,000 profit was split $10,000 for dividends and $20,000 in retained earnings. At the beginning of the second year the retained earnings account should show a balance of $20,000. This operating capital, or retained earnings, is used to start the business in the second year. As the company grows and develops, the retained earnings account should grow. If it begins to decrease, it is an indication that the company is losing money.

Total stockholders' equity reflects the total claim the stockholders have on the company as of the date of the balance sheet. This is added to liabilities. Liabilities plus stockholders' equity always equals total assets.

Income statement

The income statement shows the activities of the company over the time period and shows whether the business has made a profit or loss. The income statement for World Travel is presented in Table 7-3. It is important to note that a one-year income statement is not sufficient for accurate analysis. Any company should include two or more years of income statements to allow analysis of the changes from year to year to see whether the company is improving or not.

The income statement follows the general form outlined in the box on p. 188. Different accountants and businesses may list additional items on the income statement, but all statements can be reduced to this general form. This form allows for comparability between companies. It is advisable that you become very familiar with the general form of the income statement.

Sales

Since sales are the most important source of income, the sales figure always appears first on the income statement. Sales are the total revenue generated by operation of the company. In the case of a racquetball club, sales might consist of revenues from memberships, daily use fees, the snack bar, and locker rentals. In a retail outlet such as a sporting goods store sales consist of revenues from sale of all goods and equipment. Sales constitute the major source of income for the company.

TABLE 7-3. World Travel, Inc., consolidated income statement Dec. 31, 19X3

	19X3	19X2
Sales	$11,000,000	$10,200,000
Cost of sales and operating expenses		
Cost of goods sold	8,200,000	7,684,000
Depreciation	300,000	275,000
Administration and selling expenses	1,400,000	1,325,000
Operating profit	$ 1,100,000	$ 916,000
Other income		
Dividends and interest	50,000	27,000
Earnings before interest and taxes	1,150,000	943,000
Less interest payments	270,000	270,000
Earnings before taxes	$ 880,000	$ 673,000
Taxes	$ 414,000	$ 302,000
Net income	$ 466,000	$ 370,000

General form of an income statement

Net sales
— Cost of goods sold
Gross margin
— Operating expenses
— Depreciation
Earnings before interest and taxes
— Interest payments
Earnings before taxes
— Tax liability
Net income

In some companies additional income is gained from interest on investments. That income appears on the income statement as "other income."

Cost of goods sold

The cost of the goods sold is the actual cost to the company of the assets that were sold. For World Travel the biggest cost of goods is for tickets. In a water theme park, where the goods sold are trips down the slides, the cost of goods sold is negligible. However, in a sporting goods store the cost of goods sold is the wholesale price of the items sold from inventory and makes up a significant portion of net sales.

Gross margin

The *gross margin* is the amount left after the cost of goods is subtracted from sales. This is the amount available for coverage of other expenses.

Operating expenses

Operating expenses include all other expenses necessary for the production of revenues, including such things as wages, salaries, the cost of advertising, rent, and utilities. These items certainly have an effect on the business and yet they are not directly related to the goods sold and are therefore accounted for separately on the income statement.

Depreciation

Depreciation is used to replace fixed assets that are used for the production of income. It is considered a cost of doing business, or expense that allows for the time when an item is no longer usable and must be replaced. Depreciation is subtracted from net sales.

Earnings before interest and taxes

This line item reflects the total revenue before subtraction of interest and taxes. It is sales minus cost of goods sold, depreciation, and operating expenses.

Interest payments

Since a company usually has to borrow some money, interest is a cost of doing business. Therefore, interest payments must be subtracted before taxes are computed for the company.

Earnings before taxes

Earnings before taxes is the amount left over after all costs of doing business have been deducted from sales.

Tax liability

The tax liability is mandated by the federal, state, and local governments and changes yearly. Taxes are computed based on the current IRS regulations and on state and local business tax rates.

Net income

Net income is the amount of money the company has made over the course of one year after all liabilities have been paid. Net income is the amount available for dividends and retained earnings.

Funds flow analysis

Funds flow analysis is very important to the evaluation of any business. It allows you to determine where funds are generated and where they are used. Funds flow analysis addresses the following questions:

1. Was there an increase in current assets?
2. Was there an increase in fixed assets?
3. What were the changes in income?
4. How was growth financed?
5. Did the business provide a profit or loss?
6. What portion of the resources used were provided by day-to-day operations?

The answers to these questions are vitally important to any business, since they reflect directly on longevity, profitability, and management. It is usually wise to compute the funds flow analysis in addition to the ratios that will be discussed in the next chapter. This is because the funds flow analysis provides a closer look at the general operation of the company over the period.

The first step in a funds flow analysis is to determine whether or not a change in the balance sheet reflects a source or use of funds. The easiest way to determine

Funds flow analysis guide

Sources of funds
1. Increase in a liability line item
2. Increase in an owners' equity line item
3. Decrease in an asset line item
4. Increase in a depreciation line item

Uses of funds
1. Increase in an asset line item
2. Decrease in a liability line item
3. Decrease in an owners' equity line item

this is by looking at the box above. For each source of funds there are four possible changes to consider. For uses of funds there are three changes. By looking for these changes in each line item on a balance sheet, you can easily analyze the flow of funds.

In the case of World Travel Table 7-4 provides an example of the changes in the balance sheet from 19X2 to 19X3. In addition we have indicated whether the item was a source or use of funds based on the rules listed in the box above. Once the changes in the balance sheet have been constructed as shown, the remaining step is to group the sources and uses and add them up. Make sure they are equal, as in the example in Table 7-5.

Table 7-5 is a summary of a funds flow analysis for World Travel. There are three substantial sources of funds; increased retained earnings, increase in depreciation, and decrease in inventory. These funds were used to buy securities, improve the building, increase cash deposits, and pay off notes. This is what you would expect from a company of this type. The management of World Travel decided that inventory was too high based on the inventory turnover ratio and reduced it. The majority of the capital generated was used to increase the securities and cash accounts. Some of the funds were used to improve the building; this should come out of retained earnings according to the suitability principle.

The *suitability principle* indicates that purchases should be funded by appropriate types of capital. For example, increases in inventory should be paid for through short-term borrowing because the sale of the inventory will generate the capital to pay off the loan. An increase in capital assets such as improvements to the building should come from long-term financing. In this case you will note that an increase of $200,000 in the building cost was funded by the increase in retained earnings of $385,000. This meets the suitability principle, since retained earnings are equity capital and is being used to increase the assets of the company.

It is also important that the decrease in notes payable, which are generally short-term loans, comes from the reduction of inventory. The $150,000 decrease in notes payable was funded from the $300,000 reduction in inventory. The analysis

TABLE 7-4. Changes in balance sheet

Line item	19X3	19X2	Change	Source or use
Assets				
Cash	$ 450,000	$ 300,000	$150,000	Use
Securities	850,000	460,000	390,000	Use
Accounts receivable	2,000,000	1,900,000	100,000	Use
Inventories	2,700,000	3,000,000	−300,000	Source
Land	450,000	450,000		
Building	3,800,000	3,600,000	200,000	Use
Equipment	950,000	850,000	100,000	Use
Office equipment	100,000	95,000	5,000	Use
Accumulated depreciation	1,800,000	1,500,000	300,000	Source
Prepayments	100,000	90,000	10,000	Use
Intangibles	100,000	100,000		
Liabilities				
Accounts payable	1,000,000	940,000	60,000	Source
Notes payable	850,000	1,100,000	−150,000	Use
Accrued expense	330,000	300,000	30,000	Source
Federal income taxes payable	320,000	290,000	30,000	Source
Long-term liabilities	2,700,000	2,700,000		
Shareholders' equity				
Class A common	600,000	600,000	—	—
Class B common	1,500,000	1,500,000	—	—
Capital surplus	700,000	700,000	—	—
Accumulated retained earnings	1,700,000	1,315,000	385,000	Source

of a funds flow statement can become quite complicated. However, the information is extremely important. A funds flow analysis accurately reflects where funds were generated as well as whether or not each use was suitable.

Pro forma statements

Having explained the intricacies of the balance sheet and income statement and having shown how they can be used to assess the standing of a company, we shall discuss how they can be used for financial planning. A pro forma statement is hypothetical, an anticipated statement of where the company will be at a specific time in the future. The main purpose of the pro forma statement is to provide a systematic projection of what should be done. This projection is based on two documents, the pro forma income statement and the pro forma balance sheet. It is important that both documents be broken into specific periods equal to or less than

TABLE 7-5. Funds flow analysis

	Amount
Sources	
Decrease in inventory	$ 300,000
Increase in depreciation	300,000
Increase in accounts payable	60,000
Increase in accrued expenses	30,000
Increase in federal income tax payable	30,000
Increase in retained earnings	385,000
Sources of funds	$1,105,000
Uses	
Increase cash	$ 150,000
Increase securities	390,000
Increase accounts receivable	100,000
Improve building	200,000
Upgrade equipment	100,000
Upgrade office equipment	5,000
Increase prepayments	10,000
Pay off notes payable	150,000
Uses of funds	$1,105,000

the accounting period of the company. If your business has seasonal sales and no general long-term growth, it is wise to prepare pro forma statements on a monthly basis. A company with strong long-term sales growth and no seasonality should use pro forma statements based on a year-end analysis for five years. A company with cyclical sales but no long-term growth should do quarterly pro forma statements over 18 months.

Pro forma statements help anticipate the future needs of the company. As a result, the pro forma statement helps the manager in four ways:

1. It helps to reduce surprises and emergencies.
2. It can be used as a standard against which to measure the effectiveness of the company.
3. It can be used to anticipate coming financial needs.
4. It is a planning document.

There are many ways to construct a pro forma statement. Such a statement is a measure of logical thinking and anticipation of the future based on history. History can be found on balance sheets and income statements. In the case of a new company history can be approximated from industry ratios. This flexibility is one of the advantages of pro forma statements.

Let us develop a pro forma statement for the year 19X4 for World Travel. First we will create the income statement and then use the information created to construct the balance sheet.

Pro forma income statement

To develop a pro forma income statement you must project sales for the coming year. Sales can be projected based on a number of different factors such as previous sales levels and trends. If sales have been increasing and trends in the industry indicate that business is improving, sales can be expected to increase. In addition, if the overall economy is strong, sales will probably go up. If the economy is weakening, it would be wise to project a decrease in sales.

A third factor is the status of the industry. Most industries are increasing their market size. However, some industries are declining. A fourth factor is competition, including new businesses. A fifth factor is population growth in the immediate area. As the population grows, more people are available to participate in recreation. This has a natural tendency to increase market size.

A sixth factor is the capacity of the facility. If a facility has reached capacity, the only way to increase sales revenue may be to increase the price. Capacity is a major factor. It is often not wise to increase capacity substantially, since in commercial recreation seasonal factors may adversely affect sales.

Pricing policies can affect sales, since an increase in price may increase revenues. However, attendance may decrease. This should be examined carefully and is treated in Chapter 8.

Based on these factors, the manager of the business makes an estimate of sales for the coming year. In the case of World Travel, assume that in 19X4 sales will increase by 10% over 19X3. This gives us sales of $12,100,000. At this stage it is important to observe the general format of the pro forma income statement. Since we have already established a format that is familiar to employees of World Travel, it makes sense to use the same general format for the pro forma income statement. If no format has been chosen, it is best to use the general format for income statements provided in the box on p. 188. Insert the sales figure. Next determine the cost of goods sold. This is historically linked to sales, so the cost of goods sold is a percentage of sales in 19X3. This turns out to be 74.5% of sales, which puts the line item for the pro forma cost of goods sold at $9,014,500.

The next item is depreciation. Assume for figuring ease that all equipment owned by World Travel is depreciated on a straight-line basis and that no new equipment has been purchased. This leaves depreciation the same in 19X4 as it was in 19X3 ($300,000). If new equipment is purchased or existing equipment is sold, it must be taken into consideration on the depreciation line.

The last item under operating expenses is administration and selling expenses. We can compute administration and selling expenses as a percentage of total sales. Historically, this turns out to be 12.7%, or $1,536,700. Subtracting cost of goods sold, depreciation, and administrative expenses from sales leaves us with an operating profit of $1,248,800. Other income depends on investments. This is a

World Travel, Inc. Pro forma income statement 19X4

Net sales	$12,100,000
Cost of goods	9,014,500
Depreciation	300,000
Administration & selling expenses	1,536,700
Operating profit	$ 1,248,800
Other income	50,000
EBIT	$ 1,298,800
Interest	270,000
EBT	1,028,800
Taxes (50%)	514,400
Net income	514,400

value that cannot be accurately ascertained without additional information. Therefore, assume there is no change in other income. This leaves $50,000, which, added to operating profit, equals earnings before interest and tax of $1,298,800.

The last item is interest payments. Since we have not anticipated borrowing additional capital, the interest payments should remain the same at $270,000. This leaves pretax earnings of $1,028,800. This is taxed at 50%, leaving a net income of $514,400. This entire pro forma income statement is laid out in the box above. This constitutes anticipated income of World Travel on a 10% increase in sales for the year 19X4.

Pro forma balance sheet

The easiest format for the pro forma balance sheet is the one we have been using. It is easy to use a blank sheet with simple headings as shown in the World Travel example. Once this is done, fill in the line items based on anticipated changes. See the box on page 195.

The best place to begin is with fixed assets. Fixed assets take into consideration new purchases to be made and are consistent with formal planning for expansion or for selling equipment.

Assume World Travel is not going to acquire any new fixed assets or sell any existing assets. The fixed assets portion of the balance sheet will show only one change: accumulated depreciation has increased by $300,000. Therefore, accumulated depreciation is now $2,100,000 instead of $1,800,000. This leaves a net fixed assets total of $3,200,000.

Continuing down the balance sheet, prepayments decrease, since we have used some of the payments made last year and have made no new ones. Assume World Travel has consumed half of the insurance and other prepayments purchased in 19X3. That leaves prepayments at $50,000 instead of $100,000. We have no information concerning intangibles, so we leave it at $100,000. So far it is impossible to compute total assets, since we have not dealt with current assets.

World Travel, Inc. Pro Forma balance sheet 19X4

Assets

Current assets

Cash	$ 400,000
Marketable securities	398,400
Accounts receivable	2,178,000
Inventories	2,964,500
Total current assets	$5,940,900

Fixed assets

Land	$ 450,000
Building	3,800,000
Equipment	950,000
Office equipment	100,000
Gross fixed assets	$5,300,000
Less accumulated dep.	2,100,000
Net fixed assets	$3,200,000
Prepayments	50,000
Intangibles	100,000
Total assets	$9,290,900

Liabilities

Current liabilities

Accounts payable	$1,089,000
Note payable	931,700
Accrued expenses payable	363,000
Federal income taxes payable	350,000
Total current liabilities	$2,733,700

Long-term liabilities

First mortage bonds	
10% interest, due 19X5	1,800,000
Total liabilities	$4,533,700

Shareholders' equity

Capital stock	
Preferred stock; $100 par value; 6,000 shares authorized and issued	600,000
Common stock; $5 par value; 300,000 shares authorized and issued	1,500,000
Capital surplus	700,000
Accumulated retained earnings	1,957,200
Total stockholders' equity	$4,757,200
Total liabilities and stockholder equity	$9,290,900

Let us now move to long-term liabilities. The only long-term liability is the first mortgage bonds, which are due in 19X5. Assume that one third of the total balance of 19X3 will be paid off in 19X4. This will decrease total long-term liability by approximately $900,000, leaving a balance due of $1,800,000.

At this stage we move to the shareholders' equity account. Capital stock has not changed, since all shares are authorized and issued. These are the same as they were in 19X3, $600,000 for preferred stock and $1,500,000 for common stock.

Capital surplus has not changed, since World Travel has not sold any new stock. This remains at $700,000. Accumulated retained earnings change by the amount of net income in 19X4 left over after dividends were paid.

Assume that in 19X4 the board of directors decided to spend 50% of net income as dividends. This leaves 50% of net income, or $257,200, to be included in accumulated retained earnings. The total comes to $1,957,200. Total stockholders' equity increased to $4,757,200 (capital stock plus capital surplus plus retained income). It is time to reevaluate current liabilities and assets, beginning with current liabilities.

The problem is to determine which liability accounts are directly related to sales. Analysis of each line item reveals that accounts payable is a form of borrowing from suppliers. It makes sense to compute this as a percentage of sales. Dividing accounts payable by total sales in 19X3 and 19X2 yields approximately 9%, which comes to anticipated accounts payable for 19X4 of $1,089,000.

The same can be done for notes payable. Notes payable amount to 7.7% of sales, or $931,700. Accrued expenses may be based on the actual days since the last pay period. Usually this line item reflects salaries or interest owed but not paid. It can also be computed as a percentage of sales. The latter provides a value for accrued expenses payable of about 3% of total sales, or $363,000 for 19X4.

Since the amount of federal income tax payable is based on the total sales minus expenses, we can estimate the figure as a percentage of sales. This turns out to be approximately 2.9%, or $350,900, for 19X4.

We can now complete the liabilities and equity portion of the pro forma balance sheet by adding total current liabilities, long-term liabilities, and stockholders' equity. This amounts to the following values: current liabilities of $2,732,700; long-term liabilities of $1,800,000; and stockholders' equity of $4,757,200. This results in total liabilities and stockholders' equity of $9,290,900.

To deal with current assets, work from the bottom up. Since inventories generate sales, assume that inventory can be computed as a percentage of the total sales. This amounts to a value of approximately 24.5% of total sales. In the pro forma balance sheet for 19X4, this amounts to approximately $2,964,500. The next item up the balance sheet is accounts receivable, or the portion of total sales made on credit terms. Again, this is a percentage of total sales. Using 19X3 values, this is approximately 18%. The value for 19X4 comes to 2,178,000.

The last two items are cash and marketable securities. This can be handled by either determining the total cash on hand needed at any one time in World Travel, or last year's figure. Suppose World Travel needs about $400,000 in cash for 19X4. This estimate is based on past needs and future plans. The actual number is a best guess. Put that estimate on the cash line for current assets.

The last value is marketable securities. This can be computed by subtracting total assets from total liabilities and stockholders' equity. The amount remaining is the value of marketable securities. If assets exceed liabilities then the difference must be added to the liabilities account. This is the amount of new loans needed. Remember, assets have to equal liabilities plus stockholders' equity. This gives a value of $398,400. All monies exceeding those needed for operations are placed in marketable securities to obtain a higher rate of return than in a demand deposit account.

We can now complete our pro forma statement. Note that two line items under current assets have decreased since 19X3. These are the cash account, down by $50,000, and the marketable securities account, down by $451,600. This, along with the amount used to pay off debt, reflects a decrease in liabilities, particularly in first mortgage bonds. As a result, the manager of this company knows that he is going to have to sell off approximately $451,600 worth of marketable securities in order to cover expenses during 19X4. If sales are seasonal, this pro forma statement can be computed monthly by determining what percentage of sales takes place in each month and going through the process in basically the same way. Pro forma statements are useful items and any recreation manager should be very familiar with them.

Summary

The financial statements of a business can provide the user with a tremendous amount of information relating to profitability and operations. It is important to know the different components of each, as in the balance sheet: current assets, or monies used in the day-to-day operation of the business, and fixed assets, or plant, property, and equipment.

Current liabilities are short-term borrowing (less than a year) needed for operations, and long-term liabilities are borrowing for purchase of fixed assets. Stockholders' equity is the amount of money provided by the owners for the establishment of the company. Assets equal liabilities plus equity.

The income statement indicates company profits over a previous year. This document lists all sources of income and expenses incurred over the period indicated. Each has an important part to play in the analysis of the company and its profitability.

Each financial statement relates to the condition of the company on a given day, not to the ongoing operation of the business. They are statements of position.

Funds flow analysis allows a manager to analyze the changes in a balance sheet from year to year. Based on these changes the manager can identify sources and uses of money. It is important to match sources with uses because it allows the manager to determine whether or not the money is being used properly.

The pro forma statement projects the future. It should be used as a planning device, since it reflects what the manager thinks will happen. Pro forma statements are important because they provide a road map by which the manager can chart his business course. It is important to understand all three of these components (ratio analysis, funds flow analysis and pro forma statements), since they are the means by which he or she will be able to measure the success or failure of the enterprise.

BIBLIOGRAPHY

Baker C.R., and Hayes, R.S.: Accounting, finance, and taxation: a basic guide for small business, Boston, 1980, CBI Publishing Co.

Blecke, C.J., and Gotthilf, D.L.: Financial analysis for decision making, Englewood Cliffs, N.J., 1980, Prentice-Hall, Inc.

Gibson, C.H., and Frishkoff, P.A.: Financial statement analysis: using financial accounting information, 2d edition, Boston, 1986, Kent Publishing Co.

Haller, L.L.: Making sense of accounting information: a practical guide for understanding financial reports and their use, New York, 1985, Van Nostrand Reinhold Co.

Helfert, E.A.: Techniques of financial analysis, Homewood, Ill., 1982, Richard D. Irwin, Inc.

Johnson, L.T., and Storey, R.K.: Recognition in financial statements: underlying concepts and practical conventions, Stamford, Conn., 1982, Financial Accounting Standards Board.

Meyer, P.E.: Applied accounting theory: a financial reporting perspective, Homewood, Ill., 1986, Richard D. Irwin, Inc.

Shillinglaw, G., and Meyer, P.E.: Accounting: a management approach, Homewood, Ill., 1986, Richard D. Irwin, Inc.

Spurga, R.C.: Balance sheet basics: financial management for nonfinancial managers, New York, 1986, F. Watts.

Tracy, J.A.: How to read a financial report: wringing cash flow and other vital signs out of numbers, New York, 1980, John Wiley & Sons, Inc.

Viscione, J.A.: Flow of funds and other financial concepts, New York, 1981, National Association of Credit Management.

Winter, E.L.: A complete guide to preparing a corporate annual report, New York, 1985, Van Nostrand Reinhold.

SUGGESTED READINGS

Gibson, C.H., and Frishkoff, P.A.: Financial statement analysis, 2d edition, Boston, 1983, Kent Publishing Co.

Close analysis of financial statements; extremely technical; requires at least a basic understanding of accounting principles.

Viscione, J.A.: Flow of funds and other financial concepts, New York, 1981, National Association of Credit Management.

An easy-to-read text that presents income statements, balance sheets, funds flow analysis, and ratio analysis. Includes definitions of all terms well-illustrated with examples, and provides many important concepts.

CHAPTER 8

Profit and cost accounting techniques for commercial recreation

CHAPTER OBJECTIVES

1. To analyze financial documents to determine the soundness of an enterprise

2. To analyze and assess the financial stability and soundness of an enterprise

3. To identify the break-even point of a recreation business

4. To understand price elasticity

5. To understand pricing of a product or service

6. To know how to establish a price for a good or service

$\mathbf{N}$ow that you understand the balance sheet and the income statement, keep in mind that they are similar to a score card; that is, they tell whether you are winning (making money) or losing (not making money). As in any sport, once the game is over, the statisticians determine the box score, or how you actually did. This analysis takes place in three main steps: (1) identifying the players (establishing profit centers); (2) analysis of the game (ratio analysis); and (3) developing the strategy for the next game (pricing). Each of these concepts will be discussed in this chapter.

Profit center

In order to create profit centers, you must divide your business into its components. Examples of profit centers are park admission, the concession stand, gift shop, product lines and lodging (Fig. 8-1). Each is a unique entity, and each has certain costs and revenues associated with it. You must thoroughly analyze your business in order to identify specific profit centers.

Suppose you want to establish a profit center for the concession stand. First you designate the concession stand as a profit center. You treat it financially as a separate entity. This means you need to break down and analyze all costs associated with it.

The cost of all food for the stand is allocated strictly to the concession stand and all revenues from food sales there are identified specifically with it. Other costs associated with the concession stand are personnel and overhead.

Personnel costs are relatively easy to identify by assigning specific personnel to the concession stand and allocating their salaries to it. Overhead is somewhat different. It is necessary to take all general overhead costs—administrative expenses, advertising, office space, telephone, utilities—and allocate a portion of these to the concession stand. The easiest way to do so is to calculate the percentage of total revenues generated by the concession stand and assign that percentage of overhead to the concession stand. Share of total sales of any profit center determines share of total overhead. All administrative costs are split based on this percentage, and a portion allocated to each profit center.

There are other methods of allocating costs to profit centers. You can analyze

FIG. 8-1 One example of a profit center might include live entertainment at a theme park. A manager may define the performance as a single entity and charge admission. Another alternative would be to assign all of the costs to the food services in the area of performance. (Photograph courtesy Six Flags Great America.)

what is taking place at each operation by a negotiated or logical allocation of overhead costs to each unit. Once this is done, it is easy to see whether or not each profit center is performing up to the standards of the company.

This analysis must be done for each profit center.

Ratio analysis

An infinite number of ratios can be computed for any given balance sheet and income statement. Some are more informative than others. You can determine which ratios are the most important by breaking them down into four categories: debt, liquidity, profitability, and stock analysis.

The *debt ratios,* sometimes called the *leverage ratio* or *financial ratio,* reveal the extent to which a firm relies on borrowing to stay in business. These ratios are examined when a company tries to borrow money.

The *liquidity ratios* determine whether the firm has sufficient liquid assets to meet its current and long-term liabilities.

The *profitability ratios* are measures of the firm's ability to earn money and the effectiveness of the manager's ability to control expenses.

The *analysis ratios* are reserved for companies that trade publicly on the New York Stock Exchange or some smaller stock exchange. These ratios deal with the stock of the company and the return on investment. Since most recreation enterprises are not publicly traded, the analysis ratios are not necessarily relevant and will not be discussed in this text. The other three forms of ratios, debt, liquidity, and profitability, will be discussed.

An infinite number of ratios can be computed for any company, so the problem of which ratios are meaningful is extremely important. To identify the most important ratios, in 1981, under a grant from the Deloitte Haskins & Sells Foundation, Dr. Charles Gibson surveyed four major users and sources of ratios. These were the commercial loan departments in banks, bank loan agreements, corporate controllers, and statements of corporate objectives.

Gibson compiled a list of 59 financial ratios commonly listed in textbooks and the literature of various industries. These were sent to bank loan officers and to corporate comptrollers, who were asked to rate the top 10 ratios in each category. Table 8-1 shows the importance of the ratios to each category. The ratios are ranked by importance in each category, as is the primary measure of that ratio, such as debt, liquidity, and profitability. This list indicates 19 ratios that are probably the most common ones in use today. The remainder of this section will examine these ratios as they apply to World Travel, Inc. All of these ratios are computed using the financial documents presented in Chapter 7. These ratios will be examined in groupings to demonstrate the relationship between debt, liquidity, and profitability ratios. For illustrative purposes the balance sheet and the income statement are repeated in Tables 8-2 and 8-3.

TABLE 8-1. Most commonly used ratios

Ratio	Ranking by commercial loan dept.	Most common for loan agreements	Corporate controllers	Corporate objectives	Primary measure
Debt/equity	1	1	4	2	debt
Current ratio	2	2	10	4	liquidity
Cash flow/current maturities of long-term debt	3	4	—	—	debt
Fixed charge coverage	4	5			debt
Net profit after tax	5		3	5	profit
Times interest earned	6	6			debt
Net profit before tax	7		5	8	profit
Degree of financial leverage	8	7	—	—	debt
Inventory turnover in days	9	—	—	—	liquidity
Accounts receivable in days	10	—	—	9	liquidity
Dividend payout	—	3	8	6	*
Equity/assets	—	8	—	—	*
Cash flow/total debt	—	9	—	—	debt
Quick or acid test	—	10	—	—	liquidity
Earnings per share	—	—	1	1	profit
Return on equity after tax	—	—	2	3	profit
Return on total investment after tax	—	—	6	7	profit
Return on assets after tax	—	—	7	10	profit
Price/earnings	—	—	9	—	*

*Primary measure other than listed. Mostly used in stock analysis.

Debt ratios

Debt ratios were developed to determine three basic characteristics of a company: debt relative to equity, the ability to borrow money, and the ability to pay debts when they are due. Each is important to potential investors and lenders. Now we need to understand why to use debt to develop a company.

First, most people do not have sufficient capital to start a business without borrowing, so debt becomes an integral part of the company. Even if you are fortunate

TABLE 8-2. World Travel, Inc., balance sheet Dec. 31, 19X3

	19X3	*19X2*
Assets		
Current assets		
Cash	$ 450,000	$ 300,000
Securities	850,000	460,000
Accounts receivable	2,000,000	1,900,000
Inventories	2,700,000	3,000,000
Total current assets	$6,000,000	$5,660,000
Fixed assets		
Land	$ 450,000	$ 450,000
Building	3,800,000	3,600,000
Machinery	950,000	850,000
Office equipment	100,000	95,000
Gross fixed assets	$5,300,000	$4,995,000
Less accumulated depreciation	1,800,000	1,500,000
Net fixed assets	$3,500,000	$3,495,000
Prepayments	100,000	90,000
Intangibles	100,000	100,000
Total assets	$9,700,000	$9,345,000
Liabilities		
Current liabilities		
Accounts payable	$1,000,000	$ 940,000
Notes payable	850,000	1,000,000
Accrued expenses payable	330,000	300,000
Taxes payable	320,000	290,000
Total current liabilities	$2,500,000	$2,530,000
Long-term liabilities		
First mortgage bonds 10% interest due 19X5	$2,700,000	$2,700,000
Total liabilities	$5,200,000	$5,230,000
Shareholders' equity		
Capital stock		
Class A common: $100 par value; 6,000 shares authorized and issued	600,000	600,000
Class B common: $5 par value; 300,000 shares authorized and issued	1,500,000	1,500,000
Capital surplus	700,000	700,000
Accumulated retained earnings	1,700,000	1,315,000
Total stockholders' equity	$4,500,000	$4,115,000
Total liabilities and stockholders' equity	$9,700,000	$9,345,000

TABLE 8-3. World Travel, Inc., consolidated income statement Dec. 31, 19X3

	19X3	19X2
Sales	$11,000,000	$10,200,000
Cost of sales and operating expenses		
Cost of goods sold	8,200,000	7,684,000
Depreciation	300,000	275,000
Administration and selling expenses	1,400,000	1,325,000
Operating profit	$ 1,100,000	$ 916,000
Other income		
Dividends and interest	50,000	27,000
Earnings before interest and taxes	1,150,000	943,000
Less interest payments	270,000	270,000
Earnings before taxes	$ 880,000	$ 673,000
Taxes	414,000	302,000
Net income	$ 466,000	$ 370,000

enough to start a company without debt, at some time during its growth phase you will need to borrow money to pay for expansion.

The second reason for the use of debt is that it allows the owner of the company to improve the return on investment. This is known as leveraging. Any time you can make a higher return on someone else's money than you pay for it, you are increasing your rate of return on equity or investment.

These two factors are crucial to debt financing and are inherent in the creation of debt ratios. Now let's explain each debt ratio as it relates to World Travel, Inc.

Debt to equity ratio. The debt to equity ratio provides information concerning the relative positions of the owners and the creditors in any company. This ratio is easy to compute. Take the total debt of the company, which appears in the balance sheet as total liabilities, and divide it by total stockholders' equity. For World Travel the equation is as follows:

$$\text{Debt to equity} = \frac{\text{Total debt}}{\text{Stockholders' equity}} = \frac{5,200,000}{4,500,000} = 1.15$$

This ratio shows that the creditors of World Travel are slightly more involved in the company than are the stockholders, but by only 15%. A value of 1 would mean an equal sharing by creditors and owners. A value less than 1 would mean that the owners have invested more capital than the creditors. This value, 1.15, means that the creditors have invested approximately 15% more money in the company than have the owners.

Maturities of long-term debt. This ratio indicates how easily the company can pay off, out of cash flow, the portion of long-term debt due in a given year. In order to compute this particular value, first compute the cash flow of the company:

Cash flow = Net income + Depreciation

Depreciation is part of cash flow because it is a deduction that is allowed by the federal government to replace equipment. It is deducted prior to taxes and so represents funds available to the company.

Net income for World Travel is $466,000. Depreciation is shown on the consolidated income statement as $300,000. This amounts to a total cash flow of $766,000, which is divided by the maturities of long-term debt. This is somewhat hard to compute, since the balance sheet does not show what portion of the debt is due this year.

Assume, since the long-term debt is due over three years, that one third of it is due in 19X3. Dividing total long-term debt of $2,700,000 by 3 leaves a balance of $900,000 due in 19X3. Interest due on the total debt is $270,000 (10% of $2,700,000); $900,000 plus $270,000 equals $1,170,000, which is divided into $766,000 (cash flow) giving .655. This value indicates that cash flow is able to cover only approximately two thirds of the long-term debt due this year. World Travel is most likely going to have to obtain capital from some other source or reduce retained earnings to pay off its obligation for long-term debt in 19X3.

Note that these amounts are assumptions. It is very possible that World Travel has been allocating funds to one of its accounts to cover its principle payment. An obvious source of funds is the $850,000 of marketable securities. Even so, it is important to realize that the cash flow of World Travel is not sufficient to cover its current obligations and probably will not be until after the long-term debt is paid off in 19X5.

$$\text{Cash flow = Net income + Depreciation}$$
$$\$466,000 + \$300,000 = \$766,000$$

$$\text{Maturities of long-term debt} = \frac{\text{Cash flow}}{\text{Current maturities of long-term debt}}$$

$$= \frac{766,000}{\$1,170,000} = .655$$

Fixed-charge coverage ratio. This ratio determines whether a company can meet its interest and lease payments. Interest is the amount charged by lenders on loans. It can be found on the income statement as "interest expense." A lease payment is a form of loan in which the company has acquired an asset that it is paying for at a fixed amount per month. The main difference between a lease and a purchase is that at the end of the lease period the company does not own the asset. Interest expense and lease payments are treated the same when computing the equation for fixed charge coverage ratios:

$$\text{Fixed charge coverage} = \frac{\text{Profit before deducting interest, lease payments, and taxes}}{\text{Interest expenses and lease payments}}$$

We are interested in profit before taxes because both lease payments and interest expenses are deductible before taxes. Therefore, as they go up, they tend to lower the company's tax obligation.

World Travel's profit before deducting lease payments and taxes is shown on the income statement as earnings before interest and taxes and is $1,150,000. The denominator (interest expense plus lease payments) is the interest expense of $270,000 because World Travel does not lease any assets. Fixed charge coverage:

$$\frac{\$1,150,000}{\$270,000} = 4.259$$

This suggests that World Travel is in a very good position to pay off its fixed charge coverage, since before-interest profit is over four and a half times the amount needed in 19X3.

Times interest earned. This ratio determines how well the company is able to cover its interest payments from its earnings. The major difference between times interest earned and fixed charge coverage is the deletion of other income, or minority income (income from nonbusiness sources such as interest and investments) from the equation. The income statement shows that World Travel lists dividends and $50,000 of interest as other income. These sources of income are dependent on where and how the money is invested, so this amount can change substantially from year to year. The times interest earned ratio eliminates this variable and deals strictly with the earnings stream.

$$\text{Times interest earned} = \frac{\begin{array}{c}\text{Reoccurring earnings before interest}\\ \text{expense, tax, and minority income + the}\\ \text{interest portion of any rentals}\end{array}}{\begin{array}{c}\text{Interest expenses, including capitalized}\\ \text{interest}\end{array}}$$

$$= \frac{\$1,100,000 + 0}{\$270,000} = 4.07$$

In the case of World Travel, this means using the operating profit line of $1,100,000 (since interest received is zero) and dividing it by the interest payment amount of $270,000. The result, 4.07, indicates that World Travel is in a good position to cover its interest expenses out of earnings without the need for minority income.

Degree of financial leverage. Since interest expense is a measure of the extent to which a company is borrowing funds and leveraging its own profit upward, the financial leverage ratio is computed by dividing earnings before interest and taxes by earnings before taxes. This tells what percentage of total earnings is required to make the interest payment. World Travel's income before interest and tax is $1,150,000. Income before taxes is $880,000. Dividing the first by the second results in a ratio of 1.30, which indicates that the interest payment is approximately 30% of the total income of the company. Remember, it is important to take the interest out prior to the taxes, since interest payments are business expenses.

$$\text{Financial leverage} = \frac{\text{Earnings before interest and taxes}}{\text{Earnings before tax}}$$

$$= \frac{\$1,150,000}{\$880,000} = 1.3$$

Cash flow to total debt. This ratio determines how long it takes to pay off the total debt of the company. It is computed by dividing total cash flow by total debt. Cash flow is the sum of net income and depreciation. Total debt is the sum of current liabilities and long-term liabilities. For World Travel this amounts to $766,000 divided by $5,200,000, or .147, which interprets cash flow as 14.7% of the total debt of the company. If everything remains the same, it will take the company approximately seven years at the current cash flow rate to pay off its total liabilities.

$$\text{Cash flow to total debt} = \frac{\text{Cash flow}}{\text{Total debt}}$$

$$= \frac{\$766,000}{\$5,200,000} = .147$$

Liquidity ratios

The liquidity ratios are composed of the current ratio and the quick or acid test ratio, which measure a company's ability to pay its current obligations, plus inventory and accounts receivable ratios, which measure the ability of management to control its assets. Liquidity is a measure of how effectively management is controlling its short-term costs while covering ongoing expenses.

Current ratio. This ratio measures the extent to which current assets can cover current liabilities. The formula:

$$\text{Current ratio} = \frac{\text{Current assets}}{\text{Current liabilities}}$$

On the balance sheet total current assets and total current liabilities are clearly presented:

$$\frac{\$6,000,000}{\$2,500,000} = 2.4$$

This indicates that the current assets of World Travel can cover current debts slightly less than two and a half times. This is a fairly good current ratio.

Quick or acid test. This test, like the current ratio test, measures the company's ability to meet its current obligations. There is one major difference between the two tests. In the quick test, inventory is subtracted from current assets because when a company is in financial trouble, it is often impossible to liquidate the inventory rapidly at its full market value. The quick (or acid) test is a more conservative version of the current ratio.

$$\text{Quick or Acid test} = \frac{\text{Current assets} - \text{inventory}}{\text{Current liabilities}}$$

$$= \frac{\$6,000,000 - \$2,700,000}{\$2,500,000} = 1.3$$

World Travel still appears able to meet its current obligations, but its indicated ability to do so has dropped from almost two and a half times to approximately one and a third times, or approximately in half. This indicates that almost half of World Travel's current assets are tied up in inventory.

Inventory turnover. The inventory turnover in days is used to indicate two basic factors, the number of times a business sells out its inventory in a given year and the number of days it takes to sell the amount of inventory it is carrying. These two numbers can be used to determine whether the company is maintaining too much or too little inventory. Two figures are used to compute the inventory turnover ratio in days: inventory turnover and the number of days it takes to sell the average inventory.

$$\text{Inventory turnover} = \frac{\text{Cost of goods sold}}{\text{Average inventory}}$$

$$= \frac{\$8,200,000}{\$2,850,000} = 2.87$$

In computing the inventory turnover for World Travel, first determine the cost of goods sold from the consolidated income statement. For 19X3 the cost of goods sold is $8,200,000. The average inventory for 19X3 is computed by adding the inventory in 19X2 to the inventory in 19X3 and dividing by 2.

$$\frac{\$2,700,000 + \$3,000,000}{2} = \$2,850,000$$

The cost of goods sold is then divided by average inventory.

$$\frac{\$8,200,000}{\$2,850,000} = 2.87$$

This number indicates that in a given year such as 19X3, World Travel turned over its inventory 2.87 times.

Next, the portion of inventory sold per day can be computed by dividing 365 days by the inventory turnover:

$$\text{Inventory turnover in days} = \frac{365 \text{ days}}{2.87} = 127.1 \text{ days.}$$

This reflects the total number of days it takes World Travel to sell its entire inventory once.

Accounts receivable turnover in days. Accounts receivable turnover in days indicates the length of time required to convert credit sales into cash. This is a function not only of credit terms but of billing procedures, trends, and possibly industry averages, since World Travel is competing with other companies. This takes three steps: (1) compute daily sales, (2) figure average receivables, and (3) convert average receivables to receivables per day.

$$\text{Daily sales} = \frac{\text{Sales}}{365} = \frac{\$11,000,000}{365} = \$30,137$$

(Note: This bench mark can be used for the following year to determine how sales are progressing.)

Next compute average receivables. World Travel's accounts receivable for 19X2 were $1,900,000 and for 19X3 were $2,000,000. Add these together and divide by 2.

$$\text{Average acounts receivables} = \frac{\$1,900,000 + \$2,000,000}{2} = \$1,950,000$$

Last, divide average receivables by sales per day:

$$\text{Accounts receivable turnover} = \frac{\text{Average accounts income}}{\text{Sales per day}}$$
$$= \frac{\$1,950,000}{\$30,137} = 64.7 \text{ days}$$

This value shows that from the time of a credit sale it takes World Travel approximately 65 days to collect. This is an indicator of the effectiveness of the credit policy and billing procedures of the company.

If the credit policy of World Travel calls for accounts receivable to be paid in 30 days, we see that World Travel is in real trouble. If, on the other hand, its policy is to have accounts receivable paid in 60 days, World Travel is doing fairly well.

An adjunct to inventory turnover in days and accounts receivable turnover in days is the operating cycle. The *operating cycle* is the length of time it takes to convert inventory to cash. It is derived by adding the accounts receivable collection period in days to inventory turnover in days. This indicates how long the money must be borrowed, since it determines the entire money cycle from the purchase of inventory to the return of cash. For World Travel this is 191.8 days. The longer the operating cycle, the greater the need for permanent working capital.

$$\text{Operating cycle} = \text{Inventory turnover} + \text{Accounts receivable turnover}$$
$$= 127.1 \text{ days} + 64.7 \text{ days} = 191.8 \text{ days}$$

Profitability ratios

Profitability ratios help judge management's performance in two areas: controlling expenses and earning a return on the resources committed to the business. The majority of these ratios deal with return on investment, whether it is equity, assets, or sales.

Net profit margin after tax. This ratio reflects the tax effect on profitability and represents the final profit per dollar of sales. It is computed by dividing net income by company sales, both found on the income statement.

$$\text{Net profit margin after tax} = \frac{\text{Net income}}{\text{Sales}}$$

$$= \frac{\$466,000}{\$11,000,000} = .042$$

The profit margin of World Travel is 4.2%. On every dollar of sales World Travel will see a profit of 4.2 cents.

Net profit margin before tax. This ratio provides a more consistent basis for comparison because the tax rate of the United States is progressive. As a company makes more money, its tax rate increases. As a result, taxes can change ratios substantially. In order to compare companies in a given industry it is advisable to use the net profit margin before tax.

$$\text{Net profit margin before tax} = \frac{\text{Earnings before taxes}}{\text{Sales}}$$

$$= \frac{\$880,000}{\$11,000,000} = .08$$

This number is interpreted the same as the net profit margin after tax. The pre-tax profit of World Travel is about 8%, or 8 cents for every dollar of sales before paying taxes.

Earnings per share. Earnings per share is the amount of net income earned for each share of common stock during the accounting period. Earnings per share is calculated only on common stock outstanding. The balance sheet shows that there are two types of stock, preferred and common, outstanding for World Travel. Remember, preferred stock receives its dividends prior to common stock. To calculate earnings per share we must first know the dividend for preferred stock. Say the dividend for preferred stock in 19X3 was $5.16 per share. Since there are 6,000 shares of preferred stock, the total dividend paid to preferred stockholders was $30,960. In order to determine earnings per share, which is based on common stock, we use the following equation.

$$\text{Earnings per share} = \frac{\text{Net income} - \text{Preferred stock dividends}}{\text{Total common stock}}$$

$$= \frac{\$446,000 - \$30,960}{306,000} = \$1.36$$

Since Class A stock is both preferred and common, it is part of the total common stock. Earnings per share are important to the company's profitability, since they indirectly help set the stock price and are a measure of the return to the common shareholders of the company.

Return on equity after tax. This ratio measures the return to stockholders and represents their profits. When the return on equity is compared to the return on assets, an indication of the degree of financial leverage can be obtained.

$$\text{Return on equity after tax} = \frac{\text{Net income}}{\text{Stockholders' equity}}$$

$$= \frac{\$466,000}{\$4,500,000} = .104$$

This value indicates that the return on the money invested by the owners in World Travel is 10.4%. This value can be used to determine the relative worth of the investment. The stockholders will compare this return to other opportunities they can invest in—other businesses, stock options, bank deposits. Their return on the amount invested is 10.4 percent, and there may be other options that would provide a higher return. There are a number of other factors to be considered when determining whether or not an investment is worthwhile, such as appreciation in property values (which are not taken into account in the balance sheet) and the salary that the owner of the company, as an employee, may be drawing. However, return on equity after tax is a good indicator of the total return on the investment.

Return on total investment capital after tax. This ratio is used to determine the return on investment (or the total capital invested), including the amount borrowed, hence the effectiveness of the investment. The equation for return on total investment capital after tax assumes that the tax rate is known prior to the computation. For purposes of illustration, the tax rate for World Travel will be assumed to be 50%. This rate in all likelihood will vary given changes in government policies and company income.

$$\text{Return on total investment after taxes} = \frac{\text{Net income before minority share of earnings} + \text{interest expense} \times (1 - \text{tax rate})}{\text{Long-term debt} + \text{equity}}$$

$$= \frac{\$1,100,000 + \$270,000 \times 1\,(1-.5)}{\$2,700,000 + \$4,500,000}$$

$$= \frac{\$685,000}{\$7,200,000} = .095$$

This means that total return on the capital invested is about 9.5%. This is similar to the return on equity after tax. It is important to note the difference between the two values. If we are looking only at the equity, the return is about 1% higher. This is due to the leverage effect of the borrowed capital.

Return on assets after tax. This cumulative ratio reflects the total earning power of the company and how effectively its resources are used. Return on assets after tax is net income divided by average total assets. The reason for using average total assets is that in order to determine an accurate value of the total assets at any one time, we need to average the beginning and ending assets, as was done with inventory and accounts receivable turnover. The equation for World Travel:

$$\begin{aligned}\text{Return on assets} \atop \text{after taxes} &= \frac{\text{Net income}}{\text{Average total income}} \\ &= \frac{\$466{,}000}{(\$9{,}700{,}000 + \$9{,}345{,}000) \div 2} = .049\end{aligned}$$

The total return on all assets for World Travel is about 4.9%. When evaluating the ratio remember to take into consideration the appreciation of land and other assets in the company and any return to the owners in the form of salaries and employment.

General considerations with ratios

When you use ratio analysis to determine the efficiency, profitability, or debt ratio of a company, you must ask yourself, "What are good ratios and what are bad ratios?" The answer is "That depends." Ratios by themselves are useless. The ratios for World Travel were developed as an example of how to compute ratios. Out of context these ratios are useless.

How can we use these ratios to determine whether or not World Travel is a viable company? The answer to that is twofold. The most important use of ratios is in tracking changes over time. In order to see if World Travel is improving or having problems, compare the pertinent ratios over time to see how they change. The trend is what is important. If a ratio such as the quick ratio, which measures World Travel's ability to pay its current liabilities, decreases, World Travel may be heading toward financial problems. This is especially true during any attempt to borrow additional funds.

Another way to use ratios is to compare them for a given company to those of other companies in the same or similar industry. This can be done by obtaining ratios from any of these sources:
1. The Almanac of Business and Industrial Ratios (Prentice-Hall)
2. The Robert Morris Assoc. Annual Statement Studies (Robert Morris Assoc.)
3. Standard & Poor's Industry Surveys (Standard & Poor's Corp.)
4. Dun & Bradstreet Credit Services (Dun & Bradstreet Industry Services)
5. The Value Line Investment Survey (Value Line Corp.)

These are available in college libraries and sometimes in public libraries. They are valuable sources for ratios to analyze how effectively a business is run.

Ratios are also valuable because they project the future. Quite often companies use industry ratios to project financial statements into the future. This can be beneficial in determining whether or not a business undertaking is financially feasible.

Pricing

A key skill of commercial recreation managers is the ability to price products or services low enough that people will be willing to buy in a volume sufficient for profit and high enough to maximize that profit. This can be one of the most troubling aspects of commercial recreation. All too often commercial recreation managers set prices without giving any thought to the variables that need to be considered. The intent of this section is to enable you to approach a pricing decision intelligently and to set prices that will attract a large amount of business and make your enterprise profitable.

A theme park will provide an example (Fig. 8-2). This theme park is a major attraction and includes a food concession stand and ancillary services such as a gift shop.

You, as a manager, are concerned about whether or not your park is turning a

FIG. 8-2 Theme parks like this one have pricing problems, such as whether to charge one price for entrance to the park or separate prices for each ride. Each strategy must be evaluated and the decision must be reached in a logical manner. (Photograph courtesy Busch Gardens.)

good enough profit. In fact, you have some very strong suspicions concerning the productivity of some of your ancillary services. These service areas should be evaluated to see whether they are making a profit or losing money. If they are losing money, you may wish to change the ancillary services or the product lines. It is your job as manager to evaluate each operation within your theme park to see whether the prices of each item sold are appropriate.

These are some of the steps you need to take in order to determine whether or not the prices you have set are sufficient for profit.

Allocating costs

One of the most common methods of determining whether or not a profit center is producing properly is through break-even analysis. This is an attempt to identify at what volume, in units sold or in total sales, a particular profit center will make no profit or loss. Break-even analysis is extremely important in determining the prices of each item sold.

The break-even analysis can be divided into two parts: (1) classifying all expenses relating to the profit center into the various categories of cost, and (2) analyzing the findings to determine an optimal pricing structure and the number of units sold at which the profit center will break even.

Classifying costs. In any business costs associated with production can be broken down into three categories, fixed costs, variable costs, and mixed costs. Each category has unique characteristics that you must understand. Each kind of cost behaves in unique ways, and that behavior has a tendency to dictate what can and cannot be done in relation to pricing and cost controls. It is usually easier to control costs than selling price. Any manager has many methods of controlling costs, but the market dictates the selling price. It is extremely important to have a thorough knowledge of the types of costs involved in your enterprise.

Fixed costs. Fixed costs do not vary in relationship to the number of units produced. In most cases they are associated with the cost of doing business whether or not any product is sold. Some obvious examples include rent on a facility, advertising, and insurance. On a graph fixed costs are always a straight line that runs horizontally from left to right. A break-even analysis is always graphed using a vertical *y*-axis and a horizontal *x*-axis. The *y*-axis consists of a dollar value associated with some measure of production. This measure may be anything from hours of operation to the number of people visiting the enterprise to the number of units produced. These units are located on the *x*-axis. It is very important that the manager not feel constrained in the selection of the units to be measured in a break-even analysis. These units must be individually determined by some meaningful relationship to the business and the way in which the units will be used. There are no set values covering units of production.

Variable costs. Variable costs are associated with the direct production of a product or service and vary in a direct relationship with the number of units produced. Variable costs are always an upward-sloping line on the graph, moving left to right, indicating that as the number of units produced increases, the cost increases proportionately. This line is generally straight except in a few cases in which economies of scale come into play. The concept of economy of scale indicates that at some level of production a variable cost per unit may decrease due to manufacturers' rebates or a cheaper per-unit price or more efficient use of plant or labor. Economy of scale tends to skew the fixed costs line, but these differences are relatively minor and need not affect our assumptions. Variable costs are incurred by items that are used up in the production of the good or service.

Mixed costs. Mixed costs have some characteristics of both fixed and variable costs. Examples of mixed costs are utilities and telephone. The reason they are mixed is that most utility companies charge a fixed minimum rate for service. Once you have exceeded that minimum level, costs increase based on the amount consumed. Therefore utilities are truly mixed costs. Ideally, the most appropriate way to handle mixed costs is to split them into their respective fixed and variable portions and assign these portions accordingly. In reality this is too complex and time-consuming to be used very much, so the way mixed costs are treated depends on the manager. Each cost can be allocated either as fixed or variable depending upon the manager's judgment.

Examples of fixed and variable costs and the method of graphing each is provided in Figures 8-3 and 8-4.

FIG. 8-3 Fixed cost graph.

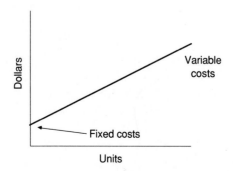

FIG. 8-4 Variable cost graph.

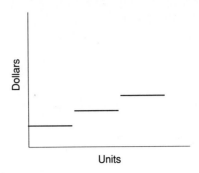

FIG. 8-5 Relevant range.

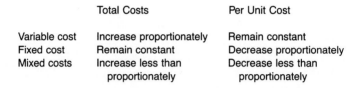

	Total Costs	Per Unit Cost
Variable cost	Increase proportionately	Remain constant
Fixed cost	Remain constant	Decrease proportionately
Mixed costs	Increase less than proportionately	Decrease less than proportionately

FIG. 8-6 Relationships between fixed costs, variable costs, and mixed costs.

The concept of the relevant period is an important consideration. Costs change from year to year or over increases in production units. A prime example is fixed costs as they change with increases in production or expansion of the facility itself.

When dealing with costs, either fixed or variable, it is important to keep in mind the concept of relevant range. This is the number of units and/or the period over which the costs have been analyzed and have been found to remain constant (Fig. 8-5). In addition, Figure 8-6 expresses the relationship among the three types of costs.

To illustrate, let's go back to our example of allocating cost to the concessions operation in our theme park. The box on page 217 shows the monthly concession stand income statement for July 31, 19X5.

A number of costs and sales are associated with this income statement. Notice that it follows the standard income statement format showing operating income and consequently it is relatively easy to break down each line item into variable, fixed, and mixed costs as shown in the box on p. 218.

It is important to understand the types of cost. The fixed category, including management and advertising, is there whether anyone buys anything from the concession stand or not. Part of these have been allocated to the concession stand because a certain percentage of the services provided by the organization benefit the concession stand. This is particularly true for legal, advertising, and management expenses. Equipment leases, taxes, and licenses are specific to the concession stand and must be borne whether or not anything is sold.

Labor and payroll deductions can be classified as mixed costs since once a business is open, it incurs a certain amount of labor costs. This begins as a fixed por-

Monthly concession stand income statement July 31, 19X5

Net sales	$3,300.00
Food	1,100.00
Paper	175.00
Total cost	$1,275.00
Gross profit	$2,025.00
Operating costs	
Labor	$ 570.00
Management	160.00
Payroll deductions	43.00
Advertising	160.00
Outside services	
Linen and supplies	70.00
Maintenance and repairs	33.00
Utilities	67.00
Office and telephone	7.00
Miscellaneous	10.00
Rent	285.00
Legal and accounting	58.00
Insurance	125.00
Taxes and licenses	40.00
Equipment leases	60.00
Depreciation and amortization	80.00
Total operating costs	$1,768.00
Net operating income	$ 257.00

tion, but as business increases and more people are purchasing goods from the concession stand, additional help is required—a variable cost. The same is true of utilities and maintenance. Some maintenance must take place even if nothing is sold, yet as use increases, maintenance costs increase.

Food and paper goods are variable costs. If nothing is sold, there is no need for the food, napkins, or packaging.

Break-even analysis

Once all costs have been identified, it is relatively easy to perform a break-even analysis by imposing the graphs over each other and including the sale price of each item as presented in Figure 8-7. Note that the fixed price is a horizontal line directly across the bottom and that variable costs start at the fixed cost line. The reason for this is that at zero units produced, there are no variable costs. At one unit of production, the total cost of that unit includes fixed costs plus variable costs. Therefore, the total cost is equal to fixed plus variable costs.

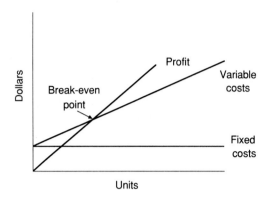

FIG. 8-7 Breakeven analysis.

Sales revenue is a straight line that slopes upward from left to right. Any point on this line represents the revenue generated from the sale of a specific number of units. The sales revenue line is computed by multiplying the number of units sold by price per unit. Therefore sales revenue is relatively independent of fixed and variable costs. The point at which the total cost line and the sales line intersect is the break-even point. If the number of units produced or sold falls to the left of the break-even point, the company loses money. If units sold falls to the right of the break-even point, the company makes a profit. Each of these is graphically illustrated in Figure 8-7.

It is important to note the amount of information available from the graph of a break-even analysis. It shows the relationship between units produced and costs and between profits and sales for a specific item. In order to clarify how break-even analysis takes place, we will return to the concession stand example and consider pricing and cost factors as they relate to one product, a bacon cheeseburger. The costs associated with the bacon cheeseburger are listed in the box on page 219, a

Examples of fixed and variable costs

Fixed	Mixed	Variable
Management	Labor	Food
Advertising	Payroll deductions	Paper goods
Insurance	Outside services	
Taxes and license	Utilities	
Equipment leases	Maintenance and repair	
Depreciation and amortization		
Office and telephone		
Miscellaneous		
Rent		
Legal and accounting		

Bacon cheeseburger cost analysis

Price	$1.25
Ingredients cost	
Meat	.22
Bun	.07
Seasoning	.003
Onion	.03
Mustard	.00
Ketchup	.008
Pickles (2)	.01
Bacon	.038
Cheese	.04
Mayonnaise	.01
Lettuce	.01
Tomato	.01
Wrapper	.01
Bag	.03
Total cost of ingredients	.539 = 43.2% of selling price

Bacon cheeseburger sales are 15% of total sales.
Daily fixed costs are $57.
Fixed costs allocated to bacon cheeseburgers $57.00 × .15 = $8.55

detailed cost analysis of one bacon cheeseburger. In reality a cost breakdown this accurate may not be possible. However, the manager estimates the cost of each item needed to produce the product.

We have established that bacon cheeseburgers account for 15% of total sales of the concession stand. Therefore, in order to establish the fixed costs associated with the production of the bacon cheeseburger, we have taken the operating costs from the box on p. 217, a monthly statement, and identified them as fixed costs for purposes of this illustration. They have been allocated on a daily basis to the bacon cheeseburger based on its percentage of total sales. This amounts to $8.55.

There are three basic techniques for establishing the break-even point. These are the graphic technique, the contribution technique, and the arithmetic, or equation, technique. Each will be discussed to determine the break-even point for the bacon cheeseburger.

Graphic technique. To demonstrate the graphic technique, we must first settle on the production units, which go on the horizontal axis. In this particular case the number of bacon cheeseburgers sold per day is the unit of production. The break-even analysis can be performed for any period, daily, monthly, yearly. Choosing the period establishes the scale for a break-even analysis.

We must first draw a fixed costs line. This is a horizontal line extending from $8.55 on the vertical axis horizontally across the graph. Next we must determine the variable costs of production. This is done on a range running from zero units to another perhaps arbitrary number of units produced. We will determine variable costs based on 30 units sold. The variable cost of bacon cheeseburgers at zero units is zero. Variable cost of the bacon cheeseburger at 30 units is 54 cents times 30, or $16.20, which is added to fixed costs of $8.55. We have now established two points on the variable costs line: $8.55 at zero units and $24.75 at 30 units. Variable costs are graphed as a straight line between these two points. (Fig. 8-8)

The remaining step is to graph the sales revenue, also a straight line running between two points. The first is zero units sold and zero sales revenue. In this case, the other is 30 units of sales. The two points for the sales revenue are zero revenues at zero units and $37.50 (30 times $1.25) at 30 units. A straight line between these points produces the revenue line. Extend the first line, which represents variable costs, from the y-axis at the fixed costs level to the point where total variable cost ($24.75) intersects with the number of units (30). Extend the second line, revenues, from zero/zero on the graph to the point where total sale amount ($37.50) intersects total units (30). The two lines cross at the break-even point, in this case about 12 cheeseburgers, or $15 (Fig. 8-8). Anything to the right of this point, as in the sale of 13 units, results in a net profit to the concession stand. Anything less than 12 units sold by the concession stand in any one day results in a loss.

Contribution method. The contribution method takes into consideration the portion of the sales price that contributes to profit and to fixed costs. Contribution per unit is defined as the selling price minus variable costs. In our example we have a selling price of $1.25 and a variable cost of 54 cents. Therefore our contribution per unit is 71 cents. We could also describe the contribution in terms of a ratio. The *contribution ratio* is the percentage of the sale price that covers fixed costs and profit. These two concepts are illustrated in the equations on page 221.

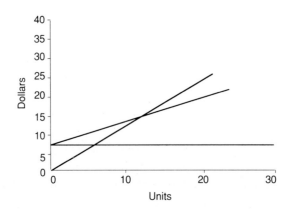

FIG. 8-8 Sales per day.

Contribution method

$$\text{Contribution per unit} = \text{Selling price} - \text{Variable costs}$$
$$= 1.25 \qquad\quad - .54$$
$$= .71$$

$$\text{Contribution ratio} = 1 - \frac{\text{Variable costs}}{\text{Sales price}}$$
$$= 1 - \frac{.54}{1.25}$$
$$= 1 - .432$$
$$= .568$$

The contribution per unit and the contribution ratio easily identify the break-even point. This can be done by determining either the number of units or the amount of sales needed to break even. If we are dealing with units, the equation is this:

$$\frac{\text{Break-even point}}{\text{in units}} = \frac{\text{Total fixed costs} + \text{Profit}}{\text{Contribution per unit}}$$
$$= \frac{8.55 + 0}{.71}$$
$$= 12.04 \text{ units}$$

The breakeven point for sales:

$$\frac{\text{Break-even point}}{\text{in sales}} = \frac{\text{Total fixed costs} + \text{Profit}}{\text{Contribution ratio}}$$
$$= \frac{8.55 + 0}{.56}$$
$$= \$15.03$$

It is interesting to note two things: First, if we multiply the break-even point in units by the sales cost, we get the break-even point in dollars. Therefore they are comparable in both cases. Second, profit in both cases was listed as zero, since at the break-even point we neither make nor lose money. However, if desired amount of profit had been determined, we could plug the profit into our equation and determine at what number of units or what number of sales we would reach our profit objective.

Equation method. The equation or formula method requires algebra. By looking at the breakdown of sales into variable expenses, fixed expenses, and profit, we can establish a simple equation in which sales equals variable expenses plus fixed expenses plus profit. If x equals the number of units required to break even, then the equation is price times x equals variable expenses times x plus fixed expenses plus profit. To determine the number of unit sales that would yield that particular profit use the following equation.

Equation method for the breakeven point in units

If x = Number of units to break even

Sales Price = Variable costs + Fixed costs + Profit

$$1.25x = .54x + 8.55 + 0$$
$$1.25x - .54x = 8.55$$
$$.71x = 8.55$$
$$x = \frac{8.55}{.71}$$
$$x = 12.04 \text{ units}$$

To determine sales in dollars at the break-even point, set sales in dollars equal to x and multiply by the percent of the unit sales price allocated to variable expenses:

Dollars

Sales in dollars = Contribution margin + Fixed costs + Profit

$$x = \text{Sales in dollars needed to break even}$$
$$x = .432x + 8.55 + 0$$
$$1x - .432x = 8.55$$
$$.568x = 8.55$$
$$x = \frac{8.55}{.568}$$
$$x = 15.03$$

The values obtained in all three methods are identical. The contribution and equation methods provide somewhat more accurate values, since they do not have to be read from a graph. Each method is extremely useful. The preferred method is left to the discretion of the user.

Special considerations. When considering these break-even analysis techniques, it is important to spend some time discussing the assumptions underlying each, since the violation of any of these assumptions may substantially affect the accuracy of the analysis. The assumptions associated with break-even analysis are as follows.

First, the behavior of revenues and expenses is linear (straight line) within the relevant range. (See Figure 8-5 for examples of relevant range.) This is a requirement due to the use of equations that represent straight lines. Sometimes figures such as total expenses or sales may deviate from a straight line, as with discounts for quantity purchases, either of your good by the public or of goods purchased by you from your supplier. This violates the straight-line assumption. It can be overcome by averaging the total costs or sale price for the units produced or purchased. Another method is to reduce the relevant range so that the sales and total expenses lines again become linear.

The second assumption requires the breakdown of expenses into fixed and variable categories. The mixed category cannot be used in break-even analysis; it must be allocated to fixed expenses or to variable expenses or split between them.

The third assumption relates to the productivity and efficiency of the operation.

The assumption states that over the relevant range there is no change in either efficiency or productivity.

The fourth assumption is that the sales mix remains constant. In the example we have used, the sales mix was the proportion of fixed costs allocated to the bacon cheeseburger. If we were to do a total break-even analysis for our concession stand, it would necessitate the development of variable costs associated with each product sold, such as hot dogs, soft drinks, and ice cream cones. We need to know what proportion of total sales is allocated to each item. This constitutes the sales mix, which remains constant in break-even analysis. The sales mix can be projected from past sales. We then figure variable costs by multiplying the percentage of each item sold from the concession stand by its associated variable cost. This provides a break-even analysis based on total dollar sales.

Assumption five states that the change in inventory levels from the beginning to the end of the period is insignificant. This factor is important if inventory has changed sufficiently that we need to restock and if these items have gone up substantially in price. For example, if we had been purchasing hamburger patties at 10 cents apiece and now they are 20 cents apiece, this substantially changes our breakeven analysis and violates the assumptions underlying it.

Pricing considerations

Pricing is a complex process in any commercial enterprise. Due to its direct relationship to the profitability of a firm, pricing has many varied components. Each component must be weighed with a logical approach to determine the maximum profit for the company while controlling costs.

Two factors relating to effective pricing are the identification of profit centers, which allows the manager to determine whether or not a specific portion of the business is profitable and priced correctly, and break-even analysis. How each contributes to the pricing process will be explained further in this section.

Pricing strategy combines five basic elements of the enterprise and the industry to form an effective and cohesive price structure. These components of business and industry:

1. The competitive structure of the industry
2. Price sensitivity
3. Cost structure of the firm
4. Legal and social considerations
5. Goals, position, and resources of the firm

Each of these will be discussed in detail.

Competitive structure of the industry. When discussing the competitive structure of the commercial recreation industry or an enterprise, economists have sorted competition into three basic categories, from least competitive to most competitive: monopoly, oligarchy, and open competition. The classifications describe the number of businesses in the marketplace at any given time.

The reason for the importance of the number of competitive firms in the industry is that as more firms compete, opportunities for controlling price decrease. In our cheeseburger example management policies affect the amount of competition the cheeseburger faces in the theme park. To establish a monopoly the manager would require that no outside food of any kind be brought into the facility. This would make it necessary for anyone wishing to eat to purchase food from the concession stand. This strategy needs to be carefully evaluated, since it might drive away potential customers of the park.

In an oligarchy people might be allowed to bring food into the facility but not to buy or sell food except at the concession stand. This produces relatively few competitors. Competition could be further limited by allowing people to enter the facility only once.

An example of open competition is allowing people to enter the park as many times as they want in a given day and having numerous fast-food outlets adjacent to the property. In this situation a customer has numerous food options and the unlimited ability to purchase goods from these outlets. The managers of the concession stand can do very little in relation to the pricing structure, since competition forces prices down. Assuming comparable quality and service, when there is competition, high prices send the customers elsewhere.

In an oligarchy, where there are relatively few competitors, there are usually price leaders. One company can affect the pricing of the entire industry simply by changing its own price. Since our concession stand is on the property, we are in a position to be a price leader for food services in the park. This is because the concession stand is conveniently located. People would be less inclined to carry in outside food if our prices were competitive. We would then be able to establish pricing strategies that would effectively create an increased demand for our product and force competitors (if our business is sufficiently large) to meet our price.

The final category is monopoly, or virtually no competition. This does not arise in commercial recreation, since true monopolies in the United States are limited to utility companies, whose prices are regulated. However, in a true monopoly you would be able to set your own price. It would be wise for you to realize that if the profits are sufficiently large, numerous other companies will be enticed to enter the business.

The ability of competitors to enter the market is limited by barriers to entry, or factors that make it difficult or expensive for competitors to enter your market. Barriers can be high start-up costs or legal issues such as copyrights and patents. You may want to set the price somewhat lower than the market would bear simply to make it harder for competitors to enter the market.

The easiest way to differentiate your product from its competitors is by offering additional products or services. Service is the factor most often used. It allows you to create something unique and different about your product simply by providing additional benefits to the purchaser. This may be additional sales help or unique product aspects. In our cheeseburger example, we may want to add a special sauce or unusual garnishes.

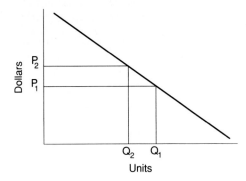

FIG. 8-9 Elastic demand.

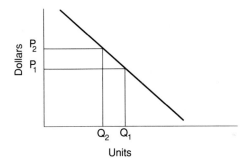

FIG. 8-10 Inelastic demand.

Price sensitivity in commercial recreation. Before attempting to discuss the price sensitivity of total industry demand or of demand for an individual firm, we need to define "price sensitivity." Demand is sensitive if volume increases or decreases substantially when prices are changed slightly. This is *elastic demand.* Conversely, if demand is affected little by price, it is *inelastic.* Fig. 8-9, a graphic representation of elastic demand, shows the number of units sold along the horizontal axis and the price along the vertical axis. The gentler the slope of the demand curve, the more elastic the demand. This can be seen by looking at the difference between P_1 and P_2. As price changes from P_1 to P_2, there is a substantially larger difference in demand from Q_1 to Q_2. This illustrates the elasticity of demand, since the change in quantity desired has decreased much more sharply than price increased.

Conversely, Fig. 8-10 illustrates inelastic demand. The polar axes of the graph are identical to those in the elastic demand graph, but the line sloping from left to right is much steeper. This indicates inelastic demand. It is illustrated by selecting two prices, P_1 and P_2, and looking at the difference in Q_1 and Q_2. It is easy to note that as the price changes, demand changes slightly, making this an example of inelastic demand.

This relationship can be expressed in the following manner:

$$\text{Price elasticity} = \frac{\text{\% changes in quantity demanded}}{\text{\% change in price}}$$

$$= \frac{(Q2 - Q1)/(Q2 + Q1)}{(P2 - P1)/(P1 + P2)}$$

This ratio has further implications for pricing. If the ratio is greater than one, demand is said to be elastic. This means that the percentage change in quantity purchased will vary more than the percentage change in price. If the value is less than one, demand is said to be inelastic; that is, the percentage change in quantity sold will change less than the percentage change in price.

Suppose we are considering changing the price of a bacon cheeseburger from $1.25 to $1.35 and we anticipate that the quantity sold will change from 20 per day at $1.25 to 19 per day at $1.35. We use this equation:

$$\text{Price elasticity} = \frac{(19 - 20)/(19 + 20)}{(1.35 - 1.25)/(1.35 + 1.25)}$$

$$= \frac{-1/39}{.1/2.6}$$

$$= \frac{-.026}{0.038}$$

$$= -.684$$

The final value of $-.684$ indicates that for every 10% increase in price, we should expect a 6.8% decrease in the number of bacon cheeseburgers sold. This equation allows us to make some intelligent decisions concerning the quantity demanded versus the price. Then we can generate a new break-even analysis to see how the change in price, and the resulting change in demand, will affect total sales.

In realistic situations the demand curve can be hard to establish. The easiest way is to find comparable products or services offered by competitors and plot each competitor's price and quantity sold on a graph similar to that in Figure 8-9. When all of the points are plotted, draw a line that best represents them. Once this is done, you can choose two prices and their corresponding quantities and compute price elasticity. This is only a rough estimate of the demand curve and the elasticity of demand. This technique should be used with caution, since it merely shows direction and a rough measure of magnitude of the change in demand for any given change in price.

Price elasticity is difficult to determine because of changes in environment, competition, and other elements of the marketing mix. The effect of price change on consumers often occurs after a time lag. Be sure to use the numbers derived from elasticity analysis as a guideline only, since there can be substantial anomalies.

Total industry demand. Price sensitivity of industry demand is very volatile, depending on many factors: importance to the consumer, saturation of need for the product, income profile of consumers, existence of substitute products or services, and segmentation of the market.

Certain purchases are very important to consumers; food, for example. In recreation many theories indicate that once a person becomes interested in a specific activity, that activity tends to become very important in that person's life and therefore be purchased in preference to other products.

In the amusement park example, the food at the concession stand may not be very important to customers. However, drinks could be very important, since the park is outdoors, heat can be oppressive, and thirst is harder to ignore than hunger. Therefore, it may be important to consumers to obtain some form of cool liquid refreshment but not necessarily bacon cheeseburgers. This is critical in pricing drinks at the concession stand. Less important items may be very sensitive to price; slight changes in price may produce relatively large changes in quantities purchased.

A second factor, perceived saturation, relates to the amount of a good or service that a person is using. For the entire amusement park the saturation point for visits may be once per month. If this is true and each person comes once a month, it would not do any good to reduce the price, since we have reached a consumer saturation point. Visitors would not be willing to increase attendance at our park even at a lower price.

A third factor, the income profile of consumers, relates directly to commercial recreation, which offers a vast number of products and services geared specifically to upper income classes. Given that market segment—individuals with a large disposable income—it is easy to see that a small price change may not significantly affect demand. This segment of the population can afford to purchase goods at a higher price. This needs to be taken into consideration when pricing the product.

A fourth factor is the existence of substitutes. Any type of commercial recreation, such as our outdoor amusement park, competes with all other forms of commercial recreation. The existence of many other recreational activities in a specific area could substantially affect pricing for entrance fees to our amusement park. Examples of other competition are bowling alleys, roller-skating rinks, and swimming pools.

A final consideration when dealing with the price sensitivity of industry demand is market segmentation. Pricing decisions are based on current or desired market share. Suppose we wished to increase our market share. We might lower prices to increase sales. Various market segments or subclasses of consumers attending our park may have different price sensitivities. If it is possible to differentiate in some way among market segments in relation to pricing, it is to our benefit to do so. Possibly we could charge lower-sensitivity customers a higher rate, while customers with higher sensitivity pay a lower rate. An example of this in our amusement park would be to use group prices. Groups are more sensitive to price than individuals. We could charge groups a lower rate and still maintain a higher rate for individuals.

When total industry demand is highly elastic (a ratio greater than 1), it may be beneficial for an industry price leader, someone with advantage over his competitors in a oligarchic industry, to start a downward price spiral. This may increase the number of people attending the facility or using the service and thereby increase total revenues at a lower margin per sale. A move of this nature may result in higher profits by increasing number of sales.

The individual commercial recreation business. Price sensitivity for the total industry is the relationship of the price to demand for the product. Price sensitivity for the individual firm can be discussed in the context of the percentage of the total market a particular commercial recreation enterprise has at any one time and how it can increase its share of the market. Market share can be increased through one of three methods.

The first is by differentiating its product through feature, style, durability, or some other tangible or intangible aspect. This could be any number of tactics, including but not limited to increased service, follow-up, serviceability of the contract, decor, and location.

The second is through promotional offerings. It is sometimes possible to acquire a premium on the purchase price by increasing the amount of advertising and thereby creating an increased demand for the product or service.

Third is the perceived status of the commercial recreation activity. In a high-service outlet a quality approach is taken and a premium is placed on service. Ways of accomplishing this are through design of the facility, ample service personnel, and the prestige given it. This can be accomplished when the product or service is offered in a very limited number of locations that are designed to attract an elite clientele. An alternative to this is a high-volume approach: the good or service is distributed through a large number of outlets, commanding a smaller margin of profit on each item while increasing the number of sales taking place.

It is impossible to determine price sensitivity for an individual commercial recreation enterprise without taking into consideration the effect of a price change. To do this first analyze the firm's marketing mix, including all aspects of the business as it relates to the customer. This is particularly true in a market with strong competition. Any drop in price will be followed by competitors as they attempt to maintain their market share, while any price rise could result in a substantial loss of market share unless there are additional services or perceived benefits associated with it. The sensitivity of demand for an individual commercial recreation enterprise is very difficult to establish and in most cases is not determined except by long-term analysis.

Cost structure. Earlier in this chapter we discussed various ways of computing the break-even point. It is important to note that the relationship of fixed costs to variable costs is also important to pricing. However, this is not the only technique, but merely one of several to use in setting a price for a given commodity. Cost figures, fixed or variable, are valid only during the period analyzed. There is nothing to indicate that fixed or variable costs will remain constant. They are simply historical trends that need to be analyzed to determine how they will affect long-term profitability.

The input for the cost structure portion of the pricing strategy should consist of three measures: (1) the ratio of fixed to variable costs, (2) the economy of scale available, and (3) costs relative to those of the competitors.

Ratio of fixed to variable costs. Once the variable and fixed costs have been identified and break-even analysis has been computed, it is easy to establish the relationship between variable and fixed costs. A company with high fixed costs and low variable costs is volume-sensitive. In this instance the easiest and most effective way to increase profit is to increase sales volume. Once fixed costs are covered, everything between total costs and the sale price is profit.

The opposite is high variable costs and low fixed costs. This situation is termed *price sensitive*. The major method of increasing profitability of price-sensitive enterprises is by raising the selling price of the product. In this case fixed costs are covered at an earlier stage, and profit is still the difference between total costs and the selling price. This is achieved at an earlier stage, increasing the profitability for the sale of additional items.

In general, commercial recreation can be assumed to be volume-sensitive. For our bacon cheeseburger fixed costs are relatively high in comparison to variable costs, typical in commercial recreation.

Economies of scale. *Economy of scale* is the ability to produce goods at a lower price given a higher volume. This may be owing to price breaks for higher quantity purchase. It relates directly to lower variable costs of providing the good. If economies of scale are available, much higher production results in lower costs per unit, allowing for a reduced price, which should increase sales volume.

Low cost position. The manager of a recreation enterprise who is producing a similar-quality product or service at a lower cost than the competitors is in a very advantageous position. The manager may very well want to reduce prices sufficiently to command a large share of the market. Since costs of producing the good are less than the competitors', if they reduce prices to match, they will be making less profit per item. If they do not reduce their price, the manager will be able to increase market share substantially, allowing an increase in productivity and profitability.

Legal and social considerations. The recreation manager may want to establish differential pricing for different classes of customers. The most obvious is quantity versus individual sales. If an individual or group is willing to buy goods or services in bulk, it stands to reason that they should be able to purchase at a lower price. One policy relating to pricing for different groups is to recognize the differences in services provided, operation costs, and the quantities of purchases. These are legitimate reasons for cost reductions. However, a manager must be careful when offering differential pricing so that it cannot be construed as discrimination against some specific group. The main consideration in this is the Robinson/Put-man Act of 1936. Under this law price discrimination is legal under certain circumstances such as meeting the price of a competitor in good faith or if the price differential is based on a lower selling cost or lower number of services provided.

Under no circumstances should competitors get together to set the price for goods or services. This is illegal and will be prosecuted.

A further concern is legal constraints placed on the sales of goods. If a manager sells a good and not services, in some states there may be fair trade laws or minimum sale prices as dictated by law. These vary from state to state, and you need to research laws in your state.

In addition to legal issues, there are many social issues relating to price. These considerations are of utmost importance to the commercial recreation manager. Since recreation may be viewed as being the right of all people, the cost factor for various minority populations can have significant social consequences on a commercial recreation enterprise. It is important that the manager firmly establish policies and guidelines to deal with these segments of the population. This allows for reduced conflict at later times, when public criticism could become substantial.

Goal, position, and resources. The goals of a recreation enterprise may include an attempt to secure a certain portion of the market share. The manager may determine that the best approach is to establish a lower entry price in an attempt to lure a portion of the market away from existing competitors.

Another goal could be to skim the high end of the market by offering something unique and by attempting to make a big profit early. This usually entails reducing the price when market saturation has been reached. Other goals may include establishing a strong social image for the company. This may reap lower profits while providing socially acceptable services to lower-income or minority populations.

The goals of the company have a definite role in pricing strategy. Quite often municipal recreation enterprises intend to provide recreation at little or no cost. This can substantially affect their pricing strategy. However, municipal recreation agencies have increasingly come under attack, not only from taxpayers who see them as wasting money, but from commercial recreation enterprises who see them as unfair competition due to lower prices.

The position of a recreation enterprise within the industry is of extreme importance. If it is considered to be the leader or the elite, that enterprise should price accordingly, that is, charge a higher price. If your company is a new business entering a highly competitive industry, it may need to be content with meeting the average price and differentiating the product with some services. This would eliminate the possibility of starting with too low a price and creating attention for yourself among your big-market competitors, who might lower prices to drive you out of business. Therefore your position in relationship to the overall market is important.

The third and final consideration is the resources of your firm. These resources can include but are not limited to financial resources, physical resources, and the talent of the managerial staff. These resources can be meager or extensive. If they are extensive, particularly financial resources, you may want to use a low-price strategy for an extended period in order to drive the competition out of the area or to establish a substantial market share. Remember, however, it is always wiser to cut prices than to raise them.

Pricing for services

Pricing for the services sector quite often follows the majority of the rules discussed in the product portion of this chapter. However, there are some interesting differences. For example, the break-even point must be calculated using fixed costs. Variable costs are personnel costs associated with producing the service. This is somewhat tricky because certain personnel costs must be allocated to administrative expenses, namely, the minimum staff required when work is not being produced. However, an attempt should be made to hold these administrative costs to a minimum.

Another pricing approach is to use a cost-plus method, wherein the costs associated with operation are all treated as fixed costs. The amount of time to complete the project or service should be established. A profit margin is added to fixed costs, and the total becomes the selling price. The selling price is a horizontal line paralleling the fixed costs line. In most cases services are billed on a per-hour or per-job basis. It is important that the manager accurately estimate the total amount of time it takes to complete a project. He multiplies that time by personnel and supplies costs. The cost per hour is based on the competitive structure of the industry, taking into consideration who the competition is, what services are provided by the competition, the differences between competing services and yours, and the ease of entry into the industry. These variables may be treated differently when dealing with services. Each of these differences is explained below.

Industry and consumer price sensitivity. In some services demand can be very inelastic. An example is environmental impact statements associated with a development on government land. In other cases demand for the service is very elastic. An example of this is a feasibility study. In spite of the importance of this process, many entrepreneurs opt not to complete one, much to their later chagrin.

Cost structure of the firm. A service firm is a highly fixed-cost entity, and this needs to be taken into consideration when setting prices. This type of business requires large volume to be profitable.

Goals, position, and resources of the firm. If you are attempting to break into a service business and if you have substantial resources, you can set prices lower and establish yourself in the industry.

This briefly outlines the ways in which pricing of services differs slightly from pricing for products. It is important to note that pricing and marketing go together and one affects the other. They are separated for clarification.

Methods of increasing profits

In profitability of a commercial recreation enterprise there are only two factors to manipulate, cost and price. The following methods of manipulating cost and price can be effective in increasing profits. Each will be discussed as it relates to the technique being applied, the expected outcome of that technique, and the underlying assumptions, so that you may determine whether or not they are effective for any given situation. These six techniques:

1. Reduced costs
2. Raised price
3. Reduced price
4. Raised costs
5. Improved marketing
6. A combination of the above.

Reduced costs

One of the most common ways of increasing profitability is through reduction of costs. There are three ways: (1) to reduce fixed costs, (2) to reduce variable costs, and (3) to establish economies of scale.

Since most commercial recreation enterprises have heavy fixed costs, this may be the best method of increasing profitability. Ways to lower fixed costs include lowering the rent, using more energy-efficient sources, making sure that water and power are not wasted, looking at the facilities for the operation of a given commercial recreation enterprise and attempting to reduce these, and reducing the variables associated with production (Fig. 8-11).

The main method of reducing variable costs is purchasing goods in quantity. Most suppliers give quantity discounts. However, this can result in a storage or shelf-life problem, so you must be careful to assess the desirability of large-scale purchases. Another method of reducing variable costs is by paying your suppliers

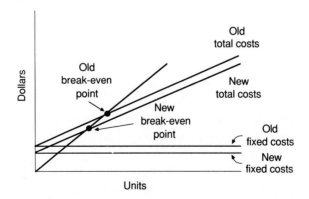

FIG. 8-11 Lowering costs—the effect on the break-even point.

earlier to take advantage of the discount for early payment. Be careful about this; the cost of money to pay the bill early may exceed the discount.

The third method of reducing cost is by taking advantage of what are called economies of scale. Suppose one cook can produce zero to 100 bacon cheeseburgers in an hour. At 30 bacon cheeseburgers per day the labor cost associated with total production of cheeseburgers does not change. This is common in recreation and service enterprises. There are economies of scale between the minimum one employee can handle and the maximum, since the costs associated with that increase will not change. This provides a variable-cost curve.

The major factor when attempting to determine whether to reduce production costs is whether sales will be unaffected. That is, reductions in cost should not significantly affect the quality of the product or service.

Raise the price of the product. One way to increase profit is to increase the price. This increases the *margin,* or sale price minus total cost. For each unit the margin increases by the increase in price. The assumption associated with increasing the product price is inelastic demand. We anticipate that people are willing to pay a higher price because there is a strong demand for our good or service (Fig. 8-12).

Reduced price. If we attempt to increase profitability, the option of reducing price does not seem obvious. However, with elastic demand and a slightly lower price the number of products sold may increase substantially. If the total units sold increase, we make a smaller profit on an increased number of units. This often increases profits, since a small profit on a substantially larger quantity is better than a larger profit on a very small quantity (Fig. 8-13).

Increased costs. As in the previous example, it does not seem logical to increase profitability by increasing costs and leaving the selling price alone. However, an increase in cost may result in an increase in the quality of the product or service provided. Given this improvement in the product or service, sales may well increase because of the better price/value relationship. This makes the product or

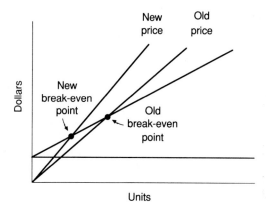

FIG. 8-12 Raising prices—the effect on the break-even point.

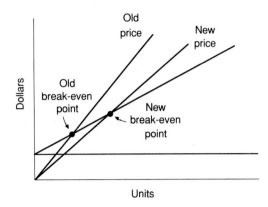

FIG. 8-13 Lowering prices—the effect on the break-even point.

service more desirable, increasing demand and total quantity sold, provided the improvement is sufficient to offset the increased price. We have then established our goal of increased profitability for the company (Fig. 8-14).

Improved marketing. This results in an increase in fixed costs. However, if we increase the desirability of the product through increased public awareness or the penetration of a new market, we can logically anticipate increased demand. This should result in more units sold at the same price, thereby increasing profits— again, provided the increased demand outdistances the increased cost (Fig. 8-15).

A combination of the above. Anything is possible when dealing with the variables of price and cost. These combinations are too extensive to discuss at this stage. However, keep in mind the assumptions underlying the previous five methods of increasing profits. If more than one of these is valid in your case, combine them.

General considerations in pricing

Listed below are a number of considerations that the commercial recreation manager should keep in mind when setting a price. Not all of these are valid in all cases, but keep them in mind.

1. Each pricing case must be carefully judged in relation to the competition, price sensitivity, the cost structure and resources of the firm, legal and social considerations and goals, and a good strong dose of common sense.
2. Assuming that supply and demand remain equal, it is not wise to cut prices just because the competition does. Instead, provide new services and/or find a new market.
3. Take into consideration the value of services over and above their cost.
4. The price charged should be a function not of the cost but of the value and benefits perceived by the end user.
5. Remember, service is the difference between success and failure, and it can be charged for.
6. Go slow when dropping prices. They are easy to lower but difficult to raise.

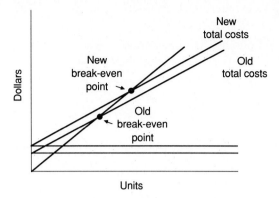

FIG. 8-14 Increasing costs — the effect on the break-even point.

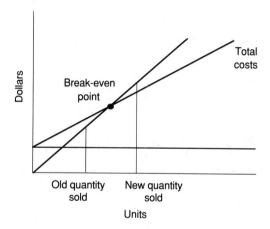

FIG. 8-15 Improving efficiency — the effect on the break-even point.

7. Set your price based on what the market will bear, not on cost alone.
8. For the sake of flexibility it is sometimes better to reduce price by using coupons or cents-off promotions than by reducing prices across the board.
9. It is better to raise prices by small amounts a number of times than by one large increase.
10. Pricing based on cost is easiest to compute. However, this eliminates opportunities for additional profit.
11. It is easy to reduce prices, but it is much more effective to develop new services to maintain your price.
12. Set prices for a new product or service low enough to make competing market entry very difficult.
13. People expect to pay an additional price for extra services.
14. Let the customer rather than the cost establish the value of the product when determining price.
15. It is a good idea to be slow to lower prices and quick to raise them.
16. There is no such thing as an obscene profit.

Summary

Profit centers and pricing strategies are of extreme importance to any commercial recreation business. They enable the manager to determine whether a specific component of his business is profitable. This is done by setting up that component as a profit center. Once this is done, a pricing analysis can determine the fixed and variable costs for that component as well as the break-even points in both volume and sales.

Then the manager can do a detailed analysis of the prices in light of the competitive nature of the industry. Then he must determine price sensitivity, or elasticity or inelasticity of demand.

The manager must evaluate the cost structure of the firm and determine whether it is price sensitive or volume sensitive. Legal and social considerations must be met, and the goals, position, and resources of the individual firm must be identified. These factors must be integrated to provide an overall pricing strategy. Once this is done various methods can be used to increase profitability. Among these are reducing costs, raising prices, reducing price, improving services, improving marketing, or some combination of the above.

Ratio analysis is used to determine liquidity, or the ability of a business to borrow more money, and indebtedness, or the extent to which that business is using other people's funds.

Funds management ratios determine how well the investors' money is being used. Profitability ratios are specifically designed to measure various returns, either before or after taxes. Profitability can be based on equity sales or borrowing.

BIBLIOGRAPHY

Armstrong, J.S.: Long-range forecasting: from crystal ball to computer, New York, 1985, John Willey & Sons, Inc.

Barron, M., and Targett, D.: The manager's guide to business forecasting: how to understand and use forecasts for better business results, New York, 1985, B. Blackwell.

Butler, W.F., Kavesh, R.A., and Platt, R.B., editors: Methods and techniques of business forecasting, Englewood Cliffs, N.J., 1974, Prentice-Hall, Inc.

Dougherty, C.: Interest and profit, London, 1980, Methuen.

Financial Forecasts and Projections Task Force: Guide for a review of a financial forecast, New York, 1980, American Institute of Certified Public Accountants.

Goodman, S.R.: Increasing corporate profitability: financial techniques for marketing, manufacturing, planning, and control, New York, 1982, John Wiley & Sons, Inc.

Hausman, D.M.: Capital, profits, and prices: an essay in the philosophy of economics, New York, 1981, Columbia University Press.

Migliaro, A., and Jain, C.L.: Understanding business forecasting, Flushing, N.Y., 1984, Graceway Publishing Co.

Milne, T.E.: Business forecasting: a managerial approach, New York and London, 1975, Longman.

Stephens, R.: Uses of financial information in bank lending decisions, Ann Arbor, Mich., 1980, University of Michigan Research Press.

Wheelright, S.C., and Makridakis, S.: Forecasting methods for management, New York, 1985, John Wiley & Sons, Inc.

Woelfel, C.J., and Mecimore, C.D.: The operating executive's guide to profit planning tools and techniques, Chicago, 1986, Probus Publishing Co.

SUGGESTED READINGS

Bailey, E.L., editor: Pricing practices and strategies, New York, 1978, Conference Board, Inc.

This small paperback deals with pricing for consumer and industrial markets. Each section provides information ranging from common fallacies in pricing to legal pitfalls. Discusses cost considerations and the influence of pricing on retail purchases. An excellent overall textbook.

Bergfeld, D.C.: Strategic pricing: protecting profit margins from inflation, New York, 1981, American Management Associations.

A simple, well-written pamphlet covering pricing basics. Included are discussions of the effect of factoring inflation into pricing modes and of direct cost pricing.

Gibson, C.H., and Frishloff, P.A.: Financial statements analysis, 2d edition, Boston, 1983, Kent Publishing Co.

Detailed analysis of financial statements including the use of ratios. Not for the nonspecialist.

Meier, G.M., editor: Pricing policy for development management, Baltimore, 1983, Johns Hopkins University Press.

A compilation of articles on pricing. The strength of this text is in public policy and prices, markets and development.

Monroe, D.B.: Pricing: making profitable decisions, New York, 1979, McGraw-Hill Book Co.

Simply written text, very applicable to commercial recreation. One section deals with pricing and demand and the use of internal costs in pricing. Other sections cover administrative decisions for pricing and special topics such as return on investments, competitive bidding, and price differentials.

Palmer, J.E.: Financial ratio analysis, New York, 1983, American Institute of Certified Public Accountants.

A management advisory aid on ratios used for analysis. Tables deal with ratios, formulas, and interpretations. Also provides comparison ratios and a sample balance sheet. Easy to read, suitable for lay readers.

Viscione, J.A.: Flow of funds and other financial concepts, New York, 1981, National Association of Credit Management.

Easy-to-read text presents funds flow analysis, ratio analysis, definitions of terms. Well-illustrated with examples; provides several important concepts including inventory pricing.

Viscione, J.A.: Analyzing ratios—a perceptive approach, New York, 1983, National Association of Credit Management.

Ratio analysis text provides specific chapters on each type. Detailed analysis of ratios with excellent explanations.

One of the biggest challenges any business faces is expansion. As a business ex-pands the drain on capital for inventory is substantial. It is at this time that a man-ager must be adequately aware of business ratios. The correct ratios can provide a manager with clues on how to regain original profitability. Closely associated with this concept is the idea of pricing. If a manager is attempting to penetrate a new market the pricing strategy is different than that of an established store. Suburban Sportswear provides an excellent example of each of these elements. As you work through the case note the different strategies at each stage of the company's de-velopment.

Suburban Sportswear*

Policy determination for a retail chain

"When I started this business I had a pretty good idea of what I wanted it to be-come," declared Steven Ridgeway, president and sole owner of Suburban Sportswear. "In the less than three years since that time I've upgraded many of my former goals and even discarded a few. Now after we appear to have successfully fought off our first ma-jor crisis I'd like to sit back and evaluate the courses open to a business such as this. Certainly there are problem areas in our operation which need attention now, but we can't lose sight of our long range objectives while meeting operational problems."

Steven Ridgeway's business consisted of a chain of seven stores, located from Santa Monica to San Diego in Southern California, which retained medium priced women's sportswear and casual dresses. The merchandise was of department store quality and price and included such brands as Jantzen, Cole of California, Jonathan Logan, and Ko-ret of California. There was no doubt that he had developed a successful business, one whose sales had skyrocketed from approximately $20,000 during its first nine months of operation in 1958 to over $300,000 in 1960. Ridgeway foresaw gross sales of one half a million dollars for 1961.

Steven Ridgeway's background

Good luck appeared to have very little to do with the success of Suburban Sports-wear. Rather it was a result of well thought out plans and adequate finances combined with Mr. Ridgeway's unusual amount of experience for a person in his early thirties. It was at least five years before he started his business, that he began planning in New York for the type of stores he wanted and the ideal location for them.

*Reprinted with permission of the Stanford University Graduate School of Business, 1961 by the Board of Trustees of the Leland Stanford Junior University.

In 1946, after attending a New England prep school and serving two years in the armed forces, Ridgeway entered New York University to major in business administration. Two and a half years later, with diploma in hand, he joined the Executive Training Program of one of the large national department store chains. He chose to work in one of the chain's smaller stores in the East, one doing about $5,000,000 in annual sales. He believed that wider experience could be gained there than in the larger stores. One year later, Ridgeway was the dress buyer for the store.

"It was actually quite accidental that I became the buyer," he stated. "The dress department was poorly run, and one day a vice president of the store came in, fired the buyer, and selected me for his place. It wasn't difficult to show an improvement in the department because of the shape it was in."

By 1951, Ridgeway had accepted a job in a larger department store doing about $50,000,000 a year. During the five years that he remained there as a buyer he built his departments up from $1,500,000 to $2,000,000 a year gross sales. It was during this period that Mr. Ridgeway decided that someday soon he wanted to be in business for himself, and conceived the idea of setting up a group of women's stores in a growing area such as the West Coast. He felt the time was not quite right, though, and while he had been gaining a great deal of retailing experience, he realized that he had a lot to learn about the operation of a retail chain.

In 1955, Ridgeway received an offer to become Southern California District Manager for one of the largest nationwide chains of inexpensive women's apparel. He accepted, and at age 30, found himself with a bright future in a large organization, a comfortable home in West Los Angeles, and a salary of $25,000 a year. However, he still wanted to enter business for himself, and saw this job only as a means of broadening his retailing experience. He felt fortunate, too, that this position was in this particular geographic area.

The beginning of Suburban Sportswear

By 1958, Mr. Ridgeway concluded that the time was about right to take the necessary steps to open his first store. His steps, however, were to be cautious ones at first. Although he had been saving a good part of his salary, he had his family responsibilities to consider. In addition, he anticipated that the operation would not be large enough at first to require all of his time.

In May of 1958, unknown to his employer, Ridgeway opened the first Suburban Sportswear store in Santa Monica, located on the coast just outside the Western city limits of Los Angeles. This site was selected because it was in a middle-class shopping district with adequate parking facilities and was expanding rapidly with new homes and apartment buildings.

Ridgeway continued to work full-time at his regular job but spent evenings, Sundays, and holidays with his own venture. He generally worked until midnight or early in the morning performing all the major functions for a retail store. His only help at first was the sales personnel; part-time clerical help was added as needed. Mr. Ridgeway, who drew no salary, did all the buying, planning, and supervising of the store's operation.

Suburban's receiving warehouse and office occupied a small area in the rear of the Santa Monica store. This store soon gained customer acceptance, and the company was breaking even financially after the first eight months, during which sales were over $20,000. Since Ridgeway had originally hoped for a chain of stores with annual sales of $50,000 each, he was more than satisfied and a little bit surprised at the initial performance with this one. The profit and loss statement covering this period appears in Exhibit A.

Mr. Ridgeway opened his second store in March of the following year. He had already studied the Southern California area and selected several sites which would be suitable for his type of store. It was really only a question of which area to enter next, and Ridgeway decided on Santa Ana. This city was the largest one in Orange County, which was the fastest growing county in Southern California. In this case Suburban Sportswear was located in a new shopping center, outside of the downtown area. Almost immediately the new store gave indications that it was going to be more successful than the Santa Monica operation.

By the summer of 1959, the pressures of Ridgeway's time had become increasingly heavy and were expected to become even greater. He realized that even when he devoted his full time to this business, which had to come soon, he would still not be able to run it efficiently by himself. Mr. Ridgeway saw the operation as including many small stores spread over all of Central and Southern California and concluded that there was room in the business for another person, probably a full partner. In the Santa Monica store sales promised to far surpass the $50,000 annually which he had expected after the store had reached its full potential. He anticipated also that Santa Ana would attain a $50,000 sales mark in its very first year. A third store was planned for a November opening in Manhattan Beach.

In September, Ridgeway approached a friend, Alan McFarland, about joining him in his venture. McFarland worked for the same firm as did Ridgeway and held a comparable position in the San Francisco office. Since he was quite interested in Ridgeway's offer, the two started working together under an informal agreement late in the same month. McFarland, whose job in San Francisco did not require working on Saturdays, would fly to Los Angeles on Friday night, spend the weekend working on Suburban Sportswear, and make the 400-mile return trip on Sunday night. The third store was opened in November and Suburban Sportswear sales during 1959 were over $130,000. Only one of the stores had been open during the entire year, one since March, and the third had been in operation less than two months. Financial statements for the year appear as Exhibit B.

March, 1960, saw the opening of the Woodland Hills store in the San Fernando Valley section of Los Angeles County and plans were made to open three more during the year. Now, with four stores, the operation required more than a part-time effort, and both men realized that they would have to devote all of their time to the business. As a result, on April 1, 1960, Suburban Sportswear was incorporated and both Ridgeway and McFarland gave notice to their employer. McFarland had only $10,000 to invest, so Ridgeway agreed to take a note for $30,000 and capitalize the business with $20,000, each owning exactly 50%. Exhibit C shows the financial statements which were drawn up at the time of incorporation, prior to recording McFarland's $10,000 investment.

By way of explanation, Ridgeway said, "I don't know what made me give up half the business on those terms. I guess I just figured that I couldn't run the corporation without Al's knowhow and help."

In the following months, store number 5 opened in the town of Ontario. Number 6 in Oceanside began operations in August and number 7 in Redlands started in November of 1960. The eighth Suburban Sportswear shop was opened at the beginning of 1961 and was located in a San Diego shopping center.

Problems after incorporation

Up until the time of incorporation, the only real problem which faced Mr. Ridgeway was the amount of time required to manage the three stores compared with the hours he had available. He continued to perform all that was expected of him in his regular job and spent his entire free time in Suburban Sportswear activities. His employers were unaware that he had been managing three noncompeting stores in addition to his regular job.

After both Mr. Ridgeway and Mr. McFarland had resigned and the company had been incorporated, the organization began to experience the typical aches and pains of a new and growing business. One of the reasons the company had not lost money during its first two years of operation was the comparatively low overhead it had had to absorb. The only nonselling salaries paid had been to one part-time bookkeeper and one part-time receiving clerk, each working 20 hours per week. Ridgeway, of course, drew no salary. After the fourth store opened, however, the company needed both a full-time and a part-time receiving clerk, a full-time bookkeeper, and a full-time person to run the warehouse. In addition both Mr. Ridgeway and Mr. McFarland were now dependent on the company for income. Each began drawing $1,000 a month salary, about one half of what they had been receiving. Space requirements had increased and the warehouse and office had been moved to a separate location. Also, 10-year leases had been signed for the fifth and sixth stores which were to open soon.

With these higher expenses the two soon faced the additional burden of disappointing sales in the stores at Manhattan Beach and Woodland Hills. These two stores gave early signs that they would reach the $50,000 annual sales mark when they matured, but that this was the highest they would go. Although this conformed with Ridgeway's original goal, there was no longer room in his plans for stores of this type.

"Why," reasoned Ridgeway, "should I be satisfied with that, when the first two stores have already doubled the figure and haven't stopped growing yet?"

Because of the disappointing sales Ridgeway sold the Woodland Hills store near the end of 1960 and was considering the same course of action for the Manhattan Beach store. He now felt that if it was clear that a store would not reach sales of about $100,000 within a few years, it should be sold so long as no contractual commitments were ignored. The inventory would then be placed in a new store and put to more profitable use.

The two men decided to specialize and divide up the work. McFarland was to be the inside man doing the buying and inventory planning, although his experience had been in buying a cheaper line of merchandise. Ridgeway was to take charge of store problems including new store locations. When they dealt with a large manufacturer, such as Jantzen, the two of them worked together. By September 1960, the firm had shown that it could absorb the increased expense of new store openings and executive salaries as Suburban Sportswear had broken even to that point. This was a favorable sign because the expected large fourth quarter would enable them to show a nice profit.

At this point, however, a new problem which had been building up since the spring made its presence known. The inventory had reached a level which the business under its current financial position could not support.

"Al was an excellent planner," stated Ridgeway, "but he just couldn't live with it. He made fine decisions as to what we were to buy and how much, but our inventory always seemed to end up much higher than that. And it wasn't because our sales weren't high enough, because they were even higher than we had anticipated."

Ridgeway believed the inventory in September should have been about $100,000 to $110,000 at retail to support the level of sales which should be forthcoming. Instead they were at a level of $180,000. Whereas the company had relied on practically no bank credit before this time it was now forced to seek help in the amount of a $40,000 loan. His goal was that once a store's sales reached a level of $100,000, its inventory should turn at least five times during the year. On the other hand, a growing store which had annual sales of only $50,000 would require an inventory of perhaps $13,000 to enable it to have enough stock to increase sales.

In September and October, sales were very good but November 1960 was disappointing for the entire industry. It looked as though the company would be unable to make its complete scheduled payments to the bank. Meanwhile store number 7 (now the sixth store) had just opened.

"Al got panicky," commented Ridgeway, "And I must admit that even though I didn't think the bank particularly wanted to run some ladies dress shops, I was a little uneasy myself."

Mr. Ridgeway concluded at this time that he could run the business by himself and do better than the two of them had done. Although they remained on friendly terms they found themselves in heated arguments more and more often. And these discussions generally centered around the inventory problem. He decided during the first week in December to offer McFarland his original investment back out of his own personal funds so as not to put further strain on the business. Mr. McFarland quickly accepted the $10,000, parted amicably, and returned to San Francisco. There he was greeted with open arms by his former employer and given his old job back at the same salary.

While Mr. McFarland's troubles appeared to have ended, Ridgeway was faced with bailing-out the business of which he was now sole owner. To him the most pressing problem was reducing the inventory to a level which the business could support. The bank gave him a generous extension and Ridgeway proceeded with what he considered to be the only solution. During December, in the midst of the peak season, he marked down much of his merchandise. Sales during the month totaled an impressive $70,000 but he had to take $10,000 in markdowns to do it.

By the end of 1960 Suburban Sportswear's inventory had been worked down to a safer level, but the items were all fall goods, whereas Ridgeway believed that the stock should have contained about half new spring clothes. Further markdowns were necessary, therefore, to reduce this inventory while building a spring line, since additional goods had been received from previously placed orders. During the first quarter of 1961, Ridgeway took markdowns totaling $25,000 to move $100,000 worth of merchandise at retail, while efficient apparel retailers would be taking around a 10% markdown during the first part of the year. Financial statements for the 9 months of 1960 since incorporation appear in Exhibit D.

Reasons for growth

Regardless of the problems that the company had experienced, Steve Ridgeway could look back on an enviable record of sales in the short time since Suburban Sportswear had been initiated. To him this record was a result of a combination of the following factors: location, store layout, nature of the clientele, sales personnel, chain operation, and their merchandising policy.

Ridgeway had decided long before that his stores would be located either on the West Coast or in the Southwest. It was in these areas that he believed customer acceptance would come the fastest.

"I didn't want to wait the rest of my life time for New Englanders to finally get around to shopping at my store," remarked Ridgeway. "In California there is a constant migration of people into the area. These people have not yet developed strong shopping preferences, and it would not be as difficult to draw them to a new store."

He determined that any one of four types of locations would be attractive to him, and actually had stores in three of these classifications by 1961. One type was the small community center location similar to the Santa Monica and Redlands stores. The Santa Ana and San Diego stores were in the second type, that of a regional shopping center, while the Ontario store was in the third class which consisted of a small town in which Suburban Sportswear would be the dominant fashion store. The fourth type, one which Ridgeway had not yet entered, was the downtown area. He was reluctant to establish a store in this type of location unless there were a lot of working women in the area. Downtown areas even in smaller towns would be avoided unless there were office buildings and, hence, secretaries, because women working in offices were likely customers for his merchandise. Ridgeway insisted that his stores be large enough and the merchandise arranged in such a manner so as to be uncluttered. Customers had easy access to the large assortments on display as all items were hanging with nothing stacked on counters.

From the beginning, Suburban Sportswear catered to three types of customers: working girls, school girls, and young housewives. The assumption was made at all times that the average customer was a young intelligent woman who possessed a good knowledge of fabrics and workmanship. This type of customer, reasoned Ridgeway, resented sales pressure. As a result, sales were conducted on an informal basis with no "pushing" on the part of the salesgirls. In addition, every attempt was made to have the same type of person as a salesgirl as were the customers. Stores were located in areas where there would be schoolgirls and young housewives who would desire part-time work.

Each store had a manager who received, as a bonus, 1% of the store's sales paid weekly. All the personnel were instructed to take back any items with which the customer was not happy, no matter how old or in what condition it was in. "We've probably been taken advantage of a few times because of this," stated Ridgeway, "but I believe it has paid off in the long run by removing one objection which some women have against trading in a small store."

As soon as the second store opened, Suburban Sportswear had one big advantage it didn't have before—it had the nucleus of a chain. Mr. Ridgeway was firmly convinced that the fact that he had more than one store was definitely in his favor. He preferred seven scattered stores doing $500,000 a year in sales to a single store doing the same amount because an unusual event in one area, such as an opening of a new shopping center, will not be as damaging if a business is not completely dependent on that area. Suburban Sportswear achieved a degree of flexibility that the single store did not have. Perpetual inventories were kept and Ridgeway knew almost constantly what each store had in stock. Then, for example, if the weather became particularly warm in Santa Ana and the demand increased for bathing suits, he could transfer part of the stock from another to it. If certain types of dresses went over particularly well in Ontario and not in San Diego, he could pull them out of San Diego and into store number 5.

From the beginning the stores' merchandising policy was set and it had never waivered. The stores carried women's sportswear and casual dresses only. In the usual case when a store reached the size of the Santa Monica or Santa Ana store it would add items such as lingerie, maybe some shoes, toiletries, and perhaps a small children's line. Suburban Sportswear had none of these items and did not intend to. Rather, if it concentrated on sportswear and casual dresses, each store's inventory would have such depth and variety that it could compete with anyone on these lines. Ridgeway was convinced that a woman in Southern California could go into one of his larger stores and find as much of a selection in his line as she could in the Broadway or the May Company Department Stores.

Advertising was done almost exclusively in newspapers which circulated in the areas which the stores served. Only on rare occasions would Ridgeway use one of the Los Angeles metropolitan papers. With the addition of the San Diego store, the Los Angeles coverage would be reduced. In the Spring of 1961, Suburban spent close to $400 on a mail order ad in the Southern edition of *Sunset* magazine. No indication had yet been received as to its effect.

Current operating problems

Mr. Ridgeway, as mentioned earlier, had current problems. The necessity of maintaining a level of inventory was only part of the whole area of cost control. Retailers generally started with a markup of 45% on the average. Ridgeway expected that with reasonable control of both cost and markdowns each store could show a net profit of 10% of sales, but in 1960 administrative and selling expenses totaled about 40%, which left little profit after markdowns.

By the end of the first quarter of 1961, Ridgeway believed that he had reduced his expenses to about 25% of sales, and looked forward to keeping his markdowns at a level no higher than 7% of sales.

In addition, Ridgeway was satisfied his inventory control methods produced accurate data from which to make decisions, but he wanted to develop a simpler and more efficient way to do it. Each day, the stores sent into the office a report of the day's sales. This reported the number of each item sold by size, style, and color. These reports were consolidated and entered on price line and style page reports every week. This process enabled Suburban Sportswear to reorder fast selling merchandise quickly and transfer or markdown slower moving items. These reports were also used for future inventory planning.

The same type of situation was true for his receiving warehouse. Items for all the stores were received at one location in West Los Angeles. Here the items were checked against the orders, marked, and made ready for distribution. While this assured an accurate check on all merchandise received and sent, it took a great deal of time and required extra transportation costs.

While Ridgeway was faced with the problem of keeping costs under control, he was also in need of additional personnel. A brief description of some of his duties might indicate the reasons. Mr. Ridgeway's working day usually began at 7:00 or 7:30 each morning when he arrived at his office. During the morning he reviewed inventory control records for each unit and made notes of what items required marking down or transfer from one store to another. This was done about three times a week. He would then get the sales figures up to date, review buying orders, and adjust sales forecasts. After going through the mail, Ridgeway would check the allocation of the incoming goods to each store.

On two mornings each week he would see salesmen in his office. By one o'clock in the afternoon, he generally was out of his office and on his way to visit the stores. He spent at least four hours and often eight hours per week in each store doing such jobs as rearranging the merchandise and generally supervising the activities. This would take him until about 7:00 each evening or 10:00 or 11:00 if the stores were open late.

Once each week Mr. Ridgeway went into downtown Los Angeles to see sportswear suppliers. For the same reason, he spent about two days each month in San Francisco and Portland, and he also went to New York for a week about five times a year to see dress suppliers.

Mr. Ridgeway confessed that although he could use additional help at the present time he wanted to wait until the business could better absorb the expense. He was thinking of the time when he could afford a profit sharing plan for all of his employees. He stated that, to him, a business was only as good as the people who made it up, and everything possible should be done to obtain the best personnel available. "If a business is successful," he reasoned, "the people in the organization should also be successful. I've seen too many companies where people are treated as numbers and not as individuals. And this will not be the case with Suburban Sportswear no matter how large we become."

The future of Suburban Sportswear

When Steven Ridgeway looked to the future he could not help feeling that Suburban Sportswear's chances for increased profits and sales were excellent. He wasn't sure, however, along what course he should follow.

"I know one thing," he emphasized, "my original plan of having 10 to 20 stores doing $50,000 annually each is outdated. With my objective of turning inventory five times each year at retail value, it wouldn't take much more than $5,000 additional cost in inventory to generate $100,000 in sales than to get $50,000. And I will insist on and get a 10% return on these sales."

Mr. Ridgeway wanted the future to be as free from debt as possible, and eventually hoped not to rely on bank credit at all. This was not going to be an easy goal to reach. Each new store opened cost about $15,000 of which $11,000 represented additional inventory and $4,000 was for fixtures. In addition, apparel manufacturers customarily granted terms of 8/10 E.O.M. which made penalties for slow payments high.

Perhaps his major concern once the immediate problems were taken care of was to determine just what size the company should aim to be and how fast it should expand.

On one hand he could attempt to keep full ownership in his own hands and take a rather slow deliberate course of expansion. Or he might attempt to have the company become publicly held sometime in the future.

Ridgeway felt that following the former course, he could reach sales of 2.5 to 3 million dollars per year within the next 10 years. Even with additional help, this would require the better part of his time and energy. On the other hand, if Suburban Sportswear issued stock to the public, Ridgeway could make a nice capital gain and diversify his own investments. He reasoned that he could still maintain active control of management and lead the corporation to sales of at least $10,000,000 with a statewide chain. These were long-range decisions but ones which he felt he must plan for now.

When asked what he would do if the business failed, Mr. Ridgeway answered: "I would retreat to one store if I had to and build that one back up again to where it was profitable. I've had a good taste of running my own business and I'll never go back to working for someone else."

EXHIBIT A

Suburban Sportswear statement of income and expenses
April 1, 1958 to December 31, 1958

Sales		$ 21,193.28
Cost of sales		
Inventory—April 1, 1958	$ —	
Purchases	19,065.17	
Freight	169.79	
	$19,234.96	
Inventory—Dec. 31, 1958	4,610.50	
Cost of sales		14,624.46
Gross profit		$6,568.82
Expenses		
Rent	$ 2,160.00	
Auto and travel	532.00	
Utilities and telephone	375.79	
Payroll taxes	115.11	
Office supplies	154.45	
Depreciation	609.17	
Salaries and wages	2,327.70	
Supplies	129.91	
Advertising	126.72	
Repairs and maintenance	295.26	
Legal and accounting	219.00	
Insurance	244.06	
Miscellaneous	370.86	
Total expenses		7,660.13
		$(1,091.31)
Other income and (expense)		
Purchase discounts	$1,312.66	
Sales discounts	(295.98)	1,016.68
Net income		$(74.63)

EXHIBIT B

Suburban Sportswear balance sheet December 31, 1959

Assets

Current assets:

Cash—change fund	$ 75.00	
Cash—in banks	15,456.38	
Accounts receivable	111.00	
Inventory	30,296.40	
Prepaid interest	275.04	
Total current assets		$ 46,213.82

Fixed assets:

Furniture and fixtures	$ 5,680.73	
Leasehold improvements	7,144.26	
Automotive equipment	3,250.00	
	$ 16,074.99	
Less accumulated depreciation	3,110.28	
		12,964.71

Other assets:

Guarantee deposit	$ 208.00	
Prepaid rent	1,236.00	
		1,444.00
Total assets		$ 60,622.53

Liabilities

Current liabilities:

Accounts payable	$ 12,333.38	
Payroll and sales taxes payable	3,034.21	
Equipment purchase contract	2,177.84	
Customers' deposits—layaways	324.00	
Total current liabilities		$ 17,869.43

Capital

Balance—January 1, 1959	$ 20,014.05	
Contribution 1959	2,500.00	
Net income	20,239.05	
Balance—December 31, 1959		42,753.10
TOTAL LIABILITIES AND CAPITAL		$ 60,622.53

Sales:		$131,717.00
Cost of sales:		
Inventory—January 1, 1959	$ 4,610.50	
Purchases	106,130.00	
Freight	1,083.51	
	$111,824.01	
Inventory—December 31, 1959	30,296.40	
Cost of sales		81,527.61
Gross profit:		$ 50,189.39
Expenses:		
Rent	$ 6,468.80	
Auto and travel	735.43	
Utilities and telephone	2,048.45	
Taxes and licenses	187.09	
Payroll taxes	914.03	
Office supplies	226.75	
Depreciation	2,501.11	
Salaries and wages	15,672.38	
Supplies	1,013.39	
Advertising	3,087.75	
Repairs and maintenance	757.79	
Legal and accounting	690.00	
Insurance	933.15	
Dues and subscriptions	193.00	
Interest and bank charges	294.70	
Miscellaneous	327.46	
Total expenses		36,051.28
		$ 14,138.11
Other income and (expenses):		
Purchase discount	$ 7,581.03	
Sales discounts	(1,480.09)	6,100.94
Net income:		$ 20,239.05

EXHIBIT C

Suburban Sportswear balance sheet April 1, 1960

Assets

Current assets
Cash—change fund	$ 171.00	
Cash—in banks	7,182.90	
Inventory	45,369.96	
Prepaid interest	206.28	
Total current assets		$52,930.14

Fixed assets
Furniture and fixtures	$ 6,623.44	
Leasehold improvements	8,413.94	
Automotive equipment	3,250.00	
	$18,287.38	
Less accumulated depreciation	4,068.96	$14,218.42

Other assets
Lease deposit	$ 1,436.00	
Other guarantee deposits	208.00	
		$ 1,644.00
Total assets		$68,792.56

Liabilities

Current liabilities
Accounts payable	$23,738.50	
Payroll and sales taxes payable	2,305.46	
Equipment purchase contract	1,944.50	
Total current liabilities		$27,988.46

Other liabilities
Loans payable—officers		30,804.10

Equity
Equity to be exchanged for capital stock		10,000.00
		$68,792.56

Sales		$38,261.92
Cost of sales		
Inventory—January 1, 1960	$30,296.40	
Purchases	38,280.63	
Freight	477.11	
	$69,054.14	
Inventory—March 31, 1960	45,369.96	
Cost of sales		23,684.18
Gross profit		$14,577.74
Expenses		
Rent	$ 2,631.38	
Auto and travel	262.78	
Utilities and telephone	812.42	
Taxes and licenses	62.00	
Payroll taxes	283.25	
Office supplies	123.35	
Depreciation	958.68	
Salaries and wages	6,805.64	
Supplies	682.27	
Advertising	659.85	
Repairs and maintenance	271.23	
Legal and accounting	565.00	
Insurance	239.77	
Dues and subscriptions	153.00	
Interest and bank charges	163.01	
Miscellaneous	210.24	
Total expenses		$14,883.87
Other income and (expenses)		$ (306.13)
Purchase discounts	$ 1,993.73	
Sales discounts	(312.60)	1,681.13
Net income		$ 1,375.00

□
EXHIBIT D

Suburban Sportswear balance sheet December 31, 1960

Assets

Current assets

Cash	$ 12,314.56	
Accounts receivable	1,019.35	
Inventory	84,922.33	
Prepaid expenses	206.28	
Total current assets		$ 98,462.52

Property, plant and equipment, at cost

Furniture and fixtures	$ 19,912.11	
Leasehold improvements	13,867.47	
Automotive equipment	3,250.00	
Office equipment	669.70	
	37,699.28	
Less accumulated depreciation	6,268.96	
		31,430.32

Other assets

Lease deposits	1,321.00	
Guarantee deposit	208.00	
		1,529.00
		$131,421.84

Liabilities and shareholder's equity

Current liabilities

Note payable, Security 1st National Bank	$ 40,000.00	
Accounts payable	27,067.33	
Accrued wages	1,695.67	
Equipment purchase contracts	1,244.48	
Payroll and sales taxes payable	7,705.86	
Total current liabilities		$ 77,713.34

Long term debt

Note payable, leasehold improvements	$ 5,940.00	
Loan payable, stockholder	26,024.50	
		31,964.50

Shareholders' equity

Capital stock:	20,000.00	
Common stock, 200 shares outstanding		
$100 par value		
Retained earnings	1,744.00	
		21,744.00
		$131,421.84

Sales		$281,442.58
Cost of sales		
Inventory—April 1, 1960	$ 45,369.26	
Purchases	222,312.76	
Freight	2,780.69	
	270,462.71	
Inventory—Dec. 31, 1960	84,922.23	185,540.38
Gross profit		95,902.20
Operating expenses		
Selling expense, (see schedule)	73,837.30	
General and administrative expense		
(see schedule)	37,021.57	
		110,858.87
		$ (14,956.67)
Other income discounts earned		16,923.63
Net income		1,966.96
Officer's life insurance premiums		222.96
Retained earnings—December 31, 1960		$ 1,744.00
Selling expenses		
Advertising		$ 6,987.76
Salaries and wages		36,288.33
Rent		16,086.65
Utilities and telephone		3,780.80
Payroll taxes		2,243.06
Taxes and licenses, other		905.85
Supplies		969.24
Maintenance and repairs		1,751.70
Depreciation		2,850.00
Charge-plan expense		1,973.91
		$ 73,837.30
General and administrative expenses		
Accounting and legal		$ 1,441.82
Auto and travel		3,087.53
Insurance		2,584.19
Interest and bank charges		1,247.63
Miscellaneous		479.22

Office expense	503.78
Office and loft salaries	9,328.23
Officers' salaries	11,600.00
Payroll taxes	1,046.41
Dues and subscriptions	505.50
Entertainment and promotion	457.97
Management expenses	450.00
Loft and office rent	510.00
Utilities and telephone	1,192.64
Loft supplies	2,606.65
	$37,021.57

Definitions

Markdown. The amount of reduction taken on an item as a percentage of the sales price.

8/10 E.O.M. An accounting shorthand term meaning that an 8% reduction in price is available if the total bill is paid in 10 days. If the bill is not paid in 10 days the full amount is due at the End Of the Month.

Questions

1. What ratios do you think are needed to evaluate the changes taking place in Suburban Sportswear? Why are these ratios important to the case?
2. Compute the ratios identified in question #1 for each year in the case. What observations can you make from this information? When should Mr. Ridgeway have noticed the inventory problem?
3. What steps do the ratios indicate are needed to solve the problems in the case? Make specific recommendations to resolve the issues.
4. Identify both the fixed and variable costs associated with Suburban Sportswear. What is the breakeven point based on these costs?
5. What impact have Mr. Ridgeway's pricing policies had on the success of his business? What pricing strategy do you feel Mr. Ridgeway has been following? Is it time for a change? If so, to what?

CHAPTER 9

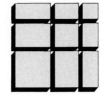

Marketing the commercial recreation enterprise

CHAPTER OBJECTIVES

1. To understand the role of marketing

2. To understand what a market segment is and how to identify it

3. To know the difference between service and product marketing

4. To understand the components of product marketing

5. To understand the components of service marketing

Have you ever been faced with a major purchase decision such as which pair of skis to buy or whether to take tennis lessons? How did you decide?

Someone who needs a new pair of skis could have decided to take up skiing and so needs the equipment, or heard of a new, more interesting model, or found that a world champion skier used that brand. Would any of these factors influence your decision?

In considering tennis lessons, our purchaser might do some analysis. Whom to take lessons from? Why take lessons in the first place—to acquire a lifetime activity that gives enjoyment, or perhaps for social mobility?

Whatever the reason, there is a similarity in the decision-making process. The first step is to recognize the fact that something important is lacking. Next is to obtain information about the chosen item. The last step is to acquire the item.

The idea of marketing is to facilitate this process. Marketing can be defined as the process by which individuals and organizations exchange services or goods for the purpose of satisfying their desires. Implicit in this definition are the exchange itself and the process that leads to the exchange. A third process is the satisfaction of human wants.

Consider these three components as they relate to the marketing of commercial recreation.

Exchange process

In any type of exchange five elements must be present:
1. The possessor of the item. For example, a local sporting goods store stocks the desired model of ski; the sporting goods store is the possessor.
2. The person wishing to buy, or the customer.
3. The item itself (the skis).
4. Some form of payment. In most cases the payment is in money.
5. The exchange of ownership.

Marketing also takes into consideration the exchange of one product for another, such as money for satisfaction. In the exchange process the customer approaches the possessor and offers him payment (usually in money) for the product. If the amount is agreeable to the possessor, he transfers the ownership rights of the skis to the purchaser, who transfers payment for the skis to the possessor. This is a complete exchange of goods; the buyer now owns the skis. This completes the exchange process.

For marketing to take place there must be two or more people, organizations, or corporations with unsatisfied wants; products (goods or services) that they are willing to give up to satisfy those wants; and some means of communicating their needs and wants to the other party.

Involvement of marketing

For the purchase of skis marketing has a threefold involvement in the process: (1) communicating the virtues of the pair of skis, (2) convincing the consumer that the skis will satisfy his or her wants, and (3) distinguishing this particular pair from all others. Let's discuss each in more detail.

Communicating information. Communication is often equated with advertising, but this is not necessarily the case. Communication in marketing is dissemination of information about the product. Communication can take many forms, from advertising to product evaluation reports by independent organizations such as *Consumer Reports*. Communication highlights the features of the goods thought to be of most interest to the consumer, including everything from color to ease of use, performance, and life of the product.

Satisfying wants. Every consumer has a personal idea of what the product should do or how it should perform. It is the role of marketing to determine what the majority of the consumers want. Once this is established, the communication process becomes easier. If we know what consumers want, we can convince them that our product can satisfy their desires better than any other product (Fig. 9-1). Selling skis is generally done by having top ski racers or Olympic gold medalists advertise how good a certain brand and model of ski is. For tennis lessons a retailer is likely to seek out a well-known professional who has won tournaments. The skier is sought out by marketing personnel to communicate the superiority of a product. Even winning tennis tournaments can be construed as a marketing ploy to display skills and draw in students.

Distinguishing between products. For any consumer desire, there are various goods or services that attempt to satisfy that want. There are at least eight or nine major brands of skis sold in the United States. How does a manufacturer distinguish his or her brand from the rest? This is done through marketing. The market-

FIG. 9-1 Every destination resort attempts to convince a potential visitor that everything he desires can be found at the resort location. Notice the number of different activities that can be identified in the photograph. (Photograph courtesy Hyatt Regency Grand Cypress.)

ing department attempts to determine what the consumers want, including colors, bottom surfaces, and suitability for the terrain. Once these factors are known, the marketing department communicates these distinguishing features to consumers. This distinguishing of one product from another is often referred to as "product differentiation."

Consumer satisfaction. The satisfaction of a consumer is related to how well the good or service meets one or more of the five *utilities,* or values placed on the item. These utilities are form, place, time, psychic, and monetary (Lovelock 1979). Each is discussed in further detail.

Form. The concept of form as it relates to consumer satisfaction ranges from complete design of a product to such purely cosmetic features as color. For tennis lessons it could be the courts and changing rooms, which affect the attractiveness of the business. The consumer may receive much greater satisfaction from a tennis lesson at a country club on well maintained courts than from one on public courts. Changing the form of the product so that the consumer receives more satisfaction is quite common in marketing. The new form may be only a cosmetic change such as fashion colors for skis or new plantings around a tennis court.

Place. Place refers mainly to the location at which the product can be acquired. The ski manufacturing company may place its wares in ski shops and mall stores, and the tennis lesson location may be chosen for convenience. Suppose it is more convenient for the consumer to take tennis lessons at the local municipal park, which is closer to home. However, is the place more important to the consumer than the form, or attractiveness of the setting? It is important to weigh both items when attempting to determine which is more important. No matter which is the final outcome, the place is extremely important. Health clubs have found this to be of utmost importance. Numerous studies indicate that the closer the health club is to a person's residence, the likelier he or she is to join and use the facility.

Time. The utility time can be the time it takes to produce the good or the time it takes to consume it. Consider the fast-food outlet. The closer to the time of consumption the hamburger is prepared, the better it tastes and the more likely it is to be sold. On the other hand, the short time it takes to acquire a precooked hamburger can be considered a convenience. If we go back to the skis, time is of the essence in that the time from when the consumer purchases the skis until they are available for use is very important. It is in the best interests of the retailer to get the bindings mounted on the skis as rapidly as possible. This is an example of time utility.

Sometimes the longer it takes for an activity to take place the more that activity is perceived as being desirable. Examples of this include the leisurely meal at an expensive restaurant versus the meal presented at a fast-food restaurant. Time is very important to both, even though they are opposites. The fast-food restaurant has built its business on being able to provide a meal rapidly. The fancy restaurant bases its reputation on its ability to present an elegant atmosphere at an unhurried pace. These are examples of producers matching their products to the desires and needs of the consumer.

Psychic value. Psychic utility provides some kind of psychological boost from acquiring the product. The best examples of this are related to the Veblen effect, which states that people are willing to pay a higher price for products perceived to be exclusive. Some consumers are willing to pay a substantially higher price for skis of limited production, which are identified as highly prestigious.

The same is also true of tennis lessons. Most people would like to take tennis lessons at an exclusive resort from a nationally ranked player. This is another example of psychic utility. People feel they are receiving something extra from the acquisition of these prestigious goods or services.

Along these same lines, the psychic approach can take form in atmosphere. The restaurant with the dim lights and the hushed service tends to command a higher price, not necessarily because the food is better but because the atmosphere is better—psychic utility.

Monetary. Monetary utility does not necessarily mean that the lower the price, the better for the consumer. Monetary utility is a measure of the price/value relationship. If you receive a much higher value for a slight increase in price, the monetary utility has increased substantially. This is very important in recreation, since many people are willing to pay a higher price for a better item if the price/value relationship is acceptable.

The other aspect of monetary utility is the ease of payment. In a lot of cases people are willing to acquire a good if the payment can be extended over a longer period or if the payment process is very simple, as by credit card. Both are examples of monetary utility, the main one being the price/value relationship.

Types of competition

Having taken into consideration exchange and satisfaction, it is important to look at the competition. Assessing the competition allows you to see how your product (good or service) differentiates itself from its competition. The important thing to remember is that your product is competing against other products at various levels. Ranging from the most to least intense, these levels are brand, product, generic, and total wants.

Brand competition is the most intense form of competition, it applies to similar products. Rossignol Skis vie directly with Head Skis. One tennis pro competes with another for tennis students.

The next level of competition is the product level: other goods or services that perform similar functions or meet similar desires. A ski rental company that offers a specific brand or a company that refinishes the skis so that they look new enables the consumer to obtain what looks like new skis without having to buy them. Instead of taking lessons from the tennis pro, a consumer may have a friend teach him or her or buy a book to improve his or her game.

The next level is the generic. At this level of competition there are other methods of satisfying the consumer. Actually there are numerous methods of meeting consumer desires. The key is to identify the participants' desired outcome. Perhaps instead of speed thrills the skier really wishes to be outdoors in a pristine environment obtaining physical exercise. If so, the competition for alpine skiing may be cross-country skiing, since this activity provides the same basic experience as alpine skiing. This opens an entirely new aspect of marketing.

The same is true for tennis lessons if the desired outcome is physical conditioning and increased opportunities for social interaction. These goals can be accomplished by playing racquetball, badminton, squash, or some other similar activity. Therefore, on the generic level, the competing product can be substantially different from yours. Substitutability has received some research attention in recreation literature. The research so far tends to indicate that the concept is valid but highly complex.

The final level of competition is that of total needs or wants. This level addresses other needs, including transportation, housing, and food. Since a person must have these to live, they are in direct competition with luxuries. For this reason recreation is said to use discretionary income and time. At the total desires level a number of things are considered more important than recreation, such as eating, sleeping, and drinking.

The levels of competition are varied and intense. The manager of a recreation enterprise needs to be aware that he or she is not competing just with people providing the same kind of activity, but with everyone in the recreation business in the area in addition to all other products. This is important to remember. Never think that you are competing only at the brand level. You are always competing at all four levels. This is extremely important when trying to establish a new business.

Marketing a commercial recreation enterprise

Now that we have defined marketing and described some of the ways in which people decide to purchase a product, the question arises: How does marketing help with the purchase process? Marketing reduces the total market population into subgroups that can be identified and served by your enterprise. The subgroup must be homogeneous enough that you can identify it, its members' wants, and their ability to purchase your product. This division into subgroups is accomplished through the process of seeking, matching, and consummating the marketing enterprise.

Seeking

This aspect of marketing management deals with the search for and identification of specific wants of the population in your area. It can range from provision of a good or service to development of a program. This seeking process identifies those areas in which recreation businesses may find sufficient population to turn a profit. Once you have identified the needs, wants, or desires of that population, move on to the next step.

Matching

Matching is connecting the needs and wants of the population, as identified through seeking, with the ability and resources of the organization to meet those needs. This facilitates the matching of customers' desires with organization objectives. Once this has taken place, you have identified a product or service that your organization may provide and that consumers will want to purchase.

Consummating

Consummation is solving all details necessary to complete the exchange. This includes providing the product to the customer in a convenient place, the exchange process, and an attempt by the company to insure that the product provided gives satisfaction. This tends to produce repeat business. This stage can include delivery of goods, or for services on site, the facilities, design, development, and location.

A fourth component to marketing management, the positioning statement, will be discussed later. There are two distinctly different approaches, depending on whether the good is a service or a product.

Another major concept is effective demand, summarized by the acronym DAM, which stands for desire, authority, and money. It is very important when pursuing the seeking and matching process to be sure that the target subgroup wants the good or service provided. If this *desire* is not present, the company is wasting its time on that subgroup. *Authority* is the power to consummate the exchange. Often in commercial recreation someone has the desire yet lacks the authority to acquire the good. This can be seen quite often in children. A child may want to purchase a skateboard, but not be allowed to do so. This leads to the third component of effective demand, *money.*

Money generally relates to the income of the individual, creditworthiness, and assets, since assets can be converted into money. Money is also a very important component of effective demand. All of these items must be present in any subgroup in order for an exchange to take place. If any of the three is missing, there will be no exchange.

Market segmentation

Marketing analysis attempts to break down the population into subgroups, or market segments. Market segments can be defined so that the organization or marketer can identify those who possess effective demand. This allows the company to better match objectives and products to the desires of the market segment.

In general a company has one of two strategies to pursue, either the undifferentiated market or market segmentation. In an undifferentiated market the company provides a good or service and advertises it to the entire population. This shotgun approach is not usually very effective.

Market segmentation is analogous to a single rifle shot. You identify your specific market and fire one image at the market that you know exists. This is a direct result of seeking and matching.

The main criterion for market segmentation is identifying some segment or subgroup of the population that can be reached. The first step is to use surveys and other similar methods to determine the wants and needs of the target subgroup. Once this has been done, it is easy to identify the characteristics of that population. This allows the marketer to determine the responsiveness of that market segment.

Responsiveness is the ability of the business to communicate the benefits of its product to the market segment. Then there must be some measure of how the market will react in a way that will result in an exchange of goods. If a market can be identified and if it is responsive, the final step can be implemented. This is to determine the size of the market, specifically whether it contains sufficient numbers of people with enough buying power to keep the company in business. If all three of these items are present, it is a viable market segment.

Market segments

Traditionally there have been four basic types of market segmentation. Ranging from the most simple to the most complex, they are state of being, state of mind, product usage, and benefits. Each is explained below.

State-of-being segmentation. *State-of-being segmentation,* the simplest and one of the earliest methods of identifying market segments, relies strictly on measuring some aspect of the consumer that is easy to measure. Among the most commonly used aspects are geography, demography, and customer type.

Geographic segmentation refers to where the market segment lives. For example, we know that approximately 25% of all visitors to a water park live within a 5-mile radius. An additional 50% come from within a 5- to 10-mile radius. This market segment is all people living within 10 miles of the park.

Demographic segmentation refers to measurable characteristics of the population. For example, the majority of the customers at the water park are between the ages of 14 and 23. The demographic segment of the market is people within that age range.

The third aspect used in state-of-being segmentation is the customer type. In some businesses a particular type of customer group is sufficiently large to require its own marketing plan. An example of this in commercial recreation is purchasers of playground equipment. A major market for swings and slides is municipal recreation departments. Therefore, municipal recreation departments constitute a specific customer type. This allows the manufacturer of playground equipment to design a marketing approach aimed specifically at municipal recreation agencies.

State-of-mind segmentation. State of mind refers to the psychological characteristics of the individual customer—such things as personality traits and the decision-making process. Quite often these psychological concepts deal with the selling of specific images that go along with a good or service. An example is selling skis associated with a specific image, usually the image projected by a world-class ski racer.

This concept is also extensively used in tourism research on psychographics. People are identified by whether they are allocentrics, who travel alone to an exotic place, or psychocentrics, who prefer to tour an area after it has been well-established as a destination point.

Another aspect of state-of-mind segmentation deals with the perceptions and preferences of certain people for specific activities. Once these activities are identified, managers can produce a marketing plan to meet that particular preference. A prime example of this is the idea that the beach is a place to relax and get away from the ratrace.

Product-usage segmentation. One of the key methods of product-usage segmentation is measuring the volume in which a market segment purchases the product. A manufacturer of running shoes bases product usage on the number of participants in major marathons or running events. These people, who typically use a pair of shoes every three months—far more than the national average—account for a large percentage of the total volume of the company. They constitute a main market segment.

The second form of segmentation in product usage is strong brand loyalty. Some people continue to purchase a certain brand regardless of whether a new or better competing item is available.

A third type of product-usage segmentation is by market factors such as cost. A portion of any market is interested only in the cost of the product. These people purchase the lower-priced item regardless of perceived quality compared with other brands.

Benefits segmentation. This aspect of market segmentation has the highest usage in recreation. It is also the hardest to identify. Benefits segmentation seeks to identify that part of the market that derives specific benefits from the product. Once this is done, these benefits are presented to this market segment to encourage additional business. The main problem with benefit segmentation is the difficulty of identifying the benefit. There have been many instances, particularly in commercial recreation, in which the marketers incorrectly identified the primary benefit to the consumer. For instance, the ski industry for many years stressed the thrill of the sport—but it has been determined that for most potential consumers the important benefits are associated with the scenic beauty and social activity that are intrinsic parts of the ski experience.

Types of marketing

In the examples of skis and tennis lessons there are two totally different types of merchandise being offered, a good and a service. Given these distinct classifications, there are a number of considerations the marketer must take into account when providing an avenue for selling the product. For example, the skis can be tried out by renting a pair or by going to a demo day to use the skis. A tennis lesson, however, may not be tried out prior to its purchase. No pro is going to give you a free lesson and then ask you whether or not you are satisfied and if so, to pay for the lesson.

Another characteristic difference between goods and services is that a good can be inspected but a true service cannot, because a true service is produced and consumed simultaneously. Very few businesses provide the opportunity to receive the benefits of a service without some commitment to purchase.

A customer can see a good prior to purchase. However, in service marketing all the purchaser can consider are surrogates of the particular service. Goods can be produced, stored, and held for future sale. A service cannot. A tennis instructor cannot take an unused hour and place it in storage to use at a later date. Once that hour is gone, it cannot be regained.

Goods are comparatively nonperishable. This means that they can be stored. This leads to the next difference, that goods can be prepared ahead of time. Given the manufacturing process of most goods, there is a low variability of output. This means that one pair of skis is similar to the next pair of skis no matter when they were made if they were produced on similar machinery. In contrast, services are individually produced and highly variable in quality. This is based on the ability or inability of the individual to eliminate personal feelings on any given day and provide the best possible service.

If the person producing the service is having a bad day or is not feeling well, the quality of the service may be drastically different from that provided on another, better day.

A good is easy to duplicate, since it is being made by equipment or machinery and consistency control is simple. However, two people cannot provide the same service; our tennis pro may provide an excellent lesson, whereas the assistant pro is not up to that standard.

This lack of consistency is responsible for a low perceived consumer risk in goods compared to services. Thus, there is an increased necessity to provide information about services. The significant differences between goods and services are highlighted in Table 9-1.

Virtually no type of recreation product is a true good or a true service. For example, skis have a service component consisting of an outlet for the goods, information for the buyer, warranties, and repairs. For virtually every good there is a service component. Conversely, in services such as tennis lessons, the good component is manifest in the ability of the teacher, the esthetics of the courts, and the

TABLE 9-1. Comparison of goods and services

Goods	Services
Can be tried out	Cannot be tried out
Can be tested	Cannot be tested
Can be inspected	Cannot be inspected
Can see product	Look at surrogates
Can be stored	Cannot be stored
Not perishable	Highly perishable
Can be produced ahead of time	Produced at time of use
Low variability of output	High variability of output
Easy to duplicate product	Hard to duplicate product
Low consumer risk	High consumer risk

quality and availability of tennis balls and other equipment. These are all examples of the goods side of service marketing.

Given this, we can construct a continuum from the true good to the true service (see the box below). It is the job of the recreational professional to decide whether the good that he is providing is more a good or a service. Once this has been determined, it is easier to provide consumers with the maximum information relating to the good and their need for it. This helps in the selling process by identifying the target market and the perceived benefits to the user.

Components of product marketing

Product marketing is generally identified as consisting of product, place, promotion, and price (McCarthy, 1975). Each of these four Ps is a unique component in marketing (see Table 9-2).

Product

The product consists of the physical good or the combination of goods and services presented to the customer. There are a number of ways to increase the prod-

---

Examples of goods and services

True good		True service
←		→
Playground equipment	Fine restaurant	Lessons
Sporting equipment		Trips
Boats		Leisure counseling
Recreational Vehicles (RVs)		Hotels

TABLE 9-2. Comparison of product and service marketing

Product marketing	Service marketing
1. Product: A physical product or some combination of goods and services that satisfies customer needs	1. Product-service mix: The combination of products and services aimed at satisfying the needs of the target market
2. Place: When, where, and by whom the goods and services are to be offered for sale	2. Presentation mix: All elements used by the business to increase the tangibility of the service in the perception of the market
3. Promotion: Any method of communicating information to the target market about the product	3. Communication mix: All communications between the firm and the target market that establish consumer expectations
4. Price: A price that makes the offering as attractive as possible	

uct's appeal. Among these are new items or additional services such as enhanced versions or changed cosmetics as with better bottoms or new colors of skis. These changes tend to increase the desirability of the product itself. Other items are additional services, for example, custom fitting of the skis.

Place

Place refers mainly to where, when, and how the goods and associated services are offered for sale. Generally the producer of the goods decides to use one of three types of distribution, exclusive, selective, or intensive. In exclusive distribution the manufacturer selects one or two very specific outlets for the product. This takes place with top-line goods such as very expensive skis. In selective distribution a manufacturer may select a number of dealers in a given area. This allows for more moderately priced products and gives better coverage of the market. In this case the marketing plan is somewhat different, particularly as it relates to pricing and availability of goods. The third type is intensive distribution, in which the marketer gets as many outlets as possible for the goods. These levels can be compared to the ski shop, the national sporting goods chain store and the discount store.

Other factors of place include transportation methods, distribution channels (whether to have a wholesaler or just a retailer), inventory, and physical quantity. These are generally lumped under logistics and are fairly straightforward. The key point is in the channel of distribution.

In commercial recreation enterprises place may be fixed by physical limitations. For example, it is virtually impossible to construct a ski resort in southern Florida. However, it would be possible to provide a Florida outlet to sell ski passes to a resort in California. Therefore, place can take on a dual meaning when dealing with recreation. It is not only the physical location of the site but also the place in which the sale takes place. Another example is registration for a soccer league. The games must be played on a soccer field, but registration can take place anywhere.

Promotion

Promotion in marketing is any method of communicating to the target market information about the product. This can take many forms of four basic channels, personal selling, advertising, sales promotion, and publicity. Personal selling is oral presentation by a person to a prospective buyer. This most often takes place in the retail outlet. Advertising is paid, nonpersonal promotion of the good or service. The most common kinds are print and broadcast media. Each will be discussed in Chapter 10.

Publicity is nonpersonal stimulation of demand by nonpaid communication. Publicity can be either positive or negative. We cannot overemphasize the importance of positive publicity in commercial recreation. The last form of promotion is sales promotion, which includes displays, exhibits, and demonstrations. The ski company demo day, during which patrons of ski resorts try out new skis is an example of a sales promotion.

Pricing

The final component of product marketing is pricing. Price should make the offering as attractive to the prospective consumer as possible. This topic is considered important enough that we have devoted most of Chapter 8 to it.

Components of service marketing

Service marketing has been defined as consisting of the product-service mix, presentation mix, and the communication mix (Renaghan, 1981).

Product-service mix

The product-service mix is the combination of products and services provided. Please note the need for identification of the market as discussed earlier in this chapter. The reason for considering the product-service mix is that most consumers expect service with the product. In fact, this mix has become so ingrained in American life that the only time a service related to a product is noticed is when it is not provided. Customers then have a tendency to switch providers. Therefore it is important that the provider of commercial recreation be aware that services are an integral part of the package and carefully choose what services to offer and at what level. For example, the tennis pro may or may not provide soft drinks for the customer at the end of the lesson, video taping of the lesson, and maybe even a tennis racquet cover to indicate that the person is a graduate of his or her course. All these services can be offered to enhance the enterprise. Each can be added at the discretion of the provider. The question is what is the most advantageous mix of services and products. A further consideration is that services are generally measured by performance—and the quality of the performance determines whether or not the customer returns.

A service can be measured in a number of different ways. One airline found that the majority of its customers were business travelers and that the most important issue to business travelers is leaving and arriving on time. Therefore the measure of performance identified by the airline was the percentage of flights that left within 5 minutes of scheduled departure time. This is one way in which service can be measured on a performance level. Another example is the number of people who win tennis matches in crosstown tournaments.

Presentation mix

The most important items in the presentation mix are the physical plant, location, atmosphere, and price.

Physical plant. In recreation enterprise the physical plant is of major importance, since it establishes the image. It includes signage, parking, building design, and facility layout. Each should be carefully designed to facilitate the flow of customers into the facility and create the atmosphere that the proprietor wishes to convey (Fig. 9-2).

Location. To a certain extent the location is dictated by the feasibility study. There are only so many locations that can support a given type of commercial recreation. This depends upon the necessary physical characteristics of the site. It is extremely important to select a site that is close to the population or has adequate transportation facilities.

Atmosphere. When we speak of atmosphere or ambience, the thing that comes to mind is the elegant restaurant. However, in any service enterprise the atmosphere is acutely important (Fig. 9-3). This can be seen by considering the atmosphere of such service areas as banks and lawyer's offices. These places project an aura of prosperity and stability that gives the prospective consumer confidence in the institution. The same holds true for a recreation enterprise. An elite country club must have a well-to-do atmosphere. The exclusive tennis resort or club must be well-situated and esthetically pleasing, with lots of surrounding green areas. The pro shop must project an image of a high-quality operation. These are all extremely important to profitability.

Price. See Chapter 8.

Communications mix

The communications mix includes all communications between the firm and the target market and establishes consumer expectations. In service marketing the communications mix is designed to persuade the consumer by making the intangible aspects of the service perceptible, usually through pictures.

In addition, the communication mix should establish and monitor the consu-

FIG. 9-2 This is an example of a resort hotel trying to provide visible proof of the physical plant, location, and atmosphere. (Photograph courtesy Hyatt Regency Grand Cypress.)

mer's expectations. The best way to monitor consumer expectations is through surveys to identify exactly what the consumers feel they should be receiving. For a summary of service marketing, see the box on page 271.

Positioning statements

The positioning statement is of great importance to the commercial recreation entrepreneur. Once you have a product or a service and have identified the target market, you need to differentiate your product from those of your competitors. In some cases there is no competition; however, if your product is profitable, you will soon have competition. This leads us to the positioning statement (Lewis, 1981).

The positioning statement relates to consumers' subjective attitudes about a

FIG. 9-3 The atmosphere of the old west is presented in these photographs of Knott's Berry Farm. (Photograph courtesy Knott's Berry Farm.)

Components of service marketing

Product-service mix
1. Most customers integrate services into the product and expect them.
2. Decide what services to offer.
3. Service is measured by performance.
4. Provide services the customers need.

Presentation mix
1. Physical plant
2. Location
3. Atmophere
4. Price
5. Employees

Communication mix
1. Persuades the consumer; includes pictures that help the customer appreciate the intangibles.
2. Establishes and monitors consumers' expectations

---

product and how it differs from the competition. Once you know how your product or service differs from that of your competitors, you can find your specific niche, and see how to become more effective at meeting your customers' needs.

The positioning statement does three things:

1. It creates an image, either good or bad depending on promotion. An effective positioning statement creates a good image of your product.
2. It promotes the perceived benefits of the product. Note the term "perceived"; very often the benefit received by the consumer is substantially different from the benefit conceived by the producer. For example, the ski manufacturer may consider the benefits of a particular ski to be ease of turning and stability in rough terrain. However, the benefit from the purchaser's point of view may well be the status derived from being seen skiing on that particular brand of ski. The same can be said of tennis lessons. The tennis instructor may think the benefit of taking lessons is the improvement of the player's game. However, the benefit from the consumer's point of view may be the status derived from taking lessons from a particular instructor or from club membership. In these examples the conceived benefit of the provider varies significantly from the perceived benefit of the user. Therefore it is important to identify the consumer's perceived benefit.
3. It differentiates the brand from the product class. The manufacturer of a specific brand of skis wants his or her product to stand out from all other skis on the market. The positioning statement quantifies differences among the various brands. This can be done by showing how the brand in question is

unique from the others. The positioning statement makes this easier by going through a process of identifying exactly what it is that makes the brand different from all others.

Let's evaluate how consumers determine which product or service they want to acquire.

Lovelock (1979) has shown that a consumer evaluates products and services based on certain utilities, form, place, time, psychic value, and monetary. When approaching these utilities from a positioning point of view, there is a unique and important difference in how each is perceived by the consumer. We shall discuss each in detail.

Form utility

The form of the utility depends upon whether the product is a good or a service. If it is a good, form refers to such characteristics as quality, style, shape, and color. We see this time and again. Skis are changed every year, not for technical reasons, but for cosmetic reasons. Styles change and new colors are coordinated with entire ski outfits.

If the product is a service, form consists of intangibles such as the attractiveness of the business and the prestige of the location. In tennis lessons the attractiveness of the pro shop plays an important part, as does the prestige of the location. The instructor can be the same, but the perceived form utility is much higher if the instructor is teaching at the local country club rather than at the municipal tennis courts.

Service form utility consists of physical attractiveness of the business or the facility and quite often relates to the physical plant.

Place utility

Place utility refers to the convenience of the location and can be directly linked to the distribution scheme. It is important whether the product is readily available through a number of retail outlets or exclusively in the higher-priced shops. A manufacturer may make skis available at numerous retail outlets, including cut-price outlets or may wish to create an image of eliteness and therefore only allow one or two expensive shops to sell them.

This is also true of services. In terms of commercial recreation the place is more a factor of the feasibility study. Recreation enterprises are usually immovable, so it is necessary to bring people to the location. There are only so many places where tennis lessons may be taught. In a municipal program the instructor may move from location to location, providing convenience of location to numerous people. However, the quality of one or more locations may leave something to be desired. This again affects marketing strategy.

Time utility

Time utility can be very confusing. In some cases the two aspects of it are in direct opposition. One concept of time is the convenience factor, or whether the service or product is offered quickly or at a convenient time. This may or may not be a factor. One of the key points in time utility for fast-food restaurants is getting a meal and getting it rapidly.

The opposite side of time utility is enjoyment. The customer may not want a meal in a fine restaurant to be over too soon. Because the concept of time utility can have two basic interpretations—or a mixture of them—it is important that the provider be aware of how the consumer perceives the time utility as it relates to the specific product or service.

Psychic utility

Psychic utility relates to the prestige associated with the good or service. This can be determined by who is the provider, the location (in terms of atmosphere), and the personal service provided.

The amount of service given by the employees of the business is very important. The employees can, by the way that they treat the customer, either enhance or detract from the psychic utility. Quite often specialty stores provide only very specific products or services and spend a great deal of time with each customer. This is usually accompanied by a higher price for the product or service.

Monetary utility

Monetary utility is the price/value relationship. If the perceived value of the product is higher than its price, the monetary utility will be considered substantial. The price/value relationship is dependent upon the other utilities. Therefore it is imperative that the marketer establish some method of translating the other utilities into a price/value relationship. Remember that ease of payment can be a very important factor to the monetary utility. It includes the use of credit cards and in a resort the ability to charge various items to the room. These tend to enhance the monetary utility and induce people to spend more.

How can marketing and the positioning statement be used to benefit the recreation enterprise? This takes place through the creation of a positioning matrix (Table 9-3). The positioning matrix shows the components of marketing across the top and the utilities down the side. For example, for a service-oriented product the product-service mix, the presentation mix, and the communication mix runs across the top, and the utilities of form, place, time, psychic, and monetary goes down the side.

All that is left is to fill in the squares. For example, the service might be tennis lessons. The product-service mix is the management decision as to what we will provide. The product-service mix for the form would be the facility, say an exclusive country club that allows the people who take lessons to use the club's facilities during lesson time.

The presentation mix portion of the positioning statement stresses such things at atmosphere, price, staff services, location, physical beauty of the courts, and how well they are maintained.

The final aspect of communication is choosing what to emphasize about the

TABLE 9-3. Positioning matrix

Utility	Product-service	Presentation	Communication
Form			
Place			
Time			
Psychic			
Monetary			

product-service mix in the presentation. This may include pictures of people playing tennis on well-maintained, esthetically pleasing courts. The picture may even show the snack bar or the lounge looking out onto the courts and show some of the other amenities students may use at the facility.

This same process is followed for each one of the four remaining utilities. Once the grid has been filled in, it helps identify the need for management decisions for the product-service mix, the presentation (what to promote for each of the utilities), and how to convey that to prospective customers. This presents a very good idea of what is provided and how to present it.

Another use of the positioning matrix is to identify a market segment. This positioning matrix would show all competitors within a given area and analyze specifically what they are providing. This matrix helps analyze weaknesses and market segments that are being overlooked by competitors. It is fairly easy to use this base for developing a new business. It allows the competition to dictate the market segment. Once the segment has been identified, it is simply a matter of determining whether it is of sufficient size to be profitable.

This same process can be repeated for a product simply by changing the headings of the columns from service components, to product components.

Summary

Marketing is a complex issue. Numerous levels of information can be provided in marketing. These relate to the different products or services being marketed.

Product marketing has four main components, product, price, place, and promotion. Service marketing components are product-service mix, communications, and presentation mix. It is important for the entrepreneur to know whether he or she is providing a product, a service, or a mix of the two. The positioning statement makes it relatively easy to tell whether there is a place in the market for the good or service.

The positioning statement shows whether the market segment is big enough to warrant providing the good or service. Remember that the market segment must be sufficiently large to be profitable and must be identifiable, communicated with, and prepared to behave in a specific manner.

BIBLIOGRAPHY

Bagozzi, R.P.: Principles of marketing management, Chicago, 1986, Science Research Associates.

Frank, N.D., and Ganly, J.V.: Data sources for business and market analysis, Metuchen, N.J., 1983, Scarecrow Press.

James, B.G.: Business wargames, Cambridge, Mass., 1985, Abacus Press.

Lewis, R.C.: The positioning statement for hotels, The Cornell H.R.A. Quarterly, May, 1981.

Lovelock, C.H.: Theoretical contributions from service and nonbusiness marketing. In Ferrell, O.C., et al.: Conceptual and theoretical developments in marketing, proceedings series, Chicago, 1979, American Marketing Association, pp. 147-165.

McCarthy, E.J., and Perreault, W.D., Jr.: Basic marketing: a managerial approach, Homewood, Ill., 1984, Richard D. Irwin, Inc.

Marketing information, Business Publication Division, Georgia State University, 1982.

O'Shaughnessy, J.: Competitive marketing: a strategic approach, Boston, 1984, Allen & Unwin.

Renaghan, L.M.: A new marketing mix for the hospitality industry, The Cornell H.R.A. Quarterly, August, 1981.

Shapiro, B.P., Dolan, R.J., and Quelch, J.A.: Marketing management, Homewood, Ill., 1985, Richard D. Irwin, Inc.

Stapleton, J.: How to prepare a marketing plan, Aldershot, Hampshire, 1983, Gower.

Stephenson, H., and Otterson, D.: Marketing your products and services successfully, Sunnyvale, Calif., 1985, Oasis Press.

Williams, L.A.: Microcomputers and marketing decisions, London, 1985, Peregrinus.

SUGGESTED READINGS

Byers, Gerald L., and Teckert, H.E.: Marketing for small businesses: what it is and why you need it, Toronto, 1980, MacMillan.

How marketing should take place for a small business. Excellent on market segmentation and marketing mix. Some ideas pertaining to marketing in the future and some examples of a marketing plan for the small business entrepreneur.

Ferrell, O.C., and Pride, W.M.: Fundamentals of marketing, Boston, 1982, Houghton-Mifflin Co.

General marketing text provides the basics on all marketing components. Good section on market segmentation, pricing, product decisions. Remainder deals strictly with product market and distribution channels.

Cotler, P.: Marketing essentials, Englewood Cliffs, N.J., 1984, Prentice-Hall, Inc.

Typical standard marketing text. Besides the main components of marketing chapters deal with product life cycle in relation to promotion, pricing, pricing policy strategies, and international marketing.

Levinson, J.C.: Guerrilla marketing: secrets for making big profits from your small business, Boston, 1980, Houghton-Mifflin Co.

Innovative approach to marketing identifies different strategies relevant to warfare or warfare concepts. How to determine where you are within your market segment and how to change your position. It is broken into mini media marketing, or small-budget marketing effects in advertising, and maxi media marketing. Simple chapter on nonmedia marketing or advertising. An excellent textbook.

Hunt, S.D.: Marketing theory, the philosophy of marketing science, Homewood, Ill., 1983, Richard D. Irwin, Inc.

Basic information on theories behind the different concepts of marketing. The background material is excellent.

Lovelock, C.H.: Services marketing: text, cases and readings, Englewood Cliffs, N.J., 1984, Prentice-Hall, Inc.

State of the art of service marketing. How to identify service markets and promote them in the organization. "Must" reading for any agency dealing specifically with services.

In any recreation business there is a tradeoff between the cost and the effectiveness of the marketing campaign. Some marketing plans do not work. It then becomes the job of the recreation manager to establish a new direction. This is the situation that Bob Mayes faces. The new marketing program must build off the old one, whether the old one was good or bad. As you read the Thousand Trails case, put yourself in Bob Mayes's place. It is now your job to develop a new marketing plan for Thousand Trails.

Thousand Trails*

It had been only three months since Jim Jensen, the new CEO, had taken over the reigns from Milt Kuolt, entrepreneur and founder of Thousand Trails, Inc. Since 1972, when the company recorded its first sale, volume had grown to over $40 million by year end 1981. 1981 had been a year of upheaval for the sales and marketing department. In late December, the Seattle-based organization was about to welcome its fourth "new" VP of Sales and Marketing, Bob Mayes.

The arrival of Jensen in September and Mayes in late December came none too soon. Many of the old sales methods were no longer working and several new ideas had recently been introduced. It was getting to the point where it was hard for the average employee to keep track of all the programs.

Jensen came to Thousand Trails with a solid background in operations, sales, and marketing. From 1974 to 1979 Jensen served as Chief Operating Officer of Grantree Furniture Rental of Portland. In that 6-year period, Grantree's revenues soared from $6 million to $70 million. Prior to Grantree, Jim Jensen worked for Encyclopedia Brittanica where, in a period of 11 years, he advanced from sales training positions to VP of Sales and Marketing and Chief Operating Officer for the Great Books division.

History

Thousand Trails had its foundation in a true entrepreneurial effort. In 1969 Milt Kuolt, a business manager for the Boeing Company in Seattle, Washington, took his family on a camping trip. What was to have been a pleasant five-day vacation turned-out to be a three-day disaster. His wife complained of the unsanitary restrooms and lack of security. Their children, after setting up camp, complained of boredom. More-

*Reprinted with permission of the Stanford University Graduate School of Business, 1982 by the Board of Trustees of the Leland Stanford Junior University.

over, as a result of trying to make life bearable for his family, Kuolt had no time to relax.

The camping disaster, however, highlighted for Kuolt the need for good, clean, out-door recreational facilities. In the ensuing year, Kuolt set out to further define what he saw as a void in the outdoor recreational industry. He passed out questionnaires to, and talked with, recreational vehicle (RV) owners and campers. He found that many of them were also dissatisfied with outdoor recreational facilities. Kuolt determined that an outdoor enthusiast generally camped at several different areas, desired clean and safe camping facilities, and often felt burdened with having to provide activities for the family when they became bored.

In 1970, Kuolt purchased 640 acres in Chehalis, Washington. With its accessible lo-cation, less than two hours from either Seattle or Portland, the spot was perfect for the concept. Milt left his job and began to construct roads and campsites in the woods. Kuolt and his three sons spent two years developing their dream. Most of his personal assets, including his wife's jewelry, were risked on the project. Kuolt put in roughly $40,000 of his savings and was able to raise $90,000 from the Canadian Imperial Bank of Commerce by using some real estate as collateral.

By July of 1972, the pioneers were ready to make their product public. Kuolt sent letters to all those who had answered his marketing questionnaire, offering them a life-time membership for a $295 contribution fee and dues of $60 a year.

The first memberships were sold in 1972, and Thousand Trails was born. It was a division of the Pacific Rim Group, a land management company started by Kuolt in 1969. The ensuing two years were devoted to the development of the Chehalis pre-serve. A 4,000-square-foot clubhouse, a swimming pool, tennis courts, all-purpose sports courts, and campsites with power and water were built. From 1972 to 1974 the number of active memberships grew slowly. In 1974, active memberships numbered 384; sales amounted to $113,000, and 18 people were employed during peak months.

In 1975, Thousand Trails acquired a second preserve near Leavenworth, Washing-ton. The Leavenworth preserve, formerly a private camping club, was perfect for Thou-sand Trails because it bordered on the Wenatchee National Forest and provided year-round recreational opportunities for members. The acquisition increased Thousand Trails' credibility. It signified to the members and the public Thousand Trails' commit-ment to multiple locations.

In 1976, two more preserves were added, one near Hood Canal, Washington, and another near Mount Vernon, Washington. Due to legal proceedings, the development of the Hood Canal preserve did not start until 1980.

Rather than acquiring new preserves in 1977, Thousand Trails devoted its capital to the development of its existing properties. During the years 1975 through 1977, the company's sales grew from $113,000 to $7,713,000, memberships rose from 384 to 3,575, and the number of employees during peak seasons increased from 18 to 175.

Thousand Trails experienced phenomenal growth in the years 1977 to 1980. The company acquired ten preserves (bringing its total to fourteen), six of which were lo-cated in California. During these 3 years, the number of existing memberships rose from 3,575 to 27,620; sales increased from $7,713,000 to $33,950,000 and the number of people employed during peak months increased from 175 to 960 (see Exhibit A).

	1976	1977	1978	1979	1980
Membership history					
Outstanding memberships	1,117	3,575	7,664	12,926	27,620
Average price per membership	$1,900	$2,725	$3,375	$3,825	$4,400
Memberships sold	614	2,826	4,263	5,581	7,704
Percentage change					
Outstanding memberships	—	220.1%	114.4%	68.7%	59.9%
Average price per membership	—	43.4%	23.9%	13.3%	15.0%
Memberships sold	—	360.3%	50.2%	30.9%	38.0%

By 1981, Milt Kuolt felt that he had made his greatest contribution to the company and began to look for a replacement. Forty-year-old Jim Jensen was chosen to take over the management of Thousand Trails in September of that year.

The Company

Thousand Trails owned and operated outdoor recreational campground resorts commonly referred to as "preserves." The Company's marketing staff, operating at these preserves, sold family memberships which entitled purchasers to use any existing or future locations for visits extending up to two weeks at a time. In contrast to most parks which were part of the National Park System or operated or franchised by Kampgrounds of America, the Thousand Trails preserve was designed to serve as a destination campground. That is, members would typically spend two or more consecutive nights at the site, most often on weekends and during vacations.

In consideration of this, as well as of the fact that memberships were sold primarily to middle-income families with children and to retired individuals, each preserve employed a staff of recreational supervisors who organized activities such as swimming and tennis lessons, dances, parties, tournaments of various types, and a large assortment of games. Amenities included swimming pools, indoor recreational centers, tennis courts, basketball and athletic courts, other outdoor game areas and fields, hiking trails, restrooms and showers, chapels, and other resort facilities. A year-round trained recreation, maintenance, and security staff was employed at each preserve.

Product

The appeal of a Thousand Trails membership consisted of several key elements. These included:

- *Effective use of an existing recreational investment.* Most Thousand Trails members had already made a major investment in their choice of outdoor recreation. Eighty-nine percent of the members were committed to utilizing their recreational vehicles. The Thousand Trails concept was designed to effectively meet that desire. By providing security, cleanliness and maintenance, supervised recreation, quality amenities, and aesthetically pleasing locations, TT attempted to meet the expressed needs of the RV owner.

- *Cost of alternatives.* Vacation homes, cabins on the lake, vacation travel, etc., had become increasingly expensive. Most consumers were not in a position financially to afford such a purchase. While a Thousand Trails preserve did not offer the same degree of privacy as an individual second home, by placing four to five campsites per acre and leaving 30%-40% of each property in an undeveloped state a certain ability to "get away from it all" was offered to the members. In addition, because of the availability of multiple locations offered by a Thousand Trails membership, the members could "pick and choose" between a mountain, desert, ocean, or lakefront environment.
- *Deterioration of public/government provided alternatives.* Due to continuing budgetary restrictions by state and federal government agencies, the alternatives available to the consuming public were diminishing. Most of the facilities offered by these agencies had a lower quality of amenities, minimal security, and a lack of maintenance. Additionally, budgetary cuts had resulted in the closure of many campgrounds across the country, further increasing occupancy pressure on a system already overcrowded with campers.
- *Security.* Perhaps the most desirable feature of a Thousand Trails membership was that of security. Controlled entry to the preserves, combined with 24-hour uniformed security personnel, provided the members with a high degree of assurance that their personal possessions would not be subject to theft or vandalism. Coincidental with funding reductions of state and national park systems had been a decrease in security provided by those organizations. Accordingly, the benefits provided a member in this area became even more apparent.
- *Supervised recreation.* The "fun" aspect of a membership in Thousand Trails was also an extremely important component of the product. Movies, dances, athletic events, instruction in sports activities, hayrides, etc. were all key elements to a happy member. Most members stated that the social experience was what they enjoyed most about Thousand Trails.

By the end of 1981, Thousand Trails was operating 15 preserves with an agreement in principle to acquire five more units. These range in size from 11 to 754 acres, with the average running 175 acres. From its roots in Washington state, the Company began its expansion south into Oregon in 1978 and California in 1979. A preserve in British Columbia opened in 1978. In selecting its preserve sites, TT considered a variety of criteria, including:

- *Proximity to a market area.* Preserves should be located within approximately 60 miles of a population center of at least 500,000.
- *Proximity to a natural amenity.* Preserves should be located on or close to a lake, river, ocean, or national forest.
- *Popularity* of a general area for outdoor recreational use.
- *Topography.* Preserves should have ample tree cover and terrain suitable to the company's typical recreational facilities.

- *Availability of domestic water supply and suitable soil conditions.*
- *Accessibility from primary roads.* Preserves should be located in close proximity to a major highway.
- *Suitability* of any existing improvements for the Company's operations.

Exhibit B summarizes the acquisitions through 1981.

Membership

A membership in Thousand Trails was similar to memberships in golf and country clubs or tennis clubs. The membership provided an unlimited right to use the Company's facilities subject only to published Company rules and guidelines. The membership was nonproprietary and the Company reserves the right to remove any property from the system subject to a "best effort" replacement in a similar geographic area.

Prior to October 1980, Company memberships permitted unlimited usage of all preserves regardless of location. After that time the Company offered two types of memberships—an Unlimited Membership entitling the member and his family to use all existing and future preserves operated by the Company; and Regional Membership which restricted usage to existing and future properties located within one of four geographic regions. Unlimited Memberships were sold at $5,795 and Regional Memberships at $4,795. A regional member could convert to an unlimited membership within one year by paying an additional $1,500. Since October 1980, approximately 90% of all new members had purchased Unlimited Memberships. Although memberships were sold on the basis of the existing preserve network, families could use facilities developed in the future, subject only to the restrictions of their particular type of membership.

Members, regardless of type of membership, could use the preserves on a first-come, first-served basis except when reservations were requested on busy holiday weekends such as Memorial Day, the Fourth of July, and Labor Day.

Memberships could not be transferred during the initial two years of ownership except to family members or by operation of law. Otherwise, memberships being sold could be transferred twice and would then expire upon the death of the second transferee. By policy, the Company had restricted memberships at each preserve to 10 times the number of constructed campsites, which prevented overcrowding of the preserves and promoted good member relations. Detailed statistical records were maintained to monitor this policy. As a preserve approached capacity, additional campsites were added. All existing properties had planned and regulatorially approved, but undeveloped, sites available for future expansion.

The customer

As mentioned earlier, 89% of Thousand Trails members were RV owners. The RV market was segmented as follows:

Motorized motor homes and vans	31%
Truck campers	20%
Travel trailers	35%
Folding camping trailers	14%

RV owners represented roughly 8.3% of vehicle-owning families in the United States. Regionally, the Western states had the highest preponderance of RVs:

	% of RV market	% of US population
West	34	21
South	29	32
North central	26	28
Northeast	11	19

Forty-eight percent of all RV owners were from households without children, 20% of RV owners had one child, 18% two children, and 14% had three or more children.

Age of household head	% owning RVs
25	3.1%
25-35	7.4%
35-44	11.7%
45-54	10.1%
55-64	10.1%
65	4.9%

Family income bracket (1980)	Share of RV market
$15,000	22%
$15,000-25,000	40%
$25,000	33%

Even with the amazing growth of the past 5 years, Thousand Trails had yet to saturate the market. With its almost 28,000 members at the end of 1981, Thousand Trails had achieved the highest penetration of RV owners in the state of Washington (5.1%). Only 1.3% of all California RV owners were members of TT. Additional data about members are listed in Exhibit C.

Competition

Management believed that the Company was in an excellent position vis-à-vis the competition. Thousand Trails did not compete directly with transient campgrounds such as Kampgrounds of America (KOA), which were generally located on or near major highways and used by recreational vehicle travelers principally on an overnight basis. Rather, the Company's preserves were developed and marketed as family "distinction" recreational resorts catering to member families for weekend and vacation use. Numerous private campgrounds existed throughout the Western USA which competed directly with TT through marketing nonexclusive membership usable at multiple destination campground locations. The two largest of these were American Campgrounds, Inc., with 30 locations and 1980 sales of $21 million, and the Great Outdoor American Adventure with 11 sites and 1980 sales of $11.1 million. In addition, there were approximately 400 "ma and pa" single site establishments. Of these 180 joined a network called Camp Coast to Coast.

In general, it was management's opinion that Thousand Trails was the industry leader by a wide margin. The vast majority of competitive personnel were former TT employees. Almost all of the pricing structures and marketing concepts were directly copied from TT. One marketing manager asserted: "We have not had the time to go out and learn about the competition; quite frankly, I just don't think they are all that important."

Organization

The Company was really four different businesses: a financial company that provided funds for expansion and managed the substantial receivables; a resort service company with a large staff dedicated to creating preserve services for members to enjoy; a construction and engineering concern that concentrated on locating and developing new properties in addition to improving existing properties; and a sales and marketing organization that focused on selling memberships to the preserves (see Exhibit D).

Each of the four subdivisions ran fairly autonomous operations. There was substantial managerial communication at the top level. The CEO played a very pivotal coordinating role in facilitating the efforts of each group.

Marketing and sales

The company marketed memberships in Thousand Trails through its own sales organization. Because the product that this firm offered was not readily available for evaluation, the marketing effort became very crucial. In fact, back in the early years of the company, Milt Kuolt saw the marketing efforts as the key constraint on growth.

Although marketing and sales were both under one vice-president, they were seen as distinctly different functions (see Exhibit E). Marketing attempted to build awareness of the product and entice people to visit the preserves for a tour. A sales force was located at each preserve and guided tours around the local facility, making a sales presentation throughout the tour. Since a sale could not be closed without inspection of the actual site, the marketing effort was concentrated on areas surrounding existing Thousand Trails preserves. The prime target base was the RV owner.

The marketing effort consisted of a number of programs whose goal was to attract members to visit a TT site. The primary methods were:

1. Member personal referral program
2. Direct mail promotion
3. Professional referral program
4. Two-step program
5. Phone sales effort
6. Attendance at fairs and shows
7. Advertising

The member personal referral program. The basic concept behind the program was the use of the existing membership base to locate prospective new sales. Members received compensation for each completed tour they generated as well as for each membership purchased as a result of referral. In more recent years Thousand Trails changed the compensation formula frequently. Prior to April 1981, members received $50 per tour generated and $200 for each generated prospect that purchased a membership. Since sales were strongest on weekends, they received an extra $50 for sales developed between Monday and Friday.

In April 1981, TT changed compensation with the initiation of The Friends of Thousand Trails program. Under this new system member compensation was determined by a very complicated award points system. Cash and/or merchandise awards were offered.

Direct mail. Thousand Trails generated a significant proportion of total prospects by mailing information about the Company to people with an interest in the outdoors. Large quantities of mail (150,000 pieces per week) were sent out to residents in areas convenient to the 15 preserves. Mailing lists utilized included the California RV ownership list, the Oregon RV ownership list (the Washington RV list was not public information), and West Coast subscribers to *Field and Stream, Campers World, Camping Journal,* and *Hunting and Fishing Review.* The Company used outside agencies to design, develop, and mail the items.

The mailers tried to sell Thousand Trails by offering free gifts in return for a visit to a preserve. The standard gifts were items like Coleman sleeping bags, Bar-B-Q grills, and cameras. Mailers offered a wide range of information on the actual product. Some pieces mentioned the product concept with little elaboration, whereas others devoted considerable space to a description of the product. Many gimmicks such as enclosing credit cards or running sweepstakes were used to get people to open the mail. The average rate (i.e., actual tours generated) was .53%. See Exhibit F for sample mail pieces. F1 is an example of an unsuccessful ad, while F2 presents a more successful one.

The large volume and diversity of mailings made the mail department a sizeable operation. Prior to the end of 1981 very few systems were in place to monitor mailing results. For example, a person who had already purchased a membership or had gone on a tour without purchasing could receive numerous additional mailings. In general, the approach was a shotgun attempt which tended to be biased towards quantity rather than quality. Very little systematic pretesting of mailers was done (see Exhibit G).

Professional referral program. The professional PR program was similar to the member PR program except for the fact that nonmembers were used to identify and send prospects to the preserve sales office for tours. Pro PR workers were paid $50 for each tour generated. They were chosen and managed by the preserve sales manager. The number of Pro PR workers used was at the discretion of the individual manager. Company management was known to change its mind frequently with regard to the value of the program and the level of support lent to it.

Two-step program. In 1981, management decided that a major disincentive for prospective customers was the distance to a Thousand Trails preserve. To deal with this issue, the Company initiated a series of presentations on the Thousand Trails concept in large population centers. These presentations generally occurred on a monthly basis. Attendees were offered free dinner and cocktails at a local hotel plus a small gift. The main sources of recruiting people for these meetings were "cold" phone calls and the membership base who were encouraged to attend with some friends.

These presentations were run by the sales manager of the local preserve. No attempt was made to close a sale. Instead these meetings were seen as a prescreening. Interested attendees were encouraged to set up a visit to the local preserve at their earliest convenience (the second step).

Phone sales effort. Thousand Trails had over ten communications centers in the western states. Each center had six phones and a supervisor. Most calls were cold calls made between 3 PM and 9 PM. The calls followed a standard format (see Exhibit H) and attempted to solicit either tours at the local preserve or attendance at a two-step presentation. Gifts were offered as enticement.

The number of centers and the organizational structure varied substantially over the years. In 1981, the number of centers ranged from 7 to 14. Centers were known to open and close within three months.

Attendance at fairs and shows. Thousand Trails participated in roughly 30 West Coast outdoor recreational fairs and shows. These activities were conducted by the Regional Sales Manager. The booths were set up and moved by a special fairs and shows staff. Company representatives informed people about the Thousand Trails concept and tried to convince them to take a sales tour. The shows were also used to generate additional leads for future mailings.

Advertising. The advertising program consisted of placing ads in media that reached areas close to the various preserves. Placement decisions were made by the Director of Marketing, who received input from the Regional Sales Managers, who in turn, received requests from preserve sales managers.

Sales

As mentioned earlier, the sales force sold memberships at the preserve sites. Each preserve sales force had a manager and, depending on the size of the preserve, the manager might also have an associate. Most of the sales manager's time was spent recruiting and training staff, developing the "team," achieving monthly and annual sales projections, scheduling the sales crew, handling sales premiums, coordinating member PR and Pro PR programs, coordinating two-step programs, and interfacing with the preserve operations manager to ensure the quality of the TT product. The 15 sales managers reported to four region managers and these managers reported to the Director of Sales and Marketing.

In 1981, the average number of salespeople was 145. The total ranged between 112 and 220. Total hires for the year numbered 440. The top-paid salesperson earned $78,500 while the average salary was a little over $40,000 on an annualized basis. The Company experienced large turnovers in the sales force, especially in the Pacific Northwest. Salespeople in Washington and Oregon eyed the greater opportunity in the newer preserves in California. Many of the salespeople from the North quit and applied for jobs when a new preserve opened.

Selling methods

When selling a membership, Thousand Trails salespeople followed a prescribed sales presentation which included the following ten steps:

- *The greeting.* A friendly greeting was given to a prospect and the prospect's family by a salesperson, welcoming them to the preserve.
- *Registration.* The greeter introduced the prospect to the receptionist who took down pertinent information such as the address and phone number, the marketing effort which influenced the prospect to visit Thousand Trails and the gifts he or she was to receive. The receptionist then assigned the prospect to a salesperson for a sales presentation. If the prospect was generated by the efforts of a specific salesman, the prospect was assigned to that salesman for the presentation.

- *Introduction to the salesperson.* The receptionist introduced the prospect and the prospect's family to the assigned salesperson who then gave them the appropriate gift. Then they went to a private room where the salesperson became further acquainted with the prospect. After preliminary introductions, the prospect was asked to fill out a consumer survey. The consumer survey provided answers about outdoor recreational preferences and interest, which alerted the salesman or saleswoman as to what Thousand Trails should emphasize during the presentation. The survey also provided the Company with information concerning consumer attitudes and demand.
- *The fact sheet.* After the prospect completed the "consumer survey," the salesperson used a "fact sheet" to acquaint the prospect with and establish the credibility of the Company. Although some salespeople presented the "fact sheet" differently, many used the format suggested in the sales manual.
- *Alternatives to Thousand Trails.* Once the prospect was given an introduction to the Company and the product, the salesperson illustrated the value of a Thousand Trails membership by presenting and comparing the alternatives—camping at state and national parks (which tended to be overcrowded, dirty, and unsafe), purchasing a private campsite (which in 1980 cost on the average over $10,000), and buying a membership to a camping club (most of which provided only one camping location).
- *Description of Thousand Trails preserves and regional memberships.* After comparing the alternatives, the salesperson showed the prospect pictures and maps of the Company's 14 preserves, described the attributes of each preserve, and then explained details of the Company's regional membership. At this point, mention was made of a special membership offer available for those who took advantage of their initial purchase opportunity. The special offer referred to was the chance to buy an unlimited membership. No details concerning the "special offer" were given at this time.
- *The video presentation.* Following the description of the preserves and the regional membership, the prospect and the prospect's family were shown a 15-minute videotape which highlighted the many merits of the Thousand Trails concept.
- *The tour.* Immediately following the videotape, the prospect and the prospect's family were given an automobile tour of the grounds. The salesperson stopped and got out of the car with the prospect and the prospect's family to view various points of interest.
- *The map presentation.* While heading back to the sales office, mention was made of additional maps of each campground which the prospect should see. While the maps were being displayed, all the benefits of membership were reviewed.
- *The close.* Finally, it was up to the salesperson to complete the sale. As an added incentive to the prospect to purchase a membership, he/she extended the "one time special offer" mentioned earlier in the presentation. The offer was the opportunity to purchase an unlimited membership if the prospect acted immediately. Salespeople often used the crew manager, the associate manager, or the preserve sales manager to help close a sale.

Immediately after a membership was sold to a prospect, the new member was told about the details and monetary benefits of the PR program, and given a schedule of preserve events. Then a picture of the new member and his family was taken and placed on display with pictures of other families who had purchased a membership at that preserve. They were now part of what the Company referred to as the "Thousand Trails family." They were welcomed to the "Thousand Trails family" by everyone in the sales office. That night, the salesperson called the new member, congratulating and again welcoming him/her to Thousand Trails, and asking if there were any questions. The following day a thank-you letter was mailed to the new member. All post-sales efforts were a means of allaying buyers' possible doubts and ensuring the satisfaction of new members with their purchases. Member satisfaction was not only essential to the image of the Company and the effectiveness of the PR program, but was important to Company personnel because they took pride in their product.

Compensation

In 1981, the Company varied its compensation plan at least three times. This caused uneasiness at the sales force level since a salesperson often did not understand how gross pay was decided. Throughout the year, this issue caused the development of a hostile attitude toward the home office in Seattle. Home office personnel were referred to as "Corporate Pukes" in the field.

Their typical sales manager's compensation package included these features: a base pay, a standard per sale ($25) rate, plus a bonus based on a monthly closing rate and percentage of target reached. Exhibit J presents a version of the compensation program.

The salesperson compensation plan included: a base pay of $200 per week, commission rate per sale based on the type of membership sold and the cash down payment and length of payment term (see Exhibits I and J), volume commission incentive, which paid an additional set fee for each sale over a certain number of sales, and a monthly bonus stock plan.

Preparing for 1982

The new management team had many issues to deal with as it entered 1982. The fourth quarter of 1981 was the firm's first losing quarter in years. Net earnings for the year 1981 were below the 1980 level, although sales were higher. The stock price had fallen from a peak of near 14 in 1980 to the current 5-7 range.

Clearly many of the major problems could be found in sales and marketing. Marketing costs as a percentage of membership sales had risen. (See Exhibit K for additional marketing statistics.)

Marketing costs as a percentage of sales

1976	1977	1978	1979	1980	1981
51.9%	46.9%	41.5%	38.1%	45.1%	49.6%

From top down the entire marketing and sales department had been in a state of upheaval throughout 1981. Four different individuals occupied the position of VP of Sales and Marketing; compensation programs changed every few months until it got to the point where staff members could barely understand their checks; rapport between the home office and the field personnel increasingly weakened; many new programs had been initiated.

Two major mistakes epitomized the misguided strategy out of Seattle:

1. *The April Mailing.* In early 1981, management decided to get away from the junk mail "gimmicky" image of its mail program. An elaborate product mailing that focused on the beauty and quality of the preserves was developed in-house instead of by one of the regular agencies. Over 1 million pieces were printed. After mailing out 400,000 units it became apparent that the response was not as high as anticipated—the return rate was only .3%. The estimated cost of this blunder was $750,000.

2. *The Friends of the Thousand Trails Program.* Around mid-1981, the VP of Sales and Marketing decided that the cash incentive for the member PR program was losing its effectiveness. He introduced an extremely complicated program which assigned bonus points to members for their referral assistance. These points translated into cash or merchandise from an extremely elaborate hardbound color catalogue. Implementing the new format cost $1.75 million and did not substantially increase member PR efforts.

As Bob Mayes accepted his position of Sales and Marketing VP in late December 1981, he was excited about the firm's tremendous potential but a bit confused about where to focus his attention. Fortunately, the firm had recently installed a sophisticated MIS system which provided good up-to-date information of sales activities. After spending some time selling in the field he drew the following conclusion: "The product is a definite 10, but our sales effort is a 2 or a 3. We really need to get things in shape quickly or the Company will lose the momentum it has built up over the years."

□

EXHIBIT A

Thousand Trails
Financial statement

	Year Ended December 31,		
	1981	1980	1979
Sales of memberships	$40,006,000	$33,950,000	$21,396,000
Costs attributable to membership sales			
Marketing expenses	19,831,000	15,323,000	8,159,000
Preserve land and improvement costs	5,753,000	4,825,000	2,832,000
General and administrative expenses	7,141,000	5,760,000	3,980,000
Provision for doubtful accounts	1,866,000	824,000	886,000
	34,591,000	26,732,000	15,857,000
Income from membership sales	5,415,000	7,218,000	5,539,000
Preserve operations			
Membership dues	3,304,000	2,048,000	1,170,000
Trading post and other sales	1,482,000	868,000	389,000
	4,786,000	2,916,000	1,559,000
Less—			
Cost of trading post sales	1,346,000	675,000	148,000
Maintenance and operations expenses	2,470,000	1,858,000	1,045,000
General and administrative expenses	801,000	524,000	498,000
	4,617,000	3,057,000	1,691,000

	Year Ended December 31,		
	1981	1980	1979
Income (loss) from preserve operations	169,000	(141,000)	(132,000)
Other income (expense)			
Interest income	4,153,000	2,530,000	1,267,000
Interest expense (Note G)	(3,213,000)	(1,332,000)	(1,470,000)
Gain on sale of property held for investment		437,000	122,000
Other	(147,000)	24,000	50,000
	793,000	1,659,000	(31,000)
Earnings before taxes	6,377,000	8,736,000	5,376,000
Deferred income taxes	3,050,000	4,200,000	2,586,000
Net earnings	$3,327,000	$4,536,000	$ 2,790,000
Net earnings per share:			
Primary	$1.06	$1.69	$1.17
Fully diluted	$1.02	$1.42	$1.17

Source: Company annual report

EXHIBIT B

Thousand Trails
preserve system ($ thousand)

Location	Year acquired	Acreage	Total planned	Existing campsites	Approved campsites	Cost of existing property and investments	Estimated cost of planned improvements
Chehalis, WA	1973	218	600	425	600	$2318	$ 775
Leavenworth, WA	1975	135	400	275	275	1666	536
Hood Canal, WA	1976	199	252	80	252	1487	1428
Mt. Vernon, WA	1976	260	500	275	275	2869	1054
La Conner, WA	1978	108	500	288	500	3042	869
Cultus Lake, BC	1978	84	530	400	530	1546	562
Bend, ORE	1978	156	520	330	530	2438	839
Pacific City, ORE	1978	108	651	251	251	1971	2607
Donner Pass, CA	1979	238	406	310	310	3879	680
Lake of the Springs, CA	1979	754	960	387	560	4446	2746
Soledad, CA	1980	230	1100	—	1100	3662	6228
Idyllwild, CA	1980	120	360	105	286	2446	1185
San Diego, CA	1980	88	600	234	234	2152	1899
San Jose, CA	1980	62	320	140	170	3631	1847
Oakzanita, CA	1981	75	350	100	142	1220	2370

EXHIBIT C

Thousand Trails
member Survey

A. Age of head of household: 52.3   Retired: 36% Yes 64% No
B. Length of time with present employer: 14.3 years.
C. Number of dependent children: 0.9   Ages: 11.2 years.
D. Do you own your place of residence? 91.9% Yes 8.1% No
E. Length of time at present residence: 11.7 years.
F. Length of paid vacation of head of household (if not retired): 3.7 weeks
G. Family income range for 1980: (percent in each income bracket)

5.7 under $10,000	12.6 $10,000–$15,000
12.4 $15,000–$20,000	18.3 $20,000–$25,000
17.9 $25,000–$30,000	12.0 $30,000–$35,000
6.7 $35,000–$40,000	5.1 $40,000–$45,000
2.5 $45,000–$50,000	6.9 over $50,000

H. Head of household by age bracket (percent in each age bracket)

2.9 under 30	14.4 30–39
23.2 40–49	26.3 50–59
16.4 60–64	16.8 over 64

EXHIBIT D

Thousand Trails
table of organization

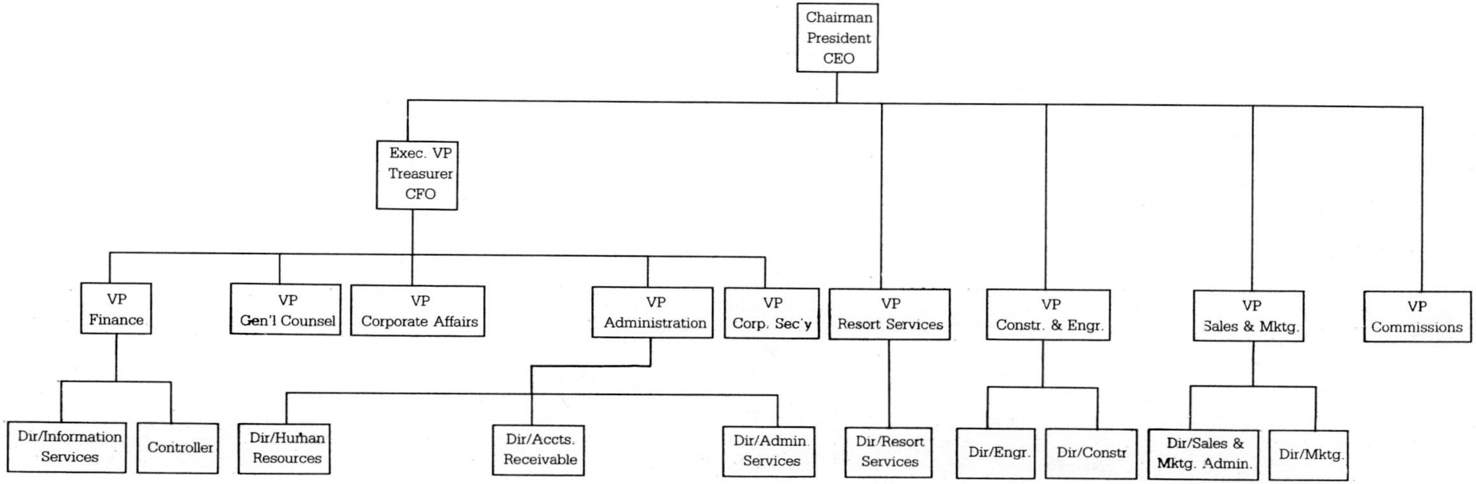

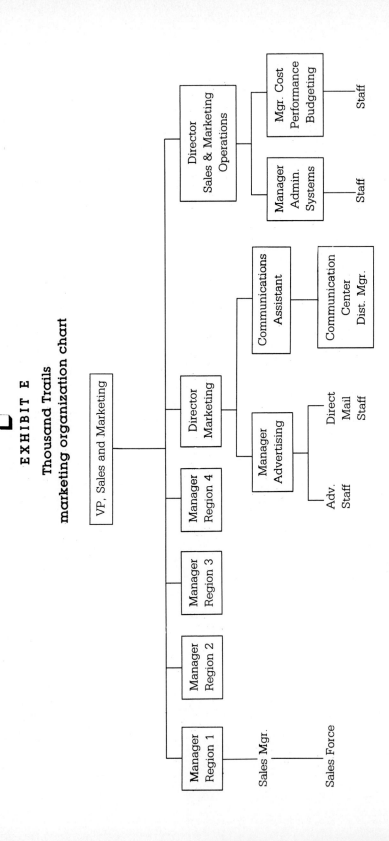

EXHIBIT E

Thousand Trails
marketing organization chart

EXHIBIT F-1

Direct mail ads

Dear friend:

We *really* want you to see Thousand Trails, so we're offering you your choice of *3 valuable free gifts* and *take a free tour* of the finest outdoor recreation preserves in the west. It's our way of saying "thank you" for driving out to hear our story and see our preserve.

When you leave for home, take with you any one of these *valuable free gifts!*

* ELECTRIC CHAR-B-QUE. A real energy-saver that ends forever the charcoal mess.
* REMINGTON CHAIN SAW. Here's a trusted name and a handy tool to have around—at home or in your RV.
* COLEMAN SLEEPING BAGS. A name synonymous with outdoor recreation for years.

Thousand Trails is *more than a dozen private preserves* from Southern California to Canada—yours whenever you plan your family's outdoor recreation.

Imagine these *exclusive resort-preserves* complete with clubhouses, swimming pools, *clean and fully equipped campsites* with recreational areas for young and old alike. PLUS acres and acres of NATURAL WILDERNESS where you can *walk and talk with your kids* and share the great outdoors—maybe just like it was when you were younger.

THOUSAND TRAILS: *A WAY OF LIFE. AN ATTITUDE.*

Honestly, one of the biggest decisions a member-family has to make is *which preserve to visit!*

The *friendly, comfortable* and *safe* environment of each Thousand Trails campground poses the dilemma to *rekindling last visit's relationships* or to head out for a *brand-new experience.* In any case, you'll be assured that your Thousand Trails neighbors will be the kind of people that you'd choose for *your own friends,* and *those of your family.*

Thousand Trails *has it all* in outdoor recreation and entertainment—we're the *original* and *the standard* for the industry to match. We're still way out front and intend to stay that way!

Come visit Thousand Trails. You deserve it.

Stu Harelik
for Thousand Trails

P.S.   Your *gift* is waiting. *Plan now* to drive out and see us. You'll like what you see and hear!

EXHIBIT F-2
Direct mail ads

$250,000

. . . Like a dream come true!

Congratulations   The Savage family has definitely won at least two prizes in the Thousand Trails $250,000 luxury sweepstakes. As a sweepstakes winner, you may have won $250,000 in cash. At least two of the following luxury gifts, with a combined minimum suggested retail value of $174.95, will definitely be yours:

		Suggested retail value
1.	$250,000 cash	$250,000.00*
2.	1982 Cadillac Coupe deVille	$ 16,009.50
3.	Ranch mink coat	$ 6,110.00
4.	Trip for 2 to London, Paris & Rome—7 nights, 8 days, airfare & accommodations	$ 4,050.00
5.	Magnavox color 25″ TV with video cassette recorder	$ 1,814.25
6.	$500 cash	$ 500.00
7.	Deluxe gas-fired, family-sized barbeque	$ 119.95
8.	$100 cash	$ 100.00
9.	AM/FM multiplex stereo with headset	$ 99.95
10.	$75 cash	$ 75.00

There's no obligation to purchase anything. To receive your prizes, simply present this mailer at the Thousand Trails information office. Your prize claim numbers will be matched to the notarized master prize list posted in the office in order to determine which specific prizes are yours.

Important . . . you must claim your prizes by November 14, 1982, or your selection as a winner in the $250,000 luxury sweepstakes will be voided. The Thousand Trails office is open for prize claims from 9:00 A.M. to dusk, Monday through Sunday. See the back of this letter for map and eligibility conditions.

Sincerely,

Julie Cooper

P.S. Visit Thousand Trails Monday through Friday and receive a mystery gift valued at $39.95.

*Prize will be paid at $12,500 per year for twenty years.

E X H I B I T   G

**Thousand Trails
direct mail results
1981 year-end***

	Total pieces mailed	Number of tours resulted	Percentage return	Actual sales	Sales closing percentage
Chehalis	237,979	870	.356%	61	7.0%
Leavenworth	19,401	176	.907%	11	6.25%
Hood Canal	11,449	91	.795%	9	9.89%
Mt. Vernon	35,009	119	.339%	9	7.56%
La Conner	197,003	790	.401%	79	10.0%
Bend	376,143	1786	.475%	102	5.7%
Pacific City	695,775	3220	.463%	204	6.3%
Donner Pass	333,669	1705	.511%	96	5.6%
LOTS	615,384	1969	.32%	251	12.7%
Soledad	940,773	5118	.544%	594	11.6%
Idyllwild	682,085	3197	.469%	342	10.7%
San Diego	830,658	5331	.642%	708	13.3%
San Jose	851,669	6187	.726%	723	11.7%
Oakzanita	31,834	199	.625%	10	5.0%
Santa Ana	22,598	270	1.19%	10	3.7%
Total as of December	5,881,429	31,028	.528%	3,209	10.3%

*This includes mailings made between 1/1/81 and 12/4/81.

◻

EXHIBIT H

Thousand Trails

Two-Step Phone Presentation*

HELLO MR. OR MRS. ＿＿. THIS IS ＿＿ CALLING FOR "THOUSAND TRAILS" AND THE PURPOSE OF MY CALL THIS EVENING IS TO INVITE YOU AND YOUR ＿＿ TO SEE A FILM PRESENTATION OF OUR THOUSAND TRAILS CAMPING AREAS. WE HAVE 12 DIFFERENT LOCATIONS FROM CANADA TO CALIFORNIA AND WE HAVE ALOT TO OFFER IN THE WAY OF CAMPING AND FAMILY RECREATION.

AND JUST FOR TAKING YOUR TIME TO SEE OUR FILM WE'D LIKE TO GIVE YOU A 3LB. SLEEPING BAG.

"HOW DOES THAT SOUND"

WE WILL SEND YOU A RESERVATION IN THE MAIL WITH COMPLETE DIRECTIONS. ALSO, WE'LL BE GIVING YOU A CALL BACK JUST TO SEE IF EVERYTHING IS O.K.

Name ＿＿ Mr. and Mrs.
Age ＿＿
Correct Addresses ＿＿
Camping Equipment ＿＿
Employment ＿＿ Works Where ＿＿

*Taken Directly from Company Literature

EXHIBIT I

Thousand Trails

Feb. 1 - April 30, 1981
Sales managers compensation
United States

Effective 2/1/81

1. Expense Allowance $2,600 per month—($1,300 paid twice monthly)
2. Base Compensation $25.00 per sale—override paid weekly
3. Performance Compensation

(To qualify for the Performance Compensation, the Preserve unit sales for the month have to be 100% of the monthly quota).

a. Closing Sales Percentage

Direct	Two-Step
16%—$30.00 per sale	28%—$30.00 per sale
17%—$35.00 per sale	30%—$35.00 per sale
18%—$45.00 per sale	32%—$45.00 per sale
19%—$55.00 per sale	34%—$55.00 per sale
20% & Over—$75.00 per sale	36% & Over—$75.00 per sale

b. 100% of Volume Target— $60.00 per sale—paid monthly (on all sales over monthly targets).

c. Quarterly Closing % Bonus—A stock bonus plan, to be used on quarterly closing rates, is currently being finalized.

EXHIBIT J

Thousand Trails
Compensation schedule
(on-site)
United States*
Effective June 13, 1981
Company Generated Sales

Length of Contract

Down payment	24 month	36 month	48 month	60 month	72 month
Cash day of sale		Unlimited regional membership—$5795			
			650		
$1995	525	500	475	425	375
$1595	500	475	450	400	350
$1295	475	450	425	375	325
$1095	455	430	405	355	305
$ 995	425	400	375	325	275
$ 795	375	350	325	275	225
All		Regional membership with option—$4795			
			200		

EXHIBIT K

Thousand Trails
marketing statistics

	1978			1979			1980			1981		
	Tours	Sales	Cost per sale	Tours	Sales	Cost per sale	Tours	Sales	Cost per sale	Tours	Sales	Cost per sale
Member PR	14,502	1,828		13,692	2,531		12,195	2,399	457	10,308	2,493	765
Pro PR	—	—		—	—		4,883	670	606	1,773	250	766
Advertising	—	—		216	21		1,607	175	1,258	548	46	1,331
Fairs & Shows/Phone	3,582	974		8,560	1,137		6,841	875	1,723	9,840	1,271	1,419
Direct Mail	1,593	302		5,683	822		17,371	1,999	600	30,721	3,221	783
Self-generated	2,511	346		1,411	282		1,644	440	N/A	1,609	364	159
Other	3,924	831		2,220	394		5,189	767	N/A	621	87	58
Total	26,112	4,281	N/A	31,782	5,187	N/A	49,730	7,325	627	55,420	7,732	847

Questions

1. What are the components of the old marketing plan that should be retained in the new one? Why?
2. How would you define the mix of product and service for Thousand Trails? What factors support your product-service mix? Do you think the mix should be changed? If so, how?
3. What are the market segments Thousand Trails should be going after? How do you support this market segmentation?
4. Construct a positioning matrix for Thousand Trails.
5. How would you, as Bob Mayes, go about marketing Thousand Trails?

CHAPTER 10

Commercial recreation advertising

CHAPTER OBJECTIVES

1. To identify the types of advertising

2. To examine each type of advertising and its parts

3. To identify the advantages and disadvantages of each type

Once you have developed a positioning statement, the next step is to communicate that information to the general public. This is accomplished through advertising and public relations.

Advertising is paid communication. It is through advertising that a product or service is portrayed in its best possible light. The positioning statement gives information about the target market, the services and products on offer, what is unique about them, and how to present each decision utility in its best light.

Advertising and public relations are the keys to creating an image. *Public relations* is planned dissemination of information about a business, product, service, or institution in order to create a positive image. Public relations differs from advertising because it attempts to influence other disseminators of information by showing the product in a positive light. You do not pay for information dissemination in public relations. Advertising is paid-for placement of information. Public relations will not be dealt with in this chapter.

There are five elements of success in advertising.

1. The advertisement must attract attention to the product, service, business, or institution through eye-catchers and innovative techniques.
2. The advertising campaign must build interest in the product or service. At-

tention without the interest to pursue or acquire the product serves no purpose.

3. Advertising must create a desire for the product. Without desire there is no sale, and the advertising is a waste of time and money.
4. Advertising must produce action, that is to say, motivate the consumer to purchase the product or service.
5. Advertising must create sales. The ultimate test of an advertisement is how many sales it generates. The effectiveness of an advertising campaign can be tested (Fig. 10-1).

The recreation manager may use two forms of advertising, print and broadcast. We shall spend a little time discussing each form.

Print media

Print media have many advantages. One is that most allow the consumer to keep a copy of an advertisement for future reference. They also allow coupon promotions, which permit the advertiser to track the effectiveness of each specific advertisement. It is important to understand some general guidelines for the use of print media and the advantages and disadvantages of each type. This section will be divided into general considerations concerning the advantages and disadvantages of the print media.

It is very important to keep in mind the following guidelines when working with the print media:

1. Make the advertisement distinctive and consistent and make it stand out from competing advertisements and articles on the page. This can be done by using white space, distinctive borders, or typeface. It is important to stay consistent with the image developed through the positioning statement.
2. Keep it simple and plain. It is better to exceed consumer expectations than to create high expectations but not fulfill them. In the case of a service the first impression is usually made through an illustration. This should be the focal point of the advertising layout.
3. Use a dominant theme. This can be directly related to the illustration. The theme or dominant element should be consistent in a particular ad as well as in the advertising campaign.
4. Offer something people want. This should be the key concept identified by the positioning statement. It should be a big enough benefit that consumers will be directly stimulated to purchase the item.
5. The product or benefit should be included in the theme of the advertisement and should be easy to see and identify.
6. Include the readers in the ad; allow them some way to identify themselves with the product. This can be done by appropriately selecting the target market and media.

FIG. 10-1 This ad uses all five steps to excellent advantage. In addition it uses the components of marketing discussed in the previous chapter. Note the identification of the target market and the graphic representation of the benefits provided. (Photograph courtesy of La Quinta.)

7. Use action words, figures, or graphics to motivate the consumer to action.
8. Above all else, be believable. Avoid offering impossible benefits. Inflating benefits will result in unbelievable advertising and in dissatisfied customers.

This short list of recommendations will benefit the advertising program. Now let's discuss the advantages and disadvantages of print advertising.

The print media consist of newspapers, magazines, outdoor advertising, point-of-purchase advertising, and direct mail advertising. Some general considerations and examples of each type will be presented and followed by a look at their advantages and disadvantages.

Newspapers

Newspapers can be divided into six major classifications:

1. National newspapers such as *USA Today* and *The Wall Street Journal* provide national information but not local news. They print regional versions to allow local ads and are suitable for advertisements of local recreation businesses because of cost and wide circulation.
2. Morning newspapers feature sports, business, and finance. They usually have wide local circulation.
3. Afternoon newspapers have more time to collect information and process it. However, decreased circulation time limits the paper to a narrower area of distribution. Their articles are usually more concerned with human interest, sales and general interest.
4. Sunday newspapers are usually full of advertisements and include special articles. On Sunday most families have the time for newspaper reading, so Sunday papers have a relatively large circulation, especially in the larger cities.
5. Nondaily newspapers are published by small communities or independent towns and the circulation is very small. They are usually patronized by local advertisers, and most are filled with local events. These newspapers have a longer life and are read more carefully than daily newspapers.
6. Shopping newspapers consist mainly of advertisements. They usually appear at midweek and control circulation by geographical location. They can be a good means for information dissemination.

Advantages

1. Newspapers have intensive market coverage. They reach more than 90% of the families in a geographical area.
2. Newspapers appeal to all ages, races, and income classes.
3. Newspapers provide specific geographic coverage and allow localized copy and text.
4. Newspapers provide seasonal promotions and special sections, allowing the advertiser to target the consumer.
5. Consumer response to newspaper ads is rapid.
6. Newspaper closing dates are relatively close to publication. This allows for rapid changes.

Limitations

1. Newspapers have very short lives.
2. Newspaper information deteriorates rapidly, so reading time is brief and hurried.
3. There is little or no chance to identify a specific geographic area in the newspaper distribution area.

Magazines

Magazines come in three classifications:

1. General consumer magazines, which are edited for the general population and which carry a large circulation. The largest of these are *Readers Digest* and *TV Guide*.
2. Special interest magazines such as for women, businesses, and sports. These can help the manager target people who are interested in a specified product or service. A new kind of specialized magazine is the regional, such as *New York Magazine*.
3. Newpaper magazines are supplements to Sunday newspapers and can be syndicated for distribution across the country, like *Parade,* or edited and published by a single newspaper, like *The New York Times Magazine*. Each type targets a geographical area well. The syndicated newspaper magazines do not allow for regional advertising.

Advantages

1. The ability to target the characteristics of a specific market.
2. Readers are generally younger and better educated than are nonreaders of magazines.
3. Confidence in the medium is high because the consumer is purchasing the magazine for a specific purpose. Many people consider magazines to be authoritative, and this lends credibility to the advertising.
4. Magazines provide national and regional coverage. Most major magazines provide regional versions as a service to regional advertisers.
5. Magazines have a relatively long life. The articles and pictures tend to remain fresh for some time, so any advertisement has a greater chance of being read.
6. Magazines provide editorial features. These may enhance the value of a product, particularly if an advertisement runs in a magazine that has an article or editorial comment relating to the product.
7. New printing techniques have created innovative types of advertising including tear-out pages, folders, and special paper.

Limitations

1. The largest limitation to using magazines is the tremendous amount of time it takes to prepare a magazine ad, particularly in color. There are also long deadlines prior to publication. There may be many months between conception and publication.
2. The advertiser is allowed infrequent communication with the consumer because magazines are usually published once a month. If an advertiser can afford it, ongoing monthly communication is possible, but when it is impossible to afford a monthly advertising campaign, exposure time is limited.
3. The cost of developing a magazine ad is high, particularly in color.

Outdoor advertising

Outdoor advertisements can be stationary or transient. Stationary ads include billboards, posters, and painted walls. Transient advertising is placed on the backs or sides of taxicabs or buses and inside the buses themselves. Inside displays are for people to read while they are riding on the bus.

Billboards

Advantages

1. Billboards demand little consumer time or effort.
2. Billboards are a mass medium that provides information to everyone.
3. Billboards are colorful and allow for dramatic and innovative techniques.
4. Timelessness is possible with billboard advertising, since it can be repeated over and over again to people passing in the area.

Limitations

1. The copy must be extremely brief.
2. It is generally a support medium for other forms of advertising.
3. Competition is high for peoples' attention in the outdoors, and chances of an ad being read are limited.
4. There is a certain amount of public resistance to billboard advertising because it blocks the scenery.

Transient advertising

Advantages

1. There is a ready-made audience, since most of the readers have nothing else to do.
2. Transportation systems provide cut rates and lower costs.
3. The competition is limited to the amount of space available inside the bus or cab. This can be of benefit.
4. Repetition is valuable. Anyone who regularly rides a bus with an advertisement on it is likely to see that advertisement every day.
5. It can have tear-off cards or brochures that can be taken by a consumer.

Limitations

1. Transient advertising is a mass medium and does not lend itself to targeting specific market segments.
2. Its message is usually limited to 25 words or less.
3. Transient advertising is an urban medium, since mass transit takes place in and between urban areas. It is not available or effective in rural sections of the country.

Point-of-purchase

Point-of-purchase advertising is located at the retail outlet. It includes displays that help to identify uses for a product and draw attention to it. Advertising methods can include clocks, such as Coca-Cola uses, store signs, and display racks. This kind of advertising can effectively stimulate point-of-purchase sales.

Advantages

1. Point-of-purchase displays tend to increase impulsive purchases.
2. They influence repeat purchases.
3. They are an advantage to both manufacturer and retailer.

Limitations

1. Point-of-purchase displays need to be changed relatively often.
2. Point-of-purchase displays may face stiff competition for floor space in stores.

Direct mail

Direct mail can be anything from a simple postcard to a full-blown catalogue. One example of direct-mail advertising is mailing small gifts embossed with a company's name. Direct mail is a highly effective method of drawing attention to your product, but it is extremely costly.

Advantages

1. This is the only medium completely controlled by the seller.
2. Direct mail is provided specifically for a given recipient and is therefore more likely to be targeted to a specific market and be read.
3. When a consumer opens the mail, there are few distractions, which allows complete concentration on advertisements.
4. Direct mail is extremely flexible and has a larger distribution with the advent of cable television. In effect, specific stations serve the purpose of targeting a specific market segment, thus allowing a specific message to be delivered to the target audience.

Broadcast media

Broadcast media are television and radio. There are three basic forms, network, spot, and local advertising.

Network advertising originates at a home office or affiliate of a television or radio station and is aired nationwide. It has the advantage of reaching large numbers of people but is extremely expensive and allows only limited audience targeting.

Spot advertising originates at the station broadcasting a local program. Spot advertisements are beginning to reach larger distribution areas on cable television.

Local television advertising originates at local stations with a relatively limited broadcast area. It is a prime medium for local areas since it targets a specific geographic area. Some local TV stations have been able to get on cable networks. This has expanded their broadcast area tremendously. Cable TV has become a major source of advertising because it facilitates local media buys and sets aside channels specifically for advertising.

Radio and television are similar in the way they put together and handle advertising, but their advantages and disadvantages are considerably different. We will deal with these later. Now, let's discuss the different types of broadcast advertising and some guidelines for effective use of it. These are the types of broadcast advertising:

1. *Story line* is a commercial that tells a story step by step, with a beginning, middle, and end.
2. *Problem/solution* states a problem at the beginning and shows how the product or service can solve that problem.
3. The *chronological* form tells a story through a series of related scenes or messages, each one growing out of the previous one. It is orderly and progressive with a logical development.
4. *Special effects* create memorability by using devices such as a musical sound, unusual technique, or unique photography. Its main purpose is to establish a mood, not to tell a story.
5. In the *testimonial* a well-known (or possibly unknown) figure gives testimony that the product or service has solved his or her problem. This is an outgrowth of word-of-mouth advertising.
6. *Satire* sells a good through caustic wit, irony, or sarcasm. This is one of the hardest forms of advertising to use effectively.
7. The *spokesman* is an individual who comments on the advantages of your product.
8. The *demonstration* is most effective on television. It shows off a product's superiority to persuade the individual to buy. Demonstrations are more difficult on radio, but new techniques can enhance this method for radio.
9. *Suspense* builds curiosity through heightened drama. Usually the product solves a specific problem.
10. *Slice of life* relates a product to an everyday scene in an individual's life. It uses people's emotions and product satisfaction to sell.
11. The *analogy* takes an extraneous example and relates it to a product's message.
12. The *fantasy* either uses fictional characters or creates a fantasy to tell a story. Examples of this are Tony the Tiger and C3P0 and R2D2.
13. *Personality* shows an actor portraying a specific personality and discusses how the product can solve the problem or demonstrates the solution. The actor in this case is not playing himself.

Guidelines for advertisements

When writing an advertisement for the broadcast media, keep the following rules in mind.

1. Do basic research. Get all of the relevant facts that you want to emphasize.
2. Analyze the research into its major and minor consumer selling points. Selling points can be found in the positioning statement.
3. Make the commercial relevant to the viewer or listener's needs and wants. Be sure not to oversell.

4. Make sure the ad attracts attention immediately. It is imperative to get the customer's attention quickly, then sell the product.

5. Use action words whenever possible to stimulate the listener or viewer to action.

6. Be sure the structure and technique correspond with the image of the product.

7. Don't waste words: keep it simple; make every word count. The fewer words, the better the ad. However, be sure you adequately discuss the benefits of the product or service.

8. Mention the product's name as often as is feasible.

9. Write the copy in a natural, conversational tone. Don't try to write poetry; this tends to cause more problems than it solves.

10. Repetition can help register the selling points and ideas. Repeat the selling point as often as possible, preferably in different ways.

11. Emotionally involve people in the ad after you have attracted their attention.

12. End the ad with a call for action. Don't let the listener question what he or she is supposed to do now.

These guidelines are applicable to both radio and television advertising. However, radio advertising allows you one additional form of advertising copy. The advertiser may provide the radio station with facts relating to the product and have an announcer ad lib a sales presentation. The main problem with this form of advertising is that it is dependent on the selling ability of the announcer. This method also leaves the advertiser without total control over the advertisement.

Here are short lists of the advantages and disadvantages of television and radio.

Television
Advantages

1. Television makes full use of visual and audio communication. It uses many innovative techniques.

2. Television is primarily a medium of close-ups. This allows you to provide details and a good look at the product.

3. Television uses motion and color to increase an individual's interest.

4. Television reaches most of the people in the United States but does not allow for as great a selectivity as other media. By placing an ad with specific programs you can achieve some degree of selectivity in advertising.

Disadvantages

1. The message is not tangible; a person cannot take it along to refer to later.

2. The message must be brief. Most commercials on television range from 15 to 60 seconds.

3. There may be time problems when using live network media. Most network programs are held for rebroadcast, but this is not possible with programs such as live sports broadcasts. A show that is broadcast at 8:00 PM on the East Coast is on at 5:00 PM on the West Coast.

4. The cost of major network advertising is prohibitive to most local recreation businesses. However, local station advertising can be effective and inexpensive.

Radio
Advantages
1. Radio coverage is extensive; 98% of the homes in the United States have radios.
2. Radios are mobile and provide information to people in their cars or away from home.
3. Radio programs are simple and not costly to produce.
4. The flexibility of radio is high, since ads can be added or cut back rapidly.
5. Radio makes little or no demand upon the listener. People can do other things while listening to the radio. This can be either negative or positive.
6. Radio does extremely well in advertising that uses the spoken word.

Disadvantages
1. Radio is nonvisual. It relies on only one of the senses and is characterized by a high degree of forgetfulness.
2. There is no physical copy of the program similar to those in television or newspapers.

There are many ways to present a concept or topic to a potential consumer. There is no one best method. In fact, studies have indicated that combinations of various methods have proven highly effective. It is up to the manager to decide what to convey and how to do it.

The costs of advertising on both radio and television vary considerably depending on station and program popularity. Popularity is measured by the Neilsen ratings for TV and the Arbitron for radio. These rating services determine how many people watch or listen to each station. The results are broken down by region and demographics. An interesting feature is how each station can interpret the data to show itself to its maximum benefit. Once the ratings have been obtained, each station assigns rates based on numbers of listeners. These vary depending on time of day and program. The important point is to match listener demographics with customer demographics. In this way it may be possible to reach a desired market without excessive cost. Advertising costs for radio and TV are based on 30- or 60-second spots. A 60-second spot costs less than two 30-second spots. You should carefully determine what message you want to project and then decide on the length of your spot.

Incentives

Some media provide incentives to encourage advertisers. Incentives range from discounts to European vacations. If an advertiser is willing to write and produce his or her own ads, as much as 15% of the cost can be saved. Still other stations offer trade-outs: the station requests a sample of your product or service (such as passes to a water park) to give to other advertisers as incentives. Some of the most elaborate incentives include overseas trips. One radio station offers a European road trip if you purchase a "qualifying amount of ads" within one year. This excellent idea brings the station's major advertisers together for 2 weeks. This may result in new advertising ideas and cooperative programs.

A media salesperson can serve another function. Once a working relationship has been established, the salesperson can put together cooperative advertising. Cooperative advertising occurs when two or more advertisers get together to create a major advertising event. These events are beneficial to everyone.

An example of a media advertising event is a summer kickoff event. The advertisers could include a soft drink company, a sporting goods store, and a recreation enterprise. The event could be held at a recreation facility as its season opening event. The other advertisers could help by providing displays, prizes, demonstrations, fashion shows, and advertising. This type of cooperative advertising is especially valuable to seasonal recreation facilities. The media and other advertisers are always looking for a place to hold a major event. As a result the recreation manager is able to have a major event at little cost.

The recreation manager should get the most exposure possible from a promotion. This can be accomplished by effective planning. Examples of maximizing this exposure could include specially printed soft drink containers, posters, store displays, coupons, entries for drawings, special events, and live broadcasts from the facility.

Personnel selling

In hotel and motel sales, travel agencies, and resorts, one of the major promotional techniques is personnel sales. The majority of personnel sales are used to persuade large groups of people to patronize the facility. Examples include inducing large ski groups to attend a resort, persuading a large group to hold its convention at a hotel, and promoting a facility to large tour operators. The majority of nonretail personnel selling takes place at trade shows and on sales calls.

Most large organizations participate in or organize trade shows. For example, every year the American Bus Association (ABA) and the National Tour Association (NTA) hold national conventions and sales meetings. Both associations attract tour operators from around the country who purchase booth space and set up appointments with operators of attractions and facilities. Facility operators try to persuade tour operators to plan stops at their facilities. This is how most of the tours for the following season are established.

A variation of the trade show is the specialty show. A company, perhaps an airline, organizes a series of ski shows for travel agents. The airline offers booths to all of the ski resorts in the areas it services. At the show each resort staffs a booth to attract the travel agents' interest. The hope is that increasing a travel agent's knowledge of the area will encourage more people to visit specific resorts. A variation of this is to open the show to the general public, which increases public awareness of an area and draws business bookings.

Once a travel agent becomes aware of a tourist facility and sends business there, he or she becomes eligible for FAM tours, or familiarization tours. This is a low- or no-cost trip to a resort area. The rationale for this approach is that the more familiar a travel agent is with an area, the more business he or she will send to it.

Summary

Advertising is complex. Choice of the method best suited for your enterprise can be based on the positioning statement. In some cases it is better to use print than broadcast media. However, in most cases a mix of the various types of advertising is beneficial. The advantages and disadvantages of each method dictate which will be the most suitable. It is extremely important to relate advertising directly to the positioning statement, since this helps identify the best means of advertising.

BIBLIOGRAPHY

Baldwin, H.: Creating effective TV commercials, Chicago, 1982, Crain Books.

Book, A.C., and Schick, D.C.: Fundamentals of copy and layout: a manual for advertising copy and layout, Chicago, 1984, Crain Books.

Borgman, H.: Advertising layout techniques, New York, 1983, Watson-Guptill Publications.

Broadbent, S.: Spending advertising money: an introduction to media planning, media buying and the uses of media research, London, 1979, Business Books.

Geis, M.L.: The language of television advertising, New York, 1982, Academic Press, Inc.

Heighton, E.J., and Cunningham, D.R.: Advertising in the broadcast media, Belmont, Calif., 1976, Wadsworth Publishing Co.

Hodgson, R.S.: The Dartnell direct mail and mail order handbook, Chicago, Ill., 1980, Dartnell Corp.

Jain, C., and Migliaro, A.: An introduction to direct marketing, New York, 1978, AMACOM.

Johnson, P.M.: How to maximize your advertising investment, Boston, 1980, CBI Publishing Co.

Konikow, R.B.: Point of purchase design: the graphics of merchandise display, New York, 1985, PBC International.

Leckenby, J.D., and Wedding, N.: Advertising management: criteria, analysis, and decision making, Columbus, Oh., 1982, Grid Publishing.

Nelson, R.P.: The design of advertising, Dubuque, Iowa, 1985, W.C. Brown Publishers.

Percy, L., and Rossiter, J.R.: Advertising strategy: a communication theory approach, New York, 1980, Praeger.

Purvis, F.K.: Marketing and marketing communications, Hicksville, N.Y., 1973, Travel Marketing Consultant Services.

Smith, L.E., editor: How to create successful catalogs, Colorado Springs, Colo., 1985, Maxwell Sroge Publishing.

Stewart, D.W., and Furse, D.H.: Effective television advertising: a study of 1000 commercials, Lexington, Mass., 1986, Lexington Books.

Stone, B.: Successful direct marketing methods, Chicago, Ill., 1979, Crain Books.

Throckmorton, J.: Winning direct response advertising: how to recognize it, evaluate it, inspire it, create it, Englewood Cliffs, N.J., 1986, Prentice-Hall, Inc.

Witek, J.: Response television: combat advertising of the 1980s, Chicago, Ill., 1981, Crain Books.

Woods, R., editor: Printing and production for promotional materials, New York, 1987, Van Nostrand Reinhold.

SUGGESTED READINGS

Anthony, Michael. Handbook: Small Business Advertising. Addison-Wesley Pub., Reading, Massachusetts, 1981.

A useful step-by-step approach to developing an advertising campaign breaks advertising strategy into its components and covers media selection and other issues. Innovative approaches to public relations and the development of the advertising budget. Informative and very effective step-by-step approach.

Dunn, S. Watson and Arnold M. Barban. Advertising: Its Role in Modern Marketing. Fifth Edition. CBS College Publishing, New York, N.Y., 1982.

Basic introductory text. Advertising organizations, how to work with advertising, how to plan a campaign, budgeting, finding the market, and measuring the effectiveness of the promotion. Also a very effective section on creating the advertising message. Good background in media advertising and promotion and in special ways to reach segments plus special advertising techniques.

Jefkins, Frank. Advertising Today. Third Edition. International Textbook Co., Holborn, London, 1984.

Closely examines each area of advertising media and how it can be effectively used for various purposes. Extensive section dealing with campaign planning.

Levinson, Conrad J. Guerrilla Marketing: Secrets for Making Big Profits from Your Small Business. Houghton-Mifflin Co., Boston, 1984.

Innovative methods for attracting new customers to businesses. Title highlights the strategy of gaining customers from other businesses. Especially interesting to entrepreneurs entering crowded markets.

Sultsky, Jeff, and Woody Woodruff. Street Fighting: Low Cost Advertising Promotion Strategies for Your Small Business. Prentice-Hall, Inc., Englewood Cliffs, N.J., 1984.

How to create cross-promotions with other agencies; publicity and how to use it. Other forms of advertising. Gives a feel for campaign planning. Concludes with a section on advertising research.

When you develop an advertising campaign there is much to think about—cost, best media to use, and what theme to run throughout the campaign. These concerns are common to the development of an effective promotional campaign, such as the one undertaken by Mr. Promo in The Western Gateway Amusement Park case.

The Western Gateway Amusement Park

The Western Gateway Amusement Park (WGAP) is being developed by a consortium of wealthy businessmen in the central Illinois area. They plan to create a regional tourist attraction that will lure visitors from a five-state area consisting of Illinois, Missouri, Iowa, Kentucky, and Indiana. It has been determined that the best location for the park is Decatur, Illinois. This site was selected because of its location—central to the major metropolitan areas of St. Louis, Chicago, Louisville, and Indianapolis. The park is located on 320 acres just outside Decatur. The town offers adequate lodging to accommodate the expected tourists. The amusement park offers multiple recreational opportunities to the public including a rollercoaster, a double loop ride, numerous other rides, live entertainment, a western village, a small zoo, food concessions, and a dinner theater. The park opened for the 1986 season. Although it was designed to be one of the country's great amusement parks, the initial attendance has not lived up to expectations. In January, 1987, Mr. John Promo was hired by the owners to design an advertising and promotional program for the 1987 season.

Situation analysis

A thorough and detailed situation analysis was not possible in the short time before the seasonal opening of the park. There were several basic issues, however, that became apparent to Mr. Promo. First, WGAP is not designed to compete with other regional parks. The prices are not excessive when compared to the competition, but the location, while central to the major population centers, did not provide a large enough population base to support the park. The major competition was determined to be Holiday World in Santa Claus, Indiana, Adventureland in Des Moines, Iowa, and Six Flags Great America in Gurnee, Illinois. Therefore, with the exception of people from St. Louis, the potential customers had to be lured past other attractions to WGAP.

It was originally hoped that word-of-mouth publicity would soon develop, but awareness of the park appeared to be low among prospective customers in the metropolitan areas. Moreover, little interest in the park or surrounding areas was being generated in the way of support from travel agencies and other travel promotion businesses such as auto clubs.

Objectives

From the situation analysis, the objectives for the promotional campaign quickly emerged. The target market was designated as prospective visitors located in a 300-mile radius of WGAP. The ideal customers were upper-middle-income families that could afford the expense of the trip to and stay in Decatur. The objective of the promotional material was to communicate the advantages, facilities, and activities offered at WGAP in a striking and unusual fashion so that visitation and revenue would rise as quickly as possible. Travel agents and writers were targeted because they could influence individuals in the key cities to visit WGAP. Methods proposed would include media ads and promotional brochures.

Budget

Although Mr. Promo did not know exactly how the promotional budget was calculated, he estimated an allocation of $200,000, an estimate based on last year's budget. This figure was apparently a percentage of the estimated revenue. The number was not exact because the owners had indicated that they were open to suggestions and if they felt the proposal would be effective they would increase the amount available. The basic strategy revolved around the development of a mailing list of travel agents, clubs and writers, and the purchase of media coverage.

The entire campaign was to be planned and implemented by Mr. Promo. It was felt that his past experiences and his ability to negotiate ad rates would provide the best results for the least amount of money spent.

Program elements

Mr. Promo's first step was to develop a promotional brochure. He obtained copies of the three competitors' brochures for the 1987 season. Each was full color and folded to fit into a standard envelope. The illustrations on pages 319-323 show the brochures before folding. Mr. Promo examined the various layouts and determined the impact each piece would have. The brochures were to be used in all aspects of the campaign including direct mail, contacts by employees, media ads, and area-wide distribution in hotels and motels.

Because of the potentially wide appeal of WGAP, Mr. Promo saw two possible strategies—mass mailings and targeted mailing to specific groups. The first strategy would cost a lot—both in printing and mailing the large number of brochures. The second strategy would require extensive time to identify the individuals who would prove to be of the greatest help to the overall campaign. In either case the brochure would be accompanied by a personalized letter explaining the park, its programs, and the facilities offered. Various approaches could be used including what appeared to be an unsolicited letter from an influential individual, a letter from someone living in the area that would receive the letter, or a testimonial about the park. The themes running through the letters included any of the possible attractions of the park, including but not limited to entertainment, rides, family fun, and excitement.

While the direct mailing reached an excellent potential market, it by no means exhausted the list of those who might be induced to visit WGAP. Therefore a series of ads were to be run in the local media. A media mix was determined to be the best approach; however the cost of production would have to be taken into account when determining what media to purchase.

The size of the ads would need to be carefully calculated to attract the most attention for the least amount of dollars. The media used would, to a large extent, determine the size of ads since print media is sold by the column inch and broadcast media is sold by time. One additional consideration was the location of the ads. What type of text or programming would reach the potential market the best? One strategy would be to carry on the theme that was developed in either the direct mail program or the brochure.

Mr. Promo debated the use of joint promotions with either local or regional companies. If a compatible cosponsor could be found for the right promotion, costs could be cut while the program's effectiveness increased. The big question was who to approach and what type of promotion to pursue.

A final aspect of the campaign was a personal sales call by either Mr. Promo or a member of his staff. This approach had the potential to be the most effective if key contact could be made. On the other hand, cost would be high and there was no guarantee that this approach would work. Another personal sales approach is the FAM tour. This approach brings key promotional individuals to the park for a first hand experience. This approach has the same drawbacks as the sales call—it is expensive and time-consuming.

Costs

Mr. Promo estimated that the cost of producing the brochure would be $30,000 for the layout, photographs, and preparation for printing in color. The printing costs would be $200 per 1000. The cost of mailing the packet, including a brochure and two sheets of paper, was estimated at $0.40 each. The cost of ads varied based on the popularity of the media. He estimated that it would cost approximately $60 per minute for a popular radio station and $12 per minute on a poor station. Print media rates averaged $50 per column inch per day, or per publication for magazine. Television spots cost $60,000 to produce per one minute spot. The ad costs ranged from $3000 per minute on a top station at prime time to $200 on a small local station in the middle of the night. Travel costs were estimated at $0.25 per mile and $100 a day per diem.

The problem

As Mr. Promo contemplated what type of overall strategy to use he was informed by his secretary that the park owners had requested a proposed advertising campaign next week. He knew that at this time he would have to provide estimated costs, ways of measuring results, and examples of all ads that he planned on using.

Questions

1. Evaluate the brochures of the three competitors. Do you see any similarities in the material? Are there market segments that appear to be left unpromoted? Use the positioning matrix to help evaluate the brochures.

2. Complete a positioning matrix for WGAP. How do you propose to provide tangible evidence of the experience provided at WGAP?
3. Develop a brochure that you would present to the owners of the park. Identify the types of photographs that you would include. Develop examples of the text you would use in the brochures. How does this relate to the positioning matrix?
4. Develop advertising copy that would be used in either the printed or broadcast media ads. What type of programs or sections of the paper would you use to promote the park?
5. Lay out the advertising campaign you would propose. Where would you spend the money and why?

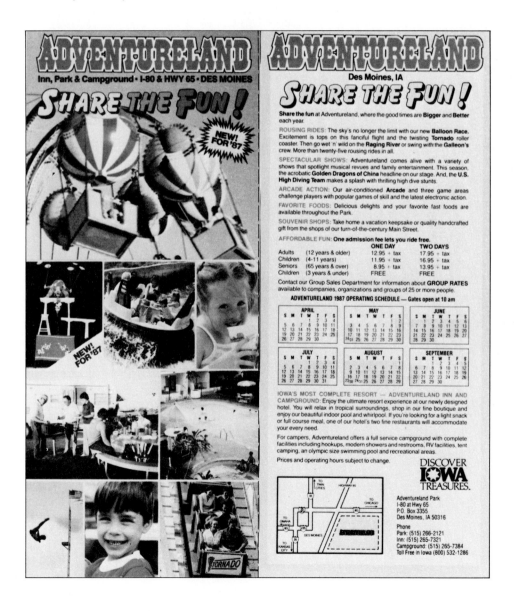

1987 Operating Schedule

MAY						
				1	2	
3	4	5	6	7	8	9
10	11	12	13	14	15	16
17	18	19	20	21	22	23
24	25	26	27	28	29	30
31						

JUNE						
	1	2	3	4	5	6
7	8	9	10	11	12	13
14	15	16	17	18	19	20
21	22	23	24	25	26	27
28	29	30				

JULY						
			1	2	3	4
5	6	7	8	9	10	11
12	13	14	15	16	17	18
19	20	21	22	23	24	25
26	27	28	29	30	31	

AUGUST						
						1
2	3	4	5	6	7	8
9	10	11	12	13	14	15
16	17	18	19	20	21	22
23	24	25	26	27	28	29
30	31					

SEPTEMBER						
		1	2	3	4	5
6	7	8	9	10	11	12
13	14	15	16	17	18	19
20	21	22	23	24	25	26
27	28	29	30			

OCTOBER						
				1	2	3
4	5	6	7	8	9	10
11	12	13	14	15	16	17
18	19	20	21	22	23	24
25	26	27	28	29	30	31

NOVEMBER						
1	2	3	4	5	6	7
8	9	10	11	12	13	14
15	16	17	18	19	20	21
22	23	24	25	26	27	28
29	30					

1987

- ☐ 10 a.m. — 6 p.m.
- ☐ 10 a.m. — 7 p.m.
- ☐ 10 a.m. — 8 p.m.
- ☐ Park Closed

The Great American High Dive Team performs daily May 23 through August 31 and September 5, 6 and 7, 1987.

"That's Entertainment" and "Raise A Ruckus" will be presented through September 27, 1987 only.

SPECIAL CELEBRATIONS AT HOLIDAY WORLD

May 26-29 — "Special Friends Days" — For all physically & mentally handicapped & impaired persons, retirement communities, nursing homes & "special needs" individuals & groups. Reservations are required for special admission pricing on these days.

June 6, 13, 20, 27 — Fireworks

June 24 — Holland Dairy Day — Every guest gets a free Holland Dairy ice cream cone.

July 3 — Kayak Pools Day — Special giveaways by Kayak Pools.

July 18 — Happy Birthday John Shiver Day

August 18 — Ronald McDonald Day

August 24 - 28 & Aug. 31 — "Special Friends Days"

Sept. 20 — Holland Dairy Day

Oct. 4 — High Cheerleading Contest

Oct. 11 — High Cheerleading Contest

Oct. 31 & Nov. 1 — Halloween — Come and stay in full-body costume to be admitted free of charge to all rides and attractions.

1987 PARK ADMISSION

Holiday World has a pay-one-price admission, which entitles the guest to ride all the rides (except where safety regulations impose height and weight restrictions) and see all the shows and attractions during the day of admission. There are no refunds or rainchecks.

Regular Admission	$8.50 per person
Children 2 and under	FREE
Senior Citizens (60 and over)	$7.00 per person

Not yet established

Group Rates: For groups of 25 or more, the park offers a special discount. Contact the Group Sales Office for information and/or required reservations.

All prices and schedules are subject to change without notice. Admission includes all rides, shows and attractions in operation for the day.

MasterCard and Visa honored.

Holiday World

P.O. Box 179   Santa Claus, Indiana 47579   Phone (812)937-4401

Holiday World Neighbors

Southwestern Indiana is a super vacation destination! Plan to spend several days or a week full of fun here!

Within an hour's drive from Holiday World!

Experience History, Nature, Technology, Recreation, and Attractions Unique in the World!

To recommend just a few...

CHRISTMAS LAKE GOLF CLUB
Santa Claus, Indiana 47579
(812) 544-2271

ENERGY INFORMATION CENTER
Rockport, Indiana 47635
(812) 649-4061

"YOUNG ABE LINCOLN"
Historical Outdoor Drama
Lincoln City, Indiana 47552
(812) 937-4493

MARENGO CAVE PARK
Marengo, Indiana 47140
(812) 365-2705

LINCOLN BOYHOOD NATIONAL MEMORIAL
Lincoln City, Indiana 47552
(812) 937-4757

FRENCH LICK SCENIC RAILWAY
French Lick, Indiana 47432
(812) 936-2405

DR. TED'S MUSICAL MARVELS
Santa Claus, Indiana 47579
(812) 937-4250

SKI PAOLI PEAKS
Paoli, Indiana 47454
(812) 723-4696

SANTA CLAUS POST OFFICE
Santa Claus, Indiana 47579
(812) 937-4469

Holiday World proudly recommends our in-park Sponsors:
Kayak Pools and Holland Dairy.
☆ ☆ ☆ ☆ ☆ ☆ ☆ ☆

Coming to you from Great America...

Here's What's New in 1987...

After you're thrilled by rocking, hanging and looping on POWER DIVE, you'll see two captivating movies on the world's largest movie screen...the "spacetacular" THE DREAM IS ALIVE, the story of America's space shuttle program, and ON THE WING, the dramatic story of man's fascination with flight. You'll experience the breathtaking art of Chinese Acrobatics when the troupe visits Great America for an extended engagement, June 6 – August 14. You'll cheer the intricate diving routines of the undefeated world champion U.S. HIGH DIVING TEAM in The Wilderness Theater and hum and tap along with the new STARS & STRIPES REVUE! Then, you'll be charmed by BUGS BUNNY™ LAND, our special children's area, doubled in size this year. It's the best entertainment package anywhere.

TM indicates Trademark of Warner Bros. Inc. © 1987

Now showing at the Pictorium: the IMAX® films THE DREAM IS ALIVE and ON THE WING

Fun for the Whole Family!

Great America brings you great rides and attractions, live shows, movies and special events. Be sure not to miss our celebration for the young and young-at-heart, Kidsfest, July 6–26, and the fall season celebration, Country Crafts Jamboree, weekends starting in September.

Tempt your taste buds with everything from scrumptious waffle cone sundaes to succulent chicken dinners. Explore our shops for some of the finest merchandise in the country.

You'll want to come back for the time after time of your life!

SIX FLAGS GREAT AMERICA

CHAPTER 11

The role of computers in commercial recreation

CHAPTER OBJECTIVES

1. To understand the role of computers in commercial recreation

2. To understand the difference between hardware and software

3. To understand how the different types of software can be used in commercial recreation

4. To know how to select a computer

Computers have touched every facet of our lives. They control telephone switching circuits, bank cards for night deposits, optical scanners at the grocery store, and energy control systems for large buildings. Businesses have used computers for a number of years. Accounting and word processing have been easily adapted to computer usage because they use a standard set of procedures that computers perform well.

Innovations in computer technology have changed and expanded the use of computers for commercial recreation. The most prominent example of this is the use of computers in existing recreation enterprises. The manager of a ski resort has been quoted as saying, "I can now receive 10 times the information I received before computerization, in one tenth of the time to generate it." (*Managing the Leisure Facility*, Jan. 1982.) In another example the owners of a prominent Northeast sports arena, after extensive energy-saving renovations, purchased a computerized system to control temperature and lighting before hockey games. The computer system cost the arena $27,000 and was paid for over nine months through energy savings alone. (*Managing the Leisure Facility,* Jan. 1982.) These examples indicate how computers have had tremendous impact on commercial recreation enterprises.

Standard programs such as word processors, electronic spread sheets, database management, and graphics programs have substantially changed the way we operate. Word processing produces instantaneously changed documents and form letter personalization. Database management systems are extremely effective in maintaining and updating huge banks of data and information. An electronic spreadsheet is capable of instantaneous recalculation of numbers and figures, allowing a manager to analyze business decisions. A graphics package allows managers to represent themselves better when presenting information to owners or boards of directors.

Each of these innovations is made possible through computer technology. This technology is composed of software, hardware, and the system. *Software* is the instructions that tell the computer how to handle information or data stored in it. *Hardware* is the physical machinery, wires, tubes and microchips. The *system* is the total integration of all hardware and software into one unit. This system consists of the computer, printer, software, and any other devices connected to the computer to collect and analyze data.

Software

Computer software has undergone tremendous changes since the late 1940s. The first computer programs consisted of a series of 0s and 1s that only the computer and a very few programmers could understand. The original computer code was similar to Morse code and was called machine language. The first programs were written by technicians for very specific repetitive and standardized procedures such as accounting.

In order to ease the task of programming computers, the compiler was developed. A compiler translates a programming language that is easy for the programmer to understand into code or instruction that the computer can execute. The compiler allowed the development of computer languages as we know them today. Some of the most popular computer languages are BASIC, FORTRAN, COBOL, PASCAL, C, and FORTH. These languages made it easier to program computers.

As an increasing number of programmers developed programs, they began selling them to others. The result was a proliferation of canned programs, general in nature so that they can be used by many individuals.

Software is either canned or customized. Canned software can be purchased from a local distributor. It is usually general in nature and allows for multiple uses. Customized software is written on commission for a client or to perform one task. The advantage of canned software is that it transfers easily from one computer system to another and is understood by many people. It has effective and detailed documentation (the instruction package) and can be adapted to many situations.

Customized software is written by one person so that only that individual knows how to modify the program if there are problems. It is not readily transferable between locations or computer systems. It usually has poor documentation.

In commercial recreation canned software works the best and is the most sensible choice. The most common types of canned software include electronic spreadsheets, database management, word processing, and graphics packages. While the functions differ little between different software manufacturers, the specific commands and the amount of data the software can manipulate vary greatly from manufacturer to manufacturer. This short discussion will deal with each briefly to give you some feeling for what functions they perform.

Electronic spreadsheet

This is a general-purpose tool. Anything that can be performed with a calculator, a pencil, and a piece of paper can be done much more efficiently by using an electronic spreadsheet such as Lotus 1-2-3 or SuperCalc 4. A departmental budget can be developed, maintained, and continually updated in a recreation enterprise. These programs allow instantaneous changes in case the budget amount for each division is changed, or as credits or debits arrive for the ledger.

Spreadsheets are useful in the analysis of balance sheets and income statements as well as in ratio analysis, covered in Chapter 8. Pro forma statements can be developed on spreadsheets and are easily changed to account for new sales information or changes in any expense item.

Another typical use of spreadsheets in commercial recreation is for break-even analysis and the creation of demand curves. All that is required is to base the spreadsheet on the information and on the equations for analysis of the material. If any of the variables change, these can be revised for an updated spreadsheet.

Database management programs

Database management programs are similar to an office file cabinet. In a drawer of the file cabinet is the file folder, and in the file folder is information on a specific topic. A database management program works the same way; it can store massive amounts of information and swiftly retrieve data based on specific criteria. This allows the program to perform such mundane tasks as inventory control and maintenance of mailing lists and files of prospective customers or suppliers. This program can rapidly create a report of all people meeting the criteria in question. Examples of data base management system are Dbase III, RBase, and Q&A.

Word processing

This type of program operates in a similar way to an office typewriter. The advantage of word processing is that a mistake on a document can be changed instantly without retyping the page. Another advantage of word processing is rapid insertion or deletion of entire passages prior to printing. More recent programs correct spelling and grammar. Word processing used in tandem with the database management system can develop personalized letters at a rate of 12 pages every minute. These letters may include personal information such as name, address, and amount owed. The saving in typist salaries is usually sufficient to pay for the system. Examples of word processing programs are WordPerfect, WordStar, Volkswriter, and Microsoft Word.

Graphics

A graphics program can take numbers entered from a spreadsheet or database manager or by hand and create graphic representations of it, including bar graphs, line graphs, pie charts, and so forth. Some programs and printers produce full-color graphics. This helps in the presentation and development of the manager's viewpoint and impresses the person receiving the document. Graphics programs can be separate, such as a program called chart, or be included in the spreadsheet, as in Lotus 1-2-3 or SuperCalc 4.

Integrated programs

During the last few years there has been a new development, integrated programs such as Symphony and Enable. They allow managers to move information easily between any of the preceding types of programs. A manager may type up a notice to all of the people in the database management program, select from the electronic spreadsheet the financial information needed to enhance that information, create graphics based on the spreadsheet and prepare it for printing with the word processor. This is time-saving and beneficial to a recreation manager.

Specialized commercial recreation software

Specialized software allows a manager to do specific tasks such as payroll, accounting, accounts payable, accounts receivable, recreation registration, league scheduling, and maintenance. Many companies provide total accounting packages for small businesses. Two that are easily adaptable to commercial recreation enterprises are Peachtree and Macola Financial Software. This type of canned specialized software is often cheaper, easier to use, and more adaptable to other programs than customized software.

Software specifically designed for recreation businesses has become prevalent in recent years. It is possible for the creative manager to develop procedures to meet most, if not all, needs of a recreation department with standard programs such as Lotus 1-2-3, Dbase III, Twin, and RBase. If a member of the staff has the skill, it is best to use one of these programs. If these skills or the time to create a system is not available, a specialized program may help.

This section will discuss some of the programs available. The programs discussed are only representative; the list is not exhaustive or an endorsement of any single program. The programs are presented from the simplest to the most complex.

Market Computing has developed two recreation programs, CRIS (class registration information system) and LMS (league management software). CRIS maintains a catalogue on class schedules, including classes and dates, instructors, and class location. Student information includes enrollment, waiting list, and receipt printing. The program also handles fees and refunds, including instructor payments. LMS maintains records on team registration; scheduling, including byes and changes; and game results. Standard reports include league schedules, team schedules, standings, manager rosters, mailing labels, and sports statistics. For further information contact Market Computing, P.O. Box 6245, Huntington Beach, CA 92615; (714) 953-8722.

A similar product for class registration is available from CityTIME. This software coordinates class registrations, produces class rosters, notes full classes, keeps participant records, prints class reports, and produces revenue reports by class and by facility. In addition to maintaining class registrations, the program also handles facility reservations to prevent double scheduling and maintains a calendar of facility use. For more information contact Foresight Solutions, Inc., 804 New Hampshire, Lawrence, KS 66044; (913) 842-7526.

Recreation Management Software II combines many modules to form a small integrated system. The modular system allows the purchaser the freedom to select only those components he or she needs. This allows expansion and compatibility between components. The various modules include class registration, league scheduling, special event registration, aquatic registration, activity and expense analysis, facility reservations, sports registration, and mailing lists. These eight modules fit together in a manner similar to the configuration in Figure 11-1. For further information contact Programmed for Success, 23611 Golden Springs Dr., Suite 7, Diamond Bar, CA 91765; (714) 861-3133.

The Work Management System is designed as an aid to productivity and service. This program helps develop work plans, schedules, and resource allocation. Its strength is in maintenance and cost reduction. The major components of the program:

1. Planning work, including facilities/infrastructure data, development and tracking of preventative/predictive programs, and analysis of proposed capital investments
2. Evaluating productivity
3. Controlling material, including inventory, reserving material, and material lists
4. Tracking crew performance and cost estimates
5. Work scheduling to minimize costs
6. Analyzing service levels to maintain consistency and to allocate resources

For further information contact LWFW Group, 12700 Park Central, Suite 1805, Dallas, TX 75251; (214) 233-5561.

One of the more versatile integrated programs is offered by Amerisoft. This program allows for data sharing between program registration, parks maintenance management, budgets, cash receipts, payroll, accounts payable, general ledger, and facility scheduling (Figure 11-2). Some of the highlights include automatic posting of receipts to a general ledger; refund check preparation; revenue genera-

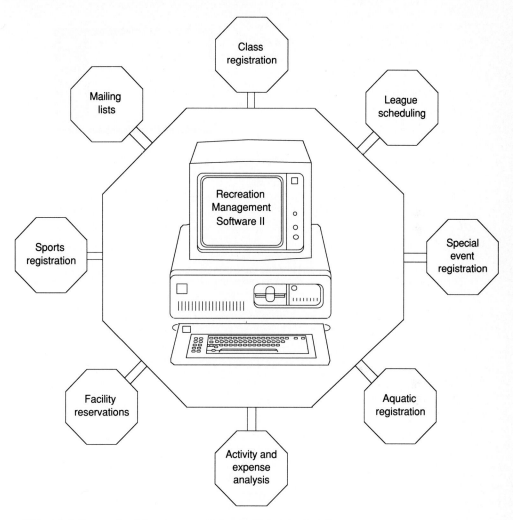

FIG. 11-1 Recreation Management Software II and its functions.

tion by date and department; sales tax reports; labor breakdown by type, tasks, and activities; payroll; automatic inventory updates; preparation of W2s; demographic statistics for participants; and facilities scheduling up to one year in advance. For more information contact Amerisoft, 96 W. Moreland Avenue, Addison, IL 60101; (312) 628-0666.

Perhaps the most sophisticated of all integrated programs is Decision Aide by Arthur Young. This accounting firm has developed a very efficient system that can do just about anything you will ever need. Decision Aide ranges from general ledger operations to court usage analysis. This program includes accounts payable and receivable, mail management, word processing, utility usage, graphics, league scheduling, court and tee reservations, budget analysis and participant usage. For

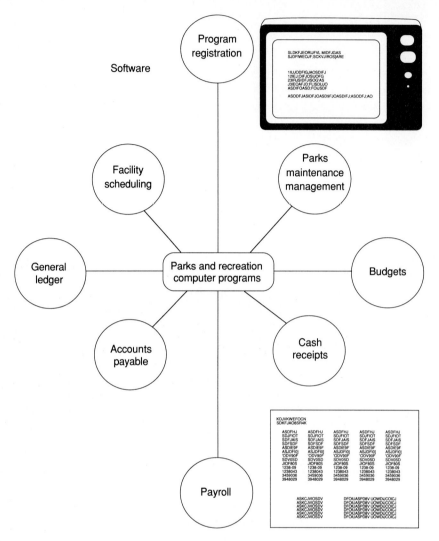

FIG. 11-2 Integrated program offered by Amerisoft.

city and county governments, additional modules can be added to help run the entire governmental entity. For more information contact Arthur Young, 201 North Central, Suite 1700, Phoenix, AZ 85073; (602) 258-4831.

Hardware

Computer hardware has evolved from the abacus used by the Chinese over 2000 years ago to the highly sophisticated terminal we know today. The first change occurred when Charles Babbage (1792-1871) invented his calculating machine, whose answers were calculated by gears turned by hand. This evolved to the electric calculating and adding machines of the 1930s and 40s. Next, Eniac, the first electronic computer, was developed in the late 1940s. This computer consisted of 18,000 vacuum tubes and required an air conditioning unit to keep the 20′ by 40′ room cool. Even omitting size comparisons, the $4.95 calculator you buy today has greater flexibility and power than Eniac. The trend in computer hardware has been toward miniaturization and lower cost. This has been accomplished by improved technology and production methods.

Computer hardware is the physical components and adjuncts of the computer. The "brain box" of a small computer houses disk drives for data storage on floppy disks that can be inserted and that appear similar to small records. The keyboard is also hardware. It facilitates data input into the computer and is more or less similar to a typewriter keyboard. A third hardware component is the CRT, or display screen. The CRT allows you to see what is being typed into or stored on the computer. The printer provides a hard copy of the document; most are either dot matrix or letter quality. The difference is that dot-matrix print is usually slightly fuzzy and square-looking, whereas letter-quality print is impossible to distinguish from normal typewriter print (Fig. 11-3).

Another piece of hardware is the modem, which allows the computer to "talk" on the telephone with a computer in another location. It also allows for data transfer and updating of information between remote locations.

An additional piece of hardware is a plotter. This allows the computer to draw intricate graphs or charts, and sometimes, as in architectural design, actual pictures. Plotters are expensive and are used only in specialized situations.

The final item that needs to be understood by a recreation manager is computer terminology. Computers are evaluated in terms of their storage space, as follows: "This computer has 256K RAM." Translated this means that the computer is capable of storing over 256,000 characters (letters, numbers, special characters, and spaces) within its random access memory (RAM). RAM refers to the storage or work space that allows the computer to perform its functions. The K in the notation stands for thousands. You can store approximately 256,000 characters, or slightly over 100 pages of typewritten document, in the memory of a 256K computer. This is a relatively powerful computer, but it has a small amount of work space.

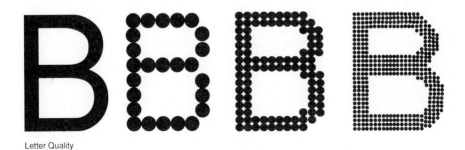

Letter Quality

FIG. 11-3 Various densities of dot matrix printers.

The operating system translates human commands into instructions that the computer can follow. Various manufacturers have developed their own operating systems to eliminate the possibility of software being transferred from one brand of computer to another. MS-DOS, which stands for "Microsoft Disk Operating System," is the prevalent one today. It is the responsibility of the recreation manager to determine which computer system would be the best for use in his or her business.

Selecting the right computer system

If you decide to purchase a computer, you need to explore some of the reasons for your decision. Is it because: everyone else is buying one; people who have computers are considered a little more advanced because they know new technology; the computer is a status symbol; or computers are good for playing games? None of these is an adequate consideration when purchasing a computer system for a commercial recreation business. You have the right idea for the wrong reasons.

Here are some good reasons: (1) Computers can increase efficiency by speeding up routine operations. (2) You can demonstrate a good payback. This is how long it will take to pay back the cost of the computer in terms of increased work performance. (3) You will make better decisions based on improved information.

These are the right reasons for selecting a computer system. Now, what can a computer do for you? It can store large amounts of information and produce it rapidly, sort information based on criteria defined by you, and make logical decisions, including mathematical calculations. How do these three functions translate into work processes? The ability to store large amounts of information and retrieve it quickly is extremely useful in inventory control, in keeping track of the budget, and in making slight revisions to form letters. Sorting can be useful when you want to select certain pieces of information from the computer's data banks. Sorts can also place the information in a specific order, alphabetic or numeric. The ability to make logical decisions is useful when you need to do mathematical computations such as budgetary work, planning, or scheduling. Scheduling is a good example of a logical decision: the computer will make a large number of comparisons to determine the optimum schedule for a department. These three functions can help make you a better decision-maker simply by improving the information available to you.

Determine needs

How do you determine what kind of computer you need? The first question is what you need to accomplish. First determine the needs of the commercial recreation business. This can be done in a relatively routine manner. List the following: (1) The kinds of auxiliary equipment available for a specific computer. You need to know this because some computers are capable of operating a number of peripheral devices such as printers and telephone modems. (2) The kinds of jobs the computer is to perform. (3) The volume of work required for each job identified in step two.

The most important aspects of computer equipment are the operating system and the format that each piece of equipment uses. The operating system determines how the computer reads data from its storage system and performs functions. You could have different peripherals that need to be controlled by different types of computer connections. These different connections need to be taken into consideration to be sure whatever you purchase will be compatible with existing equipment.

When identifying the types of jobs a computer can do for your department, keep in mind the three functions a computer can perform. Once you have identified the jobs to be performed, you need to determine the flow of work within each job. This is done by developing a flow chart, which should include the following:

1. Where the information comes from
2. The format of the information
3. Who handles that information
4. What is done to the information
5. What type of output is needed

In order to determine the amount of storage space for each job, you need to know how a computer handles information. Start with the *field,* a specific piece of information such as a name. Fields are combined to form records. *Records* contain all the information pertaining to that name (i.e., the person or piece of equipment). Records combine to form files. A file could contain all participants in a Little League baseball program. Within this file a record would describe each participant. Each record would contain fields such as name, address, and age.

When you know how many records and how many files you have, count the number of characters for each record. A character is a letter, number, space, or special character. Multiply the number of characters times the number of records. This information can be presented to a dealer, who can help you to determine your basic storage and work capacity for the system. He or she can also determine the work space you will need for each program.

You must also identify any special needs, including security, reliability of information, and special outputs such as graphics or the ability to access information from a central computer.

Select dealer

Dealer selection takes place in two steps. First determine the dealer's reputation, and then assess the support system. Usually dealers fall into two categories, branches of national companies and local dealers. Either can be reliable, so don't be misled by national companies. The local branch of a national company is usually a franchise and may be unreliable. The easiest way to determine dealer reliability is to talk to people who are using computers. Find out what they think of the different dealers in town.

The second step in selecting a dealer is examining the support system. First, what type of hardware support is available? A main concern is repair time. Does it have to be sent back to the factory or can it be repaired locally? This can be a major consideration when you have massive amounts of information stored in computer format. Second, can the dealer answer your questions about the software? If not, can you rapidly get the information at little or no cost? This is a major concern, since questions always arise. Third, how helpful are the salespeople? Are they willing to answer questions? Do they seem knowledgeable and willing to find answers to your software problems? This is critical. You must be able to get along with the sales personnel. They must be able to answer your questions and provide you with the information you need.

Software

Software should be selected based on three criteria: (1) Does it have the capability to handle the information you need? For example, if a file contains 500 records, will your software adequately sort 500 records? Some word processing programs do not have underlining. Be sure the software selected meets your needs in size and special functions. (2) Is the form of input compatible with your needs? Can your forms be modified so that they are compatible with the program without making severe changes in your system? (3) Is the output compatible with your needs? For example, if you need graphics, does the program supply them?

When you have identified several software packages that will meet your needs, have the dealer demonstrate the software on a small project involving 10 records or less. Watch how the information is entered and make sure the functions that you are interested in can be performed and produce an appropriate output so that you can obtain a clear idea of how the computer will work for you.

The last major consideration for software involves documentation. (This is the instruction manual for the software.) To test the documentation open the manual to the beginning of any section and try to perform the procedure that is explained. If you cannot easily follow the directions, consider other software. If one section is not understandable, the rest of the manual will probably not be understandable either.

Hardware

You are now ready to perform the last step in the selection of a computer system. Select hardware to complement the software you have chosen. Be sure the hardware is compatible with the software. This is a function of the operating system. Some software is compatible with more than one brand of computer. Be sure to select a computer with the capability for expansion beyond your current needs. The purchase of a "first" computer is usually made with a specific task in mind, but soon additional uses require additional memory and storage capacity. Also, files have a tendency to grow, so you need to be able to expand to meet future needs. You also need to consider the ability of the computer system to support peripherals. For example, if you need a printer, will the computer support one?

When choosing a computer, take a good look at the keyboard. It should be in a standard typewriter format. Some computers do not use a standard typewriter keyboard. This requires retraining personnel. If you are entering large amounts of number information, you may be interested in a ten-key pad. This could be part of the keyboard or added as a peripheral. The keyboard should provide some type of tactile identification, such as a roughness on the key pads themselves, so that you know what position your fingers are in on the keyboard. Some kind of an indicator to signal when the key has been fully depressed is also valuable. Some keyboards do not indicate whether the information has been entered into the computer so you must look at the screen to make that judgment.

Another major keyboard consideration is "n key rollover." Some people can type faster than the computer can read the information. With a five-key rollover the computer will remember up to five characters prior to placing them on the screen. This allows an operator to enter data at normal speed without losing information.

A major concern is the location of the break key. Many programs use the break key to terminate the program or stop whatever process is taking place. If the break key is located near the return or enter key, it is possible to hit it by accident, terminating the program. This results in the loss of whatever data you have entered into the computer system at that time. It is best if the break key is located well away from the return key.

The last consideration when selecting computer hardware is its data storage capability. In most small systems information is stored on a floppy disk. Floppy disks resemble records in jackets, only they are flexible. Various amounts of storage can be provided by a floppy disk, depending upon the hardware. When selecting data storage capacity, be sure it meets your needs and is expandable, by the addition of either floppy disks or a hard disk drive.

Several considerations should be discussed relevant to selecting a computer system. Be sure to ask the dealer for references concerning the hardware and software. Don't be afraid to contact those references and obtain users' opinions.

What other software is available for the operating system that you have selected? You should be able to select additional software and perform other functions. Some operating systems have larger amounts of software available to them than others. This may be a consideration.

No games should be purchased for a business computer system. Games can result in a tremendous loss in employee and computer productivity.

Don't worry about new developments. Advances are continuing at a rapid rate, and whatever computer system you buy will probably be outdated in six months. However, if you have selected an appropriate system, it will handle the tasks well into the future. The advantages of purchasing a computer system now and using it to improve efficiency far outweigh the advantages of waiting for a better system.

When purchasing a computer system, don't expect instant success. You will probably have to change some procedures and train employees, which take time. Depending upon the amount of data you have, entering this could involve an extensive effort. Careful selection of a system after analysis of your needs should result in a computer that will meet those needs and greatly increase your business efficiency. Definitely, a computer system is well worth the cost and effort involved in acquiring it.

Summary

Commercial recreation has been directly affected by computers, so recreation managers must be aware of the ways in which computers can aid them. Know the various computer components, hardware and software, and the differences between canned and customized software. Once these are understood, a manager can determine how he or she will use the computer and use these criteria to select a system that will benefit the business and expand to meet its needs for the extended future. Most recreation enterprises will use computers in the future.

Computer systems are composed of hardware and software. Hardware is the physical machinery, and software is the set of instructions. The software is of primary importance. The manager must decide among canned and custom software. Canned software is the least expensive and must be adapted to fit the situation. Custom software is expensive and tailored to fit the situation.

To summarize the steps in the selection of a computer system:

1. Assess the needs of the department.
2. Locate a reputable dealer.
3. Determine what software will fill your needs.
4. Select hardware compatible with the software and your needs.

In order to compete in today's business environment, a recreation manager needs quick access to accurate information. The computer is the most cost-effective method for obtaining information. A recreation manager must become familiar with computers, their use, and the available software.

BIBLIOGRAPHY

Computerized system gives ski resort a lift, Managing the Leisure Facility, Jan., 1982, p. 6.

Maine Hall cuts costs with computer, Managing the Leisure Facility, Jan., 1982, p. 15.

Chou, G.T.: dBase III plus handbook, Indianapolis, Ind., 1985, QUE Corporation.

Cobb, D., and Anderson, L.: 1-2-3 for business, Indianapolis, Ind., 1987, QUE Corporation.

Dwyer, T., and Critchfield, M.: BASIC and the personal computer, Reading, Mass., 1983, Addison-Wesley Publishing Co.

Goldstein, L.J.: Microcomputer applications: a hands on approach to problem solving, Reading, Mass., 1987, Addison-Wesley Publishing Co.

Koffman, E.B.: PASCAL: a problem solving approach, Reading, Mass., 1982, Addison-Wesley Publishing Co.

Norton, P.: Inside the IBM PC, Englewood Cliffs, N.J., 1986, Prentice-Hall Inc.

Norton, P.: PC-DOS: introduction to high-performance computing, Englewood Cliffs, N.J., 1985, Prentice-Hall Inc.

Perry, J.T., and Lateer, J.G.: Using SuperCalc 4, Indianapolis, Ind., 1987, QUE Corporation.

Popyk, M.K.: Up and running: microcomputer applications, Reading, Mass., 1987, Addison-Wesley Publishing Co.

SUGGESTED READINGS

Books

Bitter, G.G.: Computers in today's world, New York, 1984, John Wiley & Sons, Inc.

This text introduces the nonuser to computers. It talks about computer basics and history and how computers work. Also details the basic computer system. Discusses general and scientific uses of computers. It is well documented with pictures and easy-to-read text.

Blissmer, R.H.: Computer Annual, New York, 1985, John Wiley & Sons, Inc.

Updated annually, this text presents computers in their current stages. Well-written text details all component parts of computers. Examines networking, systems analysis, and the parts of the computer. One of the best introductory texts.

Magazines

Byte.

Excellent monthly source of general information. No brand or operating system affiliation. Products are reviewed and help columns provide solutions to some continually recurring problems.

MacUser.

Similar in style and format to Byte, but dedicated to the Apple product line. Emphasis on the MacIntosh and its developments.

PC Magazine.

Biweekly publication is concerned with IBM and compatibles. Each issue provides tests and evaluations of hardware or software. Valuable when selecting new products.

PC Week.

Weekly magazine is dedicated to new products in IBM-standard microcomputing. Sometimes covers new products not yet released. Insight into industry trends.

Computers are very useful when one attempts to arrive at a decision based on un-certainty. A simple program can be used to repeat a series of random events sev-eral times. An analysis of the repeated outcomes can help a commercial recreation manager arrive at a better decision. Football Concessions is such a case. There are many variables associated with a football season, such as the win/loss record of the team and the weather. Each of these can be simulated through the use of random numbers. In this case a technique called a decision tree is used to approximate the expected outcome. By repeatedly using this decision tree for various outcomes, the manager can approximate the true outcome.

Football Concessions (B)*

Mr. Michael Reeves, an enterprising Stanford MBA student, has recently learned of an opportunity to purchase rights to the hot dog concession at Stanford Stadium for the 1970 football season. In order to operate this concession Mr. Reeves must pay the University a $1000 fee, purchase a $200 vendor's permit from Santa Clara County, and con-struct a booth containing dog and bun steamers and a cash register. Since Mr. Reeves will be the sole operator, revenues exceeding the cost of his materials will be gross profit used to repay the investment and return a dividend.

Mr. Reeves is not without doubt as to the ultimate "values" of several parameters of this investment decision problem. For example, the investment required might vary due to uncertainties in the costs of constructing a booth and buying equipment. Simi-larly, he can only guess what his profit per hot dog sold will be as meat prices fluctuate freely. Also, only crude estimates of total sales for the season can be made. Sales may be expected to increase from past years since in 1970 Stanford will be a bowl contender and meet such national powers as the Boilermakers, Ducks, Bears, Bruins, Spartans, Trojans and Gauls.

Hoping to analyze this problem in a rigorous fashion, Mr. Reeves chose to develop subjective probability distributions over the three uncertain outcomes—investment, unit profit, and total sales—rather than make a certainty equivalent type of point esti-mate. For total season sales, he imagined a normal distribution with mean of 40,000 and standard deviation of 7000 hot dogs would accurately describe his prior beliefs

---

*Reprinted with permission of the Stanford University Graduate School of Business, 1970 by the Board of Trustees of the Leland Stanford Junior University.

about the problem. Distribution for total investment (including rights and permit fees) and profit per unit are given in the table below:

Subjective probability of events

Total investment		Profit per unit	
Dollars	Probability	Dollars	Probability
2000	.10	0.10	.05
3000	.15	0.11	.05
4000	.15	0.12	.10
5000	.20	0.13	.20
6000	.15	0.14	.45
7000	.10	0.15	.10
8000	.10	0.16	.05
9000	.05		1.00
	1.00		

Although Mr. Reeves is perfectly capable of completing the analysis of his problem, you are asked to do the following things:

1. Construct a decision tree structure assuming as an alternative Mr. Reeves can do nothing and receive zero net gain.
2. Develop certainty equivalents for each of the uncertain events.
3. Complete the analysis using these certainty equivalents.

Analysis of Football Concessions (B)

The discrete and continuous event fans present in this problem represent no new challenge to decision analysis methods. The decision tree on page 336 can be evaluated in the traditional manner by folding back the branches via "backwards induction." Each event fan can be evaluated to produce an expected value of total sales, unit profit, and investment. However, the combination of all three of these expected values may not constitute an event per se or may produce a biased value for net profit which is a function of all three uncertain events. Bias may be introduced when the distributions of one or more uncertain quantities is not symmetric about its mean. Thus the ultimate measure of project success, since it is not a strictly linear (additive) or quadratic (multiplicative) transformation of individual events, may show different values if computed as an event of averages as opposed to an average of events.

In using the Monte Carlo method to evaluate the three event fans in this problem, a uniformly distributed random deviate on the interval [1100] is associated with a value of total investment or profit per unit—total sales is a continuous distribution and is treated a bit differently. The tables on page 336 indicate the way in which a given random number is related with a value of investment and unit profit.

The total sales event fan is treated by simple random sampling from the standard normal distribution and then transforming the resulting deviate by adding the mean and standard deviation multiplied by the deviate ($X = \mu + \sigma z$).

Football Concessions decisions tree

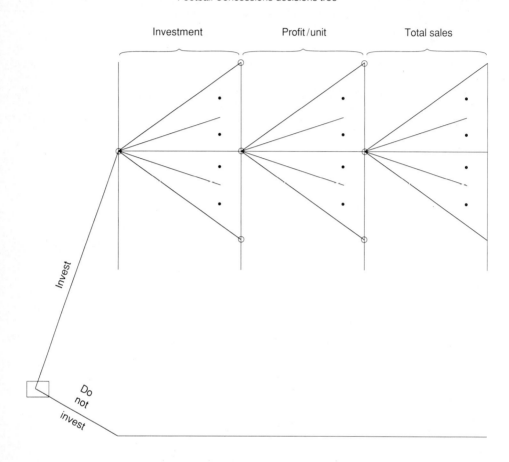

Total investment		Profit per unit	
Random number	Investment	Random number	Profit
1-10	$2000	1-5	$0.10
11-25	3000	6-10	0.11
26-40	4000	11-20	0.12
41-60	5000	21-40	0.13
61-75	6000	41-85	0.14
76-85	7000	86-95	0.15
86-95	8000	96-100	0.16
96-100	9000		

A listing of a BASIC program written to analyze this problem and illustrative output is attached.

```
100.    REM  PROGRAM 'DOG' PERFORMS FOOTBALL CONCESSIONS (B)
             ANALYSIS
110.    REM
120.    REM  DIMENSION ALL ARRAYS
```

```
130.    REM  A = INVESTMENT; B = UNIT PROFIT; C = SALES
140.    REM  D = NET PROFIT; E = PROFIT INDEX; F = PROFITABIL-
             ITY
150.    REM
160.    DIM  A(100),B(100),C(100),D(100),E(100),F(20)
170.    REM
180.    REM  DEFINITION OF OTHER VARIABLES AND INITIALIZATION
190.    REM  A1 = AVERAGE INVESTMENT AND ACCUMULATOR
200.    REM  B1 = AVERAGE UNIT PROFIT AND ACCUMULATOR
210.    REM  C1 = AVERAGE TOTAL SALES AND ACCUMULATOR
220.    REM  D1 = AVERAGE NET PROFIT AND ACCUMULATOR
230.    REM  E1 = AVERAGE PROFIT INDEX AND ACCUMULATOR
240.    REM  N = NUMBER OF TRIALS SIMULATED
250.    REM  X = ARGUMENT OF "RND" OPERATOR (DUMMY)
260.    REM  Z = RESULT OF RANDOM VARIABLE GENERATION
270.    REM
280.    LET A1 = 0
290.    LET B1 = 0
300.    LET C1 = 0
310.    LET D1 = 0
320.    LET E1 = 0
330.    REM
340.    PRINT "NUMBER OF TRIALS TO BE SIMULATED"
350.    INPUT N
360.    REM
370.    REM  GENERATE VALUES OF INVESTMENT, UNIT PROFIT AND
             SALES FOR I = 1,N
380.    REM  THEN COMPUTE NET PROFIT AND PROFIT INDEX
390.    REM
400.    FOR I = 1 to N
410.    REM
420.    REM  COMPUTATION OF PROJECT INVESTMENT
430.    REM
440.        LET Z = INT(100 * RND(X) + 1)
450.        IF Z < 11 THEN 550
460.        IF Z < 26 THEN 570
470.        IF Z < 41 THEN 590
480.        IF Z < 61 THEN 610
490.        IF Z < 76 THEN 630
500.        IF Z < 86 THEN 650
510.        IF Z < 96 THEN 670
520.        IF Z < 101 THEN 690
530.        PRINT "ERROR--RND(X) RETURN OUT OF BOUNDS"
540.        STOP
550.        LET A(I) = 2000
560.        GO TO 700
570.        LET A(I) = 3000
```

```
580.            GO TO 700
590.            LET A(I) = 4000
600.            GO TO 700
610.            LET A(I) = 5000
620.            GO TO 700
630.            LET A(I) = 6000
640.            GO TO 700
650.            LET A(I) = 7000
660.            GO TO 700
670.            LET A(I) = 8000
680.            GO TO 700
690.            LET A(I) = 9000
700.            LET A1 = A1 + A(I)
710.    REM
720.    REM    COMPUTATION OF PROJECT PROFIT PER UNIT
730.    REM
740.            LET Z = INT(100 * RND(X) + 1)
750.            IF Z < 6 THEN 840
760.            IF Z < 11 THEN 860
770.            IF Z < 21 THEN 880
780.            IF Z < 41 THEN 900
790.            IF Z < 86 THEN 920
800.            IF Z < 96 THEN 940
810.            IF Z < 101 THEN 960
820.            PRINT "ERROR--RND(X) RETURN OUT OF BOUNDS"
830.            STOP
840.            LET B(I) = .10
850.            GO TO 970
860.            LET B(I) = .11
870.            GO TO 970
880.            LET B(I) = .12
890.            GO TO 970
900.            LET B(I) = .13
910.            GO TO 970
920.            LET B(I) = .14
930.            GO TO 970
940.            LET B(I) = .15
950.            GO TO 970
960.            LET B(I) = .16
970.            LET B1 = B1 + B(I)
980.    REM
990.    REM    COMPUTATION OF PROJECT TOTAL SALES
1000.   REM
1010.           LET Z = 0
1020.           FOR J = 1 to 12
1030.               LET Z = Z + RND(X)
1040.           NEXT J
```

```
1050.          LET Z = Z - 6
1060.          LET C(I) = 40000 + 7000 * Z
1070.          LET C1 = C1 + C(I)
1080.     REM
1090.     REM   COMPUTATION OF NET PROFIT AND PROFIT INDEX
1100.     REM
1110.          LET D(I) = B(I) * C(I) - A(I)
1120.          LET E(I) = D(I) / A(I)
1130.          LET D1 = D1 + D(I)
1140.          LET E1 = E1 + E(I)
1150.     NEXT I
1160.     REM
1170.     REM   DETERMINE PI PROBABILITIES ON SCALE -.2 TO .5
1180.     REM
1190.     FOR I = 1 TO N
1200.          IF E(I) < -.20 THEN 1350
1210.          IF E(I) < -.15 THEN 1370
1220.          IF E(I) < -.10 THEN 1390
1230.          IF E(I) < -.05 THEN 1410
1240.          IF E(I) <   0 THEN 1430
1250.          IF E(I) <  .05 THEN 1450
1260.          IF E(I) <  .10 THEN 1470
1270.          IF E(I) <  .15 THEN 1490
1280.          IF E(I) <  .20 THEN 1510
1290.          IF E(I) <  .25 THEN 1530
1300.          IF E(I) <  .30 THEN 1550
1310.          IF E(I) <  .35 THEN 1570
1320.          IF E(I) <  .40 THEN 1590
1330.          IF E(I) <  .45 THEN 1610
1340.          GO TO 1630
1350.          F(1) = F(1) + 1
1360.          GO TO 1640
1370.          F(2) = F(2) + 1
1380.          GO TO 1640
1390.          F(3) = F(3) + 1
1400.          GO TO 1640
1410.          F(4) = F(4) + 1
1420.          GO TO 1640
1430.          F(5) = F(5) + 1
1440.          GO TO 1640
1450.          F(6) = F(6) + 1
1460.          GO TO 1640
1470.          F(7) = F(7) + 1
1480.          GO TO 1640
1490.          F(8) = F(8) + 1
1500.          GO TO 1640
1510.          F(9) = F(9) + 1
```

```
1520.        GO TO 1640
1530.        F(10) = F(10) + 1
1540.        GO TO 1640
1550.        F(11) = F(11) + 1
1560.        GO TO 1640
1570.        F(12) = F(12) + 1
1580.        GO TO 1640
1590.        F(13) = F(13) + 1
1600.        GO TO 1640
1610.        F(14) = F(14) + 1
1620.        GO TO 1640
1630.        F(15) = F(15) + 1
1640.   NEXT I
1650.   REM
1660.   REM  TRANSLATE F(J) COUNTERS INTO PROBABILITY
             STATEMENT LEVELS
1670.   REM
1680.   FOR J = 1 to 15
1690.        LET F(J) = F(J) / N
1700.   NEXT J
1710.   REM
1720.   REM  TALLY FINAL AVERAGES
1730.   REM
1740.   REM
1750.        LET A1 = A1 / N
1760.        LET B1 = B1 / N
1770.        LET C1 = C1 / N
1780.        LET D1 = D1 / N
1790.        LET E1 = E1 / N
1800.   REM
1810.   REM
1820.   REM  ENTER PRINT PHASES
1830.   REM  PHASE ONE PRINTS AVERAGES AND OUTCOME
             DISTRIBUTIONS
1840.   REM  PHASE TWO PRINTS DETAILS OF SIMULATION
1850.   REM
1860.   REM
1870.   PRINT
1880.   PRINT "ANALYSIS OF FOOTBALL CONCESSIONS (B)" N
             "SIMULATIONS"
1890.   PRINT
1900.   PRINT
1910.   PRINT "AVERAGE VALUES FOR UNCERTAIN EVENTS"
1920.   PRINT
1930.   PRINT "        INVESTMENT REQUIRED", A1
1940.   PRINT "        PROFIT PER UNIT (¢)", B1
1950.   PRINT "        TOTAL HOT DOGS SOLD", C1
```

```
1960.    PRINT "          PROJECT NET PROFIT",D1
1970.    PRINT "          PROFITABILITY INDEX",E1
1980.    PRINT
1990.    PRINT "DISTRIBUTION OF PROJECT PROFITABILITY"
2000.    PRINT
2010.    PRINT "          PROFITABILITY INDEX
            PROBABILITY"
2020.    PRINT
2030.    LET X = -.20
2040.    FOR J = 1 to 15
2050.        PRINT "        ",X,"         ",F(J)
2060.      LET X = X + .050000
2070.    NEXT J
2080.    PRINT
2090.    PRINT "FOR LISTING OF SIMULATION TRIALS TYPE 1;
            OTHERWISE 0"
2100.    INPUT I
2110.    IF I = 1 THEN 2130
2120.    STOP
2130.    PRINT "DETAILS OF",N,"SIMULATIONS"
2140.    PRINT
2150.    PRINT "TRIAL","INVESTMENT","UNIT PROFIT","TOTAL
            SALES","NET PROFIT","PROFIT INDEX"
2155.    PRINT
2160.    FOR I = 1 to N
2170.        PRINT I,A(I),B(I),C(I),D(I),E(I)
2171.
2180.    NEXT I
2190.    STOP
2200.    END
```

NUMBER OF TRIALS TO BE SIMULATED
25

ANALYSIS OF FOOTBALL CONCESSIONS (B) 25 SIMULATIONS

AVERAGE VALUES FOR UNCERTAIN EVENTS

INVESTMENT REQUIRED   4800
PROFIT PER UNIT (¢)   .1347996
TOTAL HOT DOGS SOLD   39167.4
PROJECT NET PROFIT   459.4573
PROFITABILITY INDEX   .2983784

DISTRIBUTION OF PROJECT PROFITABILITY

PROFITABILITY INDEX	PROBABILITY
-.2	.2
-.15	0
-9.999996E-02	0
-4.999997E-02	7.999998E-02
2.980232E-08	.04
5.000003E-02	.1199999
.10000002	.04
.15	0
.1999999	7.999998E-02
.2499999	0
.2999998	0
.3499998	7.999998E-02
.3999997	7.999998E-02
.4499997	0
.4999996	.28

FOR LISTING OF SIMULATION TRIALS TYPE 1; OTHERWISE 0
1
DETAILS OF 25 SIMULATIONS

TRIAL	INVEST-MENT	UNIT PROFIT	TOTAL SALES	NET PROFIT	PROFIT INDEX
1	3000	9.999996E-02	40868.79	1086.877	.3622925
2	7000	.14	35716.82	-1999.648	-.285664
3	6000	.15	41986.49	297.9727	4.966211E-02
4	3000	.11	45694.87	2026.43	.6754766
5	4000	.14	41987.16	1878.199	.4695498
6	6000	.14	44402.11	216.293	3.604883E-02
7	5000	.14	42436.94	941.168	.1882336
8	2000	.13	36638.94	2763.059	1.381529
9	5000	.13	51637.14	1712.824	.3425648
10	9000	.1199999	40216.32	-4174.047	-.463783
11	5000	.11	41721.8	-410.6055	-8.212107E-02
12	3000	.14	39772.07	2568.086	.8560286
13	5000	.13	30442.87	-1042.4275	-.2084855
14	2000	.15	33774.8	3066.219	1.533109
15	5000	.14	42642.94	970.0078	.1940016
16	5000	.1199999	41715.41	5.84375	1.168750E-03
17	5000	.14	35415.22	-41.87109	-8.374218E-03
18	5000	.16	43485.9	1957.742	.3915484
19	9000	.14	38951.41	-3546.805	-.3940894
20	2000	.15	39945.71	3991.855	1.995927
21	3000	.13	37076.73	1819.973	.6066575
22	7000	.15	24675.88	-3298.619	-.4712312
23	3000	.14	28472.59	986.1626	.3287208
24	6000	.13	41920.12	-550.3867	-9.173107E-02
25	5000	.14	37586.76	262.1445	.0524289

ANALYSIS OF FOOTBALL CONCESSIONS (B) 50 SIMULATIONS

AVERAGE VALUES FOR UNCERTAIN EVENTS

      INVESTMENT REQUIRED   4600
      PROFIT PER UNIT (¢)   .1337995
      TOTAL HOT DOGS SOLD   41236.28
      PROJECT NET PROFIT   885.9456
      PROFITABILITY INDEX   .4784436

DISTRIBUTION OF PROJECT PROFITABILITY

PROFITABILITY INDEX	PROBABILITY
$-.2$	.16
$-.15$	.04
$-9.999996E-02$	.02
$-4.999997E-02$	.04
$2.980232E-08$	.02
$5.000003E-02$	.1199999
.10000002	.04
.15	0
.1999999	.04
.2499999	0
.2999998	.04
.3499998	.04
.3999997	.06
.4499997	0
.4999996	.38

ANALYSIS OF FOOTBALL CONCESSIONS (B) 100 SIMULATIONS

AVERAGE VALUES FOR UNCERTAIN EVENTS

INVESTMENT REQUIRED   4890
PROFIT PER UNIT (¢)   .1333995
TOTAL HOT DOGS SOLD   40408.81
PROJECT NET PROFIT   472.5005
PROFITABILITY INDEX   .3405191

DISTRIBUTION OF PROJECT PROFITABILITY

PROFITABILITY INDEX	PROBABILITY
−.2	.23
−.15	.03
−9.999996E−02	.04
−4.999997E−02	.05
2.980232E−08	9.999998E−03
5.000003E−02	6.999999E−02
.10000002	.05
.15	0
.1999999	.02
.2499999	.03
.2999998	.05
.3499998	.05
.3999997	.04
.4499997	.02
.4999996	.3099999

Definitions

Normal distribution. A continuous distribution represented by the familiar bell-shaped curve.

Mean. The arithmetic average.

Standard deviation. A measure of dispersion of the subject about the mean.

Monte Carlo method. A simulation model of the artificial construction of a history of random occurrences, based upon a probability distribution.

Questions

1. Based on the two results presented in the case, would you purchase the concession rights? Explain your answer.
2. Is the answer to question 1 different than you would have expected without the computer analysis? If so, how is it different?
3. Could this type of computer analysis be used in other aspects of commercial recreation? Compile a list of other possible uses or examples.
4. If you have access to a computer, enter the program and insert different values for the total investment in program lines 540 to 660. Change only the numbers that correspond to those in the first table. Do the same for profit per unit in lines 830 to 970. Does this change your decision? Note how the different values change the outcomes.

CHAPTER 12

The future of commercial recreation

CHAPTER OBJECTIVES

1. To discuss anticipated changes in the field of commercial recreation

2. To look at trends that may affect commercial recreation

3. To present ideas and directions for the commercial recreation student

The technical skills of a recreation manager are extremely important. One additional skill must be developed if a commercial recreation manager is to succeed in today's business climate: the ability to foresee future events and trends. A manager must accurately forecast various aspects of the economy in order to foresee recreation markets. A recreation student can learn how to identify new business niches. It involves extracting and assimilating information from various sources.

To demonstrate this procedure, we will attempt to make predictions for the economic situation in the United States, population trends, deregulation, and insurance. Please keep in mind that these are examples of dynamic trends, and current events can rapidly change the scenarios. Also remember that the information alluded to in this section is readily available from general-interest publications. A student must identify the important information, and synthesize and rearrange it into a form that can be profitable to a recreation business.

Economic trends

The United States economy is controlled somewhat by the actions of government. The government wears four "hats": It is a financial executive, levying taxes, regulating the money supply, printing money, borrowing money from the population, providing subsidies and tax breaks to industry segments, lending money, and guaranteeing bank loans. It is a policeman, regulating industries; enforcing the health, clean air and safety rules of the country; controlling exports and imports; and setting the minimum wage and prices for certain commodities. It is an industrialist, buying, manufacturing, and selling goods and services; delivering the mail; training workers, and operating health facilities. It is a paymaster, employing more than 5 million people and providing funds for welfare programs and employee retirement. (*U.S. News and World Report,* April 26, 1982)

Tremendous changes can be made in the economy depending on how the government chooses to exercise its powers. For example, the tax changes of 1986 have affected various recreation industries. It is anticipated that restaurants and country clubs will suffer setbacks due to the reduced deductions (from 100% to 80%) of business lunch costs from individual and corporate income taxes. This is because restaurants that provide business lunches and country clubs are also used for social purposes (Weinstein, 1987). The loss of the 10% investment tax credit may force purchasers, particularly restaurant equipment purchasers, to eliminate or postpone property renovations (Helfand, 1987). The government acting under each of its other hats can also affect commercial recreation. The recreation entrepreneur must continually monitor each governmental role and assess its effects on the recreation industry.

Foreign exports can affect and are affected by the financial and policeman roles of the government. Government intervention has decreased the value of the dollar against foreign currencies such as the German mark and the Japanese yen, so foreign goods are now more expensive in the United States.

Import quotas and tariffs involve the government in its role as policeman. A prime example is the import tariff on motorcycles with engine capacity over 750cc, imposed at the instigation of Harley-Davidson to protect its domestic business. An increase in the price of goods to the U.S. consumer is the result of tariffs, limited supplies, and the decreasing value of the dollar. This increased cost of foreign goods gives American manufacturers an opportunity to compete more effectively with foreign firms.

In the hotel industry the weakening of the dollar is regarded as a benefit because it increases travel to the United States while encouraging Americans to stay home. If this trend continues, it will provide substantial benefits to the domestic travel and tourism industry.

The U.S. economy was once considered one industry; however, in the early 1980s analysts split the economy into manufacturing, services, finance, energy, and farming. Each of these subeconomies competes with the others for monetary and human resources. In simple terms, each segment is performing differently. For example, manufacturing's share of the nation's gross national product has remained at about 24%. As a goods producer manufacturing isn't dying. However, as an employer it is declining rapidly.

Service is considered the fast track of the new American economy. In order to obtain and keep good service jobs, applicants will need to continue training and education.

In finance, the trend is toward a shakeout of weaker institutions, resulting in megacompanies that will provide comprehensive financial services.

The energy segment of the economy is behaving much like the financial segment. Most experts agree that it is in a slump, but by the mid 1990s the energy segment will be doing well because the United States will again need domestic oil supplies because of shortages of supply from foreign importers.

Farming, the fifth segment of the economy, has been aided by strong government subsidies. Small farms are continuing to go broke or merge into large conglomerates. A cheaper dollar should increase farm exports because they will become more affordable (Karmin et al., 1986).

Each market segment needs to be watched by the recreation entrepreneur for changes that may require resources from the other segments and for targeting possible areas to locate businesses. The changing balance of power and centralizing of these segments in various parts of the country offer opportunities for commercial recreation location and expansion. As each of these segments changes, a corresponding change will take place in recreation enterprises. A recreation manager must be aware of the ramifications and proceed appropriately.

Government spending must be controlled in the future. As the government goes further into debt, it competes with private industry for revenue and capital. Government revenue is acquired through taxes. Raising capital becomes hard when the federal government competes with private enterprise for loans from citizens through the purchase and selling of Treasury bills. As U.S. debt increases, interest payments on the debt also increase, driving the government further into debt. As a result, the money borrowed by the government reduces the debt capital available to businesses. The U.S. government is approaching a $2 trillion debt. Two trillion $1 bills, placed end to end, would stretch 186 million miles, the distance from the earth to the sun and back (Scherschel and Morse, 1985).

The passage of the Gramm-Rudman Act was an attempt by Congress to reduce the national debt. Gramm-Rudman was supposed to force a spending compromise and provide elected officials political protection for agreeing to the compromise while trying to reduce government spending (Thomas, 1985). Currently, the president proposes a budget, which is amended and passed by the Congress of the United States. If a measure in the proposed budget eliminates jobs in a Congressional district, the Representative of that district will vote against that measure. This process tends to increase the federal debt by encouraging spending when revenue is not present. If Gramm-Rudman is allowed to work effectively, we should see a reduction in the national debt, a strengthening of the economy, and an increase in available money for recreation businesses.

The future looks good. Interest rates have dropped in recent years. If the national debt can be maintained or reduced and the supply of money remains good, we should see continued prosperity and growth, particularly in commercial recreation. As companies become more profitable and their employees have increased discretionary income, it becomes feasible for more people to participate in recreation.

There are potential problems. Paul Erdman, in his new book, *The Panic of '89*, talks about the possibility that third-world countries will fail to make the payments on the $1 trillion they owe to U.S. banks. If this should happen, Erdman hypothesizes, the U.S. economy will completely collapse. An interesting illustration of the problem is the decision of the Brazilian government, which owes American banks $110 billion, to declare a moratorium on interest payments. Brazil appears to be leading debtor nations toward an attempt to renegotiate their debts. Edward Mervosh (1987) indicated that debtor countries' problems are getting worse while the foundation for dealing with them is getting shakier. He went on to state that the Baker plan (an outline for debt repayment by third world countries proposed by Howard Baker) is not working and the power of the international monetary fund, or anyone, to impose repayment discipline on third-world debtors is weakening. If foreign countries refuse to repay the U.S. banks, we will see, at the least, a substantial tightening of the money supply due to the tremendous loss in revenues and assets these banks would entail. This eventuality, if it took place, would definitely have an adverse effect on commercial recreation until the problem was resolved.

Population trends

John Naisbitt in his book *Megatrends* and *U.S. News and World Report* in its special report "Ten Forces Reshaping America" (1984) have commented on the changing patterns of the U.S. population and the influence they will have on the future. One of the most important is the baby boomers, that 4.3 million people born in the United States between 1946 and 1964 (U.S. News and World Report, 1984). This population has already substantially changed the U.S. economy. They are different from their parents in a number of ways: As the baby boomers grow older, they want stronger family and religious ties and exhibit a greater respect for authority. They are also the most highly educated generation ever seen in this country, with 35% having college degrees.

Three fifths of this population are employed in white-collar jobs. They are marrying later than their parents did and delaying starting their families. These combined facts make this generation one of the most accessible to recreation entrepreneurs. Various studies have indicated that the higher the education an individual has, the more likely he or she is to participate in recreation. Also, as income increases, there is more discretionary income to spend on recreational activities. Hotels, ski resorts, and other recreation enterprises are beginning to cater to this segment of the population through programs specifically intended for families (Fig. 12-1).

FIG. 12-1 Ski resorts are catering to children as one means of increasing their portion of the market. Changes in the population have resulted in the need to provide new services to attract customers. (Photograph courtesy Aspen Skiing Company.)

Physical fitness and convenience are two major concerns of this highly mobile population.

An offshoot of the baby boomers is the single population. Because most of the baby boomers are electing to marry and start families later, many individuals are able to spend more time on vacations and on themselves. The single population, which numbers about 19.4 million, is composed of those who have never been married and those who are divorced or widowed. Those who have never been married are generally younger; they accounted for about 6 million people in 1981.

Numbers of people who are single as a result of divorce or death are up 78% from 1970 to 1982 (Sanoff, 1983).

This unmarried population can be divided into three age groups: those under 34, mostly never married, account for 27%; those 35 to 64, mainly divorced or widowed, account for 33%; the remainder are 65 and over. The tremendous increase in the baby boomer population and in each of the three segments has provided commercial recreation with unique opportunities for business development. For example, the increase in single persons and women in the work force has resulted in a tremendous change in the hotel industry. Among these is an increased emphasis on rooms and room security for individuals traveling alone. Another development is the establishment of businesses catering to the social life of unmarried adults. There has also been a tremendous increase in group tours specifically designed for the elderly to encourage travel and provide the social life this population needs.

The older population has also had a tremendous influence on commercial recreation businesses. Spending as a percentage of pretax income for people over 50 increased from 84% in 1973 to 91% in 1983. In fact, the 50-plus generation, which accounts for 35% of the adult population, is responsible for 42% of the total after-tax income in the United States and 77% of the total household financial holdings. Further studies indicate that the over-50 population has a 20% higher discretionary income than the rest of the population, and this segment will grow steadily as the baby boomers age (Berger, 1985). Remember, this population has additional time to spend in recreational pursuits. Children have left home, there are two persons per household, and they have increased time to do as they wish. This market segment is extremely profitable and will continue to grow as the baby boom generation matures. This is one segment for which the recreation entrepreneur must be very astute in providing services.

Deregulation

During the late 1970s the federal government deregulated many industries, including the airlines and railroads. As a result of deregulation, airline fares, after being adjusted for inflation, have declined about 13% since 1978. However, the market share of the top six or so companies that dominate the airline industry is growing rapidly, with few or no new entries into the marketplace. The six largest airline carriers now control approximately 84% of the market as opposed to 73% in 1978. Consultant Lee R. Howard of Airline Economic, Inc., foresees that by 1990 a tight oligopoly with a share of not more than 90% will exist among these carriers (Welles et al., 1986).

A further result of deregulation has been extended delays in airline travel. The delays have been blamed on a number of factors, including deregulation and crowding on popular flights. Flying has become so congested that one traveler making a short flight was delayed nine hours, missed a meeting, and was not even allowed to get off the plane. As a result Senator Abourezk filed a $200,000 lawsuit claiming false imprisonment by the airline (Chaze et al., 1986). If the trend toward oligopoly continues in the airline industry, and as competition for specific routes decreases, air fares will increase substantially, resulting in more troubles for the airline traveler.

Associated with this is the vertical integration of the airline industry with rental car companies and hotels, which has allowed discounts not only in airline fares but also in hotel reservations. In the future a traveler will be able to make one phone call to an airline company and reserve everything for a vacation trip, including rental cars and hotels. Once this happens, competition in the travel agency business will decrease and prices will increase.

Insurance

The last issue to be addressed is insurance. Recreation enterprises are dependent on insurance for business operation. Liability insurance premiums have increased rapidly in recent years. For example, Alpine Meadows Ski Resort had its liability insurance premium increase from $400,000 in 1985 to $800,000 in 1986, resulting in an increase in the lift ticket price of $2 (Church, 1986). Squaw Valley's costs increased by 350% while deductibles increased 10%, reducing the overall coverage (Yannish, 1986).

Combined with rapidly increasing insurance rates for certain types of recreation businesses is the fact that insurers are refusing to cover certain kinds of risks and industries. Among the most prominent of these are water parks, ski resorts, amusement parks, and high-risk activities such as mountain climbing and river running. This trend has forced rapid fee increases and has required that the recreation industry combine related entities to act as self-insurers. Some businesses have elected to "go bare," or not carry any insurance at all. This is drastic and short-sighted, since a major lawsuit would close a company down. The main reason for the increase in insurance rates has been an evolution in liability law that in recent years has led to high jury awards and an increase in the number of lawsuits. From 1977 to 1981 the number of lawsuits in the United States grew four times as fast as the population (Church, 1986).

The concept of joint and several liability has also affected insurance rates. This concept allows a plaintiff to sue everyone who might share in responsibility for an accident. If any defendant is found to be partially at fault, that defendant may be forced to pay the entire monetary judgment (Church, 1986). The result of this is that the entity named in the lawsuit that has the most money is the most likely to pay the judgment.

There is also the contention that insurance companies are partially to blame for the increase in rates. Interest rates paid to insurance companies have lowered, and so have revenues available to cover claims. Also, many secondary insurers, notably

Lloyds of London, are located overseas. These insurers are profoundly affected by the drastic changes in the value of the dollar.

To offset this situation some proposed ideas could have tremendous influence to mitigate damage awards: limits on pain and suffering, stricter standards for proving who bears how much blame for an accident, the abolishment of the doctrine of joint and several liability—already passed by some states—and a limitation of contingency fees to lawyers. This last would reduce their interest in taking lawsuits and attempting to raise the awards (Church, 1986).

If these ideas are adopted by the states, commercial recreation could see lower insurance rates and greater viability in the marketplace. This area is of utmost importance to the recreation entrepreneur. If insurance rates do not come down, it is very possible that there will be a reduction in commercial recreation businesses and partial or total elimination of some high-risk activities in the United States.

Summary

We have discussed four major trends in the United States as they relate to commercial recreation. The economy appears to encourage recreation enterprises. In fact, some businesses are finding it easier to find financing for startup and development costs. The population of the United States is changing rapidly in ways that will improve business prospects. Deregulation has been shown in the short term to increase travel in the United States, but over the long term the outcome is still in question. It appears that there is a potential for oligopolies and higher rates, resulting in less travel or travel within a specific company's domain.

Insurance is a major issue for commercial recreation. It is to be hoped that the future will provide changes and new directions to mitigate this problem. The future of commercial recreation appears to be sound. Current market changes tend to indicate increased prosperity in the future, particularly for specific market segments.

BIBLIOGRAPHY

Berger, J.: The new old: where the economic action is, Business Week, Nov. 25, 1985, pp. 138-140.

Chaze, W.L.: The late, late show, U.S. News and World Report, Dec. 22, 1986, pp. 14-19.

Church, G.J.: Sorry your policy is canceled, Time, March 24, 1986, pp. 16-23.

The ever-present hand of government, U.S. News and World Report, April 26, 1982, pp. 43-46.

Helfand, S.: Tax reform, Outside Business, January, 1987.

Here come the baby boomers, U.S. News and World Report, Nov. 5, 1984, pp. 68-73.

Karmin, et al.: Brave new economy, U.S. News and World Report, March 31, 1986, pp. 42-48.

Karmin, M.W., Manning, R.A., and Dworkin, P.: Economic outlook, U.S. News and World Report, March 9, 1987, p. 52.

Mervosh, E.: Economic outlook, U.S. News and World Report, Feb. 2, 1987, p. 57.

Richman, T.: Mr. Megatrend, Review, Jan., 1983, p. 85.

Sanoff, A.P.: Nineteen million singles, their joys and frustrations, U.S. News and World Report, Feb. 21, 1983, pp. 53-56.

Scherschel, P.M., and Morse, R.J.: Soaring national debt, what is really means, U.S. News and World Report, Sept. 16, 1985, pp. 33-34.

10 forces shaping America, U.S. News and World Report, March 19, 1984, pp. 40-52.

Thomas, E.: Look Ma! No Hands!, Time, Dec. 23, 1985, pp. 18-21.

Weinstein, J.: 1987 annual report, Restaurants and Institutions, Jan. 1987, p. 46.

Welles, C., et al.: Is deregulation working?, Business Week, Dec. 22, 1986, pp. 50-55.

Yannish, D.: Liability rates for ski areas snowball, Business Insurance, Jan. 6, 1986, p. 3.

Index

A numeral in italics indicates an illustration; a numeral followed by "t" indicates a table.